NATIONAL MINORITIES IN ROMANIA
CHANGE IN TRANSYLVANIA

ELEMÉR ILLYÉS

EAST EUROPEAN MONOGRAPHS, BOULDER
DISTRIBUTED BY COLUMBIA UNIVERSITY PRESS, NEW YORK

1982

EAST EUROPEAN MONOGRAPHS, NO. CXII

Copyright © 1982 by Elemér Illyés
Library of Congress Card Catalog Number 82-70729
ISBN 0-88033-055-8
Printed in the United States of America

CONTENTS

INTRODUCTION 1
TERRITORY AND POPULATION 9
   A Brief History of Transylvania and Its Peoples 9
   The Hungarians 10
   The Saxons 12
   The Romanians 14
   Population Movements and Changes 16
   Later Immigrants 18
   The Effect of Two World Wars on Transylvania's
   Territory and Population 21
TERRITORIAL AND POPULATION CHANGES SINCE WORLD WAR I 29
   The Territorial Distribution of the National Minorities 31
   Later Population Changes (1966–1977) 48
   The Effects of Urbanization and Romanianization on the
   Population of the Cities and Towns 55
   The National Distribution in the Urban and
   Rural Population 63
   The Occupational Distribution and Social Structure
   of the Population 66
THE POSSIBILITIES FOR MINORITY COEXISTENCE
IN ROMANIA, 1918–1956 71
   The National Minorities in Romania Between
   1918 and 1944 71

Laws and Decrees Between 1918 and 1940 Relating to
  the National Minorities.. 86
  Political Developments in Romania, 1944–1948.............. 94
  The Legal Status of the Minorities From the War Until
  the Foundation of the Totalitarian State 106
  The Totalitarian State: The Romanian People's Republic.... 111
  The Nationality Policy of the Romanian
  People's Republic 114

ROMANIAN POLITICS AND NATIONALITY POLICY
SINCE 1956 123
  The Socialist National State — National Communism 127
  The Nationality Policy of the Romanian Socialist
  Republic 130
  The 1970s — Moves Toward Assimilation................. 138
  International Conferences in the 1970s.................... 150
  National, Linguistic, and Ethnic Affiliation............... 151

NATIONAL-MINORITY EDUCATION IN ROMANIA....... 155
  Methodological Problems 155
  Historical Background 157
  Education for the National Minorities Between the
  Two World Wars.. 159
  National-Minority Education After 1945 164
  The Present System of National-Minority Education 184
  The Educational Status of the Csángó Hungarians of
  Moldavia... 201
  The Supervision of National-Minority Education 202
  Teachers Training 203
  Textbooks... 204
  Conclusion 205

THE CHURCHES OF THE NATIONAL MINORITIES IN
ROMANIA 213
  Historical Background and the Period Between the
  Two World Wars.. 213
  The Legal Position After the Second World War 218
  Relations Between Church and State 235

THE NATIONAL-MINORITY PRESS AND PUBLISHING
INDUSTRY IN ROMANIA 239
  The Press 239
  Development Since 1945................................ 241
  The Dogmatic Period 245
  The Desatellitization Process — Liberalizing Trends 246

Contents

    The Cultural Policy of the 1970s 249
    Book Publishing 254
NOTES 259
SELECTED BIBLIOGRAPHY 305
NAME INDEX 337
PLACE NAME INDEX 345
SUBJECT INDEX 351

INTRODUCTION

In this work an attempt has been made for the first time to analyze thoroughly the political, ethnical, cultural, socioeconomic, and historical situation, particularly between 1944 and 1980, of the national minorities in Romania. The author's main objective is to give a factual account of the existing conditions among the nationalities, also considering, however, the period between the two world wars.

This is a topic of considerable complexity. In order to give an objective picture of the situation it was necessary to use almost all the more detailed scientific works and studies published in the West, as well as other written material. This included an analysis of official Romanian data; declarations and reports in the press that were not always free of political and ideological doctrine; information provided by sources that were not published but were considered reliable; and, finally, the personal experience of the author in the country as well as his analysis of the limited available material from Romania concerning the immediate postwar years.

Transylvania and its fateful historical development are the center of interest. A short summary of its history, indispensable for a better understanding, follows.

The two largest and most significant national minorities, the Hungarians and the Germans, played a dominant role in the historical development of the country and the evolution of its culture. The situation of other nationalities is also analyzed, particularly that of the Jewish minority which today is numerically insignificant but which once played an important role in the development of the country's culture. It must be pointed out here that the Romanian people, as the national majority, have always had very different social, economic, and cultural traditions than the national minorities in present-day Romania; and significant differences still prevail. These may be explained primarily by peculiarities in historical development. It must also be taken into account that the relation of the Romanian majority to the national minorities is still determined to a great extent by great power interests and contradictory ideas and opinions. It is very difficult for an outsider to obtain reliable and sufficiently detailed information about the result of all this. Consequently, the public is poorly informed about the situation of those more than three million people who are members of national minorities in Romania today and about the changes in their culture and society during the last quarter of a century.

The notion Transylvania will be explained in the chapter "Territory and Population." Suffice to say, here, that the old Hungarian name of that territory is "Erdély" or "Erdőelve", (since the ninth or tenth centuries) from which the Romanian designation "Ardeal" derives. Like the original Hungarian name, the Latin translation "Transilvania" means "the country beyond the forest," coming from the west, *i.e.*, from Hungary. This name is used by Romanian authors and others to designate the entire territory, which belonged to Hungary before 1919. The German name "Siebenbürgen" refers to the historical territory of the independent Transylvanian Principality. This name originates, according to one of several hypotheses, from "Cibinburg" in the region of Hermannstadt. Divided from the territory of Old Romania by the Carpathian mountains, about 20 to 35 miles wide and in some places more than 6,500 feet high, Transylvania is not only a geographic unity but differs greatly from the other areas of present-day Romania, also in its western-oriented cultural history, its historical development, and its religious traditions.

This work deals with the peoples that have been part of the history of Transylvania ever since the Hungarian conquest in 896 AD. Soon after that conquest, the Hungarian kings were forced by frequent incursions from the east to develop defenses in Transylvania. Besides such peoples as Cumanians, Uzes, Petchenegues, and Yaziges, German settlers (*hospites*), the so-called Transylvanian Saxons, were called in during the 12th century. In the territory of Transylaniva, Romanians (Vlachs) first were mentioned in historical records from the 13th century.

INTRODUCTION

The basis of the development of the feudal system, which started in the 13th–15th centuries was the alliance of the three nations: the Hungarian nobles in the counties, the Széklers, and the free peasants and tradesmen of the autonomous Saxon territories. The federative alliance of the three "nations" (*Unio trium nationum Transsylvaniae*), concluded in 1437, was aimed mainly at the revolting peasants. In the following year, 1438, the alliance was confirmed; and at that time, as a consequence of the weakening of the Habsburgs' power, its character as a defensive pact against the Turkish incursions was emphasized. This pact was renewed in 1542 and remained the basis of the state administration for more than four centuries. It was not conceived in a democratic spirit; the Hungarian and Saxon bondsmen (free peasants and serfs) as well as the Romanian peasants were not included among those permitted to exercise political rights. The changes in the situation of the bondsmen occurred parallel to the development of the feudal system.

As a result of the penetration of Ottoman Turkish power into Central Europe, the medieval Hungarian kingdom disintegrated into three parts (1541). Transylvania as a principality was relatively independent between 1542 and 1688, without giving up its ties with Hungary.

Under the leadership of Hungarian dukes the Transylvanian Principality had a certain degree of sovereignty, a viable state organization, an independent army and financial system, and diplomatic connections as a vassal state in loose feudal dependence on the Turkish Empire. It paid tribute but was free from Turkish occupation and strived to preserve its internal independence between the Turkish and the Habsburg Empires by a policy of balance. It resisted successfully all Turkish attempts at invasion for one-and-a-half centuries.

In this epoch, Transylvania was in close contact with the western spiritual movements and became the most developed cultural center of the Danubian territory, a country of religious tolerance and of peaceful coexistence between the different nationalities.

At the turn of the 16th century (1591–1606) the unity of Transylvania was destroyed by civil wars between rival dukes, and the country finally was forced to give up its independence owing to the power politics of the Turks and the Habsburgs. A couple of years later, an outstanding personality, Duke Gabriel Bethlen (1613–1629) renewed stability and order in Transylvania.

After the defeat of the Turks, the Habsburgs made Transylvania into an Austrian crown colony (1687), ruled according to special statutes as Grand Principality (1688–1867). The legal basis of the Austrian administration (*Gubernium*) with its seat in Hermannstadt was established by an agreement between Transylvania and the Habsburgs, the Leopoldine Diploma (1691), and was confirmed in the peace treaty of Karlowitz in 1699. Although the Leopoldine Diploma secured the autonomous constitution of Transylvania, the domination of Austria resulted in the decrease in significance of the autonomous nations; important decisions were made by Vienna.

The Habsburg rule contributed beyond doubt to the stability and development of western culture in Transylvania. It should not pass without mention, however, that misuse of power by the government and the use of forceful methods such as punitive expeditions against the nationalities, particularly the Hungarians, occurred and, the privileges of the Transylvanian Saxons were considerably restricted. The causes of this included internal disagreements, the desire for centralization in Vienna, and finally the restriction of traditional religious tolerance by the Counter Reformation. The curtailment of the national rights of the Hungarians led finally, under the leadership of Duke Ferenc Rákóczi II (1703–1711), to the revolt of the *Kuruces* striving for national independence.

A century of political activity, lively in every respect, followed in which the Transylvanian nationalities' aspirations to emancipation and demands for social reform were of increasing significance. The Romanians based their demands on the ideas of the "Transylvanian School" [*Şcoala Ardeleană*] which was founded by Greek Catholic (Orthodox turned Roman Catholic) intellectuals and was of extreme importance in the development of national consciousness. In their petition *Supplex Libellus Valachorum* they demanded national autonomous rights and more social liberalization. Emperor Joseph II's attempt to introduce the German language into the administration later contributed to the development of Hungarian nationalism.

Finally, in the revolution of 1848–1849, earlier tensions exploded into armed conflict. This revolution, with its sharpening of antagonism among the nationalities of Transylvania, heralded a new epoch in the history of the country. Wanting to defend their rights, the Saxons, together with the Romanians who aspired to national recognition, supported the Habsburgs against the Hungarian revolutionaries, who fought for national independence. In 1849 the Hungarian revolutionary government seceded from Austria, and the Transylvanian Diet declared the unification of Transylvania with Hungary. This revolution was defeated by the Habsburg army with the help of Russian army units. The personalities who led this revolutionary movement, included among the Saxons, Stephan Ludwig Roth, who fought for the liberation of the serfs; among the Hungarians, Lajos Kossuth and the freedom poet Alexander Petőfi; and, among the Romanians, Nicolae Bălcescu who, from beyond the Carpathians and Avram Iancu, organized the revolutionary Romanians in Transylvania.

With respect to the significance of 1848–1849, each of the three Transylvanian nationalities had its own view. It is nevertheless certain that, apart from the abolition of serfdom, none of the nations was content with the events of the revolution. An era followed (1849–1860), a period called Neo-absolutism, in which Vienna suppressed all initiative shown by the nationalities. After the reintroduction of the autonomous Transylvanian constitution, by the Diploma of October 1860, the Austrian government, under the influence of the dominant European ideas of the epoch, was liberalized to a certain extent. At the Diet of Hermannstadt in 1863–1864, the Romanians were represented by their own deputies for the first time. This was the first attempt to bring about an autonomous Transylvania in a democratic spirit and to create the basis for peaceful coexistence among its nationalities. The resolutions of the Diet were, however, never fulfilled.

The unsuccessful wars led by the Habsburgs against Prussia in 1859–1860 and 1866, as well as the desire to reunite Transylvania with Hungary, eventually led to the historical compromise (*Ausgleich*) of 1867 and the creation of the Austro-Hungarian Monarchy which was a real union under one monarch. The union of Transylvania with Hungary was confirmed. Neither the Transylvanian Saxons nor the Romanians considered this compromise satisfactory—the Saxons, because they were afraid that their traditional rights would be restricted in a Hungarian national state; and the Romanians because of their struggle for an independent state. Article 44 of the Hungarian nationality law of 1868, which controlled the rights of the nationalities in the Hungarian half of the monarchy, guaranteed equal rights to all nationalities. The liberal provisions of this law were not, however, respected by the entire political leadership. Parliamentary freedom, in any case, existed at that time (although restricted by the so-called class election system), and the national minorities were in the position to develop their economy and culture freely. The Transylvanian Romanians had made demands that none of the Hungarian governments were able to fulfill. Towards the end of the First World War, attempts at Hungarian-Romanian rapprochement were unsuccessful.

After the dissolution of the Austro-Hungarian Monarchy at the end of the First World War, the Romanian National Assembly proclaimed in the declaration of Alba Iulia/Gyulafehérvár on December 1, 1918, joining Transylvania to Romania in spite of Hungarian protests. This was confirmed by the Allied and Associated Great Powers in the peace treaty of Trianon (June 4, 1920). It must be pointed out here that the annexation of Transylvania, the eastern territories of Hungary, and the eastern part of the Banat by Romania had been agreed upon secretly between Romania and the Allied powers from August 4, 1916, as a reward to Romania for changing sides in the First World War.

Because the resolutions of Alba Iulia secured the cultural autonomy of the nationalities, the Transylvanian Saxons, although not unanimously, joined the Romanians in the Declaration of Union of Mediasch on January 8, 1919. The German population of the Banat (Swabians) were initially against the division of their territory and its partial unification with Romania. After the Romanian army had occupied the eastern part of the Banat and the peace treaty of Trianon was ratified, these Banat Swabians joined the Saxons and the Romanians.

In the peace treaty of Trianon, Romania received not only historical Transylvania but also large areas of eastern Hungary: Máramaros/Maramureş, Szatmár/Satu Mare, Körösvidék/Crişana, and the eastern part of the Banat. The decision was based on the numerical superiority of Romanians, although their absolute majority of 53.8% was not very significant. In this way a multinational and multiconfessional Greater Romania was created that has had to deal with the problem of the national minorities ever since.

* * *

The appendix contains a subject index, an index of names, and a list of place names in three languages. The place names given here are those used officially today in Romania; the Hungarian names are applied according to the historical forms on the basis of the statistics established in 1910; and the German place names are given in their generally used historical forms.

Data and material available up to January 1981 have been used in this work. In conclusion, I wish to express my greatest thanks to my

INTRODUCTION 7

dear Anna, who has played a considerable part in the completion of this work, as well as to the Southeast European Institute in Munich and the Transylvanian Library in Gundelsheim from which I have received valuable material. I would also like to thank Professor Stephen Fischer-Galati, Editor of the East European Quarterly, Boulder, for making the publishing of this work possible, and Dr. Ernst Wagner, who read the manuscript and contributed valuable remarks and suggestions.

Schliersee, January 1981. *Elemér Illyés*

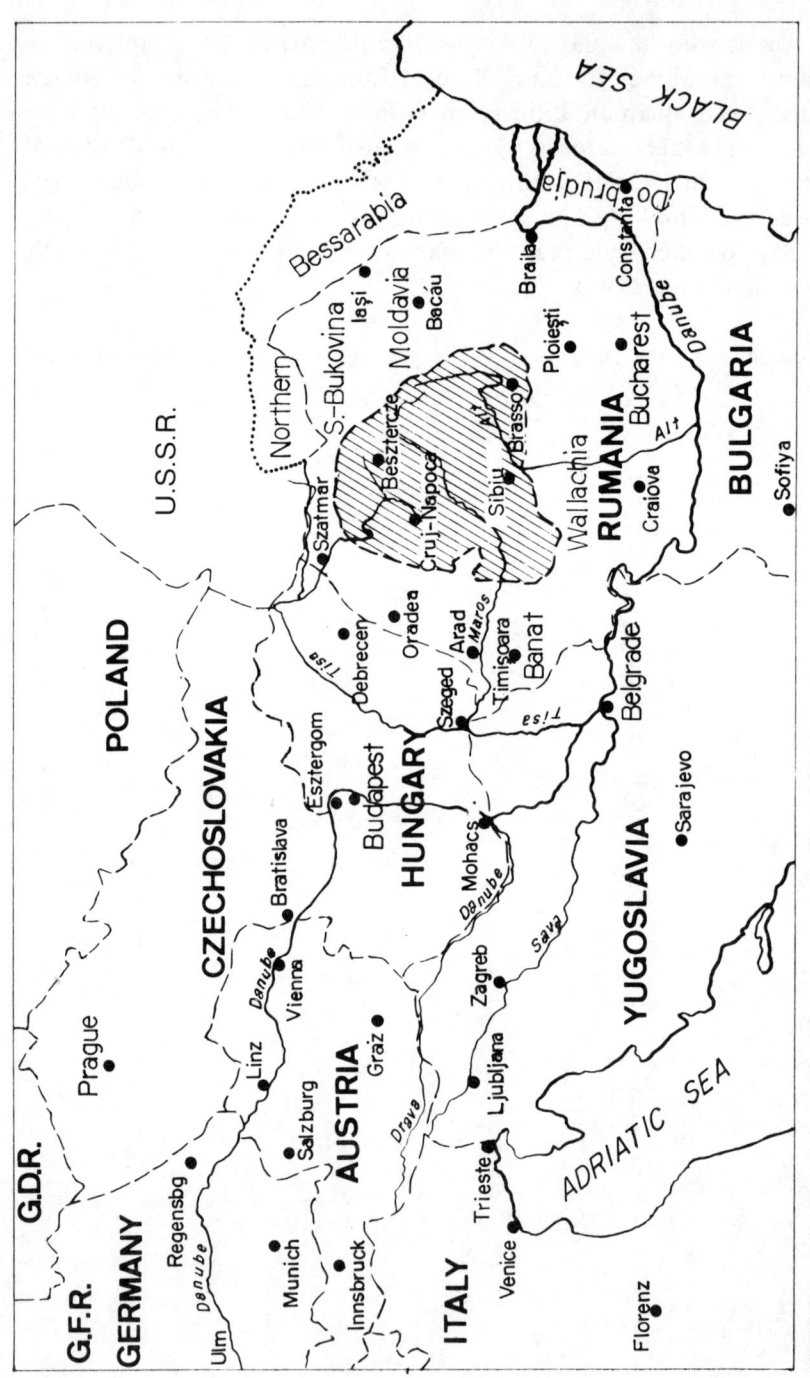

Transylvania — Part of the Danube Carpathian Basin

1

TERRITORY AND POPULATION

A Brief History of Transylvania and Its Peoples.

The history of Transylvania and its nationalities is a specific phenomenon in the development of Europe. Transylvania's ethnic composition is very different from that in the rest of present-day Romania—not only geographically but also historically, culturally, and economically. Even though the ways the national groups have lived and the goals they have pursued have diverged over the centuries, the peoples of the province have nonetheless been linked by a number of shared traditions and a common history. But at least as much as any other factor, European great-power politics have determined much of Transylvania's history and prevented true integration of the nationalities.

Today the name Transylvania is applied to all the territory transferred from Hungary to Romania by the Trianon Treaty of June 4, 1920—a region of about 103,000 square kilometers.[1] Before 1920, however, "Transylvania" connoted only part of the Trianon grant—the area of "historical Transylvania" respectively Transylvanian Principality, thus excluded the areas of the Great Hungarian Plain. Historic Transylvania covered 56,883 to 61,622 square kilometers without the area known as the *Partium,* or *"Partes regni Hungariae applicatae".* The *Partium* referred to those parts of Hungary that came under the sovereignty of the Princes of Transylvania, but did not become part of the Principality. The *Partium's* territory varied from period to period, at times including territories of northern Hungary, the counties Bihar,

Szatmár, Ugocsa, and Máramaros. In time, however, the term *Partium* came to be restricted to Zaránd, Kraszna, and Közép-Szolnok Counties and the Kővár region; areas that had belonged almost permanently to Transylvania (these counties are immediately to the west of historical Transylvania).

The Hungarians

Around 2000 B.C. the territory of present-day Transylvania was inhabited by Indo-Germanic tribes. The Agathurs appeared in the fifth century B.C., followed by the Scythians, who were in turn replaced by the Thracian-Geto-Dacian state. That state was overthrown between 105 and 107 A.D. by the Roman legions of Trajan, and Dacia (a part of present-day Transylvania) became a Roman province. In 271 the area was occupied by the Goths, who a century later (in 376) were expelled by the Huns. The Gepids and the Avars later occupied the area of present-day Transylvania. The Avar Empire, which also extended over the Hungarian Plane, was overthrown by the armies of Charlemagne at the end of the eighth century. Finally, at the beginning of the ninth century, Transylvania came under Bulgarian sovereignty, a change of rule that brought no significant change in the region's ethnic composition: remnants of the peoples of the Avar Empire, including widely dispersed Bulgarian-Slavonic tribes who had been swept into the area by the Avars.

Toward the end of the ninth century the migrations of peoples and the frequent change in sovereignty were brought to an end by the Magyar conquest of the Carpathian Basin. The Hungarians brought order and stability and were the first to establish a permanent state in the area. On the basis of recent archeological research, it seems likely that the Hungarians appeared in the Carpathian Basin centuries before the actual conquest,[2] which occurred between the ninth and eleventh centuries. The conquest and the subsequent Christianization of the area made Transylvania part of Western civilization; the region, in turn, served as a bastion of protection for that civilization. From the time of the conquest until 1918, Transylvania shared in the historical development of the Hungarian kingdom and was an integral part of the framework of the Hungarian state.[3]

As Transylvania became consolidated politically, three groups or "nations" assumed a leading role—the Magyar, the Székler, and the

TERRITORY AND POPULATION

Saxon. After the Reformation the churches of these nations constituted the four "received" religions (Catholic, Reformed or Calvinist, Evangelical or Lutheran, and Unitarian).

The Széklers, about one-third of the Hungarians in Transylvania, differ neither linguistically nor ethnically from the other Hungarians; the name was an inheritance from their historical development.[4] The rulers of Hungary ordered the Széklers to protect the kingdom's eastern frontiers at a time when Transylvania became consolidated in the Carpathian Basin. The Széklers were "free border guards" with privileges similar to those granted to the Saxon settlers. Although most of the Széklers were of peasant origin, a large proportion of them were granted nobility by the Hungarian kings as a reward for outstanding military service. By the fifteenth century the feudal political structure in Transylvania had consolidated and was organized locally into Hungarian counties and the Székler and Saxon "seat" (*szék, Stuhl*), an organization of public administration that lasted for four centuries.[5]

The Székler region, the area where they settled in the early Middle Ages, in southeastern and central Transylvania, consisted of the following counties: Udvarhely/Odorhei, Csík/Ciuc, Háromszék/Trei Scaune, Maros-Torda/Mureş, Aranyosszék, and Brassó/Braşov.[6] At the time of the annexation of Transylvania by Romania, there were approximately 600,000 Széklers in the region. The Transylvanian Hungarians and Széklers are largely Roman Catholic, Reformed, or Unitarian.

Another group of ethnic Magyars, separated in the course of time from the Széklers, is the Csángó Hungarians:[7] the Gyimes Csángós in Transylvania in the Trotuş/Tatros River valley; the Hétfalu Csángós in and around the town of Săcele/Szecseleváros near Braşov/Brassó; and other Csángós living outside Transylvania and the Carpathian Basin, in the territory of present-day Moldavia and Bucovina.[8] Exactly when the Csángós settled in the area between the Carpathian Mountain and the Siret/Szeret River has not been conclusively established. It is probable that they migrated from northern Transylvania in the twelfth or thirteenth century when the Árpád kings ruled the kingdom, but several Hungarian historians claim that the Moldavian Hungarians are a splinter group that separated from the Hungarians at the time of the conquest.[9] Other historians support the view that the Moldavian Csángó settlements along with all Hungarian settlements beyond the Carpathians must be regarded as the final phase in the conquest.[10]

The historical vicissitudes of the region tended to increase the number of Moldavian Magyars; but the process of Romanianization, already begun in the seventeenth century, continued into the nineteenth century and increased as a result of the oppressive Romanian nationality policy pursued by the Bucharest government between the two world wars. The four-century policy of Romanianization has yielded some results. As early as the eighteenth century, the Romanian language and Orthodox religion gained the upper hand in the towns and cities where the Magyars were assimilated by the Romanians. But in the villages the Hungarians retained their identity; and although Hungarian-language schools functioned only between 1949 and 1956, the people have managed to preserve their archaic dialect, their ancient folk culture, and their Catholic religion to this day.[11]

According to the 1930 Romanian census, if counted by national origin there were 20,964 Hungarians in Moldavia; if by native language, 23,894. Yet at the same time the census recorded 109,953 Catholics in the area, most of whom had to be Hungarian, since the Romanians of Moldavia belong to the Orthodox Church. The number of Csángó-Hungarians with Hungarian as their mother tongue can therefore be estimated in 1979 at roughly 100,000, if their high birthrate is also considered. Those whose mother tongue is not Hungarian—that is, those who speak Romanian—are hard to estimate; but on the basis of the number of Catholics shown in the older statistics their number can be put at roughly 60,000 to 80,000. These people are, however, Hungarian by ethnic origin as well as by their way of life.

The Saxons

The first group of German-speaking people to migrate to Transylvania were the Saxons (*Siebenbürger Sachsen*). It is now generally accepted, that the Transylvanian Saxons immigrated primarily from middle Franconia (Moselle-Franconia) and the left banks of the Rhine and Moselle rivers (Cologne, Lüttich, Aachen, Trier and Luxembourg). A small part of them came from Westfalia, Hesse, Bavaria, and Thuringia.[12] The Hungarian King Géza II (1141–1162) called (*vocati*) these Saxons to come to Transylvania as "guests" (*hospites*) to defend the southeastern frontier and to settle in the so-called *Königsboden* region[13] then uninhabited and lying between Hermannstadt/Sibiu

(Altland), Leschkirch and Grosschenk. The Germans were also settled in northeastern Transylvania near Bistritz/Bistriţa (Nösnerland), Rodna, and Sächsisch-Regen/Reghin during Géza II's reign. In 1211 King Endre II (1205-1235) permitted the Teutonic Order to settle in the Burzenland/Barcaság/Ţara Bîrsei,[14] an area that had been depopulated by repeated Cumanian incursions. The Teutonic Order built protective forts and also established several towns beyond the Carpathians but was soon expelled because of its independent political ambitions (1225). However, the settlements near Kronstadt/Braşov continued to be inhabited by Germans.

In 1224 Endre II granted territorial, political, and religious autonomy to the Saxons in his so-called "Golden Charter" (*Goldener Brief, Andreanum*).[15] The Saxons now formed the third privileged "nation" (alongside the Hungarian nobles in the counties and Széklers) in Transylvania. In 1486 the privileges granted in the *Andreanum* were confirmed and extended to other Saxon settlements by King Matthias Corvinus (1458-1490). This second grant established a basis for the so-called "University of the Saxon Nation" (*Sächsische Nationsuniversität, Universitas Saxonum*), i.e., the whole of the Saxon settlements and also an institution that represented the interests of the entire Saxon nation and for centuries guided the destiny of the Saxon people. The University's sphere of authority included the administration of justice, the management of the Saxon economy, and the working out of internal regulations. The University was headed by the Count of the Saxons (*Sachsengraf, Comes Saxonum*), who was freely elected and whose seat was in Hermannstadt. The Saxon Assembly (*Sachsentag*) was both an advisory and an executive body. The Transylvanian Saxons have been Lutherans since the Reformation.

The autonomy of the *Königsboden* and of the Transylvanian Saxons was temporarily abolished by the reforms of the Habsburg Emperor Joseph II (1780-1790) but was restored by his brother and successor Leopold II (1790-1792). In 1876, many of the Saxon privileges dating from the Middle Ages were eliminated, namely, those that had guaranteed the territorial autonomy of the *Königsboden*. However, the Saxon Assembly remained, and the University of the Saxon Nation was retained as a cultural foundation.

The historic privileges enjoyed by the Transylvanian Saxons were severely limited when the province passed to Romania.[16] The Romanian land reforms destroyed the Saxon communal landholdings; and on

March 20, 1937, the University of the Saxon Nation was abolished and its remaining property divided between Saxons and Romanians. The Transylvanian Saxon Evangelical Church became and has remained the legal heir of the Saxon part of that legacy. A common national and political consciousness among ethnic Germans in present-day Transylvania did not develop until the period between the two world wars—a phenomenon that was a result of their different origins, language, and time of settlement.

The intellectual and economic development of Transylvania owes a great deal to the Saxons. They founded the great majority of the province's towns and cities, pioneered its education, and contributed greatly to the development of an urban bourgeoisie. They laid the foundations of banking institutions and of industry in the mid-nineteenth century through their industrial associations, system of guilds, cooperatives, and credit institutions, most of which were significant economic factors in Transylvania right up to the end of the Second World War.

The vitality and survival of the Saxons in Transylvania has been due primarily to their first-rate cultural institutions and their ecclesiastical, economic, and democratic political organizations. At the time of the Romanian annexation of the province in 1920, there were approximately 234,000 Transylvanian Saxons. At present they represent the remnants of the eastern-most limit of German culture.

The Romanians

The origin of this southeast European people is still disputed and subject to various interpretations, which are not analyzed in this work. According to Romanian and certain other historiographers, the Romanian people grew out of the intermingling of Dacians with Romans (the Daco-Roman theory).[17] Documents place their final settlement in the southern Carpathians at the end of the twelfth and beginning of the thirteenth centuries,[18] at a time when Transylvania's inhabitants also included, in addition to the Hungarians and Saxons, some sparsely settled Slav-Bulgarian tribes. Documents show that small patriarchal Slavonic-Romanian communities—smaller or larger clans acting as the early cells of social development—were found in

Transylvania only after 1200. These Romanian hamlets, according to later (thirteenth- and fourteenth-century) documents were administered by the Hungarian state when fortified border areas were organized and put under the direction of a Hungarian official, the *ispán*.[19] But because they were semi-nomadic shepherds, the Romanians were not able to develop well-defined territorial settlements until much later. When the first semi-nomadic Romanians arrived in Transylvania, they sought refuge from invading and marauding Turks and found it in the mountains and isolated valleys of the region. By the fourteenth century they had begun to give up their nomadic way of life and to settle in villages. But the process was still incomplete as late as the eighteenth century, and a Romanian middle class did not develop until the nineteenth century.

At first the Romanians enjoyed certain autonomous rights under their leaders (called *voivod* and *knezen*); but with the development of the feudal order these leaders, who were largely of non-Romanian origin (Cumanian, Slav, Petchenegue or Hungarian), became nobles and the Romanian people sank into serfdom; their small communities remained primitive; and their own leaders now became their oppressors. The Transylvanian Romanians did not constitute one of the privileged "nations", nor was their Orthodox Church one of the "received" religions.

The development of Romanian national consciousness began around 1700. At that time a part of the Transylvanian Romanian intelligentsia[20] adopted the Uniate (or Greek Catholic) faith with its spiritual center at Rome, and hence they came into contact with Western culture and with the national consciousness that began to develop in Central Europe in the course of the eighteenth century. Although the national endeavors of the Transylvanian Romanians found some support in the policies of the Habsburg rulers, for various reasons none of the Romanian demands for political rights was fulfilled prior to 1848 when the old feudal order was abolished and the Romanian serfs were emancipated. Under the Dual Monarchy of Austria-Hungary and its nationality law of 1868, the Transylvanian Romanians became a lawful Transylvanian nation (alongside the Hungarians, Széklers, and Saxons) even though their collective rights were still not guaranteed.

From the last quarter of the nineteenth century on, there was increasing deterioration in the relations between the Hungarians and the other nationalities living under Magyar rule. The Transylvanian Romanians became more and more anti-Hungarian as their own national movement grew. But political power in the Hungarian lands remained a privilege in the hands of a few, until finally the alienated nationalities began to call for their own independent national states.

Population Movements and Changes

In the area of present-day Transylvania the ethnic Hungarians enjoyed a numerical preponderance until the eighteenth century.[21] In the first centuries of the Hungarian kingdom (tenth to thirteenth centuries) the Hungarians were virtually the only group within the Carpathian Basin, but at the beginning of the thirteenth century (1211) the Hungarian population of the Barcaság region was almost completely wiped out by Cumanian incursions. In this same period, especially after the settlement of the first Germans, smaller Romanian ethnic groups appeared in Transylvania for the first time, spurred to migrate by the first great Tatar invasion (1241). As a result, the expansion of the Hungarians beyond the Carpathians was halted.[22]

From the fifteenth century on, Romanians were settled in Transylvania in a regular manner. Their growth was augmented by the high Romanian birthrate and by the continuous decline in the Hungarian and German populations decimated in the defensive wars: the Hungarians and Germans living on the plains and in the river valleys were the first to encounter the invaders, while the Romanian shepherds were safe in their mountain hiding places. Romanian settlers also moved in to take the places left by Hungarian serfs, who were moving to the towns as the process of urbanization began. This migration of Romanians from the mountains to the river valleys began in the fifteenth century and resulted in greater contact between the Romanian, Hungarian, and German populations; dual place names and borrowed words are an indication of that contact.

Beginning with the period following the Reformation, population data were collected according to denomination and/or nationality. According to certain sources from the end of the sixteenth century, in historic Transylvania there were 255,000 Hungarians, 100,000 Romanians, and 70,000 Germans.[23] At the same time, another source records that the total population of Transylvania rose from 425,000 at the end of the fifteenth century to 700,000 by the end of the sixteenth century.[24]

The continued settlement of the Romanians in Transylvania in the sixteenth and seventeenth centuries[25] was the consequence of the vast movement of peoples that occurred in East-Central Europe under the pressure created by the Ottoman Turks as they moved through the Balkans into Europe. This increase in the Romanian population was exacerbated by the extension of Turkish rule over the Romanian principalities[26] and by the destruction wreaked by Turkish-Tatar punitive expeditions (1599 to 1661) into Transylvania. Further contributing factors were the invasion of Transylvania by Voivod Michael the Brave of Wallachia (1599) and the reign of terror that the Habsburg General Basta exercised over Transylvania (1600–1604), as well as sickness and starvation, (1628 to 1636 and 1640 to 1646) all of which hit the Hungarian and German populations living on the plains and in the valleys. The Romanianization of the Transylvanian areas with a mixed population took place particularly rapidly.

At the end of the seventeenth century the Great Hungarian Plain was liberated from Turkish rule, and the movement of the Hungarian population from the Great Plain into Transylvania abated. But since the Danubian Principalities remained under Turkish rule for another 150 years, the Romanian population there, seeking refuge from Turkish oppression, now fled to Transylvania. The result was that by the beginning of the eighteenth century the national composition of the Transylvanian population had changed significantly.

During the entire eighteenth century and right up to 1821 when the rule of the Fanariots[27] in the Danubian Principalities ended, the migration of Romanians into Transylvania continued. The number of Romanians who settled in the territory of the entire Habsburg Monarchy between 1720 and 1787 has been estimated at between 350,000 and 400,000.[28] In 1730, according to Austrian statistics, the total population of Transylvania was approximately 725,000, of which 420,000 were Romanian, 190,000 Hungarian, and 110,000 Saxon.[29] Hóman and Szekfű record that in 1765 the total Transylvanian population was one million, of which 550,000 were Romanian, 260,000 Hungarian, and 120,680 Saxon.[30]

In the eighteenth century most of the Romanians in Transylvania were still new settlers or at most the descendants of the first generation born in Transylvania. The deteriorating economic and social situation of that time was better weathered by the Romanians, who were used to poor circumstances, than by the Germans or Hungarians, who were accustomed to higher standards of living. Serfdom, an important factor in the demographic developments, underwent many changes in that century. While, for example, the more demanding Hungarian population left the serf-holdings en masse and either migrated out of the province or sought a livelihood in the Transylvanian towns, the Transylvanian landlords, left without serfs, were glad to take on the cheaper labor force they found in the less demanding Romanians.

According to Austrian statistics of 1857, the population of historical Transylvania included 1,287,883 Romanians, 569,742 Hungarians, and 202,114 Transylvanian Saxons;[31] by the end of the century the 1890 census showed 1,276,890 Romanians, 697,945 Hungarians, and 217,670 Germans on the same territory. At the turn of the century, as recorded in the 1900 census, the population of Transylvania totaled 2,450,000: 1,397,282 Romanians, 814,994 Hungarians, and 233,019 Germans by nationality.[32]

Later Immigrants

The so-called Swabians of the Banat[33] are another large ethnic German group in present-day Transylvania. The most of them came originally from middle Franconia (Moselle-Franconia) and the left banks of the Rhine River (Rhineland-Palatinate, Trier, Lorraine), while a small part of them immigrated from Württemberg, Bavaria and Austria in the course of the eighteenth century. (1718 to 1739 and 1756 to 1766). They came in response to a Habsburg appeal and settled in the Banat,[34] a region that had been devastated by the Turks. In a virtually enclosed area of the eastern Banat, the Swabians formed one of the largest nationalities—almost one-third of the population of Timiș-Torontal/Temes-Torontál County. Those in the Banat Hegyvidék (*Banater Bergland*) came from Austria, Bohemia, and Slovakia (the Zips Germans). The Romanian census combines the population of the German settlements in Arad County with the Swabians of the Banat, calling them all "Swabian."

The Swabians created an exemplary agricultural system in the devastated, infertile, marshy Banat. A middle class made up of artisans, merchants, and intelligentsia also developed, as did a wealthy peasantry; and important local political decisions were made by the Swabian

Council (*Schwabenrat*). But unlike the Transylvanian Saxons, the Banat Swabians never achieved a national-political representation, because of their distinct historical development. Certainly, the fact that a large part of the German intellectuals in the Banat in the last century were assimilated by the Hungarians played no small role in this development.

The Banat Swabians were by and large Roman Catholic; by the time Romania annexed Transylvania and the eastern part of the Banat, there were 293,000 Swabians in the Banat and another 30,000 to 40,000 around Arad.

Groups of German settlers arrived in the region of present-day Satu Mare/Szatmár as early as the thirteenth century, but they were annihilated in the struggles of later centuries. The settling of the present-day Szatmár Swabians (*Sathmarer Schwaben*), who came from the Württemberg region of the German Empire, began in the early eighteenth century (1712). They, too, came as part of the *Impopulatio* or repopulation program of the Habsburgs after the Turks had been pushed out of the region.

The Szatmár Swabians live in northwestern Transylvania, primarily in the town Carei/Gross Karol/Nagykároly and in the neighboring villages. The 1920 Romanian statistics show about 36,000 Szatmár Swabians, while another source[35] puts their number at 43,000 at the beginning of the 1920s, in addition to another 4,200 ethnic Germans in Bihor/Bihar County. A large proportion of these Swabians were assimilated by the area's Hungarian population, but the Romanian authorities have been re-Germanizing them since 1921.

The first Armenian immigrants appeared in Transylvania in the Middle Ages; a second group arrived between 1654 and 1672, seeking refuge from religious persecution; but the bulk of them settled in the course of the eighteenth century, when Gherla/Szamosújvár, and Dumbrăveni/Erzsébetváros were founded, although Armenians also lived in and around Gheorgheni/Gyergyószentmiklós. By religion Gregorian-Armenian and since 1686 Armenian-Catholic, they developed a lively commerce and a sizable intelligentsia. Over the past century most of them have been almost completely assimilated by the Hungarians around them: in 1850 there were approximately 7,000 Armenians in Transylvania and by the turn of the century 12,000;[36] but by 1930 only 1,041 and in 1956 a mere 365 claimed Armenian nationality, of which 57 percent spoke Hungarian, 23 percent Armenian, 16 percent Romanian, and 2 percent other languages as well as their mother tongue.[37]

The settlement of the Jewish population in present-day Transylvania occurred at the end of the eighteenth and the beginning of the nineteenth century. The Jews came mainly from the eastern European area, after the dismemberment of Poland (1772 and 1793) and settled in Maramureş/Máramaros (about 30,000 to 40,000) and others in Satu Mare/Szatmár and Bihor/Bihar Counties. They were not counted as a separate nationality until the 1920 Romanian population registration: those of Jewish nationality, who did not list Yiddish as their mother tongue, considered themselves members of the Hungarian, Romanian, German, or other nationalities. According to the 1920 data, they numbered 171,443 in Transylvania.

Like the Armenians, the Transylvanian Jews have engaged almost exclusively in commerce. But a stratum of the intellectuals who regarded themselves as Hungarian have enriched the Transylvanian press, literature, and the arts with outstanding creations, particularly in the period between the two world wars.

At the time of the annexation of Transylvania, Jews lived all over the province, but they were concentrated in the larger towns and cities; about 11 percent of the urban population and 2 percent of the rural population belonged to the Jewish faith, and most of them regarded their mother-tongue as Hungarian.[38] In the Romanian Banat a third part of the Jewish population regarded their mother-tongue as German.

The ethnic groups of Slav origin settled in Transylvania mainly in the course of the nineteenth and twentieth centuries. However, there had been Slav tribes in Transylvania as early as the Middle Ages. Although at first they adopted Hungarian language and culture, they were later assimilated by the Romanians, a process facilitated by a shared Orthodox religious faith. Of the ethnic Slavs in Transylvania, the South Slavs and Bulgarians live in the Banat; here, one can hardly speak of assimilation. In the Romanian Banat, for instance, there are six Czech settlements as well as 8,000 ethnic Croats in the Kroschowa/Karasova District. The Slovaks, who came as forestry workers in the nineteenth century, and the Ruthenians live in the northwestern and middle parts of Transylvania.

Wandering gypsies appeared in Transylvania for the first time during the Turkish wars. The gypsies who settled in the region have lived primarily on the periphery of towns and villages, in separate districts.

TERRITORY AND POPULATION

According to the Hungarian census of December 31, 1910,[39] and similar Romanian statistics, there were about 5 million inhabitants in the territory of present-day Transylvania. Table I-1 shows that population according to language, as given in the census reports.

The Effect of Two World Wars on Transylvania's Territory and Population

Transylvania: Territorial and Demographic Changes

The two world wars significantly changed the frontiers of the East-Central European countries and, in turn, the fate of the peoples living there. According to the Treaty of Trianon (June 4, 1920), about two-thirds (233,349 square kilometers) of the total territory of historical Hungary[40] was transferred to neighboring states[41]—most of them carved out of the pre-war Austro-Hungarian Empire. Table I-2 shows the Hungarian territorial losses after World War I.

The approximately 103,000 square kilometers transferred to Romania included more than historical Transylvania. There were also parts of eastern Hungary: the eastern Banat, the Körös/Crişana region, Szatmár/Satu Mare and Máramaros/Maramureş. Almost half the population of this area was not Romanian by nationality at the time of the annexation; the ethnic Romanians were represented by a slight majority of about 53.8 percent.

This study will now examine the phenomena of the nationality transformation during the past sixty years in the territory of present-day Transylvania—on the basis of the available demographic data and the conclusions that they permit. The task is made extremely difficult by the frequent territorial changes, territorial-administrative reorganizations, and the loss of population resulting from the two world wars, as well as from deportations and other arbitrary measures.

In 1914 on the eve of World War I, the Kingdom of Romania had a population of about 7,900,000 and an area of 137,903 square kilometers, including Moldavia, Wallachia (later renamed Muntenia and Oltenia), and Dobrugea. Together these territories are known in Romanian terminology and in scholarly usage as *Vechiul Regat* (Old Kingdom), and in everyday usage simply as the Regat.[42]

TABLE I-1

Population of Transylvania in 1910 According to Language

	Hungarian Statistics		Romanian Statistics	
Romanian	2,824,177	53.8%	2,871,733	54.7%
Hungarian	1,660,488	31.7%	1,618,246	30.8%
German	556,009	10.6%	556,009	10.0%
Slovak, Czech	42,000	0.8%		
Ruthenian	20,482	0.3%		
Serb, Croatian	54,055	0.9%		
Other	106,071	1.9%		
	5,263,282	100.0%	5,248,540	

Source: note 39

With the conclusion of the First World War and the dismemberment of the Austro-Hungarian Empire, the territory of Romania more than doubled, to 295,049 square kilometers; its population reached 18,000,000, of which, however, some 5,200,000 (28%) were not ethnic Romanians. In addition to the territories annexed from Hungary, Romania's territorial gains included Bessarabia from tsarist Russia (44,422 square kilometers), the Bucovina from Austria on the basis of the Treaty of St. Germain (10,442 square kilometers),[43] and some small border areas from Bulgaria and Dobrugea on the basis of the Treaty of Neuilly (23,262 square kilometers).[44] In the Greater Romania thus created, the national minorities comprised one-third of the population; and the province of Transylvania thus created included one-third of the territory of that Romanian state. But the vicissitudes of the Second World War and its aftermath meant border and territorial changes not only for Romania but for Transylvania as well. The Second Vienna Award, concluded on August 30, 1940, divided the province into Northern and Southern Transylvania: the 43,492 square kilometers and 2,580,372 inhabitants of Northern Transylvania were returned to Hungary, while Southern Transylvania (59,295 square kilometers and 3,331,642 inhabitants) remained part of Romania. Combined with other pre-World War II territorial changes, it meant that the territory of Romania was decreased by about one-third. After

TABLE I-2

Hungary's Territorial Losses After World War I

To Romania	102,787 square kilometers
To Yugoslavia	63,497 square kilometers
To Czechoslovakia	62,353 square kilometers
To Austria	4,107 square kilometers
To Poland	584 square kilometers
The Free City of Fiume	21 square kilometers
Total territorial loss	233,349 square kilometers
Retained by Hungary	93,343 square kilometers

Source: note 41.

the Second World War, Transylvania was reunited and again became a province of Romania by the Paris Peace Treaties of February 10, 1947.

Changes in Population

Every change of territory has resulted in alterations in the ethnic structure of the area's population. Between the change of power in 1920 and 1924, the territory of Transylvania lost about 197,000 Hungarians, including those who left voluntarily, were expelled, or escaped.[45] At the same time a large number of Romanians migrated to Transylvania from the Regat, among them officials, merchants, soldiers, and peasants. By 1922 approximately 25,000 had left Romania, 93 percent of them from Transylvania.[46]

The national minorities were hard hit by the direct results of the Second World War—political and territorial changes, forced resettlement, and deportation. The demographical picture underwent a drastic change. The first substantial shift of population resulted from the territorial realignments of 1940. The Soviet annexation of Bessarabia and Northern Bucovina precipitated the flight of 40,000 people; other major relocation projects from this area were also in the offing. According to official Romanian statistics 90,000 Germans from Bessarabia and 35,000 from Northern Bucovina were resettled as per the German-Soviet agreement of 23 August 1939; the actual numbers were, however, 93,000 and 43,600 respectively. After the agreement of September 5 and October 9, 1940 between Germany and Romania, about 77,500 ethnic Germans were resettled:[47] 52,100 ethnic Germans from Romanian-ruled Southern Bucovina, 15,400 from Northern Dobrugea,[48] and 10,000 from other areas of the Regat. Most of the resettled ethnic German population, 88,000 from Bessarabia and 23,900 from Bucovina went to the eastern part of Germany. Nevertheless, about 35,000 came under Hungarian rule in Northern Transylvania, but after the Romanian *coup d'état* of August 23, 1944, they were transferred to Austria, from where approximately 10,000 found their way to Germany at the end of the war.

Another result of the Second Vienna Award was, of course, that Hungary gained all of Northern Transylvania's population: 1,380,758 (or 1,380,506) Hungarians, 1,029,343 (or 1,029,470) Romanians, some 45,645 Germans,[49] and about 124,626 persons of other nationalities. Southern Transylvania, which remained part of Romania, then had a population that consisted of 2,274,138 Romanians, 490,000 Germans, 363,000 Hungarians, and about 205,000 belonging to other nationalities.[50] Approximately 160,000 to 190,000 of Southern Transylvania's inhabitants went to Northern Transylvania, either voluntarily, by escape, or by removal. These refugees were roughly 79 percent Hungarian; also included were 1,400 Romanians, about 1,000 Germans, 430 Slovaks, 60 Ruthenians, 30 Gypsies, and about 300 persons belonging to other nationalities.[51] Of the approximately 1 million Romanians in Northern Transylvania, about 200,000 left after the area's annexation to Hungary. After the Romanian *coup d'état* in August 1944, the Romanian population that had escaped to Southern Transylvania returned to Northern Transylvania; in turn about 125,000 Hungarians and about 50,000 Germans from this area fled or joined the retreating German army as the Soviet and Romanian troops moved in.

Of Northern Transylvania's Jewish population, approximately two-thirds claimed Hungarian nationality; as a result, the security of their lives and property was guaranteed until the spring of 1944, when the German deportations began, abetted by a Germanophile Hungarian government.

TERRITORY AND POPULATION

The Loss of Population

The two world wars brought about radical changes in the population of Transylvania, as in general in Central and Eastern Europe. Three nationality groups in the province—the Germans, the Jews, and the Hungarians—were particularly reduced in number. The number of Romania's national minority inhabitants—including those from Transylvania—who died, were killed, or deported, or disappeared in the Second World War has been estimated at between 700,000 and 800,000; of these about 350,000 to 400,000 were Jewish; 200,000 were German; and 150,000 to 200,000 Hungarian.

The German population in Romania as a whole was almost halved by the war.[52] According to information now available, the losses suffered by Romania's German population during the 1940s were as follows: 35,000 soldiers who died or disappeared,[53] and another 50,000 who escaped from the Soviet-Romanian army, or were evacuated by the German army from Northern Transylvania to the West. In addition 27,000 Transylvanian Saxons, 35,000 Swabians from the Banat and another 18,000 individuals from different parts of Romania were deported to the Soviet Union in January 1945. The sources vary on the exact number taken, but findings so far indicate that approximately 90,000 to 100,000 people were involved, about 15 to 20 percent of whom never came back. Approximately half of those who did return settled in either the German Federal Republic or Austria.[54]

The German population in Romania suffered another blow in the forced resettlement carried out in June 1951: 40,000 Swabians from the Banat were sent to the area of the Bărăgan Steppes in the Regat and made to perform forced labor amid horrifying circumstances.[55] Some of those thus deported were permitted to return in 1955, but in their absence their homes and property were taken by new settlers (Romanians and Gypsies).[56]

The 1939 to 1941 population transfer agreements that Bucharest signed with both Berlin and Moscow also sharply reduced the number of Germans in Romania, through the relocation of the German population of Bessarabia, Bucovina and Dobrugea.

The extent of the population loss suffered by the Germans in Romania can be readily seen by comparing the official figures for 1930 and 1948, as shown in Table I-3. These figures, however, are not entirely realistic since some of the Germans, fearing repression and deporta-

TABLE I-3

German Population of Romania, 1930-1948

Year	Transylvanian Saxons	Banat Swabians	Total Population of Romania by language	by national origin
1930	237,416	275,369	760,687	745,421
1948	157,715	171,022*	343,913	

* Including Arad county

tion, did not claim German as their mother tongue in 1948 and others had not yet been returned from Soviet deportation.

A large proportion of the ethnic Germans in post-war Romania have opted for emigration. The destruction of the basis of their economic and cultural life and Romania's nationality policy with its assimilative thrust, so destructive of ethnic characteristics, have forced many members of national minorities to leave. By the end of the 1970s, the number of Germans in Romania had decreased by 358,732, of which about 170,000 were Transylvanian Saxons and 159,738 were Banat Swabians, including those from Arad County. The policy of allowing families to be reunited has permitted thousands of Romania's ethnic German to emigrate to the German Federal Republic: as early as 1945 to 1949, 15,000 Germans emigrated to the West; they were followed by another 90,242 from 1945 to 1979 who left to be reunited with their families. The number of those emigrating to the Federal Republic Germany is constantly increasing; experts estimate that 80 percent of the Germans in Romania want to emigrate.[57]

A catastrophe of almost incalculable proportions befell the East and Central European Jews from the early 1930s until the end of the Second World War. It differed in intensity, if not in basic nature, from country to country; their number of pre-war Romania was decreased by half during the course of the war: a large proportion fell victim to the racial hatred which escalated from the anti-Semitic excesses into mass murder. Others disappeared as a result of the deportations and a sizable number either emigrated or escaped. The scale of annihilation and emigration is best illustrated by again comparing the census data for the years 1930 and 1948. The 1930 census showed 518,754 Jewish inhabitants, or 2.9 percent of the whole population of Romania, when calculated on the basis of language; 728,115 or 4 percent on the basis of national origin or religion. By contrast, the 1948 census showed 138,795 Jewish inhabitants in Romania as a whole, using language as the criterion.[58]

The data concerning the population losses suffered by the Romanian Jews (including those due to emigration) are somewhat contradictory. Using the category of nationality in the 1930 census as the basis for calculations and comparing them with the data for the year 1956, the loss amounted to 27 percent of the total population—209,214 including 15,000 from the Regat, Southern Transylvania, and Southern Bucovina combined; 103,919 from Northern Bucovina and Herța District, and 90,295 from Northern Transylvania.[59] According to another source, by 1956 only 32.4 percent of the Romanian Jewish population of 1930 still lived on Romanian territory and by 1966 only 9.5 percent.[60]

It can be assumed, however, that the numerical losses were considerably higher, amounting perhaps to 50–53 percent of the total Jewish population of pre-war Romania or, according to estimates, about 400,000 individuals.[61] The largest proportion of the victims were inhabitants of the territories that were taken away from Romania: about 200,000 Romanian Jews either escaped from Bessarabia and Moldavia to the Soviet Union, fleeing the German-Romanian occupation, or lost their lives in the 1941–1942 mass murders carried out under the Antonescu government (the pogrom of Iași).[62] In Northern Bucovina approximately 80,000 Jews died or disappeared; and of the 178,799 Jewish inhabitants of Transylvania (with nationality as the criterion) approximately 100,000 lost their lives in Northern Transylvania in 1944, after the German occupation of Hungary.[63]

After the war Jewish emigration began immediately—most of it ultimately to the state of Israel created in 1948. The frequent territorial changes and illegal emigration make precise estimates difficult. Between 1948 and August 1952, according to some sources, 128,609 Jews arrived in Israel from Romania.[64] Other sources for roughly the same period (1949–1954) say that only about 93,000 Jews emigrated from Romania.[65] Nonetheless, emigration has continued; in both 1975 and 1976 more than 2,300 Romanian Jews were given permits to emigrate to Israel.[66]

The scale of emigration is obvious: the 1977 edition of the *Jewish Yearbook* puts the number of Jews living in Romania at 60,000, of whom approximately 40,000 resided in Bucharest.[67] According to the provisional data of the 1977 official Romanian census, the number of Jews in Romania was 25,686 or 0.119 percent of the total population.[68] The decrease can be attributed to Jewish emigration under the pressure of the present regime and a decline in the Jewish birthrate since 1935, in part a result of the fear of anti-Semitic persecution and in part an effect of assimilation.[69]

There are no precise data concerning the losses suffered by Romania's Hungarians during World War II; but based on comparisons made with pre-war population figures, the losses are estimated at 150,000 to 200,000.

2

TERRITORIAL AND POPULATION CHANGES SINCE WORLD WAR I

Territorial and Administrative Changes Within the New Transylvania

The territorial-administrative reorganizations and the constant changing of place names, which the Romanian state carried out between 1925 and 1968 in its province of Transylvania, are extraordinary phenomena, almost unique in the Danubian region. Contrary to international usage, the place names have been changed with every change in political parties and modification in the state structure.[1] The Romanianized place names often bear no relation to the original historical (Hungarian or German) place names. The primary reason for changing them has been that the traditional names did not sound Romanian. The new place names are in many instances variations on those of localities in the Old Kingdom, or they are names of noted Romanians.[2]

The frequent changes in provincial and local administration not only ran counter to the spirit of the historical traditions and patterns but were frequently carried out in a manner detrimental to the national minorities. These changes were part of a latent policy of assimilation and exerted a negative influence on the development of the minorities—on their population, their education and in general on every manifestation of their intellectual, economic, and social life. Every new administrative measure, every new territorial alteration tended to narrow further the rights of the national minorities.

Until 1925, the enlarged Romania which had emerged after World War I retained the old Hungarian units of administration in the areas annexed from the former Magyar kingdom: the system of counties or *vármegye*,[3] which had existed since the time of King Stephen, (970-7-1038) was continued. Then, in 1925,[4] Romania divided its new territory into three provinces: the Banat/Bánság with three counties; Crișana-Maramureș/Körösvidék-Máramaros with five counties; and Transylvania proper with fifteen counties. However, the new law also proved to be a turning point in Transylvania's territorial-administrative history in several other respects:

a) The territorial unity of historical Transylvania was violated for the first time when two parishes from the old Bistrița-Năsăud/Beszterce-Naszód County were transferred to Suceava County in the Regat.[5]
b) The historical names of some of the Transylvanian counties were altered, as well as some of the villages and towns.
c) Some of the ancient county seats were moved to new towns, a measure clearly designed to ensure that wherever possible a majority of the town's population would be Romanian.
d) The most significant change, however, was the new territorial division of the counties. The boundaries of all but two counties (Maramureș and Caraș-Severin) were redrawn, and again the purpose was primarily to create a relative Romanian majority in as many counties as possible.

The 1925 Public Administration Act and its county division were changed on numerous subsequent occasions, modified in accordance with the interests of the frequently changing governments. The process was finally halted by a new Public Administration Law[6] introduced by the royal dictatorship of Carol II on August 14, 1938. This new law divided the country into ten provinces and placed the counties, which by now had lost their significance and even their legal identity, under the authority of the royal governors of the provinces; the law also excluded all forms of self-government. The purpose of this new territorial arrangement was political: to weaken further the role of the national minorities, particularly the Hungarians.[7]

After the dissolution of Greater Romania in 1940, the provinces were abolished. The fragmented counties which resulted from the new frontiers drawn by the Vienna Award were merged, both by the Hun-

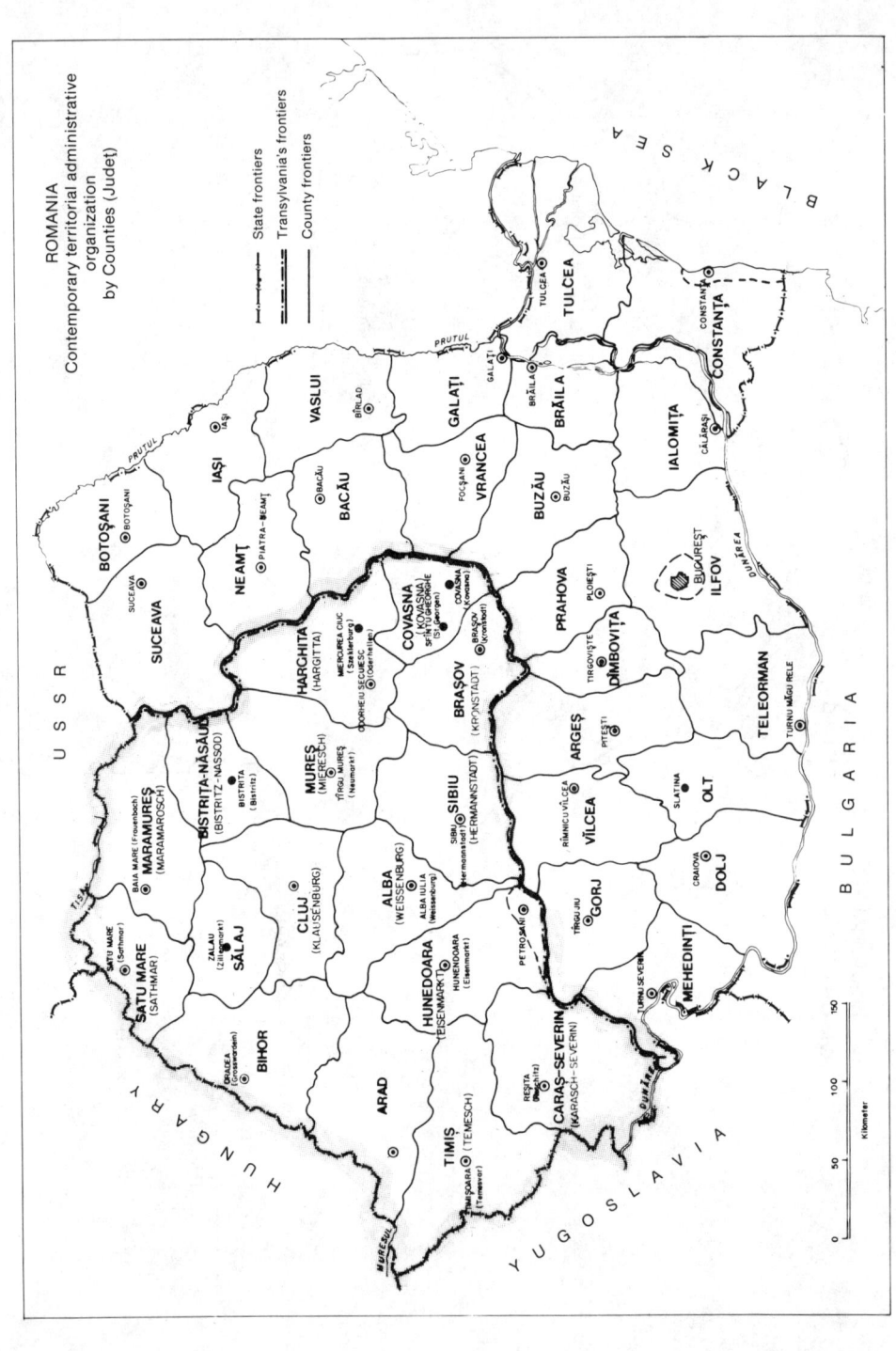

garian and by the Romanian governments, with the various neighboring counties.

After the Second World War the territory of Northern Transylvania was returned to Romania. The county boundaries of the 1925 Public Administration Act were essentially restored and remained in effect until 1950, with one exception. In 1948 a new constitution abolished Romania's historical provinces[8] (to emphasize the unitary character of the country) and divided Romania into new provinces, counties, districts, and parishes. By that time the territory of historical Transylvania had been significantly reduced.[9]

A new law of the Romanian People's Republic from 5 September 1950[10] once more abolished the county system and redivided the country, with the Soviet Union as a model, into regions (*regiune*), districts (*raion*), villages (*comune*), and towns, each with its own people's council or soviet. By 1952, however, the number of regions had been reduced to 18,[11] and in 1956 they were reduced yet again to 16;[12] by 1968 the area, names, and number of districts and their boundaries had again been altered on countless occasions.

The present system of counties came into effect on February 16, 1968, the result of a new territorial-administrative reorganization which divided the territory of Romania into 39 counties (*judeţ*), 236 towns and cities, and 2,706 parishes.[13] The purpose of the new county network was to improve the position of the ethnic Romanians, so once again historical traditions were completely ignored in drawing up the new boundaries: areas which had been united historically, geographically and ethnographically were dismembered and portions of them attached to faraway county seats with which they had had no previous connection of any sort.[14] Of the 39 counties in the new county system, 16 are in Transylvania; thus, of the 22 or 23 old Transylvanian counties, six have been abolished.[15] As a result of the various boundary revisions, by 1966 the territory of Transylvania had already been reduced to 99,837 square kilometers.

The Territorial Distribution of the National Minorities

In the territories of present-day Romania, the national minorities—primarily the ethnic Hungarians and to some extent the ethnic Germans—have with minor changes remained in their original historical places of settlement; and their territorial distribution to some extent is an indication of their social organization and structure.

One part of the ethnic Hungarian population lives in almost self-contained enclaves; others, while in regions that can still be clearly delineated, are intermingled with the Romanian people or with other national minorities; and there are also scattered groups of Hungarians living in urban areas or beyond the Carpathians, in the territory of the Regat. Approximately 60 percent of the Hungarians still form a connected, compact ethnic group in sizable areas of Transylvania (the Székler region, Bihor, Satu Mare, Sălaj and Cluj Counties); a further 30 percent live in the Transylvanian towns and cities (in certain urban areas they constitute the overwhelming majority of the population) or in their suburban areas, or elsewhere in scattered groups; while a further 8 percent are found beyond the Carpathian Mountains in areas where there are small linguistic islands. Table II-1 shows the distribution of Hungarians in the various regions of Romania as of 1979. The estimated figures are based on indirect calculations and deductions and contradict official government statistics.[16]

According to the March 15, 1966 census,[17] the Hungarians constitute an absolute majority in two of Transylvania's sixteen counties: Harghita and Covasna; they exceed 40 percent in two other counties, 30 percent in one county, 20 percent in two counties, and 10 percent in four counties. To a greater or lesser extent, there are Hungarians in all the 39 counties of Romania.

As a result of resettlements and frontier changes carried out during the Second World War, only part of the second-largest national minority in Romania, the Germans—except in the territory of the Old Kingdom—has been able to stay in their original areas of settlement: in Transylvania there were about 170,000 (47.4%), in the Banat, inclusive Arad, 159,738 (44.5%), Satu Mare 6,482 (1.8%), Maramureş about 3,430 (1.0%), Bucovina about 2,200 (0.6%), Bucharest 5,002 (1.4%), and in other areas about 11,880 (3.3%), total 358,732 people.[18]

The Ukrainian-Ruthenian nationality is the most numerous Slavic group in Transylvania—55,000 individuals, most of them living in an almost ethnically pure block in part of Maramureş County in Northern Transylvania, an area adjacent to the Soviet Carpatho-Ukraine. The greater share of the Lipovans, who are of Russian nationality (about 32,000 people) as well as the Turkish-Tatar ethnic group was settled in northern Dobrugea. Czech, Bulgarian, Serbian, and Croat-Karashovan ethnic groups are to be found in the Banat.

TABLE II-1

Distribution of Hungarians in the Various Regions in Romania (1979)

Area	Hungarian Population in Area	% of Total Population in Area
Along the Romanian-Hungarian frontier, including the one-time Partium and the Banat	710,000	31.0
Székler region, with the Tîrgu Mureş area	690,000	30.7
The Cluj area together with Mezőség region, Kalotaszeg and the Arieş (Aranyos), Mureş (Maros) and Someş (Szamos) river valleys	200,000	8.8
The Braşov, Făgăraş, Sibiu, and the Jiul Valley area	130,000	5.7
Other Transylvanian urban areas and scattered settlements	300,000	13.5
The Old Kingdom (Regat)	240,000	10.3
Total	2,270,000	100.00

The Romanian Census and the Distribution of the National Minorities

Determining the exact numbers of the national minority populations in Romania in the period following the annexation of Transylvania is a task fraught with difficulties. Romania was the only European state that failed to conduct a census in accordance with the international regulations after the conclusion of the First World War. Romanian demographic literature, though it often refers to the 1920 demographic register,[19] does not recognize it as an official census. The validity of this 1920 data, based largely on estimates, is highly debatable, but nonetheless it offers some guidance as the first population register issued by the Romanian authorities after the First World War. According to the 1920 compilation, the population of the enlarged Romania

TABLE II-2

1920 Population of Romania

National Group	Number	Percent
Romanian	11,545,300	71.9
Hungarian	1,463,600	9.1
German	713,600	4.5
Jewish	778,100	4.9
Ukrainian	500,500	3.1
Russian	174,300	1.1
Bulgarian	351,300	2.2
Gypsy	133,000	0.8
Turkish and Tatar	222,400	1.4
Gagaus (Turkish tribe)	—	—
Slovak	26,900	0.2
Serbian	52,600	0.3
Polish	35,000	0.2
Other	48,700	0.3
Total	16,045,300	100.0

Source: note 19.

was about 16.8 to 17.1 million. The distribution of the population is given in Table II-2.

As a result of the war, Romania had more than doubled its territory, but it had not attained a level of economic, cultural, or moral development sufficient to deal with its new tasks, and primarily with the problems of the national minorities. At the time of the annexation it appeared that the minorities would receive the same treatment as the Romanians—that there would be free scope for their ethnic, cultural, economic, and social development; but soon after Romania took over its new territories, hope for equal treatment was dashed by measures such as the 1921 agrarian reform and the restrictions enacted in the sphere of education. That agrarian reform, as well as the general deterioration of economic life, the corruption in the new Romanian administrative system, the general insecurity of the national minorities and the policy of oppression against them all exerted a negative influence on their development.

TABLE II-3

1930 Population of Romania

National Group	By Language		By National Origin	
	Number	Percent	Number	Percent
Romanian	13,180,936	73.0	12,981,324	71.9
Hungarian	1,554,525	8.6	1,425,507	7.9
German	760,687	4.2	745,421	4.1
Jewish	518,754	2.9	728,115	4.0
Ruthenian-Ukrainian	641,485	3.6	582,115	3.2
Russian	450,981	2.5	409,150	2.3
Bulgarian	364,373	2.0	366,384	2.0
Turkish, Tatar, Gagaus	288,073	1.6	282,663	1.6
Gypsy	101,015	0.6	262,501	1.5
Serbian, Croatian, Slovene	47,724	0.3	51,062	0.3
Other (Czech, Slovak, Polish, Greek, Armenian, etc.)	148,475	0.7	222,786	1.2
Total	18,057,028	100.0	18,057,028	100.00

Source: note 20.

The first official Romanian census, and at the same time the last one prior to the outbreak of World War II, was conducted in 1930 and provided more reliable data concerning the ethnic and national breakdown of Romania's population.[20] The data indicate that of Romania's total population, 28.1 percent, about 5,075,704, were members of national minorities.

This 1930 census showed 18,057,028 inhabitants in the whole of Romania and their distribution according to language and national origin, as given in Table II-3. For Transylvania the 1930 census showed a population of 5,549,806 divided according to their language and national origin, as shown in Table II-4.

The classification on the basis of language and national origin merits a closer look. The difference between the mother tongue and the ethnic origin of 129,000 people among the Hungarians, for example, can only be explained by the categorizing itself, false evaluation of mixed marriages or religious affiliation, or the manipulation of the data on

TABLE II-4

1930 Population of Transylvania

National Group	By Language		By National Origin	
	Number	Percent	Number	Percent
Romanian	3,233,362	58.2	3,208,804	57.8
Hungarian	1,481,164	26.7	1,355,496	24.4
German	542,068	9.8	545,138	9.8
Jewish	109,868	2.0	178,799	3.2
Gypsy	43,000	0.8	107,202	2.0
Other	140,344	2.5	154,367	2.8
Total	5,549,806	100.0	5,549,806	100.0

Source: note 20.

individuals. Only in a very small number of cases can it be explained by the adoption of Hungarian as a mother language by ethnic Jews, Germans, Gypsies, and other minorities. In areas with a mixed population, for example, the local authorities and the environment can often play a decisive part in the classifications. For example, in the case of mixed marriages, if the husband was Romanian, the whole family was declared to be Romanian.

Nationality data based on religious denominations has proved fairly reliable in the multi-denominational Romania, but it can also be a source of distortion if it is used as a means to manipulate the numerical differences between the majority nation and the national minorities. For example, Romanian censuses in many cases categorized citizens who—like the majority of Romanians—belonged to the Greek Catholic (Uniate) or the Orthodox denominations, but were not of Romanian nationality, as Romanian.

It is interesting to compare two statistical tables of denominations, both dating from the same period. Table II-5 shows the denominational distribution and increase in the Transylvanian population from 1924 to 1933, based on the preliminary data of the 1930 census published in 1934. Table II-6 uses the same source.[21] A comparison between the two tables reveals that the numbers of the national minorities' churches, with the exception of the Jewish denomination, are

TABLE II-5

Population of Transylvania in 1934 According to Religion

Religious Denominations	Denominations in 1934		Average Natural Increase in Denominations 1924-1933		
	Number of Adherents	Percent of Total	Numerical Increase	Percent of Total Population	Increase Per 1,000
Eastern Orthodox	1,932,356	34.8	12,434	27.1	6.4
Greek Catholic (Uniate)	1,385,445	25.0	17,261	37.6	12.5
Roman Catholic	947,351	17.1	5,921	12.9	6.3
Reformed (Calvinist)	696,320	12.6	5,707	12.4	8.2
Evangelical (Lutheran)	274,415	4.9	1,840	4.0	6.7
Jewish	192,833	3.5	1,623	3.5	8.4
Unitarian	68,330	1.2	628	1.4	9.2
Other	51,313	0.9	467	1.1	9.3
Total	5,548,363	100.0	45,881	100.0	8.3

noticeably lower in Table II-6, while the total for the entirely Romanian Eastern Orthodox Church is 200,000 higher than in Table II-5, even though both sets of statistics date from the same period. What is more, one can draw interesting conclusions about the growth of the various nationalities by observing the natural increase within the various religious denominations.

In the decade under discussion, the Eastern Orthodox Church, numerically the strongest Romanian Church, to which 60 percent of the Transylvanian Romanians (except for the Ukrainian/Ruthenian ethnic groups) belong, shows the lowest natural rate of growth: only 6.4 per thousand. In contrast, the other major religious group, the Greek Catholic (Uniate) Church, shows the highest natural growth rate; its adherents also included, however, members of other nationalities. The largest rate of increase among the religious denominations was in the Hungarian Unitarian Church (9.2 per thousand); second place went to the Jews (8.4 per thousand); third to the Hungarian Reformed Church (8.2 per thousand); the Roman Catholic Church was in last

TABLE II-6

Population of Transylvania in 1934 According to Religion

Religious Denominations	Denominations in 1934		Average Natural Increase in Denominations 1924-1933		
	Number of Adherents	Percent of Total	Numerical Increase	Percent of Total Population	Increase Per 1,000
Eastern Orthodox	2,156,324	38.9	12,434	27.1	5.7
Greek Catholic (Uniate)	1,219,515	22.0	17,261	37.6	13.5
Roman Catholic	881,377	15.9	5,921	12.9	6.6
Reformed (Calvinist)	670,733	12.1	5,707	12.4	8.3
Jewish	282,706	5.1	1,623	3.5	5.7
Evangelical (Lutheran)	266,076	4.8	1,840	4.0	6.8
Unitarian	66,519	1.2	628	1.4	9.2
Other	—	—	467	1.1	—
Total	5,543,250	100.0	45,881	100.00	8.1

place (6.3 per thousand), at least in part because this Church included the Swabian population which had a low birthrate.

The conclusions reached differ, however, from the official statistics, if calculations are made with the 8.8 per thousand ratio for the period between 1920 and 1930. The natural increase in uniformly Hungarian areas, such as 10.3 per thousand in the Székler region, was higher than the Transylvanian average and considerably higher than the 6.8 per thousand rate in those Transylvanian counties with an overwhelmingly Romanian population. If a comparison of this natural increase is made between and among the various Transylvanian counties between 1920 and 1939, an inverse relationship emerges between the percentage of Romanians in any county and the natural increase: the higher the Romanian population in a geographical area, the lower the average natural increase in that area. (See Table II-7).

Using statistical data, it is difficult to determine the direction of demographic development of the German nationality in this period since there are no suitable data from earlier years to compare with the 1930 figures. The ethnic population of the Banat stagnated as a result of the low birthrate and the amount of emigration;[22] on the

TABLE II-7

The Natural Increase in the Homogeneous Areas in Transylvania, 1920-1939

Areas	Estimated Population July 1, 1930				Natural Increase per 1,000		
		Percent			10-year Average		20-year Average
	Total	Roman-ian	Hungar-ian	Other	1920-1929	1930-1939	1920-1939
Counties with overwhelming Romanian population: Alba, Făgăraş, Hunedoara	629,067	83.1	11.1	5.8	8.3	5.3	6.8
Over 70 percent Romanian counties: Someş, Severin, Turda, Bistriţa-Năsăud, Caraş	984,737	75.6	10.6	13.8	7.6	6.4	7.0
Over 60 percent Romanian counties: Sibiu, Bihor, Arad, Cluj	1,451,417	61.9	26.5	11.6	8.3	6.9	7.6
Over 30 percent Romanian counties: Satu Mare, Maramureş, Sălaj, Tîrnava Mică, Braşov, Mureş, Tîrnava Mare, Timiş	2,044,364	49.5	26.9	23.6	9.5	8.5	9.0
Counties with overwhelming Hungarian population: Odorhei, Ciuc, Trei Scaune	410,980	9.7	89.0	1.3	11.0	9.5	10.3
For all of Transylvania	5,520,565	58.3	26.7	15.0	8.8	7.4	8.1

Source: Recensământul general al populaţiei României din 29 decemvrie 1930, vol. II, Bucharest 1938, pp. 1-180.

TABLE II-8

1948 Population of Romania by Language

National Group	Number	Percent
Romanian	13,597,613	85.7
Hungarian	1,499,851	9.4
German	343,913	2.2
Russian	39,332	0.2
Ukrainian	37,582	0.2
Serbian, Croatian, Slovene	45,447	0.3
Bulgarian	13,408	0.1
Czech and Slovak	35,143	0.2
Polish	6,753	—
Jewish	138,795	0.9
Greek	8,696	0.1
Albanian	735	—
Armenian	6,987	—
Turkish-Tatar	28,782	0.2
Gypsy	53,425	0.3
Other	15,639	0.2
Indeterminable	523	—
Total	15,872,624	100.0

Source: note 25.

other hand, a considerable increase can be shown among the German peasantry of Bessarabia.

The period from 1920 to 1930 does not show a sufficient demographic perspective to draw basic conclusions about either the natural shift in the ratio between the country's national minorities and its Romanian majority or the changing demographic structure. An analysis of the reliability of official statistics will be discussed later.

The next official census conducted in 1941 did not include the territories of Northern Transylvania, Bessarabia, Northern Bucovina, and Southern Dobrugea—all taken from Romania early in the war. At the beginning of 1941 the Hungarian authorities conducted a census in Northern Transylvania,[23] and in the spring of 1941 the Romanians did the same in Southern Transylvania.[24] One categorization used in the Romanian census was that of "ethnic origin"; this was also the last

TABLE II-9

**1948 Population of Transylvania Classified
According to Language**

National Group	Number
Romanians	3,752,269
Hungarians	1,482,000
Germans	332,066[a]
Other	194,792
Total	5,761,127

[a]Including 157,105 Transylvanian Saxons, 171,022 Banat Swabians, and 3,939 Szatmár Swabians.
Source: note 25.

census whose results were published in terms of each locality. Combining the results of both censuses, the population of Transylvania was 5,913,305, of which 2,610,000 or 44.1 percent were not Romanian.

The Second World War brought about radical changes in the composition of the nationality population in Transylvania, as well as in Romania as a whole. The numbers of the three large national minorities—Hungarian, German, and Jewish—were reduced considerably by resettlement and population losses discussed earlier.

The first post-war demographic data on national minorities in Romania were published in the census of January 25, 1948.[25] The data are fairly reliable and provide a basis for further calculations, because the events of the war, the resettlements and other large-scale movements connected with the stabilization of the altered frontiers had by then largely come to an end. Furthermore, the old statistical office carried out the calculations. On the other hand, since the 1948 census refers to nationality only in terms of language and the official Romanian statistics in the post-1945 period have not indicated religious denominations, it is difficult to carry out precise evaluations of nationality. The number of those with Yiddish as their mother tongue, for example, does not provide a realistic figure of the Jewish population, a large proportion of whom spoke Hungarian, German, or Romanian as their mother tongue. Similarly, in the post-war period, many Germans did not dare to claim German for their mother tongue, fearing reprisals and forced resettlement.

According to the 1948 census Romania had a population of 15,872,624 broken down in terms of language as shown in Table II-8.

TABLE II-10

1956 Population of Romania Classified According to Language and National Origin

National Group	National Origin Number	Percent	Language Number	Percent
Romanian	14,996,114	85.7	15,080,686	86.2
Hungarian	1,587,675	9.1	1,653,700	9.4
German	384,708	2.2	395,374	2.2
Jewish	146,264	0.8	34,337	0.2
Ukrainian	60,479	0.4	68,252	0.4
South Slav	46,517	0.3	43,057	0.3
Russian	38,731	0.2	45,029	0.3
Tatar	20,469	0.1	20,574	0.1
Turkish	14,329	0.1	14,228	0.1
Bulgarian	12,040	0.1	13,189	0.1
Other	182,124	1.0	121,024	0.7
Total	17,489,450	100	17,489,450	100.0

Source: note 26.

Compared with the data of the 1930 census, the 13.5 million Romanian-speakers of 1948 were confronted by 2.28 million who spoke the languages of the national minorities. The population of Transylvania in 1948 was 5.76 million—roughly one-third of Romania's population. The distribution of that population according to language is given in Table II-9, which shows a significant decline in the national minority populations, especially the Germans and the other nationalities, as a result of the war and the territorial annexations.

The 1948 census data show that the number of Romanians in Transylvania increased after the Second World War to the same extent as the national minorities diminished. Considering the losses suffered in the war, this was largely the result of new settlement. Demographic development from 1910 to 1948 shows that without affecting settlements from the Regat, and excluding war losses, the Romanian population of Transylvania in 1948 could not have been significantly larger than in 1910.

TABLE II-11

**1956 Population of Transylvania Classified
According to
National Origin and Language**

National Group	National Origin	Language
Romanian	4,051,603	4,081,080
Hungarian	1,583,631	1,616,199
German	368,255	372,806
Jewish	43,814	9,744
Other	185,009	152,483

Source: note 26.

The census of February 21, 1956,[26] which was conducted according to the regions (*regiune*) of that time, categorized the population as it had been in the 1930 census, according to language and national origin. Table II-10 shows the 1956 population of Romania classified according to both of these categories. And Transylvania, according to the 1956 figures, had a population of over 6 million, broken down as shown in Table II-11.

What is striking about an analysis of the data from 1956 census are both the rapid growth of the Romanian population of Transylvania in comparison with that of the national minorities and the discrepancies between the national origin and mother tongue categories of the minorities.

The next official census conducted March 15, 1966[27] showed the total population of Romania at 19,103,163, divided according to national origin as shown in Table II-12. According to these figures, the non-Romanian population amounted to 2,356,653 or 12.2 percent. Transylvania, after various parishes were transferred to the Old Kingdom, had a population of 6,719,555, distributed according to ethnic composition as shown in Table II-13.

The periods covered by these censuses, 1948–1956 and 1956–1966, deserve close attention for several reasons. First is the surprisingly large actual increase in the numbers of Transylvanian Romanians from 58.2 percent in 1930 to 68.05 percent in 1966, coupled with a small

TABLE II-12

Population of Romania in 1966 Classified According to National Origin

National Group	Number	Percent
Romanian	16,746,510	87.7
Hungarian	1,619,592	8.5
German	382,595	2.0
Gipsy	64,197	0.3
Ukrainian-Ruthenian	54,705	0.3
Serbian, Croatian, Slovene	44,236	0.2
Russian-Lipovan	39,483	0.2
Jewish	42,888	0.2
Tatar	22,151	0.1
Slovak	22,221	0.1
Turkish	18,046	0.09
Bulgarian	11,193	0.07
Czech	9,978	0.07
Greek	9,088	0.05
Polish	5,860	0.05
Armenian	3,436	0.02
Other	4,681	0.02
Unknown	2,303	0.01
Total	19,103,163	100.00

Source: note 27.

increase in the national minority population, particularly in the second ten-year period. The sudden weakening in the national minorities' population was the result either of emigration, assimilation, or a statistical bias toward underestimation.

The number of ethnic Germans in all Romania decreased when categorized by ethnic origin by 2,113 between 1956 and 1966, which can be explained either by assimilation, a low birthrate, or emigration; yet, in the same period, their numbers in Transylvania increased

TABLE II-13

1966 Population of Transylvania Classified According to National Origin and Language

National Group	National Origin		Language	
	Number	Percent	Number	Percent
Romanian	4,559,232	67.9	4,569,546	68.0
Hungarian	1,597,438	23.8	1,627,702	24.2
German	371,881	5.5	373,933	5.6
Slav	101,000	1.5	96,000	1.4
Jewish	14,000	0.2	1,000	0.0
Gypsy	48,000	0.7	31,000	0.5
Other	28,004	0.4	20,374	0.3
Total	6,719,555	100.0	6,719,555	100.0

Source: note 27.

slightly despite a low birthrate noted as early as the 1930s, mainly because of the inheritance problems resulting from the custom of having only one child. While the yearly growth rate of the Transylvanian Saxon population was only 6.8 per thousand from 1956 to 1966, it stagnated among the Swabians of the Banat to a mere 1.3 per thousand.

The great drop in the Jewish population from 0.8 percent in 1956 to 0.2 percent in 1966 was the result of two factors: the large number who emigrated, and the number of the remaining Jews who assimilated.

Turkish ethnic groups registered a small increase in population from 1956 to 1966. The Ukrainian, Ruthenian, Russian, Slovak, and Tatar minorities, on the other hand, showed neither significant increases nor declines in population. Even more difficult to explain is the fact that the number of Hungarians in Romania increased by 2 percent from 1956 to 1966 when classified according to national origin but remained stagnant when counted according to mother tongue. Just as surprising is the small number of Hungarians listed as living in the Old Kingdom during the same period.

In the figures for Romania as a whole between 1956 and 1966, it is difficult to find an explanation for the scarcely 2 percent increase in the

Hungarian nationality, or for the low figures[28] for the Hungarian population in the Regat. One must look for the answer in an underestimation of the number of national minorities in the official statistics and the tendency of exaggerating the numbers of the Romanian population at the expense of the national minorities,[29] because assimilation, infrequent mixed marriages, emigration, and a low birthrate cannot account for the insignificant increase in the Hungarian population. In fact, according to some authoritative demographers, at the time of the 1966 census the Hungarian nationality in Romania as whole was closer to a minimum of 2 million and a maximum of 2.5 million than to the 1.6 million disclosed in the official statistics.[30]

Before a separate analysis can be made to check the correctness of the official statistics, one must remember that it is exceptionally difficult or even impossible to gain access to statistics in Romania, especially if they have not been made public.[31] Furthermore, the general party ideological considerations are not the only factors that play a part in the policy of weakening the national minorities in Romania; there is also the nationalist policy of the present regime, a factor that brings into doubt the reliability of the demographic data.[32] Therefore, realistic estimates of the nationality population can be made only by indirect calculations from the data for Romania as a whole.

The official statistics show that if the population is classified according to ethnic origin, between 1948 and 1956 the Romanian nationality increased by 1,398,000 (a 10.3 percent increase) and the Hungarians by 88,000 (a 5.9 percent increase). Thus, the Romanian rate of increase in the same period based on nationality, is almost double that of the Hungarian, which cannot be attributed exclusively to the readiness of the group with so-called "uncertain nationality" to assimilate. It is difficult to find an explanation for the fact that while only 0.56 percent of those whose vernacular was Romanian claimed to belong to a nationality other than Romanian, 4 percent of those with Hungarian as their mother tongue were registered as Romanians by nationality. Investigations exclude the possibility of a greater rate of assimilation for the Hungarians; and it can also be questioned whether, as the official data claim, more than 10 percent of those with Ruthenian, Russian, or Polish as their mother tongue and more than 20 percent of those who claim Bulgarian had assimilated in the period in question. One must also question the 1956 figures that show the number of Hungarians living in the Regat as 4,044 according to nationality and

37,501 according to language; both these figures are far below a realistic level.

It has already been mentioned that the category in which any individual is placed is determined by a number of factors: the individual, in naming his nationality, is affected by personal interests, career considerations, fear, and other motivations—all subjective factors; but categorization according to language is determined by genuine objective facts, primarily the mother tongue. For this reason classification based on mother tongue is more acceptable: it has become more justified in multinational states and is more frequently used in international practice.

Statistics based on language have therefore been found to be more reliable, and these calculations use the 1956 census as the point of departure. The 1956 figure for Romania as a whole showed 1,653,700 people claiming Hungarian as their mother tongue and 1,588,000 claiming Hungarian nationality. The 1966 census listed some 1,652,000 Hungarians according to language and 1,620,000 according to nationality. This would indicate that in the course of 10 years the Hungarian population decreased by 2,000 according to language but increased by 32,000 when classified by nationality. This contradictory phenomenon—which is practiced in other ways in the statistics of the Soviet Union—in and of itself brings into question the reliability of the data, and the suspicion becomes even more justified if one compares the data for the increase of the total population with that for the Romanians. While the total population increased by 1,614,000 or 9.2 percent between 1956 and 1966, all the national minorities with the exception of the Hungarians and the Turkish-Tatars showed a numerical decrease. By contrast, the Romanians increased by 1,690,000 when classified according to language and by 1,751,000 or 11.7 percent when based on ethnic origin. The numerical increase of the Romanians, according to official statistics, exceeded the increase of the total population by 137,000; and this figure, taking into account the rate of natural increase of both the Romanians and the national minorities, is precisely equal to the numerical losses suffered by the national minorities. In other words, according to official data, the Romanian population increased in the same proportion as that of the nationalities decreased.

The assumption that the official census data on the Hungarian population are open to question is strengthened by the official figures on mobility, which show that between 1956 and 1966 the natural increase in the Regat was 11.4 percent and in Transylvania 7.7 percent. Yet the Hungarian natural increase over this ten-year period could not have been less than the Transylvanian average, because the natural increase in the population of the most compact Hungarian-inhabited counties (the Székler region) was much higher: Harghita County had the highest rate of natural increase among Transylvania's counties with 99.3 per thousand in 1969; Covasna was third with 97.0 per thousand.[33] The birthrate of the Hungarian rural population was therefore at least as high as, if not higher than, that of the Romanians.[34] The increase in the number of Hungarians during the period in question should therefore have been at least 127,000.

From another point of view, if the birthrate in Transylvania has always been lower than that of the Regat,[35] the changes in the actual rates of increase of the population can have only one explanation: namely, the influx of the excess population from the Regat, with its higher birthrate, a process that has been accelerating ever since the end of the Second World War.[36] And as a result of the policy of Romanianization pursued between 1948 and 1966, the population of Transylvania increased by as much as it had between 1869 and 1910, but in the more recent instance as a result of planned settlement rather than natural increase.

The state-controlled resettlement of Romanians from the Regat into Transylvania, known as "labor force regrouping" in the official terminology—can be observed mainly in those counties where the birthrate was low but where there is nonetheless a large-scale increase in the population far beyond the average rate of 28.4 per 1,000.[37] The counties where this has occurred are those where industrial centers have recently developed. One result of this industrialization has been that young women emigrated in large numbers from the Regat to Transylvania, especially women of childbearing age, in contrast to a retrogressive tendency in the Regat.[38] In this context it is interesting to note that about half the people who moved to the industrial centers of Transylvania (*e.g.* Brașov and Hunedoara Counties) came from the Old Kingdom (Regat).[39]

Later Population Changes (1966–1977)

The increase of the Hungarian population in the 1966–1977 period should be examined with the same considerations as were necessary

TABLE II-14

A Comparison of Romania's Population in 1966 and 1977

Territory	Population 1966	1977	Actual Rates of Increase In number	Percent
Romania	19,103,200	21,559,500	2,456,300	12.9
Transylvania	6,719,600	7,500,400	780,800	11.6
Regat	12,383,600	14,059,100	1,675,500	13.5

above. On the basis of the mobility data gathered in the counties, a picture emerges, as shown in Table II-14. These figures indicate that the rate of increase of the Transylvanian population was almost 2 percent lower than that of the population of the Regat. If we assume that it was an exclusively natural increase, the growth rate of the Hungarian population once again had to reach an average of 11.6 percent for Transylvania. On this basis the natural increase of the Hungarian nationality during this ten-year period must be estimated at least 207,000—in other words, 120,000 more than the increase of 87,000 shown in the official statistics. Table II-15 compares the official data for the years 1956 and 1977, showing the changes in Romania's population.

Increases in the Romanian population accounted for 98.5 percent of the country's total population increase between 1956 and 1977, even though in 1956 their proportion was only 85.7 percent; and by 1977 the Hungarians were shown as a mere 2.9 percent, even though they had represented 9.1 percent in 1956. (In 1979 the Romanians accounted for 88.117 percent and the Hungarians 7.9 percent).

Knowing the proportion of the natural increase of the Hungarian population in the given period, which was considerable even on a national scale, it is beyond doubt that the Hungarian population living in Romania considerably exceeded the two million level in 1977. Consequently, it appears that almost half a million Hungarians were statistically lost between the 1956 and the 1977 Romanian censuses.

The population development of the other nationalities in Romania shows different characteristics; the general decrease can be explained

TABLE II-15

Changes in Romania's Population Between 1956 and 1977

	Population		Change in Population	
	1956	*1977*	*Number*	*Percent*
Total Population of Romania	17,489,450	21,559,416	4,069,000	23.3
Romanians	14,996,114	19,001,721	4,008,005	23.0
Hungarians	1,587,675	1,706,874	119,000	7.5
Other nationalities			-57,000	-6.3

by assimilation and by emigration. The Germans and Jews showed a decrease during the 1956–1977 period. As already mentioned, from 1945 to 1980 some 115,000 people of German origin (more than 90 percent of them from Transylvania alone) emigrated to the German Federal Republic. The number of Jewish emigrants, about half of whom were from Transylvania, amounted to some 260,000 from 1948 to 1978. To these may be added the emigrants to the USA, Canada, Austria, Hungary, East Germany, and other countries, reaching a total of approximately 400,000 people of non-Romanian origin to leave the country since 1948: of these about 300,000 came from Transylvania. This loss of population through emigration was compensated for mostly by an influx of people from the Regat. The 1956 census shows approximately 385,000 Germans and 146,000 Jews in Romania; by 1977 there were 26,000 fewer Germans and 121,000 fewer Jews.

The population of the smaller Slav ethnic groups also dropped. Among these were the Slovak village groups that had settled in Transylvania in the course of the nineteenth century, as well as the Czech and Bulgarian-Krassovan settlements of the Banat and the Serbo-Croatian villages. The populations of these Slav islands increased while they were under Hungarian rule, but the more recent data of the Romanian censuses indicate that these Slavic settlements are gradually disappearing. The situation is similar for Romania's Russian ethnic group: the 1966 census showed 39,483 Russians, including the Lipovans, compared with the 1977 census which showed a mere 32,147.

It is also difficult to explain the very small increase or virtual stagnation in the Ukrainian-Ruthenian ethnic group since their high birth rate is well known and no significant emigration is reported. The 1956 census recorded more than 60,000 Ruthenian-Ukrainians in Romania, but the 1977 census recorded a decrease of 5,000.

A further analysis of the period between the censuses of 1966 and 1977 gives additional information about the ethnic composition of Romania. According to the official census of January 1977,[40] the total population of Romania was 21,559,416, and was distributed by nationality as shown in Table II-16.

Although in 1930 data the proportion of Romanians in the country was only 71.9 percent, by 1977 it had increased to 88.1 percent. Correspondingly, the proportion of the national minorities decreased from 28.1 percent to 11.9 percent. As already mentioned, the losses suffered by the Jews were the most extensive. The German national minority also lost nearly half of its population. The decrease in the Hungarian nationality—at a rate less than half that of the average birthrate, or a mere 20 percent in almost half a century—cannot be explained by losses suffered in the war.

According to the 1977 census, the population of Romania had increased by almost 2.5 million, from 19.1 million to 21.5 million, since the previous census in 1966. This means that in just under 11 years the population growth rate was 12.9 percent, or a yearly average of 1.1 percent, attributed officially to natural increases derived from a yearly average birthrate of 20.8 per thousand and a decrease in the mortality rate. Recent demographic developments in Romania have indeed been determined by two main factors: a fairly high rate of natural increase despite a decrease in the total number of births; and a tendency toward a longer life span. In addition, there has been an increase in the number of marriages and a lower rate of divorce.

The rapid fall in the birthrate reached its nadir in 1966, with 14.3 per thousand. Toward the end of 1960, the Romanian government began to take steps to stop the falling birthrate. The 1967 law regulating abortion,[41] the so-called family supplement paid to families with many children, and the 1967 law regarding the introduction of the child-care grant, for example, were aimed at raising the birthrate. The sudden rise in 1967 (27.4 per thousand) was the result of such legal, economic, and demographic measures. Although the birthrate has shown a diminishing tendency since 1967–1968, the 20.8 per thousand ratio since the 1966 census appears to be valid; and the mortality rate, on the basis

TABLE II-16

1977 Nationality Distribution in Romania

National Group	Number	Percent		
Romanian	19,001,721	88.137		
Hungarian	1,705,810	7.912	1,706,874	7.917
Székler	1,064	0.005		
German	348,444	1.616		
Saxon	5,930	0.028	358,732	1.664
Swabian	4,358	0.020		
Gipsy	229,986	1.067		
Ukrainian	54,429	0.252	55,417	0.257
Ruthenian	988	0.005		
Serbian	34,034	0.158		
Croatian	7,617	0.035	42,358	0.196
Slovene	707	0.003		
Russian	20,653	0.096	32,147	0.149
Lipovan	11,494	0.053		
Jewish	25,686	0.119		
Turkish	23,303	0.108		
Tatar	23,107	0.107		
Slovak	23,037	0.102		
Bulgarian	10,467	0.049		
Czech	7,756	0.036		
Greek	6,607	0.031		
Polish	4,756	0.022		
Armenian	2,436	0.011		
Macedoromanian	1,179	0.005		
Arumun	644	0.003		
Other	4,141	0.019		
Unknown	62	—		
Total	21,559,416			

Source: note 40.

of the data for the years 1966 to 1975, can be determined as 9.1 per thousand, which, in combination with the index of births, produces the average 11.5 per thousand natural increase in that ten-year period.

According to the statistical yearbooks, the natural increase in the population of Romania during the decade between 1966 and 1975 was 2,338,000—a yearly average of approximately 234,000. If we assume that the natural increase in 1976 was close to the ten-year average, then in eleven years the natural increase exceeded the actual increase by approximately 118,000, which in turn indicates a loss of over 100,000 through emigration. This assumption is strengthened by the fact that in the 1948–1966 period the balance of the actual and natural increase had already shown a loss through emigration of 245,000, that is, 1.6 percent.

In the 1977 census—in accordance with the Soviet census-model—a new model was used for determining nationality. For the first time, the Romanian census placed ethnic communities belonging to the same nationality into different categories. For example, besides the 1,707,000 individuals recorded as Hungarian, another 1,064 Széklers are recorded as a separate nationality. Despite the insignificant percentage involved (a mere 0.05 percent), this procedure is surprising. The 1930 census, for example, recorded not only the Széklers but also the Csángó Hungarians of Moldavia as belonging to the Hungarian nationality, since both ethnic groups are indeed Hungarian by language and culture. The ethnic Germans also fell victim to the new method of classification; the 1977 Romanian census divided them into three groups: 5,930 Saxons, 4,358 Swabians, and another 348,444 listed merely as of German nationality. Since all three groups are in fact German by nationality, the divisions would seem absurd.

The 1977 census' separation of the Lipovans from the Russian nationality is yet another example. The Lipovans, most of whom live in Northern Dobrugea, are Russian both by ethnic origin and language; they differ from those actually called Russian only by religion. Even the 1912 and 1930 censuses, which recorded the nationality of the population only in Dobrugea, categorized them as Russian, counting them separately only in the denominational statistics, as belonging to a separate religious community. They were categorized in the same way in all subsequent censuses prior to 1977, which was the first to qualify a religious community as a separate ethnic group. The consequence was that the number of ethnic Russians in Romania was diminished by more than a quarter.

This new method of Romanian census-taking reflected Romania's current nationality policy, which appears to aim at eroding the ethnic blocks of the nationalities and reducing their proportion in the population.[42]

If the increase in the population is examined according to nationality, it is seen that between 1966 and 1977 the total increase was 2,456,000; of this actual increase, approximately 2,257,000 or almost 92 percent was attributed to Romanians. Thus, while the total population increased at a rate of 12.9 percent, the Romanian population increased by 13.5 percent; and as a consequence the proportion of Romanians in the total population increased from 87.7 percent to 88.1 percent.

The non-Romanian nationalities numbered 2,356,000 or 12.3 percent in 1966; in 1977 they were approximately 2,555,000 or 11.9 percent of the total, which amounts to an increase of 199,000 or 8.4 percent. If the Gypsies are omitted, the actual increase in the other nationalities drops to 33,000 or 1.4 percent. If this figure is then reduced by the 87,000 by which the Hungarian nationality increased, the numbers belonging to the German, Jewish, and Slav ethnic groups decreased by 54,000 (or 8.0 percent).

The Hungarian nationality in Romania is therefore the only one to show any significant increase; but the 5.4 percent rate of this increase is not even half the 12.9 percent increase in the population as a whole or the 13.5 percent in the Romanian population.

Looking at a 21 year period, the ratio of Romanians to Hungarians, based on ethnic origin decreased from 100:10.6 in 1956 to only 100:8.9 by 1977. If, however, the 1956 statistics concerning language (100:11) are used as the basis for the calculations, it is found that while the Romanians increased by 3,922,000 or 26 percent between 1956 and 1977, the increase in the Hungarian population during the same 21-year period was only 53,000 or 3.2 percent; and consequently the ratio between the increase in the Romanian and the Hungarian populations was only 100:1.35.

Therefore, those official statistics that indicate that during the last 21 years the increase in the Hungarian population amounted to only 7.5 percent, as compared with 23.3 percent in the total population and 26.7 percent in the Romanian population, would seem to show the existence of an inexplicable disproportion. Their validity must therefore be called into question.

Table II-17 provides a general picture in both total numbers and percentages of the increases and decreases in the population of present-day Transylvania in the periods between the censuses from 1880 to 1966, according to official data.

With the exception of a part of the German population, the national minorities in Romania generally live in larger or smaller dispersed communities, and their population are consequently more exposed to the danger of assimilation. The ranks of Germans and Jews are also being thinned by emigration, quite apart from their low birthrates. As has already been pointed out, the Hungarians are the only nationality in Romania to inhabit significant areas of Transylvania, in several places forming a majority of the population. It therefore becomes obvious that the demographic question of the Hungarian population must be evaluated on a different basis than the other nationality populations.

First of all, the Hungarian population in Romania as a whole has not decreased during almost sixty years of Romanian rule. The decennial censuses have shown a constantly rising population, but the war, the collectivization of agriculture (that is, the abolition of private farming), industrialization and urbanization, the general socioeconomic handicaps, the exclusion, or at least the severe restriction in numbers, of the population from the Transylvanian urban areas, the frequent territorial-administrative reorganizations, and the psychological factors have all inevitably exerted a negative influence on demographic development.

The Effects of Urbanization and Romanianization on the Population of the Cities and Towns

Historical Background

Transylvanian towns had reached a very high level of development by the fourteenth century, when there was not a sign of medieval urbanization anywhere to the southeast as far as Byzantium. And as late as the eighteenth century in the two Romanian Danubian Principalities, one cannot refer to towns in a strict sense, but only of market places.[43] In the market towns of the principalities agriculture was the source of livelihood, even in the nineteenth century.[44] As late as 1930, the share of the population that was agrarian in several Regat towns

TABLE II-17

The Distribution of the Population of Historical Transylvania, of Crişana/Körösvidék, of Maramureş/Máramaros, and of the Banat According to Nationality Between 1880 and 1966
(In Figures and Percentages)

Year	Total Population		Romanian		Hungarian		German
	Number	%	Number	%	Number	%	Number
1880							
Total Population	4,026,872	100,0	2,299,255	57,0	1,041,344	25,9	457,796
Urban Population	402,440	100,0	79,625	19,8	216,763	53,9	77,762
Rural Population	3,624,432	100,0	2,219,630	61,2	824,581	22,8	380,034
1890							
Total Population	4,418,557	100,0	2,475,081	56,0	1,200,276	27,2	500,751
Urban Population	450,376	100,0	85,843	19,1	259,602	57,6	79,266
Rural Population	3,968,181	100,0	2,389,238	60,2	940,674	23,7	421,485
1900							
Total Population	4,872,414	100,0	2,685,036	55,1	1,438,464	29,5	532,609
Urban Population	577,185	100,0	107,665	18,7	351,045	60,8	93,713
Rural Population	4,295,229	100,0	2,577,371	60,0	1,087,419	25,3	438,896
1910							
Total Population	5,263,282	100,0	2,829,925	53,8	1,664,324	31,6	515,717
Urban Population	678,423	100,0	119,121	17,6	438,859	64,7	97,274
Rural Population	4,584,859	100,0	2,710,804	59,1	1,225,465	26,7	418,443
1920							
Total Population	5,138,528	100,0	2,922,996	56,9	1,321,707	25,7	555,208
Urban Population	721,546	100,0	181,678	25,2	330,447	45,8	105,664
Rural Population	4,416,982	100,0	2,741,318	62,1	991,260	22,4	449,544
1930							
Total Population	5,548,363	100,0	3,207,880	57,8	1,353,276	24,4	543,852
Urban Population	963,418	100,0	336,756	35,0	365,008	37,9	123,936
Rural Population	4,584,945	100,0	2,871,124	62,6	988,268	21,6	416,916
1941							
Total Population	5,912,014	100,0	3,303,481	55,9	1,743,539	29,5	535,212
Urban Population	1,138,612	100,0	384,816	33,8	546,564	48,0	135,558
Rural Population	4,773,402	100,0	2,918,665	61,1	1,196,975	25,1	399,654
1948							
Total Population	5,761,127	100,0	3,752,269	65,1	1,481,903	25,7	332,066
Urban Population	1,095,621	100,0	547,502	50,0	434,855	39,7	74,319
Rural Population	4,665,506	100,0	3,204,767	68,7	1,047,048	22,5	257,747
1956							
Total Population	6,232,312	100,0	4,051,603	65,0	1,558,631	25,0	368,255
Urban Population	1,753,844	100,0	985,584	56,2	554,324	31,6	141,981
Rural Population	4,478,468	100,0	3,066,019	68,5	1,004,307	22,4	226,274
1966							
Total Population	6,719,555	100,0	4,559,432	67,9	1,597,438	23,8	371,881
Urban Population	2,619,925	100,0	1,695,869	64,7	702,188	26,8	164,287
Rural Population	4,099,630	100,0	2,863,563	69,8	895,250	21,8	207,594

POPULATION CHANGES SINCE WORLD WAR I 57

| | Other Nationalities | | Of the Other Nationalities: | | | | | |
| | | | Slavs | | Jews | | Gypsies | |
%	Number	%	Number	%	Number	%	Number	%
11,4	228,477	5,7	101,903	2,5	40,959	1,0	64,708	1,5
19,3	28,290	7,0	7,290	1,8	10,833	2,7	3,998	1,0
10,5	200,187	5,5	94,613	2,6	30,126	0,8	60,710	1,7
11,3	242,449	5,5	112,367	2,5	48,361	1,1	66,382	1,5
17,6	25,665	5,7	6,360	1,4	9,774	2,2	5,672	1,3
10,6	216,784	5,5	106,007	2,7	38,587	1,0	60,710	1,5
10,9	216,305	4,5	132,066	2,7	49,334	1,2	30,259	0,6
16,2	24,762	4,3	9,267	1,6	10,046	1,7	1,969	0,3
10,2	191,543	4,5	122,799	2,9	39,288	0,9	28,290	0,7
9,8	253,316	4,8	140,369	2,7	49,496	0,9	60,174	1,2
14,3	23,169	3,4	11,026	1,6	7,237	1,1	3,120	0,5
9,1	230,147	5,1	129,343	2,8	42,259	0,9	57,054	1,2
10,8	338,617	6,6	—	—	178,997	3,5	—	—
14,6	103,757	14,4	—	—	91,113	12,6	—	—
10,2	234,860	5,3	—	—	87,884	2,0	—	—
9,8	443,355	8,0	141,814	2,6	178,699	3,2	109,156	2,0
13,2	134,718	13,9	19,583	2,0	100,413	10,4	10,869	1,1
9,1	308,637	6,7	122,231	2,8	78,286	1,7	98,287	2,1
9,1	329,782	5,5	—	—	—	—	—	—
11,9	71,674	6,3	—	—	—	—	—	—
8,4	258,108	5,4	—	—	—	—	—	—
5,8	194,889	3,4	—	—	30,039	0,5	—	—
6,8	38,945	3,5	—	—	22,912	2,1	—	—
5,5	155,944	3,3	—	—	7,127	0,2	—	—
5,9	253,823	4,1	124,694	2,0	43,814	0,7	78,362	1,3
8,1	71,955	4,1	21,021	1,2	38,725	2,2	8,277	0,5
5,1	181,868	4,0	103,673	2,3	5,089	0,1	70,085	1,6
5,5	190,804	2,8	122,995	1,8	13,530	0,2	49,105	0,7
6,3	57,581	2,2	31,296	1,2	13,002	0,5	9,345	0,4
5,1	133,223	3,3	91,699	2,2	528	—	39,760	1,0

exceeded 50 percent, and some towns had 80–85 percent of their population living off the land.[45] What is more, as late as 1948 these towns were overwhelmingly of an agrarian character, with most of them lacking even the most basic public utilities.[46]

The culture of Transylvania has differed from the culture found in the Regat from the very beginning.[47] The difference in the cultural level between the two areas is best illustrated by the extent of illiteracy: in the Regat towns approximately half the population was illiterate as compared with one-quarter of the population in the Transylvanian towns.

From 1899 to 1900 the illiteracy rate in the Old Kingdom among those over seven years of age amounted to about 78 percent; the number sank, however, to 38.2 percent in 1930 and 23.1 percent in 1948. Despite all the efforts of the regime from the annexation of Transylvania to the present, parity in the cultural levels of Transylvania and the Regat has not taken place.

Romanianization

In the following pages those manifestations of ethnic mobility and history that have led to the large degree of Romanianization in Transylvanian towns that had once been Saxon or Hungarian will be analyzed. Wherever necessary, the old Hungarian and/or German names of the towns will be given as well as their present-day official Romanian names, some of which have been changed from time to time.

At the time of the annexation of Transylvania by Romania, the population and character of the Transylvanian towns were overwhelmingly Hungarian or German;[48] apart from a few smaller towns the Romanians were still a minor element. Of the 49 Transylvanian towns and cities, 32 had a Hungarian and 9 a German majority; only 8 insignificant towns had a Romanian majority.[49] The Germans and Hungarians were clearly the urbanizing elements in Transylvania. According to the 1910 Hungarian census, Transylvania's urban population totaled 678,423, of which 438,859 were Hungarians, 119,121 Romanians, 97,274 Germans, and 23,169 other nationalities (11,026 Slavs and 7,237 Jews by "nationality" with 76,423 belonging to the Jewish faith).

The Number and Proportion of Illiterates

	Number 1899	Percent 1900	Number 1910	Percent 1910	Number 1930	Percent 1930	Number 1948	Percent 1948
Regat towns (total)	471,755	50.6	387,084	34.1	448,675	25.0	294,800	12.5
Bucharest only	88,203	37.4	76,331	25.6	103,933	18.2	80,369	8.4
Transylvanian towns	151,658	27.4	128,325	21.5	111,921	13.1	68,271	6.7

In the 1920s Romanian state policy already included the Romanianization of the Transylvanian towns.[50] The administrative reform No. 2465 of 1925 declared nine localities with Romanian majorities to be towns, thereby raising the proportion of the urban Romanian population from 17.7 to 31.1 percent. Soon afterward the settlers from the Romanian middle class began to move into Transylvanian cities; the process of active Romanianization, however, began only later, after the Second World War. Table II-18 shows the development of the urban and rural population of Transylvania. Using this table it is possible to trace the gains made by the Romanian element and the numerical losses suffered by the Hungarian, German, and Jewish populations from the 1880 census through 1966.

The Romanianization of the Transylvanian urban areas has occurred on two levels: through the influx of the population into towns from surrounding areas which were largely Romanian; and as a result of a systematic settlement policy carried out by the authorities. While the influx of a rural population into the towns is a normal part of urbanization and industrialization, this process occurred in Transylvania under abnormal conditions, dictated by the Romanian government's policy of planned settlement. This includes restricting permits for members of national minorities to settle in urban areas; obstacles in allocating them apartments in new housing developments;[51] various administrative, economic, and educational measures; elevating Romanian villages to the status of towns or cities, and favoring settlements attached to these new towns; excluding the minority populations from industrial occupations and technical training; and finally forcibly dispersing these groups over the entire territory of the country. All this is done in the name of what is called "ethnic homogenization," a policy aimed at the Romanianization of the Transylvanian towns and cities and the reduction of the influence of the national minorities in urban

TABLE II-18

The Development of the Urban and Rural Population of Historical Transylvania, of Crişana/Körösvidék, of Maramureş/Máramaros, and of Banat According to Nationality Between 1880 and 1966
(In Figures and Percentages)

Period	Total Population		Romanian		Hungarian		German
	Number	%	Number	%	Number	%	Number
1880-1890							
Total Population	391,685	9.7	175,826	7,6	158,932	15,3	42,955
Urban Population	47,936	11,9	6,218	7,8	42,839	19,8	1,504
Rural Population	343,749	9,5	169,608	7,6	116,093	14,1	41,451
1890-1900							
Total Population	453,857	10,3	209,955	8,5	238,188	19,8	31,858
Urban Population	126,809	28,2	21,822	25,4	91,443	35,2	14,447
Rural Population	327,048	8,2	188,133	7,9	146,745	15,6	17,411
1900-1910							
Total Population	390,868	8,0	144,889	5,4	225,860	15,7	16,892
Urban Population	101,238	17,5	11,456	10,7	87,814	25,0	3,561
Rural Population	289,630	6,7	133,433	5,2	138,046	12,7	20,453
1910-1920							
Total Population	124,754	-2,4	93,071	3,3	-342,617	-20,6	39,491
Urban Population	43,123	6,4	62,557	52,5	-108,412	-24.7	8,390
Rural Population	-167,877	-3,7	30,514	11,3	-234,205	-19,1	31,101
1920-1930							
Total Population	409,835	8,0	284,884	9,7	31,569	2,4	-11,356
Urban Population	241,872	33,5	155,078	85,4	34,561	10,5	21,272
Rural Population	167,963	3,8	129,806	4,7	2,992	- 0,3	-32,628
1930-1941							
Total Population	363,651	6,6	95,601	3,0	390,263	28,8	8,640
Urban Population	175,194	18,2	48,060	14,3	181,556	49,7	8,622
Rural Population	188,457	4,1	47,541	1,7	208,707	21,1	17,262
1941-1948							
Total Population	-150,887	-2,6	448,788	13,6	-261,636	-15,0	-203,146
Urban Population	-42,991	-3,8	162,686	42,3	-111,709	-20,4	61,239
Rural Population	-107,896	-2,3	286,102	9,8	-149,927	-12,5	141,907
1948-1956							
Total Population	471,185	8,2	299,334	8,0	76,728	5,2	36,189
Urban Population	658,223	60,1	438,082	80,0	119,469	27,5	67,662
Rural Population	-187,038	-4,0	-138,748	-4,3	- 42,741	- 4,1	-31,473
1956-1966							
Total Population	487,243	7,8	507,829	12,5	38,807	2,5	3,626
Urban Population	866,081	49,4	710,285	72,1	147,864	26,7	22,306
Rural Population	-378,838	-8,5	-202,456	-6,6	-109,057	-10,9	-18,680

POPULATION CHANGES SINCE WORLD WAR I

	Other Nationalities		Of the Other Nationalities:					
			Slavs		Jews		Gypsies	
%	Number	%	Number	%	Number	%	Number	%
9,4	13,972	6,1	10,464	10,3	7,402	18,1	6,674	2,6
1,9	2,625	9,3	930	-12,8	-1,059	- 9,8	1,674	41,9
10,9	16,597	8,3	11,394	12,0	8,461	28,1	—	—
6,4	-26,144	-10,8	619,699	17,5	973	2,0	-36,123	-54,4
18,2	- 903	3,5	2,907	45,7	272	2,8	3,703	-65,3
4,1	-25,241	-11,6	16,792	15,8	701	1,8	-32,420	-53,4
- 3,1	37,011	17,1	- 8,303	6,3	162	0,3	29,915	98,9
3,8	- 1,593	- 6,5	1,759	19,3	2,809	28,0	1,151	58,5
- 4,7	38,604	20,2	6,544	5,3	2,971	7,6	28,764	101,7
7.7	85,301	33,7	—	—	129,501	261,6	—	—
8,6	80,588	347,8	—	—	83,876	1159,0	—	—
7,4	4,713	2,0	—	—	45,625	108,9	—	—
- 2,0	104,738	30,9	—	—	298	0,1	—	—
20,1	30,961	29,8	—	—	9,300	10,2	—	—
7,3	73,777	31,4	—	—	9,598	-10,9	—	—
- 1,6	-113,573	-25,6	—	—	—	—	—	—
6,8	63,044	-46,8	—	—	—	—	—	—
- 4,1	50,529	-16,4	—	—	—	—	—	—
-38,0	-134,893	—	—	—	—	—	—	—
-45,2	32,729	—	—	—	—	—	—	—
-35,5	-102,164	-39,6	—	—	—	—	—	—
10,9	58,934	30,2	—	—	13,775	45,9	—	—
91,0	33,010	84,8	—	—	15,813	69,0	—	—
-12,2	25,924	16,6	—	—	2,038	- 28,6	—	—
1,0	63,019	-24,9	1,699	1,4	-30,284	- 66,4	1,068	12,9
15,7	-14,374	-20,0	10,275	48,9	-25,723	-66,4	1,068	12,9
- 8,3	-48,645	-26,7	-11,974	-11,6	4,561	-89,6	-30,325	-43,3

life. Unquestionably, the development of the Romanian nationality has come about at the cost of the national minorities.

The high level of planned and directed immigration to Transylvanian urban centers has been particularly marked since the creation of the Romanian socialist state, especially in the period from 1948 to 1955.[52] The result of this immigration can be clearly seen by comparing the growth of the urban population in the Regat and Transylvania. In the seven largest urban centers of the Regat (including Bucharest), 40 percent of the growth was due to natural increase and 60 percent to new settlement; in the Transylvanian cities, 83 percent of the increase was the result of the arrival of new settlers.[53]

The extent of urbanization in Romania from 1948 to 1966 was substantial: in 1930 there were 142 towns and cities in Romania with 2,865,000 inhabitants; by 1966 the number had grown to 236 towns and cities with 6,744,000 inhabitants; in Transylvania there were 49 towns in 1930 with a population of 963,000, which by 1966 had grown to 113 towns with an urban population of 2,620,000. The number of towns given for Transylvania is, however, debatable because of the markedly rural character of many of them despite their reclassification as urban areas.

The ban on settling in urban areas was at first a general ban affecting Romanians and national minorities alike; it was a measure introduced mainly to stop the population from running away from agricultural cooperatives into the towns. From the mid-1950s on, however, the ban on settling in urban areas was used exclusively against members of the national minorities,[54] as the needs of industrialization in these areas were met by settling ethnic Romanians in the towns. The government has been particularly strict about the resettlement of members of national minorities in the towns and cities with a mixed population (Cluj-Napoca/Kolozsvár,[55] Oradea/Nagyvárad, Arad or similar towns). Hungarian cultural institutions, for example, functioning in Cluj were relocated in less significant provincial towns, bilingual signs were removed and the historical character and Hungarian qualities of the city were altered. The same policy was carried out in the almost totally Hungarian area, the Székler region.

From 1953 on, most of the increase in Transylvania's urban population has come to a large extent from the resettlement of Romanians, both from the Regat and the Romanian-inhabited parts of Transylvania.

The losses in terms of numbers suffered by the nationality population, particularly the Hungarians, Germans and Jews in the Transylvanian cities, and the increase in the number of Romanians in the period between the 1910 and 1956 censuses is best illustrated by Tables II-19 and II-20.[56] The great changes in the national composition of the population, especially the growth of the Romanian element, in Transylvanian urban areas have occurred only since the end of World War II. Of the nine Transylvanian cities, according to the 1956 census, the Romanians are in a majority in six, whereas the Hungarians still predominate in three. The German population no longer holds a majority in any of the nine cities.

There are no data specifically concerning the national composition of the Transylvanian urban areas since 1956. Romanian official statistics now give the proportion of the various nationalities only for the individual counties. Numerical shifts could be suitably evaluated if percentages of the natural increases were available for comparison with other factors (such as immigration, for example) that have contributed to the growth of population. It can nevertheless be said that between 1956 and 1979 the population of certain Transylvanian cities increased by 50 to 100 percent, and this growth could only have been the result of large-scale immigration, overwhelmingly by Romanians.[57]

The National Distribution in the Urban and Rural Population

Forced industrialization has rapidly changed the character of agrarian Romania and altered the ethnic composition of both the urban and rural populations. While the changes over a 40-year period have been great, by 1969 the majority of Romania's population was still rural. (See Table II-21).[58]

By 1975 the urban population had grown to 43 percent—still not a majority.[59] Even though the urban population doubled between 1948 and 1975, in all Europe only Yugoslavia and Albania were less urbanized than Romania. Transylvania, with 46 percent of its population living in urban areas, is the most urbanized area of Romania. In the 1930s the dominant view had been that as the national minorities were increasingly excluded from the towns, they would have to preserve the biological and cultural basis of their existence in the villages. Accelerating industrialization has demolished this assumption. The excess labor force continues to move from the villages into the towns, and

TABLE II-19

Arad

	Total Population	Romanian	Hungarian	German	Other	Jews	Jewish /religion/	Slav	Gypsy
1910	63,466	10,279	46,085	4,139	2,663	226	6,295	2,218	—
1920	62,490	12,469	39,399	3,012	7,610	5,306	—	—	—
1930	77,181	30,370	29,978	6,130	10,703	7,057	—	2,994	448
1941	86,674	40,677	26,798	7,811	11,388	—	—	—	—
1948	87,291	45,819	35,325	2,234	—	1,931	—	—	—
1956	106,460	58,444	31,850	9,037	7,129	4,963	—	2,019	5

Bistriţa / Beszterce / Bistritz

1910	13,263	4,470	—	5,835	—	—	—	—	—
1920	12,364	3,716	—	5,163	—	—	—	—	—
1930	14,128	5,666	—	4,461	—	—	—	—	—
1956	20,292	13,724	—	2,594	—	—	—	—	—

Braşov / Brassó / Kronstadt

1910	41,056	11,786	17,831	10,741	698	100	1,417	368	—
1920	40,335	12,183	15,137	11,293	1,722	1,505	—	—	—
1930	59,232	19,372	23,269	13,014	3,577	2,267	—	657	58
1941	84,557	49,463	15,114	16,210	3,770	—	—	—	—
1948	82,984	55,152	17,697	8,480	1,655	1,002	—	—	—
1956	123,834	88,329	22,742	10,127	2,636	1,759	—	495	70

Cluj / Kolozsvár / Klausenburg

1910	60,808	7,562	50,704	1,231	—	445	7,046	407	—
1920	83,542	28,274	41,583	2,073	11,612	10,633	—	—	—
1930	100,844	34,895	47,689	2,500	—	13,062	—	1,173	1,043
1941	110,956	9,814	96,002	1,606	3,534	2,661	16,763	98	557
1948	117,915	47,321	67,977	360	2,257	1,625	—	—	—
1956	154,723	74,033	74,155	990	—	4,530	—	377	444

Oradea / Nagyvárad / Grosswardein

1910	64,169	3,604	58,421	1,131	1,013	285	15,155	657	—
1920	68,081	8,441	40,744	598	18,298	17,880	—	—	—
1930	82,687	22,412	42,630	927	16,718	14,764	—	1,221	571

Source: note 56.

TABLE II-20

Oradea / Nagyvárad / Grosswardein

	Total Population	Romanian	Hungarian	German	Other	Jews	Jewish /religion/	Slav	Gypsy
1941	92,942	4,385	85,383	671	2,503	1,546	21,333	184	107
1948	82,282	26,998	52,541	165	—	1,837	—	—	—
1956	98,950	35,581	58,424	343	4,602	3,610	—	377	28

Sibiu / Nagyszeben / Hermannstadt

1910	33,489	8,824	7,252	16,832	—	—	—	—	—
1920	32,748	8,553	4,291	18,218	—	—	—	—	—
1930	49,345	18,620	6,521	21,598	—	—	—	—	—
1941	63,765	33,829	4,262	23,574	—	—	—	—	—
1956	90,475	59,855	4,882	24,253	—	—	—	—	—

Sighişoara / Segesvár / Schässburg

1910	11,587	3,031	2,687	5,486	—	—	—	—	—
1920	11,561	3,488	2,253	5,620	—	—	—	—	—
1930	13,033	4,366	2,896	5,236	—	—	—	—	—
1941	17,436	8,723	2,471	5,282	—	—	—	—	—
1956	20,363	11,718	3,005	5,096	—	—	—	—	—

Timişoara / Temesvár / Temeschburg

1910	72,555	7,566	28,552	31,644	7,054	2,261	—	4,570	—
1920	82,689	15,892	26,185	29,188	11,421	8,296	—	—	—
1930	91,580	24,217	27,652	28,807	11,904	7,171	—	3,864	337
1941	110,840	44,349	20,090	30,940	15,461	25	—	—	—
1948	111,987	58,456	30,630	16,139	110	25	—	—	—
1956	142,258	75,855	29,968	24,326	12,108	6,700	—	4,941	122

Tîrgu Mureş / Marosvásárhely / Neumarkt

1910	25,517	1,717	22,790	523	—	73	2,755	170	—
1920	30,988	3,947	23,178	446	3,417	3,246	—	—	—
1930	38,517	9,795	22,387	632	—	4,828	—	290	400
1941	44,933	1,756	42,087	378	712	514	—	27	114
1948	47,043	11,007	34,943	72	—	762	—	—	—
1956	65,194	14,623	48,077	263	—	1843	—	112	208

Source: note 56.

TABLE II-21

Romania's Population, 1930–1978

Year	Total Population	Urban Population		Rural Population	
		Number	Percent	Number	Percent
1930	18,057,028	3,632,200	20.1	14,420,700	79.9
1948	15,872,624	3,713,139	23.4	12,159,485	76.6
1953	16,490,000	5,742,000	34.8	10,758,000	65.2
1956	17,489,450	5,474,264	31.3	12,015,186	68.7
1966	19,105,056	7,305,303	38.2	11,799,753	61.8
1969	20,010,178	8,096,261	40.0	11,913,917	59.5
1978	21,854,622	10,626,335	48.6	11,228,287	51.4

Sources: note 58.

this one-way territorial and social mobility has fundamentally modified not only the social structure but also the national composition of the urban population.

The Occupational Distribution and Social Structure of the Population

Industrialization and the urbanization that accompanied it have caused large-scale shifts in the way the people of Romania earn a living. The nationalization and socialization of industry and the collectivization of agriculture, the main factors in transforming the social structure, were introduced after 1948, when the communist government came to power.

In addition to being near the end of the European urbanization list, Romania is economically among the poorest countries of Eastern Europe. Since the July 1972 national conference of the Romanian Communist Party, Romania has been officially regarded as a "developing socialist country" (*ţara socialistă în curs de dezvoltare*).[60] Although the number of people engaged in agriculture has continuously declined since 1950 as a result of industrialization, in 1975 agriculture still employed more people (38.1 percent)[61] than any other occupation.

Although Romania is among the most rapidly industrializing countries in the world, the forced changes in the economic character of the country have given rise to serious internal (and external) problems: the use of dictatorial methods; the constant shortfalls in the food supply; the erosion of the patriarchal way of life; the shocks to which the peasantry has been subjected; the lack of interest shown by the younger generations toward agriculture; the policy of "socialist homogenization" which has aimed at assimilating the national minorities; the nature of the proletariat that has been recruited from the rural population and has developed along the periphery of the industrial centers, together with the problem of those who commute to work from the countryside.

Table II-22 shows the occupational distribution of the nationalities in Romania and provides a general picture of the social structure of the national minorities between 1956 and 1966.[62] The high number of German workers, followed closely by the Hungarians, with the Romanians in third place is evident. A large proportion of the former German and Hungarian landowners have become part of the industrial proletariat. The table also shows that the Jews have maintained their lead among white collar employees. The figures also show that with the influx of independent peasants into the cooperatives, the 1956 proportions between these categories had reversed by 1966.

Without doubt, the ethnic minorities are affected more adversely by Romanian domestic problems than is the majority population. The policy of ethnic discrimination in the socioeconomic sector can be seen most clearly in the changes in the professional and social structures. The national minorities, if not totally excluded, are not permitted to take part enough in the current process of industrialization to lead to their economic advancement. Even qualified workers are only offered jobs in the Old Kingdom (Regat) or, at best, in the Romanian populated industrial areas, while in the areas occupied by the minorities, industry and salaries are kept at the lowest level.

Demographic characteristics

Romania is currently in the third phase of demographic development, one that is characterized by a low ratio of births to deaths. The

TABLE II-22

Occupational Distribution of the Nationalities in Romania, 1956–1966
(in percentage)

	worker	intelligentsia	Agriculture independent	cooperative	independent (free-lancer)
1956					
Romanians	25.2	13.6	53.0	5.7	2.5
Hungarians	31.5	12.2	43.6	8.1	4.6
Germans	56.8	14.9	9.6	14.5	4.2
Jews	27.4	63.3	0.9	5.4	3.0
1966					
Romanians	38.86	12.33	5.54	39.69	3.58
Hungarians	48.86	11.60	2.98	34.20	2.36
Germans	58.49	13.58	2.04	23.58	2.31
Jews	29.01	62.45	0.00	3.33	5.21

Source: note 62.

symptoms of this demographic aging are already beginning to appear.[63]

Anuarul Statistic 1979, p. 58, shows that the birthrate indeed sank from 27.4 per thousand in 1967 to 19.1 in 1978; the latter number, however, is substantially higher than the lower point of 14.3 reached in years 1960 to 1966. As is known, the gradually declining birthrate leads to demographic aging, the symptoms of which can be seen in Romania. This tendency signaled a serious, if not alarming, change in age groups in the period from 1956 to 1966. The share of children under seven years of age sank visibly in comparison to that of eight to sixteen year olds. Moreover, the 17 to 26 year old group showed a decrease even though the share of those under 25 was still 41.5 percent of the whole on July 1, 1978. A substantial growth was registered by the 35 to 45 year old group, although the number of 46 to 50 year olds did not increase to the same degree as in the past: the 1976–1978 average was

67.42 percent for men and 72.18 percent for women. Above this age group, a general increase in population can be observed.

The growth and changes in the population of the national minorities, as has been already pointed out, are closely linked with the demographic situation of the Romanian people. The majority nation and the national minorities do not, however, benefit equally from the advantages of the current processes of social restratification, industrialization, and urbanization.

3

THE POSSIBILITIES FOR MINORITY COEXISTENCE IN ROMANIA, 1918–1956

The National Minorities in Romania Between 1918 and 1944

The break-up of the Austro-Hungarian Monarchy with its population of over fifty million and the Paris peace treaties at the end of World War I resulted in changed frontiers and artificially created multinational states. The new state borders had not been drawn along ethnic boundaries, so the territories of the newly founded or enlarged successor states—specifically Czechoslovakia, Yugoslavia, Romania—were formed at the expense of the neighboring countries[1] and their people, for strategic, economic, and other reasons.

As a result, the interests of the various nationalities and religions living in the area were not reconciled, but were, in fact, often exacerbated. Nationalities that had been majorities—often ruling majorities—before the war in many instances now found themselves a minority in the new "national" states, while previously oppressed minorities now found themselves a ruling majority. The situation provided fertile ground for later revanchist and nationalist politics.

In the period after the peace treaties of 1919–20, the question of national minorities grew into a genuine European problem and eventually into a world issue.[2] The new map of Europe meant that 40 million people—or one-quarter of the population of East-Central Europe—now found themselves living in states where they were a national minority. With regard to territorial and population losses, Hungary was one of the countries most adversely affected: as a result of the Trianon treaty she lost 71.3 percent of her territory, and 33.03 percent of her Hungarian-speaking population. Over 3.6 million ethnic Magyars now found themselves living outside the newly drawn borders of Hungary and in new countries in which they formed a minority; of this total, two million Magyars lived in compact areas along the frontiers drawn by the Trianon treaty.

In Transylvania, now part of Romania, the national minorities responded variously to their new situation. The bulk of the Hungarians—once members of the majority people and now in a minority—adopted a position of passive resistance, while a common recognition of their plight as a minority grew. Their first political move was to form an organization—the non-partisan Hungarian Federation (*Magyar Szövetség*) on January 9, 1921. The Federation's aim was to represent the Hungarians in Romania politically, economically and through their educational institutions. Although the Paris Minorities Treaty (December 9, 1919) stated that minorities had the right to form political organizations based on their national communities, the Romanian government quickly banned the activities of the Hungarian Federation. But the idea of reconstituting the Federation remained alive and reappeared toward the end of the 1930s.

On January 23, 1921 (toward the end of the month in which the Hungarian Federation was first founded), on the initiative of the Transylvanian Hungarian writer Károly Kós, a pamphlet was published under the title "*Kiáltó Szó*" ("Warning Cry"; a literal translation is "yelled word"). The pamphlet's editors called on the Hungarians of Transylvania, the Banat, Crişana and Maramureş to organize and become active politically. The pamphlet confronted issues facing the national minorities, condemned chauvinistic nationalism, and formulated a democratic program which called for coexistence of the Transylvanian national minorities with the Romanian people and marked out the political path to be followed by the Hungarians in Transylvania.

In June of 1921, again on the initiative of Károly Kós, the Hungarian People's Party (*Magyar Néppárt*) was founded with a program based on the ideas in "*Kiáltó Szó.*" This party was the first political organization of the Hungarian middle class in Transylvania. Early in the following year another—and somewhat more conservative—movement was organized: the Hungarian National Party (*Magyar Nemzeti Párt*), founded on February 12, 1922. These two groups eventually merged (December 28, 1922) to form the National Hungarian Party (*Országos Magyar Párt*).

The National Hungarian Party based its nationality policy on the Resolutions of Alba Iulia and the Paris Minorities Treaty.[3] The new organization actively represented the interests of the Hungarians in the Romanian Parliament, where the Magyars—in their first major parliamentary action—worked toward the formation of a coalition with the Romanian People's Party. The result was the "Pact of Ciucea" (in Hungarian, Csucsa)[4] on October 23, 1923.

The German minority in Transylvania (unlike the Magyars who had been part of the ruling majority before the war) had a long experience as a minority and adapted prudently to the changed situation. The Saxons were the first Transylvanian nationality to form a political organization; on September 6, 1919 under the leadership of Rudolf Brandsch, they held a meeting in Timişoara/Temesvár to develop a common electoral program. In 1921 the Federation of Germans in Romania (*Verband der Deutschen in Rumänien*) was founded. Led by the Transylvanian Saxons but comprising all the German ethnic groups in Romania, it was under the leadership of Rudolf Brandsch until 1931, from 1931 to 1935 under the Banat Swabian Kaspar Muth, and from 1935 until its end in 1945 under Hans Otto Roth. The Transylvanian Saxons also convened their popular assembly, the *Sachsentag*—this assembly also founded under the leadership of Rudolf Brandsch. They then established the German-Saxon People's Council in Transylvania (*Deutsch-Sächsische Volksrat in Siebenbürgen*), the highest political organ of their people, taking the role of the *Nationsuniversität*.

In 1920, to represent the interests of all the Germans in Romania, the German Party (*Deutsche Partei*) was founded; it functioned until 1938 under the political leadership of Rudolf Brandsch and Hans Otto Roth. The German Party fought—basing its argument on the Resolutions of Alba Iulia—for a new law that would guarantee the national rights of the German minority in Romania. Between the two world wars, the interests of the German national minority were represented in the Romanian parliament by one to eleven members of parliament and two to four senators. The German Party—like the Hungarian Party—fought for the right of self-determination but without achieving more than minor concessions.

In 1927 the National Hungarian Party joined forces with the German Party and fought side by side with them for several national election campaigns. In the July elections of that year, there were eight Hungarians and seven Germans in the lower house of Parliament and one Hungarian in the Senate. The idea of creating a joint electoral organization was advocated by Hans Otto Roth; however, the pact was never realized because part of the German minority came to an agreement with the Romanian Peasant Party instead. The reason for joining forces with this Romanian party was the Germans' dispersed geographical situation: in order to be represented in the Romanian Parliament, the Germans had to come to terms with the government in power.

The Transylvanian Jews, the third politically relevant nationality, also organized in the 1920s, founding the Transylvanian Jewish National Federation. Because the official Romanian policy aimed at splintering the nationalities, the government supported Zionism and the Yiddish-language school network in an unsuccessful attempt to separate the Jewish minority from the Hungarian camp—at a time when 11.1 percent of the urban and 2.1 percent of the rural population of Transylvania belonged to the Jewish religion and a decisive majority of them claimed Hungarian as their native tongue.[5]

Romania's National Liberal Party, which was based on the French statist-centralist model and which followed a nationalist policy, was primarily responsible for the oppression of the national minorities and the neglect of their rights.[6] But the National Peasant Party was not much better when it came to discriminatory measures. It must be said, however, that between the two world wars it was still possible, under the protection of the institutions which defended the minorities to voice complaints against transgressions of minority rights and to cite supporting international agreements on protection of national minorities. Even if the results were insignificant, it was at least possible for national minorities to speak out before international forums, one the rights of self-determination promised to them, without incurring reprisals for their efforts by their government.[7]

From the 1920s on, Romania's minorities turned increasingly to the League of Nations in Geneva with their grievances concerning the government's repressive nationality policy. For example, C. Angelescu, a Liberal and Minister of Religion and Education from 1922–1926 and 1933–1937, drafted educational legislation which destroyed the national-minority school networks, brought into question the future of the property of the national minority churches, and contained economic, social and cultural measures. Complaints against these oppressive measures were often placed before the League of Nations. Thus, for example, between 1920 and 1940 a total of 47 complaints by the Hungarian minority in Romania were submitted to the League.[8]

After an unsuccessful political struggle to gain equal rights, the Transylvanian national minorities realized they could fight oppression only on the intellectual level; yet, they did not totally abandon their political claims either. The result was that politics and literature became inseparably intertwined; and the idea of Transylvanism arose, an idea which proclaimed the mutual cooperation of the Transylvanian peoples—Hungarians, Romanians and Saxons. The ideal of national solidarity, however, took root only in literature, under the influence of the Hungarian and Saxon writers. The Saxon writers particularly welcomed the alliance because they saw in it a way to protect themselves against the official dictates of Greater Romanian nationalism. And as the Saxon Otto Folberth wrote: "It is certain that there has never been a more suitable time for the spiritual meeting between Hungarians and Saxons."[9] The idea of Transylvanism, however, evoked hardly any reaction from the Romanians of the region.[10]

The thought of Transylvanism led to a renewal of sufficiently realistic Transylvanian ideals, of national self-evaluation and of interest in historical traditions. The Hungarian and Saxon intellectual leadership in Transylvania endeavored to shape their national consciousness and self-identity by a study of their historical past.

A gradual trend toward democratization coincided with this period of self-examination in intellectual life, softening to some extent the hitherto more rigid stance of the various nationality groups. It was most clearly manifested by the Hungarians in the founding of the Hungarian People's Party (*Magyar Néppárt*), democratic in spirit, in 1927; the Hungarian Smallholders' Party (*Magyar Kisgazda Párt*) and the National Hungarian Party Opposition (*Országos Magyarpárti Ellenzék*) in 1933; and the left-wing Hungarian National Workers' Federation (*Magyar Dolgozók Országos Szövetsége*—MADOSZ) in 1934. In Transylvania the Hungarian liberal publicist, Miklós Krenner (Spectator) had criticized the separatist policies of the Hungarian Party as early as 1926 and called on the Hungarians to work for a more wide-ranging and active democratic organization. The so-called "reform group" which formed around him, as well as the Hungarian Party, gave voice to the Hungarians' grievances. The reform group's authoritative journal, the *Keleti Újság* (Eastern News), published in

Cluj/Kolozsvár devoted a series of articles to discussing the problems of national minority existence in Transylvania.

Toward the end of the 1920s representatives of the national minorities in the Romanian Parliament once again became active. It was during this period that the parliamentary debates on the church and school grievances led to the signing of a Concordat between the Romanian government and the Holy See (May 10, 1927). The purpose of the Concordat was to resolve the controversial relationship between the Roman Catholic Church and the Romanian (overwhelmingly Orthodox) state. But the Concordat also brought new restrictions, primarily by subordinating the centuries-old autonomy of the Transylvanian Catholic Church to the Romanian Catholic Archbishop, whose seat was in Bucharest.

The end of the 1920s also saw significant changes in the political life of ethnic Germans in Romania. The cooperative construction organization "*Selbsthilfe*" (Self-Help), which had been founded at the middle of the decade to deal with economic problems, assumed a political character with the advance of National Socialism, and the group changed its name to "*Nationale Selbsthilfebewegung der Deutschen in Rumänien*" (NSDR—National Self-Help Movement of the Germans in Romania), which in turn later changed its name to "*Nationalsozialistische Erneuerungsbewegung der Deutschen in Rumänien*" (NEDR—The National Socialist Movement for Renewal of the Germans in Romania). At the *Sachsentag* elections of October 1, 1933, this party won 62 percent of the votes.[11] The more conservative German stratum—particularly the Evangelical Church in Transylvania, and the Catholic Church in the Banat, to a lesser degree,—resisted these new directions. The highest organ representing the German minority, the *Volksrat* (People's Council), continued to function democratically; but by the end of the 1930s the political weight of Berlin was increasingly felt. The result was the fusion in 1935 of the opposition and the new movement into the "*Nationalsozialistische Deutsche Arbeiterpartei*" (NSDAP, National Socialist German Workers' Party). After the dismissal of Fritz Fabritius, the political fate of the German minority in Romania was placed in the hands of Andreas Schmidt, a man who, under the guidance of Berlin, acted as "*Volksgruppenführer*."

A certain polarization could be observed at the beginning of the 1930s, a polarization which initially acted as a kind of psychological release for the national minorities. The government of the historian Nicolae Iorga (April 1931–May 1932) attempted to settle the national minority question by appointing a so-called Undersecretary for Minorities to the office of the Prime Minister. The Transylvanian Saxon Rudolf Brandsch became minority undersecretary; and the Hungarian Árpád Bitay, a professor of theology, became special advisor to the minister. But the minority undersecretariat's duties were limited to acting in an advisory capacity; and on October 28, 1932 the Peasant Party abolished the short-lived office.

The next initiative came from an article which appeared in the Hungarian-language daily *Ellenzék* (Opposition) on January 10, 1932. Entitled "Let Us Build a Bridge" ("*Verjünk hidat*") and written by the journalist Miklós Krenner,[12] the article proposed a spiritual reconciliation with the Romanians. The idea of "bridge building," however, evoked no response from the Romanians.

The rift between the Romanian people and their country's national minorities deepened increasingly in the 1930s because of the territorial demands made by Hungary on its neighbors, the creation of the Romanian "Anti-Revisionist League," the anti-minority campaign of the extreme nationalist Romanian daily *Universul,* and the emergence of the extreme right-wing political organization, the Iron Guard.[13] The negative aspects of growing Romanian nationalism were directed against the national minorities, and were manifested primarily in anti-Semitic and anti-Hungarian excesses.

With the fall of the not yet quite fascist Goga-Cuza government of the National Christian Party, which had come to power on December 28, 1937, outright fascism took over in Romania. The Constitution of February 20, 1938 eliminated parliamentary democracy and established a royal dictatorship. The state of emergency, which had been introduced in 1933 and which lasted until 1940, now assumed an even more rigid form.

After political parties were banned, the nationalities in Transylvania turned to economic organization. At the same time a democratically oriented national resistance began to take shape; and the new Transylvanian realism became evident at the Conclave of Vásárhely,[14] held October 2-4, 1937. The 187 Hungarian participants in the conclave came from groups with highly divergent and even conflicting ideologies. The outcome was that the Conclave could not draft a lasting program, and that the various factions soon broke with each other.

In the meantime, the royal dictatorship of King Carol II (1938-1940) abolished all existing political parties—including those of the national minorities, and by a decree issued on December 16, 1938, they were merged into the National Regeneration Front (*Frontul Renașterii Naționale*). By the time the Hungarian People's Community (*Magyar Népközösség*) was founded on February 11, 1939, the constantly worsening situation of the Hungarian minority made it impossible for the new organization to have any significant effect.

The Transylvanian Saxons lost their traditional independence when on March 10, 1937, the Romanian state abolished their centuries-old economic basis, the institutionalized *Nationsuniversität* and *Sieben-Richter-Waldungen,* dividing their property between the Romanian Orthodox and Saxon Lutheran Churches.[15]

Official public opinion rejected the National Socialism of the German minority in Romania, but early German successes in the war brought about an improvement in their position, as Romania realigned itself politically toward the German Reich. On February 6, 1938, before it fell from power, the Goga-Cuza government had recognized, by a direct settlement with Berlin, the People's Community of the Germans in Romania (*Volksgemeinschaft der Deutschen in Rumänien*). The significant turning point in German-Romanian relations came with the bilateral economic treaty signed by the two governments on March 23, 1939. The outbreak of the war six months later signalled the establishment of close ties with Berlin.

The New Political Orientation

In 1940 a series of international events determined Romania's political path and the fate of its minorities: primarily, the advances of the German Reich in East Central Europe, the outbreak of the German-Soviet war, and Romania's own territorial losses (Bessarabia, Northern Bucovina, Southern Dobrugea, and Northern Transylvania). These losses had far-reaching effects on Romanian domestic and foreign policies.

The German orientation of Romanian foreign policy was unquestionably influenced by the territorial losses. The reorientation toward the Reich was made official in September 1940 when the Gigurtu government resigned and the pro-German general, Ion Antonescu (ruled 1940–1944), came to power on September 5. This was followed a day later by the forced abdication of King Carol II and his escape from the country; his situation had become untenable because of the territorial losses. His son Michael then ascended the throne but only as a figurehead; real political power lay with General Ion Antonescu, until now Minister of War and backed by the Iron Guard. Antonescu, together with the Iron Guard, assumed unlimited power as "*Conducător*" (Leader).

The Antonescu-Horia Sima government proclaimed the "National Legionary State,"[16] and adopted a domestic policy that was extremely nationalistic, anti-Semitic and anti-Hungarian. The regime's foreign policy was one of unqualified support for the Axis powers. On November 23, 1940 Romania adhered to the three-power alliance of Germany, Italy, and Japan, and on June 22, 1941 joined Hitler's military campaign against the Soviet Union.

The failure of Romania's foreign policy to regain the lost territories cast a shadow on domestic politics: the Antonescu government blamed the national minorities, particularly the Jewish and Hungarian populations, for this lack of success. In contrast the German national minority's protection was ensured because it was under the protection of the German Reich.

On August 30, 1940, a German-Romanian protocol—without consulting the German ethnic group in Romania— was signed.[17] It guaranteed, with reference to the Resolutions of Alba Iulia, complete legal equality for the Germans in Romania. The protocol was followed on November 20, 1940, by the so-called "*Volksgruppen Gesetz*"[18] regulating relations between the German ethnic group (*Volksgruppe*) and the state; by this decree, the Antonescu government with reference to the Resolutions of Alba Iulia accorded legal recognition to the "German Ethnic Group in Romania." On October 12, 1940 so-called German military "instructors" (*Lehrtruppen*) arrived in Romania, beginning what was, for all practical purposes, a military occupation. The pro-German policy pursued by Romania during this period had social, economic, and cultural as well as political consequences for the German minority in Romania: its economic position improved, and its autonomous educational network was further developed.

The character of Hungarian-Romanian relations was markedly different: here nationalism was the guiding force, and tensions became so great in the summer of 1940 that, in order to avoid armed conflict, great power intervention was necessary. When, after the failure of Hungarian-Romanian negotiations in Turnu-Severin,[19] the Romanian royal government and Hitler learned that the Hungarians intended to take armed action against Romania, King Carol asked Hitler—on various occasions—to act as arbitrator in the debate over Transylvania.[20] There could hardly have been a more appropriate moment, psychologically, for Hungarian military intervention than the eve of the conflict between the Soviet Union and Germany. Following the signing of the German-Romanian economic treaty in 1939, the Soviet Union had indicated its approval of Hungarian territorial demands: at that moment, it considered Romania, rapidly moving toward fascism, to be a greater danger than the still rather conservative Hungarian regime. Additional moral support for the territorial demands of the Hungarian government was provided by the Soviet annexation of Bessarabia, Northern Bucovina and a small area of northern Moldavia (from the Herța-district) on June 28–July 2, 1940, after giving Romania no more than twenty-four hours to reply to an ultimatum. At the same time Bulgaria also realized its long-standing territorial claims against Romania by occupying Southern Dobrugea.[21]

Given his military plans, Hitler could not afford an armed conflict between Romania and Hungary. He therefore had Ribbentrop issue a two-day ultimatum calling on the representatives of the Hungarian and Romanian governments formally to request arbitration.

Ultimately, on August 30, 1940, the Axis powers issued the Second Vienna Award[22] dividing Transylvania into two parts: Northern and Southern Transylvania. Northern Transylvania, with an area of 43,492 square kilometers, with 1,380,506 Hungarian and 1,029,470 Romanian inhabitants, was awarded to Hungary, leaving Southern Transylvania, with an area of 59,295 square kilometers, and approximately half a million Hungarian inhabitants, in the possession of Romania.[23]

The real motive behind the Second Vienna Award was to play Hungary and Romania off against each other, ensuring a balance of power in the Danube area by exacerbating tensions between the two countries. In this way, Hitler was better able to exert his control over the area, and to use the countries as pawns in his overall military strategy. Thus, Hitler was able to use Hungarian territorial revisionism and the revanchist policy of Romania that resulted from these territorial losses to secure increasing military support from both countries, as well as control of the Romanian oilfields. The Gigurtu government would actually have been willing—for the first time in Romanian history—to agree to minor territorial revisions in favor of Hungary but constantly growing extreme Romanian nationalist feelings in other quarters thwarted all such initiatives.

During the ensuing period, the conflict between Romania and Hungary was expressed most clearly in their treatment of the other's ethnic minority in their respective parts of Transylvania.

Under the guise of an anti-Semitic campaign, attacks were made by the Romanian government against the Hungarians of Southern Transylvania. In turn, the Hungarian government reacted with energetic retaliatory measures against the Romanians of Northern Transylvania, measures which were not justified in every instance and were sometimes excessive. Viewed from a historical perspective, the discriminatory measures of the Romanian government were more drastic than those taken by the Hungarian government; the Romanian measures were also more numerous and more effective. The Romanians perceived themselves to be in a position of strength: Hitler had a greater interest in Romania than in Hungary and Romania's contribution to the war effort was greater than Hungary's. Thus, the Romanians believed that, in case of an armed conflict between the two countries, they would receive more support from Germany and that an armed conflict could therefore only result in a more favorable solution to the territorial dispute. Romania had little to lose after the loss of considerable parts of its territory, and those losses, particularly the loss of Northern Transylvania, had angered Romanian public opinion considerably; the flames of outrage were further fanned by the government's propaganda for territorial revisionism. It is therefore understandable that the Romanian leadership was psychologically more prone to aggression than was the Hungarian government, that it took the initiative more frequently in instituting discriminatory and retaliatory nationality measures, and that its measures were more provocative in character than their Hungarian counterparts.

Just as Hungary's military strategy was focused, however, on the Transylvanian question till the very end, the fear of losing Transylvania lay at the heart of Romania's military strategy: in this way, an unbridgeable chasm developed between the two states, precluding any possibility of a reconciliation. The two countries' participation in the war, Romania's withdrawal from the Axis, and Hungary's attempt to do so and to compete for Hitler's favor were all determined by these territorial considerations. The Romanian army fought in the east to restore its western frontiers, not to recapture Bessarabia. Neither Antonescu nor Horthy sent their elite formations to fight on the Soviet front: each kept them on guard against the other.

Hungarian-Romanian tensions lessened only with the approach of the "common danger," the Soviet army (and even then, they lessened only temporarily). Both sides hoped for Anglo-American intervention, but, by that point in the war, it was impossible to act without the approval of the Soviet Union. Despite this threat, however, when the idea of Hungarian-Romanian discussions was proposed in March 1943, the Romanian representative, Iuliu Maniu, refused to coordinate Romania's efforts to encourage an Anglo-American occupation with similar Hungarian plans. Maniu's interest in knowing about the Hungarian plans was only part of an effort to forestall Hungarian diplomatic maneuvers in Transylvania.

The Years of Decisive Changes

The entry of Romania into the war on June 22, 1941, and its campaign against the Soviet Union had a considerable effect on the status of the national minorities living in its territory. Romania gave greater military support to Germany against the Soviet Union than did any other Axis ally.[24] Whatever tensions had existed earlier between the Antonescu government and the German minority in Romania were relaxed by the joint campaign against the Soviet Union. No fewer than 45,000 Transylvanian Saxons and Swabians from the Banat fought in the Romanian army, and 60,000 Germans from Romania participated in the SS formations established, at the instigation of Berlin, in the spring of 1943 on the basis of a German-Romanian agreement. These developments were later to have serious consequences.

The Hungarian population of Southern Transylvania found themselves in a very different situation from the German minority. As "unreliable elements," many were either sent to the front in so-called "death brigades" or deployed behind the front lines in "labor service brigades."

A series of anti-Jewish laws were issued as well. For example, permits for Jewish-owned monopolies were withdrawn on December 31, 1940. A measure went into effect on April 1, 1941, that ordered the expropriation of all Jewish real estate in urban areas as well as the property of Jewish communities;[25] only synagogues and the homes of rabbis were exempted. The expropriated property was entrusted to the National Center for Romanianization (*Centrul Național de Românizare*). Furthermore, after August 1, 1941, Jewish males between the ages of 18 and 50 were drafted into "labor service brigades" and sent to work at the front under unspeakable conditions. According to the official 1942 census, the Jewish population of Romania numbered approximately 300,000, of whom 50,000–60,000 were engaged in permanent labor service.[26] In addition to forced labor at the front and elsewhere, a significant proportion of the Jewish population fell victim to ultra-nationalist pogroms and deportations.

With the collapse of the German offensive in the Soviet Union and the approach of the Red Army to the frontiers of Romania, the idea of withdrawal from the war began to find support in Romanian political circles. Secret diplomatic contacts, aimed at preparing for this withdrawal, were made via the Czech statesman Beneš, living in London,[27] and through the German embassies in Ankara and in Teheran. Most Romanian politicians with the exception of Antonescu and his closest military advisors considered Hitler's war to be lost. It was at that time that the idea of withdrawing from the war arose. Two factors lay behind such thinking: one was the turn of the fortunes of war in favor of the Allied powers and the psychological impact of the entry of the Soviet army into Romania. The desire to withdraw was also based on the expectation of many Romanians that the Allies would invalidate the Second Vienna Award; the Soviets had, in fact, promised to return Transylvania to Romania as compensation for the loss of Bessarabia and Northern Bucovina, and as an encouragement for Romania to launch an attack on German and Hungarian troops. This intention was confirmed by Beneš, in a letter to the leader of the Romanian Peasant Party, Maniu, in which he wrote: "Romania obligates itself to compensate the Soviet Union in part for the damage it caused to the latter; [Romania] recognizes the rightful demands of the Soviet Union concerning Bessarabia and Bucovina, while the Allies, on the other hand, regard the Second Vienna Award, which they have never recognized, as invalid."[28]

On April 2, 1944, when the Soviet army reached the line of the Pruth and Siret Rivers the so-called "Focşani defense line," a new chapter in the history of East Central Europe was begun. Thereafter the affairs of this area were to be shaped by the great power policies of the Soviet Union. The first significant change occurred on August 23, 1944, when Romania capitulated and the Soviet army had occupied the country. It had become obvious to the Romanian leadership that Germany was going to lose the war and that Romania could regain even a part of its territorial losses only by changing sides and joining with the Allied powers, who had promised before the capitulation that Romania would regain Transylvania or at least "the greater part of it."[29]

The coup d'état of August 23, 1944 was carried out by King Michael I with the aid of the National Peasant Party, the Socialist Party, General Sănătescu and other non- or anti-Communists. Following the coup d'état, the king had Marshal Antonescu arrested and formed a new government headed by General Sănătescu. The new government ended the war against the Soviet Union and, on August 25th, declared war on Romania's erstwhile allies.

The Romanian capitulation of August 23, 1944, had immeasurably grave consequences for Southeastern Europe, both in terms of the general political and social situation and from the point of view of the national minorities. Romania's change of sides came unexpectedly for the German military leadership; the Balkan front collapsed and the Soviet army was able to advance unopposed toward Northern Transylvania and Hungary. The Romanian army, now fighting on the side of the Soviets against German and Hungarian forces, became increasingly hostile to the German and Hungarian populations it encountered: it regarded "the liberation" of Northern Transylvania "as a national war."[30]

The German population of Romania in its threatened situation continued to expect protection from the German army. It soon appeared, however, that the small German forces stationed in Southern Transylvania and the Banat region had also retreated. The new Romanian government immediately began mass arrests among the Hungarians and German population. Only a few people managed to flee to Northern Transylvania, which was still under Hungarian administration.

Although Romania's change of sides and its declaration of war on Hungary did not come as a surprise for the Hungarian leadership, it did cause a considerable disruption of Hungarian internal politics. The head of state, Admiral Horthy, (1920–1944) dismissed the pro-German Prime Minister Sztójay and appointed Colonel-General Géza Lakatos in his place; the Germans' most trusted supporters, however, still continued to be members of the government. Horthy found himself trapped by the forces and political atmosphere he had originally created to support Hungarian participation in the war; it was to prove increasingly difficult for him to pull out of the Axis alliance. The Romanian action had a much more direct effect on the Hungarian leadership of Northern Transylvania, and it led the Transylvanian

Party (*Erdélyi Párt*)[31] to become more active. The democratic-spirited Transylvanian Party, under the leadership of Béla Teleki, had already recognized that the *status quo* in Transylvania could not be maintained, and that the continuation of the war would have grave consequences for the Hungarians living there. This view was shared by left-wing Hungarian Transylvanian politicians as well, and, consequently, they made several efforts to establish closer links with the Transylvanian Party. As a result of discussions between a left-wing group and the chairman and representatives of the Transylvanian Party in the summer of 1944, it was concluded that an official action by Horthy was the only realistic means of withdrawing from the war. Subsequently, the chairman of the Transylvanian Party, Béla Teleki, and the representatives of the party, as well as Dániel Bánffy, one-time minister of agriculture, had several discussions with Regent Horthy and the members of the government. Teleki suggested, for the first time, withdrawing from the war. At that time, Horthy did not consider the situation ripe for carrying out this plan, but Prime Minister Lakatos promised to postpone the armed attack on Southern Transylvania that the Hungarian general staff had planned for the beginning of September. Despite this promise the attack on Soviet and Romanian forces in Southern Transylvania did take place, on September 5; however, by September 15, the Hungarian forces had retreated, with great loss, to Turda/Torda where they were subsequently engaged in heavy defensive fighting for several weeks. By that time, the Transylvanian Hungarian army group was no longer in any condition to fight; it was poorly equipped and consisted primarily of reserve units.

Meanwhile, the Hungarian leaders of Northern Transylvania formed an illegal Transylvanian Hungarian Council (*Erdélyi Magyar Tanács*), whose members included politicians, Church leaders, and representatives of social institutions and trade unions, supporting the Transylvanian Party's policy of withdrawal from the war. In the meantime, Béla Teleki and Dániel Bánffy, through the mediation of Ladomér Zichy, attempted to establish contact with the Soviet leaders in order to negotiate a cease-fire agreement and prevent Transylvania from becoming a battleground. Horthy instructed Prime Minister Lakatos to announce Hungary's surrender. The Council of Ministers, however, opposed this plan, and Horthy therefore decided to begin cease-fire negotiations with the Allied Powers without the knowledge of the government, following a meeting between chairman of the Transylvanian Party Béla Teleki and Regent Horthy on September 10, 1944. On September 12 the Transylvanian Hungarian Council demanded, in a memorandum, that Horthy ask the Allies for a cease-fire immediately. The Council also asked that a policy of reconciliation with the Romanians be initiated.

The memorandum of the Transylvanian Hungarian politicians had a considerable influence on Horthy's conduct but a majority of the members of the government felt that the Carpathians had to be defended against the Soviet army until the English and Americans could airlift troops into Hungary. They also hoped that if the Hungarian army could hold off Soviet forces for a few weeks, Germany would collapse and Hungary would thereby not become a theater of war.

Laws and Decrees Between 1918 and 1940 Relating to the National Minorities

The rights of the national minorities in the areas of Hungary annexed by Romania, including, above all, the right to the free use of the mother tongue, had been guaranteed by the Alba Iulia Resolutions, issued by the Romanian National Assembly on December 1, 1918,[32] as well as by the Paris Minorities Treaty, concluded between the Allied Powers[33] (Entente) and Romania on December 9, 1919. The Minorities Treaty became an integral part of, as well as a condition for, the Trianon Treaty of June 4, 1920, and guaranteed the minorities protection through the League of the Nations, the constitution and a promise to implement rights of minorities.[34] The treaties contained further the exclusion of discrimination and the guarantee of cultural autonomy. It must be noted that the Trianon Peace Treaty did not provide for any form of self-government or any autonomous legal position for the national minorities living in the areas ceded to Romania. The Allied Powers had sought to make Romania accept, prior to the signing of the peace treaty, an agreement guaranteeing the rights of the national, linguistic and religious minorities within its boundaries. When Romania hesitated, the Allies warned the Romanian government in a strong note that unless it signed a treaty protecting the rights of the minorities, they would not recognize Romanian territorial demands.[35] Only then did the signing of the treaty generally known as the Paris Minorities Treaty take place.

Article 1 of the Alba Iulia Resolutions[36] proclaimed the union of Romania and Transylvania. Article 2 stated that "until the convocation of the constituent assembly the inhabitants of these areas shall possess temporary autonomy." Article 3 guaranteed in paragraphs 2, 3, and 4 individual and national rights.

Paragraph 1 of that article proclaimed:

> full national freedom for the coexisting peoples. All of the peoples have the right to public education, public administration, and the administration of justice in their own languages, provided by individuals chosen from among their own members. All peoples will receive rights of representation in the governing of the country and in the legislative organ, in accordance with their numbers.[37]

Paragraph 2 of Article 3 guaranteed "equal rights and complete religious freedom for all religious faiths." Paragraph 3—proclaimed the "unqualified realization of a pure democratic system in every sphere of public life," while paragraph 4 guaranteed "unrestricted freedom of the press, association, and assembly, as well as the possibility for freedom of thought". (The unification of Transylvania and Romania was subsequently ordered by decree No. 3631 issued on December 11, 1918 by King Ferdinand I of Romania).

The Resolutions of Alba Iulia were enacted despite protests by the Hungarians of Transylvania[38] and without the general agreement of the German minority.[39] On the Romanian side the Social Democrats, who supported autonomy for Transylvania, also objected to these resolutions. Objective, non-Romanian historiography is unanimous in its view that the annexation of Transylvania by Romania took place not on the basis of a referendum or self-determination, but by the force of arms.[40] Ion I.C. Brătianu, Prime Minister of Romania and one of the leading figures in those historic events, later declared in the Bucharest Senate: "the integrity of the Romanian state and of the Romanian people was not the result of the Resolutions of Alba Iulia but rather of the treaty of alliance, . . . sealed by the deaths of 800,000 soldiers."[41] (He was referring to the secret agreement which Romania had concluded with the Entente on August 4, 1916, and which had already, at that point, determined the fate of Transylvania.[42])

There are divergent views concerning the legal significance of the Resolutions of Alba Iulia. From the point of view of Romanian statutory law they had no significance whatsoever, since the legislature of the new Romanian state did not incorporate them into the constitution or enact them as law; this view is confirmed by the international literature on the question.[43] Even in Romanian legal literature, the Resolutions of Alba Iulia are but rarely viewed as law or as an international treaty.[44] Of all the articles of the Resolutions of Alba Iulia, only Article 1, which proclaimed the union of Romania and Transylvania, was enacted into law (January 1, 1920). However, Romania attempted to represent the Resolutions of Alba Iulia—above all Article 3, paragraphs 1 and 2—to the international community as if its provisions guaranteeing to "all the coinhabiting nationalities wide-ranging national, cultural, and religious self-government," were integral parts of Romanian law.[45] In fact, however, the new Romanian state increasingly issued laws and decrees which, on the basis of the principle "*lex posteriori derogat priori,*" invalidated both the obligations undertaken in the Minorities Treaty and the sections of the Resolutions of Alba Iulia relating to the protection of the minorities. Despite the fact that in Article 1 of the Minorities Treaty Romania had agreed to abide by Articles 2 to 8 of that treaty as a fundamental international law, and that no law or decree contrary to the measures and provisions of that treaty could be considered valid, Romanian legal literature and the Romanian Supreme Court subsequently supported the view that international treaties had an even lower legal status than ordinary laws and that the government was entitled to disregard them at any time in pursuit of the national interest. Only rarely were dissenting viewpoints expressed by the Romanian legal community.

In the Minorities Treaty,[46] Romania had agreed: "to guarantee to all the inhabitants of the country complete personal security and full freedom" (Article 2); "it acknowledges those persons living in the territory of Romania from the time when this treaty comes into force as citizens possessing full rights" (Article 3); and, similarly, "it acknowledges those who are Austrian or Hungarian citizens but were born in areas which became Romanian as citizens with full rights" (Article 4); persons described in the last two articles "can opt for gaining foreign citizenship while at the same time retaining ownership of their real estate in Romanian territory" (Article 3); the Romanian government guaranteed "the use of the mother-tongue without restriction in private and commercial life . . . or at political meetings . . . as well as in judicial procedures" (Article 8); the minorities possessed the right "to establish, manage and control charitable, religious and social institutions, as well as teaching or other educational institutions, with the free use of the mother-tongue and the free observance of religion" (Article 9); the Romanian government "guarantees facilitation of the use of the nationality vernacular in those towns and districts where nationalities live" (Article 10); finally, Romania agreed that "the Transylvanian Székler and Saxon communities should be permitted local self-government in religious and educational matters under the supervision of the Romanian state" (Article 11). Besides establishing the general principles of national, racial, and religious equality, the agreement also obligated Romania to automatically acknowledge as Romanian citizens the approximately 300,000 Jewish inhabitants of the Regat (Old Kingdom) who had not been granted citizenship despite the categorical stipulation of the Congress of Berlin in 1878.

The newly established Greater Romania never fulfilled the obligations it had undertaken in the Minorities Treaties and the Resolutions of Alba Iulia concerning its national minorities.[47] The very fact that Romania was initially unwilling to sign the Minorities Treaty indicates that the principles of the Resolutions of Alba Iulia were also unacceptable to it. It is characteristic that the liberal government of I. Brătianu had to be dismissed before Romania would sign the Paris Minorities Treaty. An insight into the views of the Romanian government was provided during debate over the draft Constitution of 1923, when one of the leading politicians of that time, Vintilă Brătianu, stated: "The Minorities Treaty was an attempt to weaken the unified national character of the Romanian state and it pledged—in a promise which we have fortunately not fulfilled—to turn Greater Romania into a new and unfortunate Austria-Hungary."[48] All these facts demonstrate that, in practice, the Minorities Treaty provided no international protection whatsoever for the national and religious minorities in Romania.

The reorganization of the territories annexed by Romania and the tasks of a provisional government were entrusted to a Governing Council (*Consiliul Dirigent*) of fifteen members, elected by the 212-member Greater Romanian National Council (*Marele Sfat Național Român*). The Governing Council, which had its seat in Sibiu/Nagyszeben/Hermannstadt, was the executive organ for the unification of Transylvania in Romania, and had unlimited legislative and executive powers, which it exercised throughout the territory of Transylvania, supported by the Romanian army. As long as the Governing Council continued to function, Romania's promises to protect the minorities continued to be honored. However, an oppressive and restrictive nationality policy was soon to be instituted.[49]

The economic position of the national minorities in Transylvania was undermined during the first year of the Romanian seizure of power by the land reform of July 23, 1921.[50] This measure struck primarily at the owners of the large and medium-sized estates, as well as public institutions, including the churches, schools and foundations, whose lands were confiscated. Non-Romanian researchers generally share the view that the redistribution of land benefited the majority nation at the expense of the national minorities.[51] A large proportion of the expropriated wealth of the nationality churches became the property of the Romanian Orthodox Church.[52] It is characteristic of the discriminatory nature of the law that the land reform, which aimed at the expropriation of the large estates, was carried out much more strictly in Transylvania than in the Regat, even though 40 percent of the land in the latter belonged to large landowners, while the proportion in Transylvania was only 10.8 percent.[53] The indemnifications were also much smaller in Transylvania than in the Regat.[54] The 1921 agrarian reform also deprived the Széklers of the communal properties they had been granted in the 18th century in return for their services as defenders of the frontier, while the properties of Romanian border soldiers were not expropriated.[55]

It is worth mentioning, in connection with the agrarian reform, that before the annexation of Transylvania by Romania there had been a predominance of small and medium-sized (Hungarian and German) landowners, relatively few large estates, and a small group of landless peasants.[56]

The Romanian government used the land reform for propaganda abroad, proclaiming that it had instituted democratically based ownership of the land. However, the real purpose of the agrarian reform was to undermine the economic superiority of the national minorities in Transylvania and thereby change the nationality balance of power.

The new Constitution enacted on March 28, 1923[57] (published on March 29) was markedly nationalist and statist in character. It declared Romania to be a "unified, indivisible national state." Although it guaranteed equality before the law for every citizen of Romania, its provisions in this area were vague and its formulations contradictory. It did not incorporate either the Resolutions of Alba Iulia, the guarantees in the Minorities Treaty, or the cultural autonomy of the Széklers and of the Transylvanian Saxons. It guaranteed only individual, not collective, rights. In the sphere of public administration it relied on the principles of decentralization, and thus did not affect, to any great degree, the system of local and county self-government that had existed before the change of power in Transylvania.

The 1920s saw a whole series of laws and decrees restricting the freedom of religious observance by the national minorities[58] and endeavoring to destroy the network of schools providing instruction in the minority languages. This was the first occasion in the history of the Western-oriented Transylvanian nationality educational system, which dated back several hundred years, that a school system that had developed within the state system of the Balkans and was totally alien to the traditional Transylvanian spirit was established here.

These attacks against the national-minority churches and schools and other measures of this nature were part of an overall policy of Romanianization. Moreover, these discriminatory laws affected not only the school network but the whole public sector. The national minorities in the territories annexed by Romania became second-class citizens. Despite the fact that Article 8 of the Minorities Treaty provided for the unrestricted use of the mother tongue in private and commercial life, until 1926 all use of commercial signs and notices in the languages of the national minorities in the commercial sector was banned.[59] At the same time, a law dealing with public employees introduced a compulsory examination in the Romanian language for all non-Romanian officials,[60] which resulted in the mass dismissal of public employees belonging to the national minorities.[61] These dismissed minority officials were generally replaced by Romanians.[62]

The discriminatory measures against public employees were followed by language examinations for teachers belonging to the national minorities. The draft legislation on this matter was an amendment to the December 22, 1925 Act on Private Education; it prescribed that even where national-minority teachers had already passed an examination in Romanian, they could be compelled to take further language examinations at any time and, in case of failure, lose their teacher certification. The results of these compulsory examinations were devastating throughout Transylvania.

> The young teachers were failed in the qualifying examination and the older generation of teachers, who had gained their diplomas before the war, were sifted out through the language examinations. And, at the

same time, if the number of teachers in a gymnasium was reduced to less than six, the school could be closed down.[63]

A law concerning the unification of public administration, enacted in 1925,[64] abolished every form of local self-government[65] on the basis of the principle of complete state centralization, thereby initiating a period of arbitrary centralized rule.

From the first half of the 1930s Romanian economic policy aimed at weakening and taking over the economic bases of the national minorities. Despite the general economic crisis, a large proportion of the German, Hungarian and Jewish national minorities in Transylvania consisted of an economically strong middle class, with well-established industrial, commercial, and cooperative networks. In handicraft and small-scale industry alone, German participation amounted to 25 percent of the national total in the 1930s,[66] while, in 1943, 15.5 percent of all Romanian industry consisted of German enterprises.[67] The cooperative movement proved to be the most effective method in combating the government's anti-minority economic policy. The Hungarian nationality in Transylvania already had a well-developed economic, commercial, and cooperative network at the time of annexation by Romania.[68] Thus, the level of economic development of the national minorities in Transylvania exceeded in all respects the level of economic life in the Old Kingdom which stagnated in a state of corruption and underdevelopment between the two world wars. It was this difference in level of development that Romanian economic policy sought, and is still seeking, to equalize.

A legislative project for the "protection of national labor" aimed at restricting the economic life of the Romanian national minorities during the interwar period. It prescribed that at least 75 percent of the staff and 60 percent of the management of economic, industrial, commercial, and other enterprises with Romanian capital, were to be Romanians, with the remaining places going to members of the national minorities.[69] The Industry Act of April 29, 1936,[70] abolished the national-minority chambers of commerce and turned over their property to state chambers of commerce. The remaining properties of minority institutions were increasingly expropriated, even if they were not chambers of commerce.

The fiscal policy pursued by the Romanian government also contributed to the economic stagnation of the national-minority areas. According to an official publication of the Romanian Ministry of

Finance, between 1924 and 1926 direct taxation in Transylvania exceeded that in the Regat by 205 million lei.[71] Similarly, other national-minority areas also paid higher taxes.[72]

From 1938 onwards the vital national-minority cooperative network was prohibited from functioning. As has already been noted, a law enacted in 1937 abolished the centuries-old economic foundation of the Saxon people, the so-called Saxon National University (*Nationsuniversität*) and the community of the Seven Judges (*Sieben-Richter-Waldungen*); only 100 of the 35,000 yokes[73] of land originally possessed by the Saxon foundation remained after the law was put into effect.[74]

After the dissolution of the political parties, the royal dictatorship of Carol II (1938-1940) tried to find a solution to the national-minority question by way of the so-called Minority Statute of August 4, 1938[75] without, however, consultations with the nationalities. In any case, the government intended the statute merely as a piece of propaganda for foreign—particularly German—consumption. The statute was not a law, but only a statement of principle lacking the force of either a law or an executive decree. For a long time it was not even published in the internal press. This statute was supposed to guarantee, among other things, the use of a national-minority language in parishes where that nationality represented a majority of the inhabitants. During this period, for example, the post office accepted packages and letters which were not addressed in Romanian, and telegrams sent in languages other than Romanian did not require an excess charge. A few elementary and secondary schools with instruction in the languages of the nationalities were also reopened. Besides these measures, a decree of the Council of Ministers,[76] issued on August 1, 1938, guaranteed the right to use place names in the languages of the national minorities. This had been a long-time demand by the nationalities in Romania, just as it had been a demand of the Romanians under the Austro-Hungarian Dual Monarchy.

The new Constitution, enacted on February 20, 1938, and published on February 27 of that year, reinforced the royal dictatorship and introduced a further restriction of political freedom. The royal proclamation delivered on the occasion of the publication of the Constitution emphasized that "the peoples of other ethnic groups that have lived in the territory of United Romania for centuries will receive treatment identical to that of the Romanians."[77] In the text of the Constitution, however, one cannot find any conception of national minorities or of their ethnic identity; rather, rights were guaranteed only for the majority people—even though the constitution formally guaranteed them for all "Romanian citizens"—and only when discussing duties was it stated that these applied to all Romanians "irrespective of ethnic origin or religion." In formulating the new constitution, neither the Resolutions of Alba Iulia nor the articles of the Minorities Treaty were included in the text.

The decentralization of public administration was regulated by the Public Administration Act of August 14, 1938, which divided the country into ten provinces, each with a royal governor at its head. The territorial-administrative division of the provinces everywhere ran contrary to historical frontiers, and the counties comprising them were organized in such a way as to ensure a Romanian majority everywhere. The most unjust measure was the joining of the Hungarian-inhabited Trei Scaune/Háromszék region and Brasov/Brassó County, which also had a large Hungarian and German population, to the province of Bucegi, which had Bucharest as its seat; in this way the two counties were entirely excluded from the geographical and public administrative network of the Transylvanian basin.

Political Developments in Romania, 1944–48

Immediately after the conclusion of the Second World War the national minorities of Central and Southeastern Europe found themselves involved in a series of insoluble conflicts. Moreover, their political position had deteriorated considerably in comparison with the period after the First World War. The fateful errors of the peace treaties concluding the First World War survived or were even revived in the peace treaties at the end of the Second World War, and the consequences of the misguided national minority policy of the interwar period became increasingly manifest. The main sources of conflict remained the same: territory and ethnicity. There was one difference from the period after the First World War: now neither the "mother countries" nor international institutions would protect the minorities. It became a general principle that nationality questions must be treated as internal affairs: a policy of silence about minority problems manifested itself, often interpreted as fitting punishment for the "historical guilt" of those minorities. Punishment gained official sanction. Its intensity and time-scale varied, according to the country in question, from nationality discrimination to a complete deprivation of rights, from deportation to genocide.

The People's Democratic Interlude

Following the coup d'état of August 23, 1944, King Michael of Romania entrusted General Constantin Sănătescu, a political moderate, with the task of forming a new government, in which, alongside the representatives of the historical parties (the National Peasant Party and the Liberals), the Communist Lucrețiu Pătrășcanu also took part. At this point, the formation of the government still took place on a democratic basis. The first measure of the new government—the decree of August 31, 1944—was the re-establishment of the 1923 Constitution.[78]

In the meantime, a start was made toward the preparation of the Armistice Agreement between the Allies and Romania, that was to determine the fate of Romania. Already on April 2, 1944, the Soviet Union had assured Romania through Molotov that it had no intention of changing the existing social order and political system of the country.[79] A communiqué issued on August 25 once again confirmed this promise.[80] It was in this spirit that an armistice agreement[81] was signed in Moscow on September 12, 1944, by the representatives of Romania, the Soviet Union, the USA, and Great Britain. The agreement stated, among other things, that Romania would withdraw from the war against the Allied Powers on August 24, 1944, and would fight alongside them against Hungary and Germany (Article 1). The political clauses of the armistice declared the Second Vienna Award void and confirmed the final and irrevocable annexation of Bessarabia and Northern Bucovina by the Soviet Union. The implementation of the Armistice Agreement was guaranteed by the Soviet Military High Command and the Allied Control Commission.

By declaring the Second Vienna Award null and void, the Armistice Agreement restored Romania's *de jure* possession of Transylvania, while leaving open the possibility of revising the frontiers in favor of Hungary: "Transylvania, or the larger part of it, shall be restored to Romania, which will be confirmed in the peace treaty." This meant that it was a matter for the peace treaty to decide whether the whole of Transylvania "as an entity or only in part is returned to Romania" (Clause 4).[82] It should be noted here that the return of Northern Transylvania to Romania was finalized by the Soviet Union—more than a year before the Paris Peace Conference—after the Groza government came to power. The conditions for the re-annexation were the formation of a popular front government and the elimination of the historical "bourgeois" political parties. The Soviet Union perceived these conditions as part of the preparation of the international proletarian revolution in Romania.

In the meantime, the left-wing was organizing, and on October 12, 1944, it founded the National Democratic Front (*Frontul Național-Democrat*), which replaced the National Democratic Bloc (*Blocul Național-Democrat*) that had been created while the August 23 change of direction was being prepared. The advance of the left-wing and the propaganda launched by the Soviet Union laid the groundwork for the reorganization of the Sănătescu government, which was carried out on November 4, through a coalition with the Național Democratic Front, which consisted largely of communists. Sănătescu continued to be prime minister, or rather Chairman of the Council of Ministers, but the post of Deputy Premier was occupied by Petru Groza, the leader of the left-wing Ploughmen's Front; the communists continued to be represented by L. Pătrășcanu and G. Gheorghiu-Dej, who occupied the post of Minister of Transport. The Liberals and the Peasant Party were still represented in this government.

The interlude of people's democracy, however, did not last long. On December 2, 1944, the second Sănătescu government was also forced to resign, and on December 6, General Nicolae Rădescu took over the coalition cabinet.

By the beginning of 1945, the Rădescu government, increasingly weakened by the regular disturbances organized by the left-wing and by conditions of chaos, found it more and more difficult to retain its position. The Soviet Union was waiting for an excuse to justify intervention, and it found it when Rădescu used armed force in an attempt to stop provocative demonstrations. Already on February 28, after the Yalta Conference, the Soviet Union, through its Foreign Minister Vishinsky, issued an ultimatum forcing the resignation of the Rădescu government and calling on King Michael to appoint a radical popular front government. Such a government was established on March 6, 1945 with Petru Groza (1945–1952) as Prime Minister.

1945 marked a new turning point in Romanian internal politics: it was the beginning of the period of people's democracy, which lasted till 1947, as well as of the transition to the dictatorship of the proletariat.

The key positions in the Groza government were occupied by communists: Teohari Georgescu was Minister of the Interior, Pătrăşcanu Minister of Justice, and Gheorghiu-Dej, the General Secretary of the Communist Party at that time, occupied the post of Minister of Labor and Economy. The police was reorganized, internal controls were strengthened, and preparations were begun for the nationalizations of June 11, 1948.

The political scene of the next year and a half was marked by a struggle for the liquidation of the so-called "historical" political parties. The National Peasant Party was the first to be eliminated: its leader, Iuliu Maniu, was arrested on a charge of treason and sentenced to life imprisonment. Barely a year later, in the first parliamentary elections, held on November 19, 1946, the "democratic forces" supported by Moscow emerged victorious; the so-called Bloc of Democratic Parties received 378 mandates out of a total of 414 (79.86 percent); by contrast the National Peasant Party received 33 mandates and the National Liberal Party a mere 3. The elections were characterized by fraudulent manipulation and political intimidation.[83]

As already noted, the Transylvanian issue played a not inconsiderable part in the appointment of the Groza government. As early as March 9, 1945, Stalin had informed the Groza government by telegram of the permanent establishment of Romanian administration in Northern Transylvania: "Taking into consideration the fact that the new Romanian government, which has just taken over the governing of the country, has accepted responsibility for securing the desired law and order in the territory of Transylvania, as well as for securing the rights of the nationalities and the undisturbed functioning of all the local institutions serving the supply of the front, the Soviet government has decided to fulfil the request of the Romanian government and permits the introduction of the public administration of the Romanian government in the territory of Transylvania, in line with the cease-fire agreement of September 12, 1944."[84]

In the meantime—while preparations for the peace treaty were still going on—the diplomatic struggle for Transylvania began on both the Romanian[85] and the Hungarian sides.[86] In April 1945, a Hungarian delegation led by Prime Minister Ferenc Nagy travelled to Moscow to request 22,000 square kilometers of Transylvanian territory; however, as an alternative it would have been satisfied with a minimum of 11,800 square kilometers.[87] Incidentally, the Hungarian demands, which related to the railroad line running along the Satu Mare-Oradea-Arad route, through a border district with an overwhelmingly Hungarian population, were not contrary to the provisions of the Soviet-Romanian Armistice Agreement, which did not deal with all of Transylvania.[88] Stalin appeared to accept the proposal of the Hungarian delegation, with the proviso that Hungary should submit them to the Paris Peace Conference and that Romania should accept them.[89] Romania, however, rejected any negotiations with Hungary[90] and the issue was not raised again by the Soviet side, even though the Western Powers did not reject the Hungarian request. Thus, for example, at the May 1946 foreign ministerial conference[91] J. F. Byrnes, American Deputy Secretary of State, recommended territorial modifications in favor of Hungary; Molotov rejected these by saying, "Stalin has already decided that the whole of Transylvania shall be returned to Romania."[92] The possibility of territorial adjustments in favor of Hungary was also not alien to the approach of the British political delegation participating in preparations for the peace conference. That delegation declared: "Having regard to the very large Hungarian minority (in Transylvania), some modification of the Trianon settlement may be desirable."[93]

It was in this atmosphere of political conflict of interest that the Paris Peace Conference was held between July 29 and October 15, 1946,[94] and the Soviet point of view finally prevailed. Molotov declared that "The Transylvanian question has been settled to the satisfaction of the Romanian people."[95] At that point the Soviet Union was more confident about the establishment of communism in Romania than in Hungary, where the Communist Party had received a mere 17 percent of the vote in the 1945 elections.

It should be noted that the Soviet Union had earlier considered an alternative solution to the Transylvanian question, when there had been a possibility of Hungary's changing its position during the war. In June 1941, the Soviet government had still offered its support to Hungary on the Transylvanian question if Hungary remained neutral in the German-Soviet war.[96]

The Elimination of Democracy

1946 and 1947 were years of political and class conflict in Romania. In the course of these struggles the Soviet Union and the Communist Party aimed at the liquidation of the former "ruling bourgeois class" and the leaders of the "historical" parties. The show trials of war criminals and the intimidation of political dissenters made open opposition impossible. However, until the conclusion of the Paris Peace Treaty between Romania and the Allies,[97] which Romania signed on February 10, 1947, such measures remained limited, largely due to the tactical considerations. Nevertheless, mass arrests began in May 1947, particularly among the ranks of the Peasant Party. On the July 15 the leaders of the Peasant Party, Iuliu Maniu and Ion Mihalache, were arrested. The arrests were not based simply on the criterion of association with the "old regime": they affected the Social Democrats and Liberals just as much. According to estimates, 60,000 people were executed in the course of the "purges" in 1946–47.[98] Developments escalated extremely rapidly as a result of the Soviet presence in Romania. Parliament was purged of democratic elements and turned into a monolithic institution; at the same time, the Groza government came to play an entirely subordinate role. As a consequence of this King Michael I was forced to abdicate in December 1947; on the 30th a Romanian People's Republic (*Republica Populară Română*) was proclaimed.[99] Soon thereafter, Parliament enacted a law[100] arbitrarily abolishing the 1923 democratic Constitution. With that act, the dictatorship of the proletariat had begun in Romania.

1944: Year of Decisive Change
for the National Minorities

The first phase of Romanian nationality policy following the Second World War developed even before the final conclusion of peace. At that time it was in the fundamental interest of the Romanian leadership, as a party to the peace negotiations, to prove to the victorious Great Powers and world public opinion that as a result of the new political course it would respect the rights of the national minorities living within its territory. Such a policy was also necessary in order to mollify the political leadership and public opinion in Hungary, so as to neutralize possible territorial demands based on the position of the Hungarian population in Transylvania. Winning over the large Hungarian population of Northern Transylvania, which had been returned to Romania, was also a matter of some importance. Providing reassuring prospects of complete freedom of development for the national minorities and of a situation diametrically opposed to the oppressive atmosphere of interwar Romania was the only means of avoiding strong resistance.

The end of the war, with Romania on the victorious side, and the measures taken by the Great Powers had a different effect on the fate of each of the national minorities in Romania. Thus, the various ethnic groups need to be discussed separately, at least when focusing on the immediate post-war period. One has to start with the fact that the two largest national minorities in Romania, the Hungarians and the Germans, belonged to the category of the Axis "satellite" peoples who had lost the war, and their position reflected this status, insofar as they were made the object of condemnation and collective punishment. Their fate was really determined not so much by their previous conduct, as by considerations of great power politics, which confronted them with a pronouncement of guilt as a *fait accompli*.

The indifference of the Great Powers toward the principle of the protection of national minorities was already observable at the Paris Peace Conference. What is more, the discussions at the Peace Conference took place in an anti-minority atmosphere. Without any hope of support from their mother countries and without any international protection, they were isolated and defenseless.

Nonetheless, in contrast to the situation in neighboring countries, the German minority in Romania was not radically eliminated; apart from a few isolated cases there were not even any anti-German excesses. Even at the time of the total collapse of the Axis cause, following the turning point of August 23, 1944, the bulk of the German population remained in their ancestral homes and did not see any reason to flee. As the situation became precarious, Hans Otto Roth, the political leader of the Germans in Romania, took the initiative and appealed to the Saxons of Transylvania and the Swabians of the Banat to remain calm.[101] His personality and influence in Romanian political circles unquestionably played a role in lessening any threat to the German population. However, subsequent events undid much of his work: he was ultimately unable to prevent discriminatory measures or a denial of rights to the German population.

A decree issued on October 8, 1944,[102] abolished the privileges granted to the German ethnic group in Romania (*Deutsche Volksgruppe in Rumänien*) in 1940. On January 8, 1945, in a surprise move, approximately 100,000 people from among the German population were selected for deportation to forced labor in the Soviet Union. Romania had agreed to this—without stipulating the nationality involved—in the Armistice Agreement, as part of its reparations payment to the Soviet Union. The deportation affected men between the ages of 17 and 45, and women between 18 and 35. Data on the precise number of people deported differ, but according to several different estimates, approximately 80,000–100,000 people were involved;[103] about 20 percent of them never returned.[104] Subsequently, the German population was subjected to further discriminatory measures. In August 1945 a considerable part of them lost their citizenship and economic assets, as will be discussed below. The electoral law of July 14, 1946 deprived them of their right to vote on the pretext of war collaboration and war crimes. In the short run, some gains were made in the cultural and economic sector, but they were only short-lived. A Decree of October 16, 1946, for example, restored the houses, land, small businesses, and workshops to the Germans who had been forcibly evacuated.[105]

As mentioned earlier, the fate of the Hungarian nationality in Romania after August 23, 1944 differed sharply from that of the Germans; in this case, a crucial role was played by the Transylvanian question. As already noted, the Soviet Union had rewarded the Romanian withdrawal from the war and its subsequent action against the German and Hungarian armies by returning Northern Transylvania—which had been re-annexed by Hungary in the Second Vienna Award—to Romania. As a consequence of this from September 12, 1944, until November 11, 1944, with the extension of Romanian administration to Northern Transylvania under Soviet supervision, the Hungarian population of the "liberated" areas lived in fear of its very existence. No sooner had Hungarian administration been withdrawn from Northern Transylvania, than Romanian nationalist circles began inciting anti-Hungarian feeling among the Romanian population. According to the notes of one contemporary writer, "the clauses in the Armistice Agreement prescribing the punishment of war criminals were interpreted as if they referred, not to Romanian war criminals, but solely and entirely to the Hungarians in Romania."[106] In the name of anti-fascism, all Hungarians, as the last allies of Hitler, could be collectively branded as fascists and therefore, as war criminals. A theoretical justification was thereby provided for the campaign of retribution beginning with the pogrom of the so-called "Maniu guard" in October 1944.[107] By quick and decisive intervention, the Soviet military administration succeeded in protecting the Hungarian population; at the same time, in the name of the Allied Control

Commission, it ordered the withdrawal of the recently established Romanian public administration from Northern Transylvania on November 11, 1944. The Soviets thereby achieved a dual purpose: they stopped conflict behind the front lines, which had interfered with the continuation of the war, and, at the same time, they gained the confidence of the terrorized Hungarian population, thus increasing the camp of Soviet sympathizers.

In this context it is worth noting that some of the Hungarians in Transylvania, though certainly not the majority, began to join left-wing organizations under the guidance of *MADOSZ* (Hungarian National Workers' Federation),[108] particularly in the towns, some out of conviction, others for more complex reasons. One motive for this movement was the growing realization that nationality survival could be secured only by organized resistance. It should be added that the interwar labor movement in Romania had been more a means of struggling for higher wages than a conscious left-wing political movement, and neither the Hungarian National Workers' Federation (*MADOSZ*) nor the Romanian Communist Party had sufficient influence to mobilize the broad masses during that period.

For a clearer understanding of the historical background it is important to note that—contrary to the view of contemporary Romanian historiography—there were hardly any Romanian communists in Transylvania at that time. The membership of the Romanian Communist Party at the end of 1944 amounted to approximately 1,000, the overwhelming majority of them Jews and Hungarians. This in turn was reflected in the composition of the top party leadership, since the leading personages in the RCP were the returned "Muscovites," Ana Pauker and László Luca, and the Romanian triumvirate, also called the "Troika," which consisted of Emil Bodnăraş, Constantin Pârvulescu, and Josif Ranghet. Only two Romanians from the "home front" succeded in entering the leading cadre, the intellectual Lucreţiu Pătrăşcanu and the worker Gheorghe Gheorghiu-Dej. Nonetheless, the number of party members belonging to the discontented national minorities steadily increased; here, as everywhere, the internationalist character of the communist parties undoubtedly played an essential role, appealing to the dissatisfaction felt by oppressed national minorities.

The efforts of the Hungarian minority in Romania to maintain its own cultural institutions and its economic and political rights during the immediate post-war period began with a certain degree of Soviet support. Stalin—using the national minorities as a means for undermining anti-communism in Romania—promised far-reaching cultural concessions and stipulated that the annexation of Northern Transylvania by Romania was conditional on "the new Romanian government securing full, equal rights for the Hungarians in Transylvania."[109]

During this transitional period the Hungarians and Romanians of Transylvania found a meeting ground for settling their differences and to establish a *modus vivendi* under the protection of a neutral power, the Soviet Union. Thus, for four months, there were no official anti-minority pronouncements, and the dominant tendency in the treatment of the nationalities continued to be one of tolerance. During this brief period, it became clear for the first time since the end of the war that the national minorities desired democracy and justifiably believed that the nationalist excesses of the past could be brought to an end: it appeared that national primacy was to be replaced by the class struggle.

It was during this period that the Hungarian People's Alliance in Romania (*Romániai Magyar Népi Szövetség*) was formed to replace the Hungarian National Workers' Federation (*MADOSZ*), which had ceased to exist in October 1944. The Hungarian press, which came back into existence at this time, fought for the survival of this new organization, whose aim was the protection of the political, economic, and cultural interests of the Hungarian national minority in Romania. The Romanian and Hungarian democratic parties joined in a coalition based on their common interests; they established village, town, and county organizations; a Central Executive Committee and a Central Advisory Board, including both Hungarians and Romanians, were formed in order to carry out the functions of the absent central authority. During this four-month period, which lasted from November 14, 1944, until March 19, 1945, a semi-autonomous, democratic self-government arose which resembled in many ways the one-time autonomous Transylvania.

Illustrative of the endeavor to promote Hungarian-Romanian coexistence on a democratic basis was the text of a declaration issued by the Hungarian People's Alliance during this period: "Just as sincerely as we profess the need for cooperation with the progressive Romanian democracy, we openly and frankly desire close economic, educational, and political cooperation with Hungary, the abolition of the need for passports, and the elimination of customs barriers."[110] The Romanian Communist Party reacted with a similar tone: ". . . fighting against nationality oppression and for the development of the science, culture, and art of the Romanian and coexisting peoples, on the basis of the principle that these should be national in form and consistently democratic in content, the United Workers' Party guarantees by the letter and spirit of its organizational rules the realization of the equal rights that are the due of the coexisting nationalities."[111]

Matters, however, were ultimately to turn out quite differently, as the situation in Romania and Transylvania worsened. The People's Front government of Petru Groza (1945–1947) promised relatively liberal autonomous rights to the nationalities; however, it fulfilled these promises to only a minimal extent. Certain members of the government, such as, Lucretiu Pătrăşcanu, the Minister of Justice, and Lotar Rădeceanu, the Minister of Labor, introduced anti-minority measures in spite of Groza's intentions. The arrests, deportations, executions, and attacks against the economic assets of the Transylvanian minorities continued.

It must be admitted, nonetheless, that under the Groza regime certain important national-minority cultural institutions were established, a start was made in organizing the literary life of the minorities, and minority representatives were elected to the nationality Secretariat of State and the Romanian Council of State and Council of Ministers.

Concessions were made particularly to the Hungarian national minority, largely because of the Transylvanian question, which had not yet been settled.[112] It was characteristic of the new political climate that on April 6, 1945, Hungarian broadcasts were transmitted by Radio Bucharest for the first time.[113] Similarly, a 1945 decree of the Lord Lieutenant of Cluj County and the city of Cluj called for the settling of various nationality political differences between the Hungarian and Romanian inhabitants, particularly the issue of the use of the mother tongue, on the basis of reciprocity.[114] At the congress of the Hungarian People's Alliance, on May 6, 1945, Prime Minister Groza proclaimed Hungarian-Romanian fraternal solidarity, in a speech delivered in Hungarian; in a speech in Cluj on March 12th, delivered in the presence of Vishinsky, the Soviet Foreign Minister, Groza promised equal civil rights for the national minorities. Some time later, he made the following statement to a journalist from Hungary: "The sense of identity that the Hungarians in Romania have with the term 'minority' must be eradicated. In the future, Hungarian-language schools can operate freely in the territory of Romania and nothing must hinder the free use of the mother tongue in the spheres of culture, public administration, and economic life."[115]

The greatest improvement that the Hungarians in Romania achieved under the Groza government was the opening of the Hungarian Bolyai University in Cluj, on the basis of a decree of June 1, 1945. At that time, Bolyai University had thirteen faculties with Hungarian teachers. At about the same time, the Csángó Hungarians of Moldavia were permitted to have schools with instruction in the mother tongue. During this period the use of both languages in shop signs and other public notices, signs, place names, and street names was to some extent a reality. The use of national-minority languages was permitted at the work place, official meetings, party conferences, and in the public sector, and the flags of the nationalities could be flown side by side with the Romanian flag. There were visiting professors from Hungary at the University of Cluj, and Hungarian newspapers could be imported in almost unlimited quantities. According to a contemporary writer, "the Groza government, which had proclaimed a democratic policy . . . wanted to create a Transylvania which would be a bridge rather than a barrier between Hungary and Romania."[116]

The third major national-minority group in Romania, the Jews, who were still a political factor at that time, found itself in a different position than the German and Hungarian nationalities at the end of the war. As already mentioned, the Jewish population of Romania had been reduced by a half as a result of the events of the war: the majority of those who had disappeared were victims of racial prejudice that first broke out in the atrocities perpetrated by the Iron Guard and subsequently escalated into mass extermination during the war, while others were lost as a result of military service and deportation.

Immediately after the Romanian coup d'état of August 23, 1944, the Jewish population was accorded a form of rehabilitation and a certain degree of toleration. This was all the more so because Romanian internal politics were preoccupied with the question of hostilities against the German and Hungarian armies. It would have been unsuitable to initiate discriminatory measures against the Jews, the victims of fascism, during or immediately after the "anti-fascist" military campaign. On the contrary, with the consolidation of the earlier left-wing movements, some of the Jews living in Romania gained a certain political role. This was reflected in the fact that a portion of the membership and leadership of the Romanian Communist Party at the end of 1944 consisted of Jewish intellectuals. The extent to which this picture was subsequently altered as a result of changes in the political constellation will be discussed later.

The first political organization of the Jewish national minority in Romania after the war, the Democratic Committee of Jews, founded in June 1945, attempted to group the Jewish population of the country into a united front. The committee consisted largely of communists and social democrats. They opposed the more traditionally oriented Federation of Romanian Jews, as well as the Jewish Party, which was soon abolished with the rise of the Romanian left. The first wave of Jewish emigration from Romania signalled a fundamental change in the political scene. In June 1947, 150,000 Romanian Jews chose to emigrate to Palestine (later Israel); by comparison, only 70,000 had emigrated before the end of 1944.[117]

With the consolidation of Stalinism, after 1949, within the framework of a developing system of nationality oppression, the Jewish national minority was also subjected to a succession of serious discriminatory measures. This was a preliminary stage of the period which began with the Rajk trial[118] in Hungary and was characterized by Stalin's anti-Semitism and a "purge" of non-Romanian elements from the Romanian Communist Party. With the emergence of this new political constellation at the beginning of 1949, Zionist leaders were arrested and all Jewish institutions in Romania were nationalized.[119]

*The Legal Status of the Minorities From the War
Until the Foundation of the Totalitarian State*

Following the Romanian coup d'état of August 23, 1944, the national minorities living in Romania found themselves in an entirely new situation, which was to decisively determine their ultimate fate. Their existence has been closely linked ever since with the social, political, and economic life of the majority Romanian people. There were no international forums to protect their rights, nor was the issue mentioned at all in the peace treaties that concluded the Second World War. This was in sharp contrast to the well-known nationality principle that played an important part in the peace treaties and related international agreements after World War I. These treaties contained two basic principles for the protection of minorities: nondiscrimination against individuals and a guarantee of collective rights. Minorities were considered collectively and were under the protection of the signatory powers; the League of Nations had the right to apply sanctions, which proved the existence of a certain degree of jurisdiction (*e.g.,* the right of petition).

The peace treaties concluded after the Second World War between the Allied Powers and the satellite states—Italy, Finland, Romania, Bulgaria, and Hungary—called for the observance of universal human rights and basic freedoms, but no mention was made of international protection for ethnic or religious minorities. Treaty stipulations apply only to individual rights (nondiscrimination against persons; see for instance, Part II of the peace treaties). Although there is implied, albeit minimal, protection for minorities,[120] collective rights, however, exist only in separate agreements (*e.g.,* Article 7 of the Austrian State Treaty of 1955). The failure to incorporate guarantees of minority rights in the peace treaties concluding World War II meant that the minority question had become an internal matter, that is, it had changed from international to national right.[121]

In the peace treaty concluded between Romania and the Allies on February 10, 1947, there are provisions, although inadequate, giving minorities a certain amount of protection against discrimination. The Political Clause (Article 3 of Part II), for example, guaranteed "equal rights for the inhabitants of Romania, regardless of race, language, religion, or nationality," as well as "the full enjoyment of human rights and fundamental freedoms," that is, "the free expression of opinions in the press or other channels of information or at public meetings, freedom of religion and assembly."

A further development toward international standards of protection for minorities can be seen in the work of the United Nations. This is especially clear in the Economic and Social Council (ECOSOC), dealing with the basic human rights of both individuals and groups. Both the UN Charter and the Universal Declaration of Human Rights (proclaimed on December 10, 1948)[122] raised protection of minorities to an international principle. In addition, after World War II there were a number of international treaties for the protection of minorities; they included the UN Convention for Prevention and Punishment of Genocide (Dec. 9, 1948); the European Convention for Protection of Human Rights and Basic Freedoms (Rome, Nov. 4, 1950); the UN Convention Against Discrimination in Education (Dec. 14, 1960); and the UN World Pact on Civil and Political Rights, Article 27 (Dec. 16, 1966). Furthermore, since 1949 the UN Commission on Human Rights has had under its jurisdiction the Subcommission on Prevention of

Discrimination and Protection of Minorities, which is primarily concerned with racial discrimination.[123]

The UN's efforts to clarify the problem of protecting minority and group rights have taken concrete forms since 1972, especially after the publication of the so-called Capotorti Reports which will be discussed later.

In conclusion it must be said that in the UN Charter there are no international standards for protection of ethnic, linguistic and religious minorities, although the international basis of the UN Charter has priority over the principle of regional jurisdiction. The limited interest in this question is found primarily in ideological quarrels (the East–West conflict), as well as in contrary territorial aspirations (Europe, Africa, etc.). One of the fundamental principles of the rights of ethnic groups, the right of an individual to belong to an ethnic group without suffering discrimination, is still lacking.

The first experiment aimed at a solution of the nationality question in Romania after the war took place during the transitional period of the people's democracy, under the Sănătescu government, with the establishment of a Ministry of Nationality Affairs.[124] This was followed by the Nationality Statute of February 6, 1945,[125] which attempted to provide a legal framework for the rights and obligations of the members of the national minorities in Romania, consolidating all those decrees in force which guaranteed the freedoms and rights of the nationalities. The statute prescribed the free use of the mother-tongue in education, in public life, and in judicial proceedings in those parishes where the national-minority population was more than 30 percent. The Nationality Statute was reconfirmed by the Groza government.[126] A further decree banned the official use of the term "minority," replacing it with the concept of "coinhabiting nationalities,"[127] in accordance with Marxist-Leninist nationality policy. However, this concept still had connotations of second-class status as compared with that of the majority nation.

The purpose of this nationality policy, which can be said to have been a liberal one, was, on the one hand, to gain sympathizers from the ranks of the national minorities for the strengthening of communism and, on the other hand, to prove to the victorious Great Powers and world public opinion that, with the onset of the democratic period, the nationality question in Romania had been solved, before the conclusion of the peace treaties and the final settlement of the Transylvanian question. The clauses protecting minorities contained in the Nationality Statute were destined, in fact, to remain valid only until the conclusion of the peace treaties.

Just how much the Nationality Statute was the result of political and tactical considerations was revealed in other aspects of nationality policy not long after it had been enacted. The agrarian reform law of March 23, 1945,[128] for example, had serious consequences for the national minorities in Romania, particularly the Germans and Hungarians. It is worth noting that the land reform affected primarily the owners of small and very small holdings, i.e., the broadest section of the population, and in large part it was shaped by considerations of war guilt. For example, according to Point c of Section II of the law, those landowners who had fled to countries at war with Romania, or had fled abroad after August 23, 1944, lost their property rights. Moreover, according to Point d, the landed and other property of "absent" individuals was also to be confiscated. It is obvious that this law affected primarily the German and Hungarian population of Transylvania; Article 3 further stipulated that the landholdings and any other agricultural property of all those Romanian citizens of German origin or of Romanian citizens or institutions who had collaborated with Hitler's Germany were to be expropriated without compensation; finally Point *a* of Article 3 stipulated that this expropriation did not apply to those Romanians who had found themselves in Hungary or in Germany as a result of wartime labor service. The law regarded as "absent" primarily those members of the German or Hungarian minorities who had fled from the Antonescu terror in Southern Transylvania to Northern Transylvania or to the West, and those who had fought in the German and Hungarian armies and had left for the West during the retreat. Those Hungarians and Germans, however, who had been deported from the battle areas, who had left their homes because of the bombing, who had been called up for military service in the Romanian army, who were disabled as a result of the war or were under medical treatment, or who even simply happened to be abroad on private business with a passport or who, due to advanced age or ill health, were unable to cultivate their land were placed in the category of "refugee" or "absentee." The landholdings of all these individuals were expropriated.

The land reform was carried out not in accordance with social need but on the basis of nationalistic considerations: 80 percent of the redistributed land of Hungarian landowners and 98 percent of German property became Romanian property.[129] It is characteristic that 94.6

percent of the individuals affected by the expropriations and 49 percent of the land expropriated, including the expropriations in the Banat—were in Transylvania.[130]

The expropriations, as the law indicated, applied not only to landholdings but—according to Article 3—included other assets, agricultural implements, buildings, and livestock, and were also used against the cooperative, handicraft, industrial, commercial, and banking networks.[131]

In carrying out the agrarian reform, the local organs of the Committee for Land Distribution acted in a totally arbitrary manner, making decisions on their own authority and not in accordance with the law. As their decisions were not put into writing, it was impossible to determine which article of the law they had been based on.

Another discriminatory measure of the Groza government aimed at undermining the economic position of the national minorities was the so-called C.A.S.B.I. decree,[132] which established a Management and Controlling Chamber for Enemy Possessions (*Cassa pentru Administrarea și Supravegherea Bunurilor Inamice*). This body was established on the basis of Paragraph 8 of the Soviet-Romanian Armistice Agreement and was responsible for the sequestering of the property of "presumedly" hostile persons. According to the decree, all those who had fled to Germany, Hungary, or to territories occupied by these two countries in the period between August 23 and September 12, 1944, or immediately afterwards—thus at a time of complete anarchy and political uncertainty—counted as "presumedly" hostile persons. All real estate, businesses, goods, movable property, securities, and valuable objects were sequestered.

In light of the historical and political circumstances, it can be assumed that during this period only members of the German and Hungarian national minorities were refugees and, consequently, branded as "presumedly" hostile persons.

Besides economic sanctions, the national minorities in Romania were also at a serious disadvantage in the course of clarification of citizenship under the Groza government. As a result of the citizenship law of April 4, 1945,[133] and an executive directive issued on August 13, 1945,[134] relating to the population of Northern Transylvania, the citizenship of approximately 300,000–400,000 Hungarian and German refugees from Northern Transylvania was placed in doubt, as was that of those inhabitants who had voluntary served in an army officially at war with Romania or in any alien military formation and people who had left their places of habitation only temporarily because of the nearness of the front; their status now became dependent on the arbitrariness of those who interpreted the law.

The Totalitarian State: The Romanian People's Republic

After the fall of the monarchy on December 30, 1947, and the proclamation of the Romanian People's Republic (*Republica Populară Română*) there began an entirely new period of political developments in Romania. At the same time all democratic parties were eliminated, and with them all political opposition was removed. At the party conference held on February 21-23, 1948, a merger of the Communist Party and the left wing of the Social Democratic Party resulted in the formation of the Romanian Workers' Party (*Partidul Muncitoresc Român*),[135] under the leadership of General Secretary Gheorghe Gheorghiu-Dej. The unified party of the ruling working class was in fact entirely subordinate to Moscow. According to the official formulation, it had been formed as a result of "historical need." It gained a parliamentary majority through the support of otherwise insignificant left-wing organizations which it absorbed through the unification, and which had hitherto been able to function thanks to the presence of the Soviet army and Soviet advisors. On February 27, as part of the reorganization of the Workers' Party, a People's Democratic Front (*Frontul Democrației Populare*) was formed, consisting of the former Communist Party, Ploughmen's Front, National People's Party, and Hungarian People's Alliance, together with all of their party-controlled mass organizations.

The first Constitution of the Romanian People's Republic,[136] published in draft form in the Romanian press on March 6, 1948, was enacted on April 13, 1948. It had been drawn up by the People's Democratic Front on the basis of the Soviet Constitution of 1936, although it diverged in many respects from its model. Like the constitutions of the other socialist countries, it was based on the principle that state power is embodied in the people, whose will is expressed through local people's councils (soviets), and through its representatives in the Grand National Assembly. The constitution made no mention of the Soviet Union, and the creation of the People's Democracy was described in Article 2 as a Romanian achievement.

The establishment of the People's Republic and the enactment of the new constitution fundamentally altered the political, social, and economic structure of Romania; the dictatorship of the proletariat was thereby given legal sanction, and by 1948 the foundations had been laid for the building of socialism in Romania.

As the government and the system in general consolidated their position, a rapid series of measures based on the Soviet model were taken, aiming at the transformation of Romania's society, economy, and educational system. On the basis of the new constitution, a decree of June 11, 1948, nationalized the larger industrial, mining, metallurgical, insurance, transport, and banking enterprises.[137] By March 1952 the major phase of nationalization was completed, with 96.5 percent of all industrial enterprises, 85 percent of the transport sector, 76 percent of the commercial sector, and 16 percent of the land in the hands of the state.[138] The nationalization, which resulted in the destruction of the middle class, was carried out using the same Soviet schema as in other Eastern European countries. The collectivization of agriculture was in fact first begun at the time of the 1945 agrarian reform, but the effective organization of large-scale collective farms began only in 1949, owing to the stubborn resistance of the peasant population.

The ideological re-education of youth was begun with the educational reform of August 3, 1948.[139] The educational system was restructured once again according to a Soviet model—on the basis of Marxist-Leninist principles. At a congress on March 19-21, 1949, hitherto separate youth organizations were merged to create a Union of Working Youth (*UTM—Uniunea Tineretului Muncitoresc*) modeled on the Soviet Komsomol, charged with the task of indoctrination in the schools. This mass communist organization, to which (until 1966) the subsequently-formed Pioneer organization also belonged, became an organic part of the party system.[140]

With the launching of the educational campaign aimed at an ideological transformation, the so-called "Roller period" (1947–1954)[141] also began, a period characterized by the rewriting of Romanian history in the spirit of proletarian internationalism and Romanian-Soviet friendship.

As part of the general process of Sovietization, the Grand National Assembly enacted a new territorial-administrative law on September 6, 1950,[142] dividing the country, in accordance with the Soviet model, into regions (*Regiune*), districts (*Raion*), communes and towns. This arrangement of public administration was aimed, on the one hand, at the further development of the system of people's councils (local administration),[143] which had been established in January 1949, and the intensification of government control[144] and, on the other hand, at the organization of a territorial framework for carrying out the industrialization plan.

The second Constitution of the Romanian People's Republic, enacted on September 24, 1952,[145] was even more closely modelled on that of the Soviet Union. In fact, it was and is the most "Sovietized" of the constitutions of the Eastern European people's democracies, even incorporating various articles from the 1936 Stalin Constitution. The new constitution represented a certain modification of the 1948 Constitution, introducing among other things the division of the Romanian People's Republic into new territorial–administrative units.[146]

Although the new constitution guaranteed the rights of all the inhabitants of the country, it did so in a form which subordinated them entirely to the goal of building socialism. This meant, in practice, that the rights of the citizens vis-à-vis the state were placed in doubt. The absolute power of the state (the dictatorship of the proletariat) was proclaimed in Article 1, while Article 86 declared the Romanian Workers' Party to be "the leading organ of the working people and the state," thereby investing it with sovereign power.

Part of the Romanian population had offered considerable resistance to the dictatorial regime of 1947, but as the government and the system consolidated their position, terror aimed at overcoming that resistance increased. By 1948, the enemy outside the party had been dealt with. Thereafter, until 1952, as a result of internal power struggles, the party, and particularly its lower and middle strata underwent a series of purges. These purges provided an opportunity for a new figure, Gheorghe Gheorghiu-Dej, to consolidate his own power, by placing his followers in key positions and thereby gradually gaining total control of the whole state apparatus.

A major political change came in Romania—as elsewhere in Eastern Europe—with the consolidation of Stalinism in 1949, following the Rajk trial in Hungary. First Party Secretary Gheorghiu-Dej took advantage of the opportunity to strengthen his own position by executing his only serious rival, the intellectual Pătrăşcanu. The Rajk trial also provided an opportunity for a showdown between the largely alien "Muscovites," who were not of proletarian origin, and the proletarian "home-based" communists of Romanian origin.[147]

However, the really fundamental change came in 1952. In the spring of 1952, Gheorghiu-Dej finally seized power (which he was to maintain until 1964). Taking advantage of Stalin's anti-Semitic and nationalist course, he expelled the Muscovites Ana Pauker and László Luca from the leadership as "foreigners" and agents of Moscow on the grounds of political "deviation," at a plenary session of the Central Committee on May 26–27. The development of a new policy with Gheorghiu-Dej, a policy whose fundamental principles are still in force, became the task of the "national cadres," even though not all rivals had yet been liquidated. As already mentioned "purges" began, first among the members of the government, and then in the various ministries, which henceforth took on a "national" character. Prime Minister Groza, who was by then merely a figurehead, was elected—purely for the sake of appearances—President of the Grand National Assembly, while on the same day Gheorghiu-Dej replaced him as Chairman of the Council of Ministers. The communist internationalist orientation represented by Ana Pauker, László Luca, Teohari Georgescu, Miron Constantinescu and Iosif Chişinevski was thereby replaced by a Romanian nationalist one. The relatively more tolerant and democratic line that had characterized post-war Romanian politics heretofore was now replaced by terror dressed in nationalistic colors. The wave of arrests which followed struck particularly against members of the old leadership, Social Democrats, intellectuals, non-Romanian elements, and persons of Jewish origin.[148] Every new measure was accompanied by a new wave of arrests. Some of those arrested were condemned to death; others were deported to long-term forced labor on the Danube-Black Sea canal or in the camps of the Danube delta.[149]

The Nationality Policy of the Romanian People's Republic

The fundamental rights of the national minorities, as formulated in the April 13, 1948 Constitution of the People's Republic, followed the prescriptions of the still-valid Nationality Statute of February 6, 1945 in "guaranteeing the free use of the mother-tongue and the organization of education in the language of the coinhabiting nationalities" (Article 24). The Constitution of September 24, 1952, referred in several places to the equal rights possessed by the national minorities.[150] The preamble of the Constitution guaranteed the "legal equality of the national minorities" with the Romanian people and gave territorial-administrative autonomy to the Székler region, a compact Hungarian area. Article 82 stated that "in the Romanian People's Republic the national minorities are guaranteed the free use of their own language and the right to have books, newspapers, journals, theaters, and education in their own languages." Finally, Article 81 contained sanctions for the protection of national-minority rights.

There is no doubt that the young Romanian People's Republic initially endeavored to win the support of the national minorities by its ideological statements. Thus, for example, a resolution introduced at the second session of the Central Committee of the Romanian Workers' Party, held on June 10–11, 1948, stated that the party "seeks to solve the problem of the German population of Transylvania and the Banat in a democratic manner."[151] Similarly, the December session of the Workers' Party approached the nationality question in the spirit of Stalin's formulation: "equal rights for the nationalities liberated from the class yoke."[152] The persecution of the national minorities was condemned.

Shortly thereafter, an official celebration of German-Romanian friendship was organized.[153] The so-called "German Anti-Fascist Committee in Romania," which had been formed in 1945, was reorganized in February 1949 as the "Anti-Fascist Committee of German Workers in Romania,"[154] with the task of organizing the German working masses in support of the regime. Official bilingualism was introduced, and minority-language schools were established in areas with large minority populations.

This phase of Romanian nationality policy represented an experiment at finding a Marxist-Leninist solution to the nationality problem, giving priority to the class struggle rather than to nationalistic considerations. This program was in many respects successful. On the other hand, however, behind the concessions made to the national minorities lay the goal of consolidating the regime, in other words, of strengthening the dictatorship of the proletariat, as a result of which particular national features would lose their meaning. According to the official formulation concerning national culture under socialism, "the form remains national, while the content is socialist."

As soon as the position of the government and the system had been consolidated, Romanian internal politics began to focus on the national minorities. A type of anti-nationality system began to develop, implemented by a consistent, but formally "secret," policy. Romanians were given an increasing role in the middle and upper leadership organs in areas inhabited by the national minorities.[155] The rights which had been won by the minorities in the preceding period were soon eliminated by an awakening spirit of Romanian nationalism. As early as September 1949, the Western signatories of the peace treaties protested to the UN about violations of human rights in Romania.[156]

The first arrests, it is true, struck primarily against the ranks of the Romanian middle class. These arrests, however, based on the criterion of "class enemy", soon affected the national minorities as well. Discrimination against the national minorities was not yet open, at least not officially. This was all part of the program of general political "purges."

The first direct attack on the national minorities was a result of the Rajk trials in Hungary. A campaign was undertaken against the Hungarian People's Alliance, an organization which had broad mass support and had given strong backing to Prime Minister Groza. Its best known leaders, men who had at first sincerely believed in democracy and in the possibility of cooperation with the Groza government, were almost all arrested. Having opposed the old bourgeois regime, they had believed that their left-wing radicalism would enable them to protect Hungarian interests, but when they refused to make any further concessions at the expense of the Hungarian minority, they were imprisoned.

On the basis of a trumped-up charge of espionage, the backbone of a national-minority social and political organization was broken. This provided a good opportunity for changing the national composition of the party, as well as for weakening or eliminating entirely the cultural institutions of the national minorities. Despite protests, age-old cultural and economic institutions of the national minorities were abolished. The Hungarian Bolyai University of Cluj, for example, was reduced by the "purges" to the level of a secondary school. At the same time, Romania was increasingly isolated from other countries; journeys and contacts abroad were made more difficult, a development that affected the Hungarians of Transylvania in particular, since of all the minorities, the Hungarians had maintained the strongest links with their mother country. A campaign was also launched against the Roman Catholic Church because of its foreign—in official terminology, "espionage"—links.

When the Székler region,[157] a compact Hungarian-inhabited area in southeast Transylvania, gained nominal autonomous rights as the

Magyar Autonomous Region (*Regiunea Autonomă Maghiară*) in 1952, it was possible to predict that the Hungarian People's Alliance would be abolished, and indeed this did occur in 1953. Its abolition was justified by the argument that the rights of the Hungarian national minority would be protected in the future by the policy of the party, and that there was no need, therefore, for a separate organization. At the time no one attributed particular significance to this measure.

It should be remembered that the establishment of the Magyar Autonomous Region, which was included under Section II, Articles 19 and 20, of the 1952 Constitution of the Romanian People's Republic, and was based on the Soviet model of autonomous territorial organization and Marxist-Leninist teaching on national minorities, was a measure prompted by Soviet pressure. Its creation was the result of two tactical considerations: the external propaganda role that the Region could serve and the Region's potential within Romania as a means of enabling the government to achieve its goals within the framework of a Romanian nationalist minority policy. The Region was officially presented as the basic means for maintaining the existence of the Hungarian minority, and it was therefore possible to use it to divert attention away from endeavors aimed at the elimination of the Hungarian national character outside the Autonomous Region. Everywhere else, repression became more open. That was why the area comprising the Autonomous Region was made as small as possible; in any case, it was as far as possible from the Hungarian border, was surrounded by counties with a majority of Romanian inhabitants, and contained barely a third of the Hungarians in Transylvania; the Hungarians outside the Region, who represented two-thirds of Transylvania's Hungarian population, were left to be discriminated against as second-class citizens. As a result of the new territorial-administrative reorganization, the proportion of Hungarians outside the Autonomous Region nowhere exceeded 6.5 to 28.4 percent, and the proportion of Germans, 16.5 percent.

According to Article 19 of the 1952 Constitution, the Magyar Autonomous Region "contains the compact areas inhabited by the Széklers and possesses an independent administrative organ elected by the Magyar Autonomous Region." The Constitution went on to provide in Articles 20 and 21, that "the laws of the Romanian People's Republic, as well as the decisions and instructions of central state organs, are also to be applied in the area of the Magyar Autonomous Region." Moreover, according to Article 57 of the Constitution, "The organ of state power in the Magyar Autonomous Region is the State Council of the Autonomous Region, whose members draw up its governing statute which is then to be approved by the Grand National Assembly of the Romanian People's Republic."[158] It is symptomatic, that the special legal regulations contained in the fundamental statute of the Autonomous Region and prescribed in Article 21 of the Constitution were never implemented; and the legal status and administration of the region did not differ in any way from any other region in the country. Essentially, the only difference was that Hungarian could be used in dealing with the local courts and administration, and petitions could be written in Hungarian. On the other hand, the Romanian officials and judicial authorities in the Autonomous Region did not speak Hungarian. Furthermore, bilingual signs and notices were used only at the beginning.

As the foregoing passage indicates, the Magyar Autonomous Region did not possess self-government of any sort. Its fundamental statute lacked any real legal or political significance and remained a purely administrative notion to the very end. And even these administrative aspects were seriously handicapped by the public administration law of December 24, 1960, which modified the Constitution. This law changed the name of the region to the Maros-Magyar Autonomous Region (*Regiunea Mureş-Autonomă Maghiară*) and, by adding new territories and detaching others, reduced the percentage of Hungarians in the region from 77.3 percent to 62.2 percent, while almost doubling the Romanian population (which rose from 20.1 percent to 35 percent).[159] With the growth in the proportion of Romanian inhabitants, the earlier Hungarian character of the Autonomous Region was changed: it became possible to question the justification for its existence, and steps toward its gradual elimination were undertaken. The term "Magyar Autonomous" remained, merely as an external form without legal substance, but in practice the term "Mureş Region" was generally used. Article 19 of the Constitution, which had designated the Autonomous Region as those "compact areas inhabited by the Széklers," was removed, clearly indicating the trend toward elimination.

Finally, on February 15-16, 1968, the Grand National Assembly, in the course of the territorial-administrative reorganization of the country, reintroduced the old county system (*judeţ*), abolishing the 16 previously existing regions, including the Magyar Autonomous Region.[160] The purpose of the territorial-administrative reorganization was the creation of a unified Romanian state; this also involved the creation of 16 Transylvanian counties in place of the earlier 23, distributed in such a way as to ensure a Romanian majority everywhere, with the exception of the two newly organized Székler counties.

At the beginning of the 1950s, the Tito crisis, like the Rajk affair earlier,[161] provided a good pretext for retaliatory measures, this time against the Swabians of the Banat, who in the winter of 1950–51 had manifested their discontent over the constantly increasing collectivization of agriculture. In the course of forced deportations carried out in June, approximately 30–40,000 Swabians were removed from the Banat, near the Romanian-Yugoslav border, to the environs of the Bărăgan Steppes,[162] and a life of forced labor under inhuman conditions. The deportees also included Serbians, Romanians, and Hungarians.[163] Some were able to return in 1955, but in the meantime new settlers had occupied their houses and taken over their possessions.

Soon after the forced deportation of the Swabians of the Banat, at the beginning of 1952, the forced evacuation of several Transylvanian towns and villages also began.[164] The bulk of the persons forced to move belonged either to the middle strata or to the "rich" peasantry (Kulaks): that is, members of those groups branded as "war criminals," "exploiters," or "politically unreliable." There were many members of the national minorities among the deportees; no precise data are available about the number, but, according to contemporary documents, in certain Transylvanian urban areas only those belonging to the national minorities were expelled,[165] and the state confiscated the houses and property of these people.[166]

After the death of Stalin in March 1953, Romania regarded its nationality policy as an "internal affair." This new tendency manifested itself in a January 1953 statement by Party Secretary Gheorghiu-Dej, in which he announced that the nationality question had been solved.[167] By implication, the position of the national minorities could henceforth not be discussed fully or truthfully, nor could any minority statement or demands be formulated. From this time onward, the expression of any minority needs, claims or grievances was viewed as an expression of nationalism and dealt with accordingly. Nationality policy became hypocritical. Alongside public statements and official measures, secret instructions began to play an increasingly important role.

About that time, all political organizations except the RCP were abolished, thus depriving the national minorities of any organized means of protecting themselves. As a result of this process, the rights of the national minorities became purely formal, reduced from collective to individual rights, a change which amounted in reality to a deprivation of nationality rights. With that, all nationality self-defense became illegal. National-minority cultural and educational institutions were branded as fomenters of "separatism" and "nationalism," and their very existence was thereby brought into question. These same slogans were later to be the guidelines and means for denationalization.

During this period, efforts at Romanianization assumed considerable proportions and concrete forms for the first time, particularly in the Transylvanian towns and cities, which possessed a rich nationality culture. Bilingualism was hereafter gradually eliminated in these areas: the bilingual signs and notices disappeared as did bilingual advertisements and announcements. The bilinguality of party meetings also ceased; and, what is more, the use of the national-minority languages at conferences, public discussions, and in official contacts of all sorts was forbidden. This was justified by the argument that in Romania there were only "national" institutions and enterprises, and that the Romanian Communist Party was itself a "national" party: thus, the language of these institutions also had to be the "national" language. It is symptomatic of this trend that during that period the national-minority press was forced to use the Romanian forms of place names.

The Romanianization of the more important institutions of public administration also took place. A number of institutions were declared to be "national" ones, and, thus, members of the national minorities could not fill any important posts in them. This was followed by changes in the leadership and personnel of economic institutions and enterprises, wherever people belonging to the national minorities still played any significant role. These measures were carried out in such a way as to maintain the appearance that a proportion of posts were filled by members of the national minorities, while in fact only those who played no part whatsoever in decision-making or who had a servile attitude were left in their posts.

Parallel with the attack on the intelligentsia a start was made toward excluding the minorities from the upper strata of the working class. Foremen and other more highly qualified workers fell victim to this selection process, particularly in those urban areas whose Romanianization was an immediate government goal. The equalization of the historical differences in level of social development thus took place in a downward direction, through the influx of new groups that had only recently emerged from the peasantry and had hardly any experience or culture.

4

ROMANIAN POLITICS AND NATIONALITY POLICY SINCE 1956

Two events in 1956 exerted a fundamental influence on the further development of Romanian nationality policy: the Twentieth Congress of the Soviet Communist Party (February 1956) and the revolutionary ferment in the East European countries, manifested primarily in the Hungarian Revolution (October–November 1956). It was at this time that a deviation from the policies and models of the Soviet Union assumed concrete form in many Soviet-bloc countries. Similar phenomena could be observed in Romania's internal and external politics, with the difference that the Romanian Party leadership, aware of the consequences of the Hungarian Revolution, further consolidated internal security on one hand and turned its attention to Transylvania and its nationalities, particularly the Hungarians, on the other. Both the de-Stalinization, which could be observed throughout the Eastern bloc, and the Hungarian Revolution were in line with the goals of Romanian policy: to cautiously participate in the process of de-Stalinization while continuing to demonstrate, ultimately, loyalty toward the Soviet Union and, in the sphere of nationality policy, to strengthen nationalistic tendencies. These policy aims were expressed concretely in internal politics by the repression first of Hungarians and Jews and then, gradually, of the other minorities and in external politics by an anti-Soviet attitude.

It was inevitable that the Hungarian Revolution of 1956 would have significant reverberations among the Hungarians of Romania. It is well known that on October 27, there were anti-Soviet and anti-

Romanian student demonstrations in various cities of Transylvania and even in certain urban areas of the Regat. After the defeat of the revolution and with the crystallization of Romanian nationalist policy these demonstrations served as a good pretext for launching a new anti-Hungarian campaign. On this occasion, it was announced officially and at the highest level: in January 1957 Gheorghiu-Dej found the entire Hungarian nationality in Transylvania guilty of the sins of "revisionism" and "counter-revolutionary attitudes" in a speech given in Tîrgu Mureș. This was followed by a new wave of terror. Immediately, during the first few days after the defeat of the revolution, more than 1,200 individuals, including some Romanians, were arrested,[1] all of whom had sympathized with the revolutionaries, or had expressed in some way their solidarity with the Hungarians.[2] Most of those arrested were deported to the forced labor camp or to the penal camps of the Danube delta. The first waves of arrests affected approximately 10,000 persons—mainly Hungarians—but the number later grew to 40,000.[3] The prison sentences handed down ranged between ten and twenty-five years.[4] In the atmosphere of a defeated anti-Soviet uprising Romania showed the greatest rigor in punishing "reactionaries," on the pretext of "loyalty" to the Soviet Union and the defense of internal "stability"; it was impossible to determine the extent to which these reprisals were excessive. It was too easy to organize show trials and to sentence people to death or unspecified periods of forced labor on charges of conspiracy or anti-state agitation. The persons singled out for punishment were sufficiently well known for their sentences to act as a deterrent, without being so widely-respected as to give rise to general protests.

By 1959, a strong Romanian nationalist spirit became both general and official, particularly where this served the immediate aims of the government.[5]

Attempts at Emancipation from Soviet Influence—
The Romanian Socialist Republic

Romanian foreign policy from 1955 to 1964 was characterized, as is well known, by the development of relative political and economic independence from the Soviet Union. This was a time of rapid growth in Romanian national consciousness, inspired by the ideals of independence, self-reliance, and rapid economic development. These goals, reflecting a desire for national glory, mobilized the majority nation, and it was under their banner that originally muted anti-Soviet feeling came to be openly and officially proclaimed. From time to time, this feeling was given new impetus by some spectacular statement, but, at the same time, it fell short of transgressing against the fundamental interests of the Soviet Union, remaining essentially within the framework of journalistic debates. By the mid-1960s, the potential of the Transylvanian question as a tool with which the Soviet Union could counter and thereby mute open Romanian claims to Bessarabia began to become clearer.

In the 1947-1955 period no essential differences in the political approaches of the Soviet Union and Romania had as yet emerged. Joint endeavors towards the building of a socialist camp still predominated. The first signs of a move toward greater independence in Romanian politics appeared at the Seventh Congress of the Romanian Worker's Party, held on December 23-28, 1955, but a much more spectacular deviation from the Soviet line was officially formulated, as is well known, in 1964, at the April 15-22 meeting of the Romanian Workers' Party, in the so-called "April Statement," or "Declaration of Independence." According to that statement

> "The differences between the peoples and countries will continue for a long time, even after the establishment of the dictatorship of the proletariat. . . . No party occupies a privileged position or a claim to occupy one, and no party can enforce its own line or approach on another party."[6]

Romanian politics entered this phase as a result of the general process of de-satellitization taking place throughout the Soviet bloc, of which the Hungarian uprising, the East Berlin revolt, and the Poznań demonstrations of 1956 had also been a part, and following the decision to withdraw the Soviet troops from Romania on May 24, 1958. Internally, Romanian de-Russification was reflected in a reinterpretation of history, in an elimination of the Slavic-Russian approach and the rebirth of an emphasis on Daco-Roman origins. The rehabilitation of Romanian intellectuals who had been silenced for two decades because of their "patriotic-nationalist" approach was a direct consequence of the process of de-Russification. In foreign policy, Romania's efforts to assert its independence from Soviet tutelage were characterized by the development of closer relations with the Chinese leadership and by a search for political, cultural, and economic links with the West.

Romanian strivings for emancipation could hardly have been successful without the loosening ("de-satellitization") that occurred in the Soviet bloc at the end of the 1950s and the beginning of the 1960s. This was the precondition for the achievement of even relative independence. Only then could Romanian fears of total integration into the Soviet economic complex and the gradual Sovietization of Romanian culture and public life give rise to a consistent policy aimed at the assertion of greater national independence. Romania perceived in the restrictions imposed by the Soviet-Romanian economic enterprises (SOVROMS), founded in May 1945, which served exclusively Soviet interests, in the fraternal societies aiming at the establishment of closer Soviet-Romanian cultural ties (ARLUS), in the Council for Mutual Economic Assistance (COMECON), founded in 1949, and last but not least, in the Warsaw Pact Organization formed in 1955,[7] the ultimate threat of complete Soviet hegemony.

The so-called Valev plan, according to which "the objective conditions have arisen for the realization of an inter-state industrial complex on the lower reaches of the Danube,"[8] occasioned almost as much disquiet among the Romanian political leadership. The Valev plan would have merged the southeastern part of Romania, the northeastern part of Bulgaria, and the southern part of Bessarabia into one vast supranational industrial unit. The Romanian political leadership saw this plan as evidence of secret Soviet intentions to destroy Romanian national unity by political and economic means in the service of the great power interests of the Soviet Union. Consequently, Bucharest reacted sharply.[9]

In its strivings to emancipate itself from Soviet influence, Romania became the first Eastern-bloc country to re-establish diplomatic relations with Albania, in 1961. Similarly, although it had been one of the founding members of COMECON in 1949, Romania ceased to be an important member after 1959–60. Since then Romania has frequently displayed a passive and even provocative attitude toward the obligations it originally undertook in COMECON and the Warsaw Pact Organization.

Despite these facts, it can be said that the current Romanian regime, while displaying external signs of liberalization, is actually in no way different from the Soviet regime in political terms. The policies of Bucharest, which are often interpreted by Western observers as independent foreign policy endeavors, could also perhaps be understood as an organic part of Soviet diplomatic strategy.[10] What is more, despite assumptions to the contrary, Romania's relations with the Soviet Union have remained unchanged to this day. There is no doubt that by its efforts to assert its independence in the sphere of foreign policy, Romanian diplomacy gained sympathizers among the Western countries, a development that provided Romania with unexpected economic advantages: its commercial ties with the West increased from 24.6 percent of the total in 1963 to 38.1 percent in 1967; and since 1970 they have increased by 230 percent.[11] The main focus of Romania's efforts is on establishing closer ties with the USA even though the actual extent of Romanian-American cooperation is still fairly modest. The representatives of the two countries signed an agreement concerning the development of cultural and economic cooperation on December 13, 1974,[12] and this was followed by the signing of a trade agreement on April 2, 1975.[13]

The attainment of a certain degree of economic independence by Romania has had an internal price however. On the one hand this has been reflected in difficulties in repaying Western loans,[14] due to an unfavorable trade balance and, on the other hand, the efforts which the government has made to sell Romanian products, which are of inferior quality as compared with Western goods,[15] as well as the process of forced "socialist industrialization" have demanded heavy sacrifices from the population. The Party leadership has endeavored to compensate for domestic tensions and deficiencies resulting from overambitious plans and the inherent inefficiencies of the regime[16] by fanning the flames of national sentiment, by a constant reiteration of Romanian independence, and by frequent coercive measures.[17] A 1965 decree on civil procedure, for example, enables the Romanian authorities to order compulsory psychiatric treatment for persons who "disrupt working conditions of other people."[18] Party Secretary and head of state N. Ceauşescu, has frequently called on the population to accept even greater discipline and responsibility and to make further sacrifices.[19]

The Socialist National State—National Communism

The Ninth RCP Congress, held on July 19–24, 1965, ushered in a new period, politically and ideologically speaking. The concepts of "sovereign nation" and "independent state" were given added emphasis, within, however, the complex of international socialism. This tendency was actually nothing but a reformulation of Gheorghiu-Dej's stated policy of the development along "national" lines of a form which remains at the same time unswervingly "socialist," thus avoiding giving offense to Soviet interests or providing an excuse for Soviet intervention. This policy of heavily accentuated Romanian nationalism was the one pursued during the 1960s, and it remains the one pursued to this day.

It was at the Ninth RCP Congress that the name of the Party was changed from Romanian Workers' Party to Romanian Communist Party, the term "class struggle" was replaced by that of "class consciousness," and the formulations "socialist nation" and "socialist national state" were introduced, with the stress unquestionably on the "national."[20] Clearly, the concept of "nation" is in no way an outdated one: it continues to flourish under socialist conditions as well.[21]

Romanian strivings toward independence and sovereignty within the socialist camp were unmistakable in the speech of N. Ceauşescu at the Ninth Congress, which was also attended by Brezhnev. However, these aims were expressed in such a form as to ensure that they would not violate the interests of the Soviet Union: care was taken to demonstrate, using the theses of Marxism-Leninism, that the concept of "national independence and sovereignty" is not irreconcilable with international socialism. Or in other terms—to quote N. Ceauşescu—"socialist ideology precludes all idiosyncrasies or deviations between the fraternal communist parties."[22]

The basic principles of "national communism" were formulated in the August 21, 1965 Constitution of the Romanian Socialist Republic.[23] The new constitution signalled the formal transformation of the Romanian People's Republic into a Socialist Republic (Article 1). This did not, however, mean a change in the regime, or any real alteration of the form or content of state power, which continued to be a "dictatorship of the proletariat." On the other hand, the "liberation of Romania by the glorious Soviet Union" was dropped from the preamble to the Constitution. The leading role of the party was given added emphasis (Articles 3, 26, 27); in practice, this meant that the entire structure of state and public administration was subject to party supervision (Article 26, Section 2), and that the sovereign director of the system of government was the Communist Party (Article 3). The party's appointees filled the key posts in the public administration, the legislative and executive organs, and the judicial system. Articles 42-76 of Section II of the new constitution designate the Grand National Assembly, the State Council, and the President of the Romanian Socialist Republic as the supreme organs of state. As part of the development of the party's monopoly of power, law No. 1/1961 declared the State Council to be the highest organ of state power. There is no doubt that state power was concentrated in the hands of the RCP to an unprecedented extent as a result of these reforms.

Another significant event of 1965, which also had consequences for the national minorities, was the election of Nicolae Ceauşescu as General Secretary of the RCP on March 22, an action which was confirmed by the Ninth Party Congress.

The years following the Ninth RCP Congress represented a new phase in internal political consolidation. Ceauşescu further developed the national communist tendencies initiated by Gheorghiu-Dej, gradually built up support for himself through the careful appointment of party cadres, and, once he had taken real possession of state power, began the development of his personal rule. The changes of personnel also involved a further concentration of power within the Party.

There was a basic need to create a political atmosphere in which, through a constant emphasis on independence and Romanian national interests, attention could be drawn away from the gradually emerging economic difficulties, including serious inadequacies of supply, as well as from the consequences of the excessive cult of personality centered on Ceauşescu. Romanian national interests were accorded absolute priority in all areas of economic and political life.

The Soviet-led Warsaw Pact intervention in Czechoslovakia in August 1968 caused much anxiety in Bucharest and the Romanian army was mobilized. Ceauşescu's speech, on August 21, 1968,[24] in which he condemned Soviet invasion, was delivered in an atmosphere of panic. The speech attracted a great deal of attention and increased the respect felt for the party leader both at home and abroad; however, the Romanian political leadership was even more than usually careful not to interfere with Soviet interests in any way. To avoid any pretext for Soviet intervention in handling the national minority issue they practiced a policy of liberalization. However, as soon as the danger of Soviet invasion was over, restrictions on the minorities began to increase again. A period of the establishment of internal stability followed.

In the course of an internal political reorganization in 1968, the Central Committee of the RCP founded the Socialist Unity Front (F.U.S.—*Frontul Unităţii Socialiste*), on October 24, to demonstrate the "homogenization" of Romanian society. This new mass political organization, the largest in the country, signalled a new phase in the further development of socialism toward communism. The concept of a "multilaterally developed socialist society" was outlined in the resolutions of the Tenth RCP Congress, held on August 6–12, 1969.[25] The changes in personnel made after the Congress further strengthened the absolute power of Ceauşescu.

The Nationality Policy of the Romanian Socialist Republic

Romanian nationality policy in the 1960s was particularly influenced by three events: the Valev debate, which took place after 1964; the election of Ceauşescu as party First Secretary in March, 1965; and the Soviet intervention in Czechoslovakia in 1968. The significance of the Ninth RCP Congress of 1965 and of the Constitution of 1965 for nationality policy will be discussed at greater length later.

As already mentioned, the Romanian political leadership saw the Valev plan as directed at the political and economic destruction of Romanian national unity in order to advance Soviet great-power interests; for that reason it focused its attention once again on Transylvania and the national minorities living there. As a result, the nationality policy which had been developed at the beginning of the 1960s and vigorously put into practice, which had been aimed at countering the presumedly centrifugal effects of the Transylvanian nationalities— particularly the Hungarian minority—and as promoting exclusive Romanian nationalist interests, was given new motivation and justification. The guiding principles and components of this policy will be outlined later.

The year 1968 brought a further change in the handling of the nationality question, but only in the ways in which the nationalist policy was realized: rigorous, purposeful, repressive measures alternated with apparent, but often illusory concessions. As already mentioned, the previous period had been characterized by a gradual assertion of economic and political independence from the Soviet Union, while the post–1968 period was characterized more by a forceful development of Romanian national consciousness.

In the political climate of the Soviet intervention in Czechoslovakia in 1968, the Romanian leadership recognized the extreme danger of the situation and—anticipating possible active resistance by the nationalities—changed its policy, adopting a tactic of far-reaching concessions. It was no accident, therefore, that it began to show greater tolerance toward the national minorities. However, once the fear of Soviet intervention in Romania had passed, the Romanian government demanded even greater loyalty from its minorities. In the long run, therefore, there had been no abandonment of traditional principles of Romanian nationality policy.

In order to relieve tensions, a Council of Working People of the Nationalities was formed on November 15, 1968. The Romanian Party leadership continued to take great care not to overstep the limits of Soviet tolerance. In the area of nationality policy, a pattern of alternating tension and relaxation began to develop: occasional concessions of secondary importance were made only to be withdrawn subsequently and then to be granted once more. This was done in such a way as to maintain and even gradually expand oppression and the denial of minority rights. In addition to the concessions made after the Tenth RCP Congress, held on August 6–12, 1969, and the February and March sessions of the Council of Working People of the Nationalities, a whole series of formal measures were instituted which appeared to represent concern for minority rights without having, in fact, any practical significance whatsoever. Such measures were, however, useful for making propaganda both at home and abroad. In fact, however, such institutions, by creating the appearance of real concessions, provided a cover for the actual denial of minority rights. Such "window-dressing" institutions included the Council of Working People of the Nationalities, the Nationality Directorate in the Ministry of Education, and a Nationality Committee within the Romanian Writers' Association. At the 1971 meeting of the Council of Working People of the Nationalities delegates were permitted to speak publicly about nationality problems. At the March 14 session, the Hungarian Council raised such issues as bilingual signs and notices, the teaching of certain subjects in the mother-tongue, the supply of textbooks in Hungarian, and so on. (Notably, nothing was done about any of these problems.)

This policy of apparent concessions did not arise out of any sincere desire of the government to deal with these problems, but—as mentioned—was a response to the foreign political situation and aimed at neutralizing constantly increasing pressure from party activists belonging to the national minorities. The illusory nature of these concessions is proved by the fact that the more important Hungarian party activists were subsequently dismissed.

But, even so, as a result of the concessions which were granted, the intellectual life of the national minorities in Romania did develop more during those two or three years than during the previous quarter of a century.

Having succeeded in neutralizing the demands of the national minorities with partial concessions, the Romanian political leadership now began to work out systematically and in detail a new nationality policy, whose outlines were expressed in a speech by General Secretary Nicolae Ceaușescu, at the March 12, 1971 session of the Council of Working People of Hungarian Nationality:

> . . . it follows from the fact that the nation still has a long future ahead of it that the existence of the nationalities also has a long future. . . . The nationalities will possess a clearly and well defined position and role of their own and, just like the nations, will retain their own characteristic identity for a long time to come.[26]

As indicated by the above discussion, a new motif had appeared in the government's nationality ideology alongside those of the long-term historical destiny of the Romanian nation and the equality of all in Romanian society "irrespective of nationality" (themes which had long provided ideological cover for a policy of assimilation). This new motif was the view that each nationality has a parallel historical existence in relation to the nation both with regard to the time-table of its development and its economic, social, and cultural characteristics. Given the character of political life in Romania, however, where the only recommendations and claims that can be openly expressed are those whose positive practical realization has already been decided on, and given the fact that this statement was made in the presence of the General Secretary of the party, one can conclude that the "tolerant" phase following the events of 1968 was succeeded by an increasingly "intolerant" one. All subsequent measures have demonstrated that the apparent concessions served essentially to disguise a policy of continuing oppression. It was at this time that the authorities began to force various writers writing for the national-minority press to write articles condemning "national prejudice,"[27] or demanding the acquisition of

Romanian culture as the price of the cultural concessions that had been made to the nationalities.[28]

The Legal Position of the National Minorities in the Romanian Socialist Republic

The transformation of the Romanian People's Republic into a Socialist Republic and the "homogenization" of Romanian society also opened up greater possibilities for the absorption of the national minorities. "De-Russification" was followed by "Romanianization." In contrast to the constitutions of 1948 and 1952, the new socialist Constitution of 1965 made no mention of territorial autonomy or self-government. Instead there was a great emphasis on the "unified" and "indivisible" Romanian state. The problem of the national minorities continued to be a strictly internal, Romanian affair. All outside voices raised in defense of the nationalities in Romania were seen as "interfer[ing] in the domestic affairs" of Romania and as "infringing national sovereignty."

It was on the basis of these principles that the August 21, 1965 Constitution of the Romanian Socialist Republic was drawn up, whose articles affecting the national minorities are analyzed below.

Article 17 of the new and still-valid constitution guaranteed "equal rights for all citizens of the Socialist Republic of Romania in every sphere of economic, political, juridical, social, and cultural life." The article in question guaranteed these fundamental rights "irrespective of nationality, race, sex, or religion." Further, that article also stipulated that "any attempt to restrict [these rights], to make nationalist-chauvinist propaganda, or to foment racial or national hatred will be punished by law." The constitutional provisions are reiterated by, among others, Act No. 57/1968 concerning the organization and operations of the local people's councils, the educational Laws No. 11/1968 and No. 80/1972, Article 4 of the press law, and Act No. 24/1971 concerning citizenship. Furthermore, a separate decree, No. 468/1971, obligated the people's councils "in those counties where the nationalities live" to publicize the rights and obligations of citizenship "in [minority] languages as well." In addition, Article 30 of the Constitution stipulated that "freedom of conscience is guaranteed for every citizen of the Romanian Socialist Republic; anyone is free to profess, or not to profess, a religion." At the same time the Constitution also stated that "Romania is a national state also inhabited by national minorities." Along with these purely formal provisions, further statements by the political leadership and party documents also stressed the sanctity of national-minority rights.

The first and most important test of equal national rights is whether equality is accorded to both languages, whether the free use of one's mother tongue is permitted in public administration, in one's occupation, in education, and before the courts. According to Article 22 of the Constitution, these rights were to be guaranteed so that

> in those territorial administrative units where, besides the Romanian population, there is also a population belonging to a different nationality, all bodies and institutions shall use the language of that nationality as well, both in speech and in writing, and shall appoint officials from that nationality group or from among other citizens familiar with the language and customs of the local populations.

The article also stated that "in the Romanian Socialist Republic the coinhabiting nationalities are guaranteed the free use of their own language and the right to have books, newspapers, journals, theatres, and education on all levels in their own languages."

The right of the free use of the vernacular before courts was guaranteed by Articles 22 and 102 of the 1965 Constitution and was further defined by Article 8 of the Act No. 58/1968, dealing with the organization of the courts. According to this act,

> in the Romanian Socialist Republic legal proceedings are in Romanian, with provision in the counties inhabited by a non-Romanian population for the use of the vernacular of the inhabitants in question. Those parties who do not speak the language in which the court proceedings take place are given the opportunity to acquaint themselves with the contents of the records, to speak in their mother tongue, and to sum up their plea before the court with the aid of an interpreter.

According to Article 44 of the Constitution, moreover, "the judicial organs of those administrative-territorial units where there is a population belonging to a different nationality than the Romanian must have judges who are familiar with the language of the population in question."

In analyzing the rights outlined in the constitution, one must begin with the observation that they regulate relations between the state

NATIONALITY POLICY SINCE 1956

and the individual and not between the majority nation and the national minorities. Individual equal rights existed in principle, but as for the legal equality of the national minorities and the majority nation, no provision was made either in the constitution or in any other laws in Romania. The Constitution guaranteed merely the rights of the individual in the abstract and not the collective rights of the national minorities, communities with their own separate character. Collective rights as such did not figure in the Romanian Constitution. Yet oppression has been directed not against the individual but against the community, the national minority as such, in an effort to disintegrate and destroy it. In this situation, individual discrimination takes place only as a part of discrimination against the community as a whole. By referring to the concept of the national state, the authorities could reject everything that would support local autonomy. On this basis, neither bilinguality nor the duality of public administration could be realized as it had been, for example, in Yugoslavia, where there were also sizeable national-minority populations.

The law, the basis of the legal system, has, in any case, been rigid and subjective.[29] The legislator has often not been acquainted with the complex characteristics of the national minorities or with the special circumstances of their way of life. Laws which apply to a majority nation are often not appropriate for national minorities.

It is also obvious that the equal rights guaranteed by the Constitution and other laws will remain purely theoretical unless they are applied in everyday practice. Equal rights ought to mean the participation of the national minorities in proportion to their numbers, in every field of cultural, economic, social, legal and political life. But this—as we shall see presently—has not been the case.

Let us begin with the problem of bilinguality, a minimum requirement for the ensuring of human rights. In the national-minority regions or ones with a mixed population, the free use of the vernacular, the freedom to express oneself in the language which one speaks best in one's place of work, in dealing with the bureaucracy, before judicial organs and, most importantly, in education, is an indispensable requirement. As for the actual practice of bilinguality—in contrast to such areas as Switzerland, Belgium or Southern Tyrol in Italy—in the areas of Romania inhabited by national minorities—with the exception of two counties in the Székler region: Harghita, which has an absolute majority of Hungarians, and Covasna—there are no bilingual signs or announcements,[30] even where the national minorities are present in large numbers. The language of shop signs, museum exhibits, the signposts indicating towns and street names, maps, and guidebooks, is Romanian everywhere in the country, including the compact nationality areas. In the professions and other occupations and institutions Romanian is the language used generally and primarily; what is more, the use of the minority vernaculars is forbidden for government employees, even ones belonging to the nationalities. Naturally, meetings and conferences of all types are conducted in Romanian as well. This has resulted in the rise of terminological uncertainty, mixed speech, and the obscuring of concepts in the minority languages.

The use of place names is regulated by a directive issued in 1971 (which has never been published), according to which the only place names which may appear in the language of the national minorities are those which accord etymologically with the Romanian names.[31]

The Constitution of 1965 has been modified several times since its ratification. The first major modification, which significantly affected the legal position of the national minorities was a result of the territorial-administrative reorganization of the country into counties—such as existed before 1944—passed by the Grand National Assembly on February 15–16, 1968.[32] This law had a detrimental effect on the rights of the national minorities[33] inasmuch as the boundaries of new network of counties were drawn up to the advantage of the majority people. As already mentioned, the Hungarian Autonomous Region fell victim to this law. At the same time, place names almost a thousand years old were altered, such as that of Háromszék (Trei Scaune) County, changed to Covasna, or that of Udvarhely (Odorhei) in the Székler region, changed to Harghita. It was at this time, too, that the use of German place names was banned.[34] It should be noted, in this connection, that in Romania the term "areas inhabited by national minorities" is not in official usage: instead, the expression "areas with a mixed population" is used. Nor are the terms "regions or areas inhabited by Hungarians or Germans" or "Hungarian- or German-language areas" used, but rather "areas also inhabited by Hungarians or Germans" or, more frequently, "areas where other nationalities as well as Romanians live." Such terms would be justifiable, however, only as designation for areas with fewer minority inhabitants that Romanians.

The establishment of Councils of Working People of the Nationalities for the Hungarians, Germans, Serbians, and Ukrainians on November 15, 1968, was part of the nationality policy pursued in the 1960s. These organizations, which belong to the Socialist Unity Front, supposedly represent the interests of the national minorities in Romania; in reality, however, they are organs for implementing the objectives of the regime. Their organizational charter reveals their real purpose and goal: to provide help for party, state and social organs at the central and county level in mobilizing the national minorities, active participation in carrying out the current tasks of the "building of socialism" and realizing the party's policy. Their role is merely consultative; they do not represent the nationalities in a democratic sense; authority within them moves from the top downwards. The selection of their leading members is made in accordance with these considerations, and is designed chiefly to reassure the national minorities that they are not unrepresented, as well as to serve the purposes of Romanian propaganda abroad.

In examining the illusory concessions made during the 1960s, mention must be made of the absolute cooperation expected by the Romanian party leadership from the national minorities in return for those concessions. "National sovereignty" and "socialist patriotism" (on which present-day Romanian nationality policy is based)[35] demand, particularly of the national minorities, the repression of everything "liberal" or "particular" and total "loyalty" to Romanian national interests,[36] in short, the self-abnegation of the national minorities. The desire for democratization expressed among Romanian intellectuals has also been rapidly silenced.[37]

As the nationalistic policies pursued in the 1960s intensified, the Romanian national idea came to dominate Romanian public life accordingly, exceeding even the ideological engagement.[38] It is obvious that when the "national interest" assumes a preponderant position in a multinational state like Romania, this inevitably leads to a restricting or ignoring of the rights of the national minorities, to a conflict between majority and minority national interests. Further, it is obvious that an excessive emphasis on the interests of the state is a disguised form of nationalism, unmistakably aimed at the assimilation of minorities, a goal made easier by the use of proven integrational methods. In Romania this aim is also reflected in the efforts of the majority nation to achieve exclusive control of economic and cultural life and to monopolize the key positions in the party, in a conscious neglect of occupational training for the national minorities, in employment discrimination, in restrictions on the settlement of minority population in the urban areas of Transylvania, and in other measures excluding the minorities in favor of the majority nation.

The national minorities in Romania are not represented in proportion to their share of the population in public administration, the judiciary, or, least of all, positions of leadership.[39] Frequent "administrative reorganizations" and the rapid turnover of laws and decrees have provided good opportunities for disguising the disproportions between the nationalities and the exclusion of non-Romanians from major job opportunities. For example, it often happens that an enterprise is abolished and both Romanian and non-Romanian personnel are dismissed; often, however, the enterprise is reorganized within a short time, this time employing only Romanians. Every such "reorganization" further strengthens the position of the majority nation and weakens that of the national minorities.

While it is true that the "coinhabiting nationalities" represent 16 percent of the population of Romania, in Transylvania they comprise more than a third of the inhabitants, and in certain counties they represent from 40 to 88 percent of the total. Thus, nationality representation, if it is formulated simply in relation to the entire population of the country, provides a misleading picture: for example, an index of 8–9 percent, which accords with the percentage of Hungarians in the entire country, cannot be applied in areas with a 40–88 percent Hungarian population, such as the Székler region, where the majority of the population is Hungarian. However, even calculating proportions to determine minority representation is a discriminatory means of handling the nationality questions.

In short, the national minorities of Romania do not have any real right of self-determination nor can they, as long as nationalist and statist considerations remain paramount. National oppression is practiced in present-day Romania to an even greater extent than between the two world wars.[40] By contrast, under the Austro-Hungarian Monarchy, the national minorities, including the Romanian, could struggle for their nationality rights by parliamentary means, through their independent institutions and in the press; they were able to influence public opinion abroad and could rely on the support of their mother countries.

The 1970s—Moves Toward Assimilation

Romanian nationality policy in the 1970s has been shaped by periodic official statements and a series of both open and internal secret directives (*dispoziții interne*). Its major aim has unquestionably been the assimilation of the national minorities. Official statements have typically expressed two basic concepts: that of rights, etc., "irrespective of nationality" and a reformulated "class consideration" which has, to some extent, taken on a new meaning. Aside from endlessly repeating these two slogans—which merely provide a hint of what is in fact taking place below the surface—raising any question about the position of the national minorities appears to be considered a form of tactlessness, since the Party leadership clearly regards the issue as settled. However, behind the slogan "irrespective of nationality" (*indiferent de naționalitate*) lies a profoundly significant threat to the minorities.

At first sight the formulation appears to have cosmopolitan connotations, as if "irrespective of nationality" reflected a rejection of nationalism and support for a utopian supranational universalism and democratic equality under socialism. In reality, however, this slogan sanctifies a policy of assimilation into a state which insists on the exclusiveness of its national character.

The Romanian national minorities did not react openly to the underlying political challenge of the slogan "irrespective of nationality" as long as the real aims were not expressed publicly and remained a secret known only to the top political leadership. The first open protest was voiced at the March 14, 1978 joint session of the Council of Working People of Hungarian and German Nationality. To quote one speaker:

> I do not find the formulation "irrespective of nationality" entirely satisfactory. . . . A Communist cannot afford to ignore an individual's nationality. Nationality implies a particular psychology, a certain past, a good many customs and memories and contexts. We gave up the concept of "minority" a good many years ago; nonetheless, the Hungarian nationality . . . has been a national minority for the past sixty years.[41]

By this time a whole series of disenfranchising measures had been put into practice. These realized the hidden purposes of the nationality policy but did so with careful timing so that by the interposing of various campaigns it would be possible to disguise the real situation and to prevent open rebellion, while continuing and accelerating the policy of assimilation.[42] The reformulation of the "class consideration" is also part of the general ideological obfuscation: the "joint struggle" fought in the past under the aegis of classless "socialist fraternity," has now come to mean the merging of the nationalities into one large unit, the "socialist Romanian homeland."[43]

In the nationality policy of the young Romanian democracy of the first post-war years, the concept of "class consideration" still had some real substance; today, both the formulations "irrespective of nationality" and "class consideration" are little more than ideological building blocks, in a program of assimilation.

On the surface of political life, in official documents, speeches, theoretical works, statistics, and so on, the fundamental issues are avoided by glib phraseology. External threats to the continued operation of the system of assimilation are ideologically circumvented in two ways: by an energetic rejection of any right of intervention by any outside power, because of the "internal" character of the nationality question,[44] and by the pursuit of an unquestionably orthodox Marxist-Leninist policy, which serves to forestall possible Soviet intervention in response to Romania's efforts to assert its independence.

As long as conditions favorable for the assimilation of the national minorities were absent and as long as there was a certain insecurity in the position of the Romanian Party leadership, the assimilational aims of Romania's nationality policy remained disguised and no open references were made to them. The thinking behind various institutional measures was not made explicit. Only the deeds were public, not the motivation. The first open statement indicating that assimilation was ultimately the aim of the state was published in an issue of *Lupta de Clasă* (Class Struggle) in July 1971: "In a social historical sense a nationality becomes an inseparable part of the country since it professes the same ideas and interests as the people as a whole" and its development "proceeds in the direction of increasingly organic integration into a given state."[45] The assimilation of the national minorities, as a long-term goal, was given even clearer expression in a speech delivered at the Third National Conference of the RCP, held on July 19–22, 1972:

> "In the process of development into a socialist nation, the different ethnic characteristics are maintained and preserved but become . . . closer [less distinctive] during the process of homogenization of society, along the path of creating a unified communist order both in the social and in the national relations, regardless of nationality."[46]

A similar statement was made in the Program of the Eleventh RCP Congress on November 24–27, 1974, concerning the question of the nationalities under socialism: "In the treatment of the national question we should not forget, that . . . the working peoples, regardless their nationality, are in the process of creating a multilaterally developed socialist society and communism, and are increasingly integrated into the unified mass of working people of a communist society."[47] Or: "Within the foreseeable future in Romania there will be no nationalities, only a socialist nation."[48] With that, practical efforts toward the elimination of the various nationalities of Romania had taken on a definite ideological form. The integration of the national minorities into the Romanian nation is part of the overall process of socioeconomic and cultural unification that is reshaping Romanian society. Within the framework of a nation-centered and Marxist-Leninist conception, the program sees the role and future of the national minorities in Romania in their construction of a "common socialist homeland" and the realization of "socialism progressing towards communism," "irrespective of nationality." This represents a strange and in many ways contradictory application of the concepts of Marxist-Leninist nationality policy to justify Romanian nationalist goals: it foresees the merging of nations and nationalities with the growth of international socialism, while it still seeks to realize the aspirations of Romanian nationalism. This approach differs from the nationalism of the Romanian Kingdom between the two world wars only by its use of orthodox Marxist-Leninist ideology.

The program of nationality policy formulated and proclaimed at the Eleventh RCP Congress held on November 24–27, 1974, was soon followed up by open, directed measures and campaigns of various types, all with the same general aim—the assimilation of the nationalities. These were complemented by internal measures (*dispoziții interne*) which were carried out under the cover of the Romanian government's crash programs of forced industrialization and cultural revolution.

The statute issued by the Eleventh RCP Congress further strengthened the control of the Party leadership. In particular Ceaușescu's personal power was increased and broadened: already before the Party Congress, on March 28, 1974, he had been elected President of the Republic, adding this position to those of Chairman of the National Council of the Socialist Unity Front and Commander-in-Chief of the Armed Forces. Obviously, obtaining and maintaining such a great degree of personal power was possible only through the creation of a supporting network of trusted individuals, including a large number of family members, in the government and party. Thus, at the Third National Conference of the RCP, held on July 19-22, 1972, Ceauşescu's wife Elena was elected a member of the Central Committee; since that time, she has been considered to be the most powerful person in the country after her husband. This centralization of state power in the hands of one man and his close supporters has also had important consequences for nationality policy.

The Laws and the Campaign Against the Nationalities

In the Romania of the 1970s there has been a need above all, to make laws to solve the still unsettled nationality question in accordance with the ideas of the Party leadership: that is, to promote assimilation. Along with disenfranchising measures, various propaganda campaigns have been launched to legitimize those measures.

Among the discriminatory laws enacted in the 1970s, the decrees reforming the educational system must be mentioned first.[49] Similar measures, with serious consequences for the nationalities in Romania, were Act No. 63/1974 on the Protection of the National Cultural Heritage[50] and Decree No. 206/1974, issued by the State Council,[51] which modified Decree No. 472/1971 concerning the National Archives of the Socialist Republic of Romania.[52] These laws struck at the very foundations of the centuries-old cultures of the Germans and Hungarians, particularly their ecclesiastical aspects, and earned a great deal of criticism from abroad.[53] These measures were accompanied, both before and after, by an intensive campaign of internal propaganda in both the nationality and the Romanian-language press: a great deal of attention was focused on the "need to preserve the national cultural heritage."[54]

The decree dealing with the Protection of the National Cultural Heritage declared that "those historic art treasures produced over the course of thousands of years on Romanian soil as a result of literary and artistic creativity and scientific and technological research" were to be part of the Romanian national heritage and thereby state property. Paragraphs a, b, and c of Article 2, Section I of the law divided cultural treasures into three main categories: those of special artistic value, those of historic-documentary significance and those of scientific value. The first and second categories included art and architecture, historical and ancient monuments, historical documents and material sources, manuscripts, rare books, ecclesiastical objects (chalices, crucifixes, vestments, icons, etc.), rare coins, stamps, antique furniture, paintings, and other rare objects of historical value, as well as articles made of precious metals or containing precious metals and stones. However, the categories of valuables to be handed in could be expanded *ad infinitum.* According to the decree, all national cultural treasures belong to the entire people, and thus society has the right and duty to ensure their protection and safe-keeping. Article 6 of Section I ordered "the centralized state registration of all wealth comprising the national cultural treasure, as well as the securing of the conditions for their safe-keeping and for facilitating their scholarly evaluation." Article 7 of Section I prescribed that the owners of the materials listed in Articles 1 and 2 of the law, whether organizations, churches, or private individuals, were obliged to register such materials with the relevant authorities within sixty days of the law coming into force or within fifteen days of acquiring such materials. The state authorities, in turn, were to submit these lists to the county museums within the above time limit, that is, by December 31.

The intention of the law was perhaps best expressed in Article 20 of Section II, dealing with scholarly research. According to the law, if a scientific researcher received permission to carry out a project, he was to inform the Central State Committee of the National Cultural Treasury about the results of his research. This posed serious obstacles to free research, resulting in immeasurably harmful consequences for scholarship. According to Articles 19 and 20 of Section II, for example, special permission is required for photography or study of the national treasures which have been turned over to the government for safe-keeping. In general, the authorities have provided permission for research by national-minority scholars only after lengthy delays or not at all. The law has had equally harsh consequences for foreign researchers interested in the study of the Danube basin. Decree No. 472 of 1971 concerning the National Archives had already stipulated that all historical documents, archives, manuscript collections, and libraries in the possession of private individuals, religious communities, and other institutions were the property of the state, that is, of the National Archives. Although the decree permitted the continued public functioning of scientific institutions, research institutes, and Church archives under the supervision of the Central State Archives, national-minority material was increasingly consigned to the closed sections of archives. The new law, by placing the material in archives and libraries under the supervision of the Ministry of the Interior, that is, the police, restricted the possibilities for research even further. It is well known that the greater part of Romania's cultural and historical heritage comes from Transylvanian Saxons and Hungarians. The documents of the Transylvanian German Evangelical Church and the Hungarian Roman Catholic, Reformed, and Unitarian Churches come to mind immediately. The archives, manuscript collections, and libraries of the Transylvanian Saxon and Hungarian towns also contain German, Hungarian, Latin, Old Slavonic, and Greek documents of immeasurable value; Transylvanian historical scholarship would be impossible without access to them. The aim of the law, therefore, amounts to little more than robbing the national minorities of the documents of their own past, which could still act as a source of national consciousness.

No sooner had the law concerning the protection of national cultural treasures begun to be implemented than treasures of irreplaceable value for European culture began to be destroyed: national-minority libraries and archives were demolished, and their materials were reused in new buildings.[55] Neither the administration in charge of this program, nor the so-called "conservation and preservation" organs have experts in ecclesiastical history or staffs speaking the languages of the national minorities; the selection and confiscation of articles is done largely at the whim of the local authorities. Between 1971 and 1975, the State Archives forced some parishes to hand over their ecclesiastical and secular historical documents, as well as their liturgical, theological, and catechistic material, along with registers of births, marriages, and deaths, some of which date from the 16th and 17th centuries. A refusal to comply was punishable by law.

In addition to the danger of documents of great significance for the history of the national minorities being lost, the act cited above represented a violation of the freedoms and rights enjoyed by the Transylvanian churches for almost half a century. In the past, the churches had played a major role in Transylvania, acting in close cooperation with the state; the application of the new law severed these ties to an unprecedented degree.

In the same year, 1974, Act 59/1974 regulating land-holding[56] was issued, according to which "all land, irrespective of its use and ownership, forms part of the unitary land holding of the national wealth of the Romanian Socialist Republic." The law prescribed that land of any

NATIONALITY POLICY SINCE 1956 145

type was not to be alienated, that it could change hands only by way of legal inheritance. According to the act, the land of Romanian citizens who left the country was to become, automatically and without compensation, the property of the state.

Decree No. 58/1974, issued on December 1, 1974, regulated the size of plots that might be built on. In rural areas a plot utilized for building a dwelling and related structures was not to exceed 200-250 square meters. Larger plots were to be at the disposal of the state. According to Decree-Law 223/1974 of December 3, 1974,[57] only those individuals who reside in Romania may own buildings and land there. Foreigners who inherit real estate in Romania are obliged to sell it to the state.

At the beginning of the following year, 1975, a decree was published[58] making it compulsory for foreigners visiting Romania to stay in hotels. Romanian citizens could henceforth provide accommodations only for their closest relatives (parents, children, siblings, and spouses). There can be no doubt about the anti-minority and anti-democratic nature of this measure. It is well-known that the overwhelming majority of the national minorities in Romania have co-nationals in states adjacent to Romania; thus, visits by persons from those countries (not always close relatives) are frequent. It can be assumed that this law also aims at bringing about a type of isolation: to protect Romanian citizens from perceiving differences in the standard of living and freedoms arriving from the West (for example, from Hungary) shows a decreasing tendency. A new decree in 1976 modified visiting restrictions, but only in the case of former Romanian citizens.[59]

In light of further developments in nationality policy, it is impossible to ignore several aspects of Romanian economic and cultural life during the 1970s which had and still have a profoundly transforming impact on the whole of society. These changes have affected the national minorities as particular linguistic, and religious groups, on a number of different levels—social, economic, cultural, and demographic. In the course of the further integration of the society as a whole, the possibilities of a minority's being absorbed into the majority people are constantly present and are even consciously multiplied.

One type of planned—though indirect—assimilation is involved with the process of industrialization and urbanization. This has resulted in a dispersal of the population, and a consequent loosening up and breaking up of the national-minority units. Economic policy in this instance has aimed primarily at the exclusion of the national minorities from the process of urbanization and the banning of minority settlement in the Transylvanian urban areas.[60] Those members of the national minorities who cannot settle in the towns and cities of Transylvania as a result of this ban find themselves obliged to settle in Romanian-inhabited areas; thus, the surplus rural labor force and urban workers in search of new jobs have been forced to migrate to the Romanian areas, and especially to the Old Kingdom.

The state's arbitrary assignments of places of employment has also contributed to this process of dispersal: a large proportion of national-minority graduates have been given posts in the Old Kingdom (Regat).[61] On the other hand, the industrialization of Transylvania has resulted in a mass influx of Romanian white-collar and manual workers. In any case, there is a constant influx of Romanians from the Regat into Transylvania, drawn by the higher standard of living. Moreover, the policy of filling the key state and party positions with Romanians has excluded the leading strata of the national minorities, drawn largely from the older Transylvanian urban middle class.[62]

Intellectual assimilation, carried out under the banner of the 1971 and 1976 "cultural revolutions" based on the Chinese models, which extended to all aspects of Romanian cultural life, has proceeded alongside other forms of ethnic homogenization. While it is certainly true that the ideological uniformizing, schematizing effects of the new cultural policy have affected all of Romanian intellectual life, radical "homogenization" has tended to completely drain the "national" character from nationality culture. Symptomatic of this policy was the statement of the party chief and head of state Ceauşescu at the joint session of the Councils of Working People of Hungarian and German Nationality:

> At present we speak the same language of work ... people understand each other in the language of work irrespective of whether they express themselves in Romanian, German or Hungarian. This statement is valid not only as regards work but also in science and technology. Indeed: machines speak the same language, a universal language. The tendency is to create only those machines whose language is understood by everyone. ... Without speaking Romanian one cannot expect equal rights.[63]

Occasional statements condemning "past mistakes" and "discriminatory measures" against the national minorities[64] have also been part and parcel of the maneuvers of the general and fundamentally unchanged policy of assimilation. The great importance Bucharest gives to propaganda abroad, can be seen in the formal official statements and statistics published in other countries, as well as in the spectacular reports about the cultural life of the national minorities.[65] Likewise, the executive organs have continued to pursue their nationalistic anti-nationality policy. One aspect of this method of dual tactics has been to publicize the concessions—particularly the spectacular ones—made in certain areas, while revoking concessions already granted in other areas and introducing new restrictive measures. The duplicity of Romanian nationality policy is clearly reflected in a number of widely publicized articles written by second-rate writers and journalists belonging to the national minorities, hailing the slogan of "friendship and fraternity,"[66] thus providing an outward appearance of loyalty.

At the same time, however, along with slogans about the "joint struggle" and "fraternal solidarity against the common exploiting enemy" in the past, an officially inspired campaign of evoking the recent past in a hostile spirit at home and abroad, a campaign whose methods have been more diverse and complex but which have served the same aims, has also been undertaken. Its ultimate objective is to evoke in the national minorities a recognition of their second-class status vis-à-vis the majority nation and to provide, in a sense, a legitimation of an oppressive nationality policy.

A related phenomenon, which has become increasingly widespread in recent years and has signalled the revival of interwar nationalism, has already created a literature of its own. Thus, for example, a collective work by nine Romanian historians was recently published, entitled *Anti-Fascist Resistance in Northern Transylvania*;[67] it depicted Hungarian rule in Northern Transylvania between 1940 and 1944 in a way designed to evoke anti-Hungarian sentiment. Francisc Păcurariu's book *Labirintul* (The Labyrinth),[68] which has also appeared in English[69] and was publicized by Radio Bucharest,[70] Liviu Bratoloveanu's book *Reptilia* (The Reptile)[71], and the pamphlet entitled *Transilvania ultima prigoană maghiară* (Transylvania: Last Hungarian Persecution), published in Rome, also dealt with Hungarian rule in Northern Transylvania, presenting an equally falsified picture with the same emotional purpose. Anti-Hungarian sentiment was further whetted by the pamphlet *The Long St. Bartholomew's Night*[72] by the historian Ion Spălățelu, which in its treatment of the "Horthy period" in Northern

Transylvania between 1940 and 1944 viewed the activity of the Hungarians as fascist atrocities.[73] Thus, not only the press, but political and literary publications as well have played a role in the propaganda campaign against the national minorities. In this context it is worth noting that while Hungary of the 1940s is portrayed in Romanian works as a representative of Fascism, Romanian Fascist leaders and intellectuals have been rehabilitated, and the role of Romania in the 1940s is passed over in silence.[74]

Parallel to this campaign against the national minorities has been one aiming at popularizing the alleged historical primacy of the rights of the majority nation in Transylvania. Thus, for example, the plenary meeting of the CC of the RCP on October 26–27, 1977, resulted in a resolution concerning the celebration, in 1980, of the 2050th anniversary of the founding of the first independent, centralized Dacian state.[75] Another reflection of this type of overblown nationalism is the annual "Song to Romania" festival, a fete of self-glorification, based on a kind of mass psychosis. In mass events of this kind, the "coinhabiting nationalities" have been made to appear as later immigrants, in contradiction to historical reality.[76] It is obvious that a psychological atmosphere dominated by Romanian nationalism must, in time, lead to a sense of second-class racial identity among the national minorities of Romania.

Two other relevant events relating to Romanian nationality policy during the 1970s are worth discussing here. One is the letter of protest written by Károly Király, a Romanian citizen of Hungarian origin, and the other is the statement to the Western press made by Paul Goma, a dissident Romanian writer.

Károly Király, a former high-ranking party functionary, addressed three letters in the second half of 1977 to the RCP leadership, in which he revealed the contradictory character of nationality policy, listing the most recent chauvinistic discriminatory measures against the Hungarian, German, Jewish and Serbian national minorities. The note of protest was supported by former Prime Minister Ion Gheorghe Maurer and other leading party functionaries of the Hungarian minority. Király's letters were followed by a 7,000 word memorandum by Lajos Takács, a former university pro-rector, the prominent writer András Sütő, and Deputy Premier János Fazekas. The world press first learned about the event from the Belgrade office of the Reuter News Agency on January 23, 1978; thereafter, a number of Western press organs published detailed reports on the affair, as well as excerpts from Király's letter.[77]

The Király affair was of great significance inasmuch as it broke a thirty-year-old silence: this was the first occasion in the history of the Romanian communist regime in which a high-ranking party functionary, familiar with the internal affairs and regulations of the regime, revealed the contradictory nature of the nationality policy pursued by the party. The long-term policy of assimilation of the national minorities in Romania has been pursued in such a way as to keep pressure at a level which would facilitate resignation without bringing about resistance. Open resistance appeared for the first time with the Király affair.

Subsequently, the Romanian authorities took measures to silence the disquiet which arose among the Hungarian population.[78] Among other things, Károly Király was banished together with his family.[79]

The Party leadership reacted sensitively to the Király affair. It launched a campaign to gain the sympathy of the Hungarian population; for example, Ceauşescu visited the regions inhabited by the national minorities;[80] second- and third-rate writers and poets belonging to the Hungarian national minority were enlisted to write articles expressing Romanian-Hungarian friendship in the Romanian press;[81] and the Hungarian and German Councils of Working People of the Nationalities were convened in joint session on March 14, 1978.[82]

Even before the Király affair, a dissident Romanian writer, Paul Goma, one of the signatories of Charter 77,[83] made serious accusations against the Ceauşescu regime, emphasizing the oppression of the national minorities living in Romania and of the Romanian people itself, by a "totalitarian regime." His statements were published in several Western periodicals, and newspapers.[84]

On 10 February 1980 Károly Király sent a new letter of grievances to the recipient of his letter of 1977, Ilie Verdeţ, who was then responsible for minority problems and in the meantine had become Prime Minister. In his letter of protest, Király pointed to the constantly deteriorating state of ethnic minorities in Romania. He described "the complete lack of collective rights of the minorities in Romania [as] an extremely acute problem", and condemned "the unification (homogenization) of socialist society, which enforces with every possible means and at all costs the assimilation of the national minorities".

International Conferences in the 1970s

The problem of national minorities today has attracted the attention of world public opinion, and a number of international organizations and meetings have been concerned with it. The most important events in this area were the UN-sponsored seminars on minorities in the Yugoslav towns of Ljubljana in 1965[85] and Ohrid in 1974[86]; the activities of the United Nations Subcommission on Prevention of Discrimination and Protection of Minorities, including the so-called Capotorti Reports of June 25, 1973, and July 1977[87]; the European Convention for the Protection of Human Rights and Fundamental Freedoms; the activities of the International Pact on Citizenship and Political Rights; the Helsinki Conference on Security and Cooperation in Europe; and the Helsinki follow-up Conference in Belgrade and in Madrid.

The Helsinki Conference on Security and Cooperation in Europe, held from July 3 to August 1, 1975, dealt in Principles of Basket I (synonym for daily program) and in Basket III with human rights and basic freedoms, specifically with the fulfillment of international commitments. Finally, recognition of human rights and basic freedoms appeared in two places in the Helsinki Final Act Provisions passed on August 1, 1975, during the summit conference of state and government heads of the participating countries: first, in Principle VII, which postulates recognition of human rights and basic freedoms, including the freedoms of thought, conscience, religion, and conviction; and second, in the adoption of Basket III, which calls for cooperation in humanitarian and other sectors. Principle VII, Section 4, of the Final Act contains the following statement: "The participant states whose territory is inhabited by national minorities respect the right of persons belonging to such minorities to equality before the law and fully provide for them the opportunity of de facto enjoyment of human rights and fundamental freedoms and thereby protect the lawful interests of the national minorities in this sphere."[88] This statement corresponds to Article 27 of the International Pact on Citizenship and Political Rights of December 16, 1966.

From an analysis of the statements of the Helsinki Conference on Security and Cooperation in Europe, one can conclude that even if they lack the power of binding of international agreements, the basic human rights included in them have validity as a principle and are politically and morally binding through the signatures of the highest representatives of the participating states. From the context of the statements, certain allusions can be recognized that indicate protection of ethnic, linguistic, and religious minorities. From the international point of view, however, the Final Act is more concerned with the rights of the individual that with the rights of groups; it gives no recognition of the collective rights of ethnic groups and gives no legal guarantee of the stipulated rights.

Romania, too, participates in international conferences and seminars on human rights and nationality questions and has been a member of UNESCO since 1956. It is also well-known that Romania has signed some of the declarations on these subjects without, however, fulfilling their provisions. Its nationalities policy remains, as before, an internal affair.

National, Linguistic, and Ethnic Affiliation

The historical circumstances which have determined the development of the national minorities living in Romania are well known. Their relationship with the state which had sovereignty over them was closer or more limited depending on the nationality policy pursued by that state.

The situation of the Hungarian minority in Romania is determined by the current relationship between Romania and Hungary: for a long time it was considered an expression of irredentism for Hungary, the vanquished, to show any interest in its national minorities, even though more than a quarter of all Hungarians found themselves inhabitants of neighboring states. This view has not fundamentally changed to this day. Thus, for example, there are no Hungarian-Romanian treaties concerning the position of the Hungarian nationality in Romania and even so-called "fraternal visits" between the two countries are infrequent. The Transylvanian problem continues to be a heavy burden on both sides and inhibits any sincere moves toward rapprochement.

In November 1956 and January 1957, in an atmosphere colored by the recent defeat of the anti-Soviet revolution in Hungary, a Romanian delegation arrived in Budapest, led by Party Secretary Gheorghiu-Dej and Prime Minister Chivu Stoica, with the task of obtaining a declaration from the First Secretary of the CP of Hungary, János Kádár, renouncing Hungarian claims to Transylvania. There is little doubt that, in response to the events of 1956 in Hungary, the Soviet Union had prompted the Romanian demands. In a speech delivered at the January 27, 1958 session of the National Assembly, Kádár declared that "the People's Republic of Hungary has neither territorial nor any other demands on other countries."[89] One month later, the Prime Minister of Hungary, Gyula Kállai, on a visit to Romania, reiterated Kádár's statement: "Hungary has no territorial demands on Romania."[90]

Then, in the middle of the 1960s the Hungarian government began officially criticizing Romanian foreign policy, first in an article by a Hungarian Politburo member, Zoltán Komócsin, published in the September 16, 1966 issue of Moscow *Pravda.* In an interview with János Kádár, published in the July 2, 1966 issue of the Budapest daily, *Népszabadság,* he called the Trianon Peace Treaty an "imperialist dictat" which had "robbed Hungary of its territories." A seeming opportunity was offered by the Warsaw Pact invasion of Czechoslovakia in the summer of 1968; about that time, the Hungarian government formulated its relations with the Hungarians living beyond its borders in a new way: "No people would sever its ties with its torn away parts, which speak the same language and have an identical history and culture. No people would or could act like this without abandoning itself. We have an inalienable duty to preserve and cultivate these relations."[91]

Such statements, however, merely reflected the voice of the Soviet Union at a time when the first Romanian attempts to emancipate its foreign policy from that of the Soviet Union had begun, and when N. Ceauşescu had severely criticized the Soviet Occupation of Czechoslovakia.

The question of the national minority was first discussed openly by the post-war Hungarian and Romanian regimes in the summer of 1971, when, shortly after Ceauşescu's visit to China, Zoltán Komócsin, a member of the Hungarian Politburo, declared that "Hungary is interested in the fate of the Hungarian national minority living in Romania."[92] A representative of the Romanian government, Paul Niculescu-Mizil, branded Komócsin's statement as interference in Romanian internal affairs.[93]

János Kádár's speech at the Helsinki Conference on Security and Cooperation in Europe on July 31, 1975, evoked great interest. Kádár, while not touching directly on the Hungarian frontiers established at Trianon, did refer to Hungary's territorial losses in 1919–1920, speaking of a "historic tragedy" and the "injustice of Trianon."[94]

Whenever the Hungarian side has raised the issue of the Hungarians in Romania, the Romanian government has reacted sharply and referred to the principle of "non-interference in the country's domestic affairs." Usually a member of the Hungarian minority in Romania has been made to answer the charges made in the Hungarian press.[95]

In the second half of the 1970s, as the Western press began to show a greater interest in the question of national minorities in Romania, tension between Romania and Hungary also increased and debates were begun which, however, remained on the level of journalism for the time being.

The impetus for one sharp exchange between Romania and Hungary came from two articles by the prominent Hungarian writer Gyula Illyés, one entitled *"Válasz Herdernek és Adynak"* (Reply to Herder and Ady), which in a somewhat disguised form accused Romania (not by name) of pursuing a policy of apartheid towards its minorities.[96] This was answered on the Romanian side, not without prejudice, by Mihnea Gheorghiu, President of the Academy of Social and Political Sciences, in *"Hunok Párizsban"* (Huns in Paris), an article whose title was the same as one of Gyula Illyés's novels.[97] Gheorghiu's article inspired a rejoinder from the Hungarian academician Zsigmond Pál Pach, in an article entitled *"A Dunánál. Itt élned kell"* (By the Danube. You Must Live Here).[98]

In the meantime, the age-old controversy between Hungarian and Romanian historians over the so-called question of "Daco-Roman" continuity[99] was also renewed. For the first time, Constantin C. Giurescu, a Romanian historian, sharply criticized the views of Hungarian historians,[100] one of whom, the Hungarian historian László Makkai, joined in a debate with him.[101]

The study *"A dákoromán kontinuitás problémái"* (The Problems of Daco-Roman Continuity) by the Hungarian historian Antal Bartha evoked a great deal of interest. In effect, it amounted to a breaking of the post-1945 taboo on discussion of this question.[102] This was followed by *"Őstörténeti tévutak"* (An Erroneous Approach to Ancient History), also by Antal Bartha.[103] The Romanian historians D. Berciu and C. Preda wrote rejoinders to these works.[104]

The June 15–16, 1977 Romanian-Hungarian negotiations failed to bring about any substantial change in Hungarian-Romanian relations. The revision of the agreement, originally signed on June 17, 1969, expanded the border area, the so-called "little frontier zones," from 15 kilometers to 20; however, the agreement expressly forbade Hungarian citizens to visit three Transylvanian cities, Arad, Oradea/Nagyvárad and Satu Mare/Szatmár, largely inhabited by Hungarians, although these cities are situated within the agreed area. The establishment of the "little frontier zones" has served to facilitate the mutual entry and exit of the populations living in the border zone; it came into effect on November 29, 1977. However, the setting up of consulates on a bilateral basis, envisaged at the time of the negotiations, was carried out only in the spring of 1980.

Following the public debates, the position of the Hungarian minority in Romania also became a part (even if only unofficially) of Hungarian politics. It must not be forgotten, however, that the Soviet Union is not only the political and ideological mentor of the states in the Eastern bloc but also supervises and criticizes them.

The historical development of the German minority in Romania has been briefly outlined in both the historical overview and the sections on territory and population. After the historical turning-point of 1944 and the mass exodus, its relations with Germany (especially the Federal Republic) became even closer. The elimination of its economic and cultural bases and the assimilationist character of nationality policy have forced it to give up any real hope of continued existence in Romania. Today, 80 percent of the ethnic Germans living in Romania favor emigration. In fact, the RCP leadership perceives emigration as a good business: permission for the population belonging to the German minority to leave Romania has been made dependent on economic and financial support from the Federal Republic of Germany. On January 7, 1978 Helmut Schmidt, the West German Chancellor, reached an agreement with Ceauşescu in which Romania gave permission for 10,000 ethnic Germans to leave Romania each year in return for a loan of 700 million dollars.[105] At the same time, the Romanian Party leadership looks with disfavor on emigration[106] which can cause serious economic problems by depleting the numbers of skilled industrial workers belonging to the German minority.

In conclusion, it can be stated that the question of national minorities in East Central Europe has not been solved to this day. On the contrary, it remains a factor of insecurity. All attempts to find an arbitrary solution by means of forced measures, discrimination or assimilation have proven unsuccessful in the long run. The ethnic and political aspects of the national-minority problem cannot be regarded as an "internal affair," nor can it be treated as an isolated phenomenon occurring in certain countries, since it is organically tied to European and world affairs.

5

NATIONAL-MINORITY EDUCATION IN ROMANIA

Methodological Problems

The existence of an adequate number of educational institutions providing instruction in the mother tongue is essential for the survival and further development of any national group. In the long run, education in the language of a majority nation ultimately spells assimilation for any national minority. For this reason, any study of the position of the national minorities in Romania must pay close attention to the question of minority language education.

Statistical data alone cannot provide an accurate picture of the level, quality and content of minority-language education. One must also be aware of the implications and historical background of the cultural policy that lies behind the statistics, especially since such statistics are often compiled to serve propaganda objectives. If, for example, lack of proficiency in the majority language bars an ethnic minority from occupations requiring higher-level educational qualifications, then the members of such a national minority will be forced to send their children to schools which offer instruction in the majority language and this, in turn, can lead a state to the conclusion that there is no real demand for minority-language education. Or if, for example, minority-language schools are for any reason unable to provide an education comparable in quality to that provided in the schools of the majority nation, it is obvious that parents will be more likely to send their children to the latter. Furthermore, it may also be the case that institutions termed "nationality schools" are such in name only, while in reality instruction in the mother tongue is provided only partially or not at all.

In light of the above, two aspects of the question must be kept in mind when studying national-minority education. Firstly, it must be viewed in terms of the national minorities themselves, and, secondly, it must be viewed within the framework of the educational system of the country as a whole. Thus, on one hand, one can analyze the laws which guarantee education in the mother-tongue for national minorities, examining the extent to which the educational institutions contribute to securing national equality and the extent to which they carry out their "nationality" function. In this context, greater attention would be paid to the conditions under which such education takes place, including an examination of the quality of teaching, the question of textbooks and syllabi (particularly those related to teaching of literature and history), the training and composition of the teaching staff, and the ways and means used to transmit the cultural inheritance of the group in question. The important issue of the teaching of the language of the majority people, the age at which it is begun and how and with what results it is done is also part of such an approach. Nor can it be ignored that national-minority educational institutions are at the same time nationality institutions with cultural functions far broader than that of mere education: they are also the shapers and transmitters of national consciousness. On the other hand, it must also be remembered that the nationality educational institutions are also part of the overall educational system of a given state. From this perspective, one must examine the social factors that exert particular influence on the network of nationality institutions within the school system of the country; in short, one must take note of the demographic and sociological characteristics of a given minority group. The factors that need to be examined here include such questions as: whether the particular nationality lives in a fairly compact area or is widely scattered; the social stratification of that minority; and the possibilities for further education and upward social mobility open to the youth of the national minority as compared with the youth belonging to the majority nation. It is also necessary to examine each type of school separately, as well as the educational level of the nationality population and the proportion of those receiving education in their mother language as a percentage of all those of school age. The question whether national minority educational institutions and the number of pupils and students attending them correspond to the proportion of minority population must also be considered. It is extremely difficult to evaluate the level of development of a national-minority school network or, indeed, the standard of the education offered in such schools, since in both cases the problem of comparison arises. Comparing the number of institutions and pupils to the amount of nationality population in a given country, for example, is an imperfect measurement since it can often overlook the problems of a school network in serving minority population dispersed over a wide area.

A comparison of national-minority education during the interwar period with that provided at present can also lead the researcher astray. Such comparison is impossible not only because of radical changes in socio-economic conditions but also because of the transformation of the significance and role of education. Today, the development of education is a key question in every country in the world. Increasingly higher levels of training are a precondition for dynamic technological and economic development. Nor can one ignore the fact that education is most effective when provided in one's native language.

Education can often speed up the assimilation of a national minority, particularly if the use of the language of that nationality is hindered in public life or in places of employment, despite all laws and measures to the contrary. Rapid assimilation can also be facilitated by the absence of suitable minority-language schools of particular types, or if the geographical distribution of minority schools does not correspond to the geographical distribution of the minority population. General (that is, primary) and secondary education in the mother tongue is also affected negatively if entrance examinations for institutions of continuing and higher education are not offered in the minority language. All of these issues are thus complex ones requiring an examination of many factors. An analysis of every aspect of these questions cannot possibly be undertaken here; in what follows only the most important problems will be indicated. However, before discussing the education of the national minorities in Romania and the Romanian educational system in general, some aspects of the historical development of this problem should be considered.

Historical Background

The origins of the independent Saxon and Hungarian school networks in Transylvania go back to the 14th and 16th centuries, respectively.

The Transylvanian Saxons were the first European people to establish a system of compulsory education, earlier than the Austrians or Prussians and 150 years earlier than the English:[1] compulsory school attendance was introduced in the area of "*Königsboden*" in 1722. The first Saxon gymnasium was founded in Kronstadt/Brassó/Braşov in 1543 by Johannes Honterus, and the Saxon gymnasia of Hermannstadt/Nagyszeben/Sibiu, Schässburg/Segesvár/Sighişoara, and Mediasch/Medgyes/Mediaş are centuries old. Kolozsvár/Cluj was the second university city of historical Hungary: as early as 1581 the Transylvanian Prince Stephen Báthori founded a Jesuit academy there, which later became a university. Moreover, the college of the Hungarian Unitarians and Calvinists in Cluj has a 400 year-old history, and the Calvinist college in Nagyenyed/Aiud, Marosvásárhely/Tîrgu Mureş, and Székelyudvarhely/Odorhei are also centuries old.

The Transylvanian nationalities' educational traditions are inseparable from the historic role of their churches. The Saxon and Hungarian schools in Transylvania, with some exceptions, were ecclesiastical schools attached to monastic communities or episcopal institutions; this relation, however, had been changed significantly after 1868. The Saxon Evangelical and Hungarian Catholic, Calvinist, and Unitarian Churches, were the oldest ecclesiastical schools in Transylvania. The educational activity of the Romanian Uniate and Orthodox Churches in this area was much less developed.[2] This was certainly to some extent a result of the Hungarian government's neglect of its educational policies toward the national minorities, although the historically low social level and high rate of illiteracy among the Transylvanian Romanians cannot be ignored.

The significance of ecclesiastical education for the national minorities of Transylvania increased after 1868 in an Hungarian state striving for national unity. After World War I and in the first years after the Second World War, the continuity of education in the mother tongues, the survival of Hungarian and Saxon schools, and the continuing supply of minority intelligentsia were all ensured by the churches. Between the two world wars, 80-90 percent of the Hungarian school network in Romania was maintained by the financial, intellectual, and moral support of the Hungarian churches in Transylvania.[3]

After the confiscation of the property of the Transylvanian Saxon's institution of the *Nationsuniversität* in 1937, German education in Transylvania became the task of the Evangelical Church.

The education of the Banat Swabians developed differently. Because the majority of schools had been Hungarianized before 1918,[4] the Catholic Church played an important role in building up a German educational system through private schools in the now Romanian Banat. A high school for the natural sciences and a teachers college that was incorporated into a commercial school in 1936 were founded in Timişoara/Temesvár.

Education for the National Minorities Between the Two World Wars

The structure of Hungarian and German society in Transylvania at the time of that area's annexation by Romania at the end of the First World War differed significantly from the social structure of the Old Kingdom (Regat). This difference was the result of historical conditions, and especially of the fuller development of a bourgeoisie in Transylvania. The bourgeois transformation and economic and intellectual growth were particularly noticeable in the German and Hungarian cities of Transylvania. A third urban element, the Jews, also contributed significantly to intellectual and economic development.

It is well known that, as a result of historical factors, the Hungarian, German and Jewish populations of pre-war Transylvania had attained a relatively higher level of economic and cultural development than the Romanian population of Transylvania or the population of pre-war Romania.[5] Although, as a result of favorable political conditions, this difference has been considerably reduced during the past half-century, it has still not been eradicated entirely. The governments that have ruled the new, enlarged Romania since the First World War have endeavored to correct these cultural imbalances to the detriment of the Transylvanian nationalities, particularly the Hungarians and Germans. Naturally, the attainment of this goal was conceivable only as the result of a repressive and restrictive nationality policy. The extent of the destruction of the cultural institutions of the national minorities can best be measured by examining the gradual elimination of the minority school networks. It is a well known fact that during the interwar period the Romanian kingdom officially regarded state education as a means for assimilation of the national minorities.

Between the two world wars, the national minorities in Romania waged a hard struggle to save their centuries-old educational institutions. Three separate periods in this educational struggle, characterized by markedly different Romanian government policies, can be distinguished: 1919–1925, 1925–1934, and 1934–1940. The status of the minority schools changed as one government followed another. Perhaps the National Peasant Party could be said to have exhibited somewhat more tolerance than the Liberal Party. Nonetheless, all of the political parties which held power can be characterized as having been basically anti-minority.

Article 1, paragraph 3 of the December 1, 1918 Alba Iulia Resolutions stated: "Each nationality is to have education, administration, and the administration of justice in its own language, provided by members of its own group." Article 9 of the December 9, 1919 Paris Minorities Treaty provided that "those Romanian citizens who belong to a national, religious or linguistic minority" have the right "to establish, manage and supervise welfare, religious and social institutions, as well as schools and other educational institutions, at their own expense, the right to the free use of their own languages and the right to the free observance of their religions." This section of the treaty concerned state schools and private ecclesiastical schools, while Article 10 regulated the status of state schools for citizens belonging to alien nationalities. Finally, Article 11 ensured local autonomy in matters of religion and education for the Széklers and Transylvanian Saxons under the supervision of the Romanian state.

Both the Resolutions of Alba Iulia and the Minorities Treaty were to some extent an internationally formulated basis for the regulation of national minority education in Romania. The Sibiu Romanian Governing Council (*Consiliul Dirigent*), the short-lived executive organ established by the Romanian government after the annexation of Transylvania, which had charge of education, honored these rights, but as soon as it was abolished, in the 1919–1920 academic year, significant changes began to occur, and from that time onward the situation gradually deteriorated. The network of state and ecclesiastical national-minority schools was soon to be destroyed by new legislation.

The fate of the ecclesiastical national-minority schools was determined by two new laws: the act of June 30, 1924,[6] concerning general elementary education and the act of December 22, 1925, concerning private education[7] up to the elementary and secondary level. Churches owning school buildings and other educational capital received the right to select a teaching staff and to provide for their financial maintenance. By the Concordat of May 10, 1927, the Roman Catholic Church secured for itself the right to establish ecclesiastical schools and to determine the language of instruction in them in accordance with the desire of the populations they served.

However, national-minority ecclesiastical education had already been seriously handicapped by two decrees enacted in the 1923-1924 academic year.[8] As a consequence of these, one nationality school after another lost the right to provide public education and, consequently, the future of minority education became uncertain. One decree, relating to general elementary education called for the establishment, in areas with a majority of Hungarian inhabitants, of a so-called "cultural zone"[9] whose obvious purpose was the expansion of the Romanian-inhabited areas along the Hungarian border and the Romanianization of the Székler region. In these "cultural zones" teaching in the Hungarian schools was done primarily by Romanian teachers sent there from the Regat, who spoke no Hungarian; their salaries were fifty percent higher than the salaries of the teachers outside the "cultural zone." Furthermore, they receive more rapid promotion, and the state provided them with plots of land to settle on.[10] The same law also introduced the teaching of Romanian in the national minority state schools and decreed that the "national" subjects (history, geography, and constitutional studies) had to be taught in Romanian.

The December 22, 1925 law concerning private education turned national-minority ecclesiastical schools into public (state) institutions, taking away their autonomous rights, and introduced the principle of "name-analysis" (Articles 35 and 47). This meant that members of the national minorities who had Romanian-sounding names—particularly Hungarians—were declared to be of Romanian origin. (It should be noted here that the bulk of both Hungarian and German pupils attended ecclesiastical schools, and only a small group went to state schools.)

New laws and decrees of this type were issued practically every academic year, with the result that, for example, within a short space of time, the number of Hungarian schools had been reduced everywhere between 62-93 percent, depending on the type of school involved: between 1919 and 1924, the Romanian government either Romanianized or closed down 2,070 of 3,025 Hungarian rural elementary schools (68 percent), 123 of 151 lower-grade secondary schools (82 percent), 46 of 65 secondary schools (70 percent), 23 of 29 teacher training colleges (78 percent), and 27 of 29 commercial colleges (93 percent).[11] The introduction of the high school graduation (baccalaureate) law of March 7, 1925[12], was another setback for minority education. According to this law, students henceforth had to take their final examinations not from their own teachers but rather from a committee composed of Romanian teachers, who spoke none of the languages of the minorities. This meant that 70-80 percent of the pupils in the national-minority schools failed to pass the graduation examination, and that the supply of new intelligentsia for the national minorities was thereby threatened. At the same time, 51.9 percent of the pupils from the Regat succeeded in passing these examinations.[13]

In the 1933-1934 academic year, during the premiership of C. Angelescu, still more schools providing instruction in the national minority languages were closed; only 20-25 percent of Hungarian children of school age, for example, were able to attend Hungarian ecclesiastical schools. Furthermore, in 1935, the fifth, sixth, and seventh grades in German-language state schools were completely Romanianized, and in many localities, so were the lower classes;[14] independent German-language education (as opposed to programs offered in Romanian schools) ceased to exist completely.[15]

As a result of the Romanian state's closings of Hungarian-language schools and its closing of the Hungarian university in Cluj, out of the 2,641 Hungarian-language schools in 1918 there were only 1,040 in all of Romania in 1924, only 875 in 1932, and only 795 in 1938.[16] According to different data from another source, during the decade following the First World War, the Romanian authorities closed down 472 Hungarian-language ecclesiastical schools in Transylvania.[17]

The situation of national-minority education in Romania seemed to improve in 1937, but this was merely temporary. On December 15 the government sanctioned minority-language education in those parishes where there were at least thirty minority children of school age, but the Constitution of February 27, 1938, failed to make any reference to the rights of the national minorities contained in the Paris Minorities Treaty. Finally, with the introduction of the so-called Minorities Statute in 1938,[18] genuine measures were taken to facilitate education in the languages of the national minorities; these measures, however, were merely a reflection of concern over the impending world war and the fear of a possible revision of Romanian frontiers.

After the Second Vienna Award of 1940, dividing Transylvania into two parts, the pre-1918 Hungarian educational system was reestablished in the territory of Northern Transylvania, annexed by Hungary, but in Southern Transylvania, which remained under

NATIONAL-MINORITY EDUCATION

Romanian rule, the fate of the Hungarian-language schools continued to be uncertain.

The political organization of the German *Volksgruppe* in Romania, breaking with the age-old tradition of ecclesiastical education endeavored in the 1940s to take upon themselves the task of providing education in German. Given the new political orientation of the Romanian state, this endeavor of the *Volksgruppe* was supported by the Decree of November 8, 1941;[19] for the time being, however the Evangelical Church resisted these tendencies. Finally, on November 20, 1941, the Church gave way to pressure from the *Volksgruppe*, and the latter henceforth exerted control over all the German-language educational institutions in Romania. The Catholic Church of the Banat did not hand its German-language schools over to the *Volksgruppe* until March 1942.

In 1919–1920, the first academic year after the annexation of Transylvania by Romania, the following Hungarian-language state schools were in operation in Romania:[20]

- 1,686 primary schools
- 62 lower secondary schools and junior grammar schools
- 65 grammar schools (lycées)
- 14 teacher training colleges
- 9 commercial colleges

In addition, the following Hungarian-language ecclesiastical schools were in operation:

- 1,086 primary schools
- 58 lower secondary schools
- 34 grammar schools (lycées)
- 17 teacher training colleges
- 7 commercial colleges

The distribution of German-language educational institutions of the Transylvanian Saxons after the annexation of Transylvania during the 1919–1920 academic year was as follows:[21]

- 250 primary schools
- 8 lower secondary schools
- 3 junior grammar schools
- 6 grammar schools (lycée)
- 2 girls' combined grammar school and commercial colleges
- 2 teacher training colleges
- 1 nursery school teacher training college

In the Romanian Banat during the 1934–1936 academic year the
following German-language schools were in operation:[22]
- 115 state primary schools
- 65 ecclesiastical primary schools
- 16 ecclesiastical secondary and post-secondary schools
- 1 state lycée

In the Satu Mare region (Sathmar Swabians) there were during the
1930–1931 academic year:[23]
- 22 primary schools (14 ecclesiastical, 7 state schools and 1 private school).

By comparison the number of German-language educational
institutions in the whole of Romania—except Northern Transylvania
which was part of Hungary—in the 1940–1941 academic year included:
- 146 kindergartens
- 457 primary schools
- 17 secondary schools
- 10 post-secondary schools
- 4 teacher-training colleges
- 1 nursery school teacher training college

These schools were attended by 62,731 German pupils; the number of teachers was 1,669.

After the annexation of Transylvania by Romania, the educational system of the Jews there found itself in a situation similar to that of the Hungarians and Germans: the Romanian government had hindered the development of Jewish education through the closing of schools. In the academic year 1921–22, 29 of the 32 pre-war Jewish elementary schools were in operation. There were also 4 Jewish lycées with instruction in Romanian in Oradea, Timişoara, and Cluj.

National-Minority Education After 1945

Between the two world wars the oppression of the national minorities had involved a more or less open struggle; the nationalities had their defenders and also—even if only to a limited extent—the means to defend themselves. They had found support not only in their political, social, and cultural organizations, but, to a significant extent, in the minority school network as well.

After the Second World War, the national-minority ecclesiastical schools were ultimately nationalized by the Decree of August 3, 1948:

thus the role of the churches in defending and encouraging the development of the nationality cultures and languages was undermined. Since the introduction of the state monopoly in education, the school system ceased to be a means of protection of the minorities and become a means of denationalization. Since the schools today provide an education for a much broader section of the population than they did between the wars, they have become an even more effective tool of denationalization.[24]

The Romanian national-minority educational system has become what it is today as a result of a complicated series of changes in the laws and decrees issued since the Second World War, which, while appearing to make concessions, actually introduced further restrictions and a state of permanent uncertainty. The negative repercussions, however, were not immediate: in the immediate post-war period official educational policy did not aim as yet at a forced equalization of the level of education, in the more developed Transylvanian school system and the less developed system in the Old Kingdom: the educational development of the national minorities in Transylvania was not yet curbed in favor of the Romanian population.

During this early period, the state organized a national-minority school network extending to every level of education and gave a free hand to the churches. At this time the class point of view rather than the national was still paramount in the shaping of educational policy. With the abolition of the granted rights of the German *Volksgruppe,* the Transylvanian Saxon Evangelical Church as well as the Catholic Church in the Romanian Banat once again took charge of those German-language schools which had not yet been expropriated by the Romanian authorities or been turned into Romanian institutions.[25] During the 1946–1947 academic year, following the purges, a certain degree of improvement in the condition of German-language education could be discerned. A portion of the German teachers were able to return to their posts once again. However, the plan to have German teachers in all German-language schools by the end of 1947 was not realized. In most parishes only four-year German-language schools were opened, with teaching staffs that were at least partly Romanian.[26]

The deportation of much of the German population of Romania at the beginning of 1945 also had serious consequences for education in the vernacular. The decline of the German population can best be measured by the sudden drop in the numbers of children of school age. According to the 1956 census, the German nationality in Romania amounted to 2.2 percent of the total population; by contrast, during the 1956–1957 academic year German children of school age born between 1946–1950 accounted for only 0.87 percent of all the children of school age in the country.[27]

National-minority education in Romania was first regulated during the post-war period by the Nationality Statute issued on February 6, 1945. This, however, represented only a temporary stage before the final integration of Northern Transylvania into the Romanian educational system. Thereafter the use of the mother-tongue in national-minority schools, where all subjects—including history and geography—could be taught in the languages of the national minorities, was regulated by the Decree of March 15, 1946, issued by the Groza government. The Groza government partially ensured the continued operation of the existing Hungarian school network and facilitated the foundation of more schools, colleges and cultural institutions. During this period, the Catholic Church still represented a considerable force; Hungarian Catholic ecclesiastical schools were given state subsidies to permit their continuing operations.

The 1946–1947 academic year was characterized by two developments in the sphere of educational policy which were seemingly contradictory but which, in fact, organically complemented one other. On one hand, Romanian administrative organs were compelled for reasons of external and internal politics to make concessions in favor of the Hungarians on the level of higher education while, on the other hand, on the lower and local levels a free hand was given to Romanian nationalism.

An old demand of the Hungarians of Romania was realized in 1945, when the government issued a decree establishing the Hungarian-language Bolyai University in Cluj with faculties of philosophy, law, economics, and natural sciences. In addition to this new university, there were several other Hungarian-language higher educational institutions, namely, an agricultural college, a college of visual arts, a college of music, a college of dramatic arts and the Institute of Medicine and Pharmacology.

The Hungarian People's Alliance was given an important role in developing Hungarian-nationality educational policy; the educational authorities took notice of its recommendations. The work of schools offering instruction in Hungarian was initially directed by two educational-district chief directorates in Cluj/Kolozsvár and Brașov/Brassó, and by six inspectorates for primary schools in Cluj, Timișoara/Temesvár, Tîrgu Mureş/Marosvásárhely, Odorhei/Székelyudvarhely, Sfîntu Gheorghe/Sepsiszentgyörgy, all of which were headed by Hungarians. In 1947–1948, there were 2,071 Hungarian-language kindergartens and elementary schools in Romania, with approximately 4,200 teachers; there were 184 Hungarian secondary schools. This period can be said to have laid the foundations for a Hungarian-language school network proportionate in size to the number of the Hungarians in Romania and to have begun a development toward equal rights for the nationalities in the sphere of education, with the establishment of minority-language educational institutions on all levels, including the university.

National-Minority Education in the Romanian People's Republic

The first constitution of the people's democracy, enacted on April 13, 1948, and the August 3, 1948 Decree[28] on educational reform, brought about a radical change of direction in Romania's educational policy. In the pages that follow, an attempt will be made to analyze, in as great a detail as possible, the history of national-minority education from 1948 to the present, in the light of the laws and decrees, the educational system as a whole, and the various types of schools within it. The frequent and contradictory changes in nationality policy and the misleading nature of available official statistics pose significant difficulties for an analysis of this kind. (In Romania, every statistic is considered to be a state secret unless it serves the purposes of propaganda.)

Article 24 of the first people's democratic constitution, published on March 6, 1948, and ratified by the Grand National Assembly on April 13th, guaranteed the "free use of the mother-tongue for all the 'co-inhabiting nationalities,' as well as the organization of education in the mother-tongue."

The law on educational reform enacted on August 3, 1948, which was worked out by the Central Committee of the Worker's Party, and which changed the principles of the previous 1942 Education Act, represented a departure from democratic principles. The law, like the Constitution, was based on a Soviet model; it laid down the ideological foundations for the future development of the educational system. It consisted of two decrees,[29] the first of which dealt with the nationalization of school properties, administrative questions, modifications in the syllabus and guidelines for teachers. The second decree prescribed, among other things, the nationalization of all ecclesiastical and private schools, and ". . . the expropriation of the landed and other properties of the churches, congregations, and religious and private organizations which provided for the maintenance of such educational institutions" (Article 35). This measure of the decree finally destroyed the link between church and school that had traditionally played such a great role in the education of the national minorities in Romania. The law created an absolute state monopoly in the sphere of education.

Following the 1948 educational reform, class considerations became paramount, and workers and peasants were given preferential treatment. Thus, the change of regime meant the opportunity for more education for groups that had been hitherto barred by financial circumstances from schools above the primary level. On the other hand, the real aims of the law were the introduction of Marxist ideology into the new school system, the development of a new intelligentsia acquainted with Marxist-Leninist ideas, and an end to the influence of the churches, the traditional protectors of the national-minority ecclesiastical schools. The state endeavoured to achieve these objectives by dismissing a large group of teachers, the ideological re-education of the remaining teaching staff, and the introduction of a completely new syllabus. Purges and "organizing work" among the students were part and parcel of this process of re-education.

The decree guaranteed the education of the nationalities in their mother-tongue from the primary to the university level. However, the 1948 educational reform had two other striking implications for the national minorities: the introduction of the teaching of Romanian in all educational establishments, including the Hungarian university, and the radical reinterpretation and rewriting of the history syllabus. The negative Hungarian reaction in Transylvania led the party leadership to claim that these measures served the cause of "Hungarian-Romanian fraternity."

Since the history syllabus had been reinterpreted and rewritten, the history books published for the 1948–1949 academic year caused unprecedented confusion, particularly since not even the Romanian historians could develop a uniform official interpretation. Some of them continued to support the Daco-Roman continuity theory,[30] while others, under the guidance of the party leadership and Soviet influence, placed emphasis on Slavonic elements in discussing the origins of the Romanian people. The new history books were silent about the Hungarian history of Transylvania and about the important historical role of the Transylvanian Saxons and primarily emphasized the role of the Romanian people in the history of Transylvania.[31]

On the basis of the 1948 act, a compulsory seven-year system was introduced in the primary sector; in the 1963–1964 academic year this was raised to eight, and in 1969 to ten years. A later decree introduced an eleventh and a twelfth year to prepare pupils for higher education. The secondary schools, in the original meaning of the term, thereby lost their special role, and, consequently, the role played by the universities in the creation of the intellectual stratum was increased. Critics of the 1948 act complained about the neglect of technical training in secondary education; now, just as later, at the very time when technology was growing in importance, no provision was made for national-minority education in this area.

On the basis of the decree of July 21, 1948,[32] foreign schools in Romania were closed and their staffs had to leave the country. At the same time Romanian schools operating abroad were also abolished, and ties with foreign institutions were broken off.

National-minority education did not show any great decline immediately following the 1948 education reform, at least not in numbers. During the first years of the Romanian People's Republic, the authorities avoided all cruder forms of interference, in order not to frighten public opinion.

The first real step was to be the purge and "re-education" of teaching staffs, from the lowest level up to the universities. This was necessary in order to destroy the "bourgeois" school network and to abolish traditional subjects and departments, replacing them with new ones. Key positions generally went to teachers selected by the party, not so much on the basis of academic ability as on the basis of "political reliability." By the middle of the 1950s, the number of teachers whose primary task was "ideological education" had almost doubled.[33] In effect, then, the language of instruction was the only element of nationality education to be preserved, since the entire educational system had been redirected to serve the realization of proletarian internationalism. At the same time, moreover, in the course of nationalization a large number of national-minority institutions became Romanian institutions (i.e., with predominantly Romanian student bodies and with instruction chiefly in Romanian).[34] There was no separate decree providing for this; the expropriations were carried out by the local authorities.[35] In such localities if there were large numbers of national-minority pupils, national-minority sections in Romanian schools were established in place of the expropriated institutions; in villages where national-minority children of school-age were not present in sufficient numbers, the schools were filled with Romanian refugees from Bessarabia. This occurred particularly in the Székler region.[36] It was not in the interest of the people's democratic regime to cultivate and further develop the cultural heritage of the national minorities; the weakening of the cultural institutions of the national minorities began with the de-emphasis which proletarian internationalism placed on the particularity of national cultures. The authorities attempted to carry out this policy in large part through the 1950 reform measures relating primarily to education in the arts, which were aimed at institutions of higher education.

These purges reduced the Hungarian Bolyai University in Cluj—which lost its right to self-government already in March 1945 and, from which visiting professors from Hungary had already been expelled—to the level of a secondary school. At the beginning of the 1950s, an attempt was made to remove Hungarian cultural institutions and the university from Cluj to insignificant provincial localities[37] as part of the program to Romanianize the towns and cities of Transylvania in general, and Cluj in particular. This process began in 1953. The Hungarian-language monthly, *Irodalmi Almanach* (Literary Almanac) was moved to Tîrgu Mureş. Similarly, the College of Dramatic Arts and the university medical faculty, which later became the Institute of Medicine and Pharmacology, were also moved. Due to resistance by the intelligentsia, however, further steps were not taken. (Nonetheless, the Hungarian-language publishing house was later moved to Bucharest.)

At almost the same time, other nationality cultural institutions were simply abolished. Already, during the 1948–1949 academic year, the Ministry of Arts had abolished—under the guise of a temporary measure—the Hungarian School of Music and Dramatic Arts in Cluj and replaced it with a Hungarian Institute of Arts with three Hungarian faculties and one Romanian faculty. At the same time, however, the Ministry organized a Romanian Institute of Arts, which also had four faculties. In place of the Hungarian music faculty of the old School of Music and Dramatic Arts, the Romanian Gheorghe Dima Conservatory was created, including a Hungarian faculty. In the same way, the Romanian Ion Andreescu School of Plastic Arts also had a Hungarian faculty organized within it. The faculty of choreography of the old School of Music and Dramatic Arts was abolished entirely, and in its place a so-called lycée of dancing arts was established, which had no Hungarian faculty. Also about that time, the teaching of philosophy and psychology was discontinued—for a time—at the Hungarian university of Cluj, and teaching in Hungarian was finally discontinued at the College of Agriculture in Cluj. The history of how this was done throws interesting light on the methods and the situation. In the spring of 1954, two Hungarian agronomists from the college were accused of embezzlement; they defended themselves by arguing that they had not understood their instructions correctly—for linguistic reasons. Actually, this whole affair had been fabricated higher up with the aim of abolishing the Hungarian section. The decision was announced by the Politburo, thus precluding the possibility of protest. At the same time, as a concession, Hungarian courses and possibility of using Hungarian in the entrance examinations were promised. Both measures, however, failed to materialize.

The regime used this period of reshaping and reorganization to carry out purges of the teaching staff and the student body. After the abolition of the youth organizations in 1949 and the general political reorganization, mass political organizations for young people were established under the names "Young Pioneers"[38] and "Union of Working Youth" (*Uniunea Tineretului Muncitoresc*); the former was for pupils in the general schools and the latter, for students in secondary schools and institutions of continuing and higher education (90 percent of Romanian pupils and students currently belong to these organizations). Both were designed to serve as extracurricular instruments of the cultural policy of the regime. The proportion of school textbooks devoted to the revolutionary movement and to ideology also increased enormously; thus, for example, the history of the Romanian Communist Party became compulsory reading.

We have only incomplete and somewhat unreliable data on the number of national-minority schools during the post-war years. According to a report published in the Bucharest German-language paper *Neuer Weg* on March 28, 1949, there were at that time 441 German-language general schools (113 of them seven-year schools) and five German-language secondary and post-secondary schools in Romania; on December 25th of the same year the *Neuer Weg* spoke of only 396 general schools. In August 1950 there were, altogether, 361 general schools, two pedagogical schools, and ten occupational and technical secondary schools providing instruction in German in Romania.

In the 1951–1952 academic year in Romania, 2,267 general schools with 237,560 pupils, 79 general secondary schools with 13,179 pupils, 92 technical secondary schools with 11,809 pupils and 197 occupational schools and occupational courses with 11,312 pupils, had instruction in the languages of the national minorities. The Hungarian Bolyai University of Cluj consisted of seven faculties. Altogether, there was instruction in Hungarian in six higher educational institutions, and 3,045 Hungarian students completed college or university degrees in their mother tongue.[39] Particular attention should be paid to the problem of the availability of higher education in Hungarian in the areas of medicine, economics, agriculture and the arts. The Hungarian-language Institute of Medicine and Pharmacology was in operation in Tîrgu Mureş, with approximately 1,000 students; in Cluj, there were Hungarian-language sections in the agricultural college and the colleges of economics and visual arts; and from 1946 onward regular instruction was offered at the Hungarian Music Academy in Cluj.

It should be noted that in the schools where a minority language was the language of instruction, teaching was often done by Romanian staff. The Romanian administration placed Romanian teachers wherever it was possible, and the dismissal of the teachers of minority origin shook the entire national-minority educational system to its very foundations.

With the consolidation of the internal political situation, cultural policy also took a new direction in people's democratic Romania. According to the new Constitution of September 24, 1952, "the development of the culture of the Romanian people and the culture of the nationalities is socialist in content and national in form." Thus, while the spirit of the Constitution was infused with a "class" point of view, it was tolerant toward the nationalities, a fact clearly reflected in changes in policy toward the national-minority school network.

Steps were taken toward the further development of national-minority education in 1956 and 1957. The network of general secondary schools offering instruction in Hungarian was expanded, and several new specialized German-language and Hungarian-language secondary schools were organized. A party resolution on the development of higher education seemed to promise significant results. The number of Hungarian students to be admitted to Bolyai University in Cluj was increased, and young people belonging to the national minorities were given the option of taking higher educational entrance examinations in their mother-tongue. An independent Hungarian agricultural college was founded in Cluj and the Cluj Technical University established a Hungarian-language chair and lectureship. A nationalities directorate was set up within the Ministry of Education to oversee the education of the national minorities. This directorate issued a decision that, in order to begin offering instruction in one of the national-minority languages, only 15 fifth-grade pupils and only ten sixth- and seventh-grade pupils were required.

However, 1958 saw another significant turnaround in Romanian nationality policy; since that year, the national minorities have been subjected to serious infringements in many spheres of life. Several of the measures which have limited national equality have related specifically to education. In this context, it is worth noting that, according to statistical data, the amount of education in the nationality languages is growing, but the number of independent national minority schools is constantly decreasing. In fact, this process had already begun in the 1950s, as illustrated by Table V-1.

The 1956 Hungarian Revolution had a great effect on the reorganization of higher education in Romania. On the surface, it appeared that many concessions were made, but, in fact, higher education was put under more rigid control. The July 26, 1957 reform of higher education made clear the intentions of Bucharest: the ideological re-education of the future entrants into the ranks of the intellectual elite.[40] The emphasis was shifted, from the traditional examinations to determine the academic preparedness of candidates for admission to institutions of higher education, to an examination of social origins. The children of workers and peasants were to be given preferential treatment.

The 1957 law concerning higher education modified in many ways regulations of 1953[41] governing, among other things, the activities of instructors and organizational, social and student problems in institutions of higher learning.

The same ideology which claimed that the nationality question had been "solved" called for a struggle against "nationality isolation" in 1959. The hidden purpose of this campaign was the abolition of independent national-minority schools in order to facilitate—according to the official formulation—"the establishment of closer ties between the national minorities and the majority people." As part of this program, the national minorities were pressed to request the "unification" of

TABLE V-1

Minority Schools and Sections in Romania, 1948-1959

	Academic Year			
	1948/49	1951/52	1957/58	1958/59
National-minority schools (total number)	2,289	2,515	2,514	2,534
National-minority sections in schools offering instruction in another language:	111	189	457	475
Independent national-minority schools	2,178	2,326	2,057	2,059

Source: *Anuarul Statistic al R.P.R. 1959* (The Statistical Yearbook of the Romanian People's Republic, 1959), pp. 288-293.

their schools with Romanian ones; minority teachers who did not were threatened with dismissal.[42] Thus, the hitherto independent national-minority schools became mere sections in Romanian schools, thereby losing their special character as national-minority institutions. Specialized schools teaching in the languages of the minorities have thus been gradually eliminated; in the Székler region, for example, which has an absolute majority of Hungarian inhabitants, Hungarian pupils have often had to study in Romanian-language schools because of a lack of Hungarian-language ones. This policy affected national-minority education as a whole, but it had the greatest impact on institutions with instruction in Hungarian or German, as illustrated in Table V-2.

What is most striking is the constant decrease in the number of Hungarian-language four-year general schools: in the 1955–56 academic year there were 1,022, and by 1958–59, their number had been reduced to 915. During the same time the number of Hungarian sections in Romanian-language four-year general schools increased from 38 to 124. In the 1955–56 academic year there were 493 seven-year general schools offering instruction in Hungarian while in the 1958–59 academic year there were only 469, and at the same time the number of

TABLE V-2

The Development of the Hungarian and German Education for Four-year and Seven-year General Schools Between 1955 and 1959

1. Four-year General Schools

Academic Year	Hungarian		German	
	Schools	Sections	Schools	Sections
1955-1956	1022	38	146	56
1956-1957	940	163	157	69
1957-1958	943	132	170	61
1958-1959	915	124	178	70

2. Seven-year General Schools

Academic Year	Hungarian		German	
	Schools	Sections	Schools	Sections
1955-1956	493	10	132	18
1956-1957	456	33	102	20
1957-1958	455	56	94	34
1958-1959	469	77	85	34

Source: *Anuarul Statistic al R.P.R.* (Statistical Yearbook of the Romanian People's Republic), 1959, pp. 290-293.

Hungarian sections in seven-year general schools increased from 10 to 77. By contrast, the number of German-language, four-year general schools and sections shows an increase; that of seven-year schools shows a decrease, while the number of German sections in seven-year schools is increasing.

Table V-3 provides a general picture of education in the Romanian People's Republic, arranged according to types of school and language of instruction, in the academic year 1958-1959.

At the end of the 1950s Romanian nationalist tendencies were given more concrete manifestation. The merging of the national-minority schools and Romanian schools at the end of 1959, referred to as "parallelization" and "unification," is a good example of the roundabout way in which the Romanian authorities sought to undermine the equal

TABLE V-3

National-Minority Education Institutions in the Romanian People's Republic in the Academic Year 1958-1959

Types of School / Language of Instruction	Hungarian	German	Ukrainian	Russian	Serbian	Slovak	Jewish	Tatar	Turkish	Others
Four-year Elementary Schools	1039	248	88	10	30	31	—	44	19	26
Seven-year Elementary Schools	546	119	37	13	18	3	3	5	5	7
Eleven-year Elementary Schools	92	29	4	2	1	1	—	1	—	1
Pedagogical Schools	5	2	3	—	—	—	—	—	—	—
Technical Schools	15	2	3	—	—	—	—	—	—	—
Vocational Schools	67	12	—	—	—	—	—	—	—	—
University Faculties	12	—	—	—	—	—	—	—	—	—

Source: *Anuarul Statistic al R.P.R.* (Statistical Yearbook of the Romanian People's Republic), 1959, pp. 254 *et seq.*, 265, 268 *et seq.*, 272 *et seq.*, 290-293.

rights of the national minorities. This so-called "parallelization" and "unification" continues to be an important instrument for Romanianization. "Parallelization" means that Romanian-language classes are established alongside minority-language classes, even in those areas where there are only a very few Romanian pupils: in minority-language schools, a request by three Romanian pupils has been enough to have a Romanian-language class organized. The purpose of establishing the parallel classes, called sections (*"secţie"*), is to persuade—with carefully chosen methods—national-minority pupils to join the Romanian-language classes. The ultimate result of this policy has been the closing of one national-minority school after another, because of a lack of pupils for minority-language instruction.[43] At the same time, nationality sections are set up, which are later combined with the Romanian section of the school. Even the existence of nationality sections can be justified only as long as the proportion of national-minority to Romanian pupils remains constant. But an unfavorable change in this proportion is ensured by the government's efforts to introduce Romanian settlers into minority areas. As a result, for example, in some places 75 percent of the German sections are made up of Romanian pupils.[44] In the long run this process undermines the justification for the existence of nationality schools. This measure has resulted in a 50 percent reduction of the national-minority school network over the last ten years. In the course of this process frontiers between the nationalities' educational systems have taken on a national character: official educational policy has sought to encourage the development of the culturally less-advanced Romanian population by restricting the educational development of the more-advanced national minorities.

"Parallelization" and "unification" have affected every level of the educational system. The imposition of uniformity began with the merging of the independent Hungarian Bolyai University of Cluj and the Romanian Babeş University in 1959 to form Babeş-Bolyai University.[45] This merger,—which was carried out with disregard for the principle of national equality—was officially justified by the argument that the separate Hungarian university was a hotbed of "separatism" which could have only led to the emergence of "nationalism," rather than facilitating cooperation between Romanian and Hungarian students and the establishment of closer ties between them. The rector of the Hungarian university was forced to be the one to request the merger, arguing that it was impossible to separate the schools on nationality lines. It is characteristic of the atmosphere of intellectual-political terror at the time that the more uncompromising opponents of the merger were publicly humiliated at the unification rally. (The meeting was chaired by the then still relatively young Nicolae Ceauşescu). The loss of the Hungarian university's independence led to the suicide of four professors, including the famous Hungarian poet and literary scholar, László Szabédi.

The merger took place gradually. According to the unification document, each faculty was to have a separate Hungarian section, and Hungarian-speaking students were still to be taught in Hungarian, although it was not specified which subjects were to be taught in Hungarian. However, the number of lessons and lectures held in Hungarian decreased from year to year; in the 1958–1959 academic year there were twelve faculties with Hungarian lectures; after 1964 these sections were abolished, and thereafter in practice only those studying Hungarian linguistics or Hungarian and another language were taught in Hungarian. The merger document, containing a list of faculties, was never published. The Romanian authorities took strict measures against those professors and teachers who objected to the new instructions in one way or another; as a result, many were forced to resign.

Instruction in Hungarian has gradually ceased at the other Hungarian-language institutions of higher education as well. The Institute of Medicine and Pharmacology, which was transferred from Cluj to Tîrgu Mureş, had originally been an exclusively Hungarian institution, but it was transformed after 1962 into an institution with a majority of Romanian students, the result of recruiting students from the Regat; only part of the Hungarian teaching staff remained in their posts. Instruction in Hungarian continues to be offered only at the College of Dramatic Arts in Tîrgu Mureş (which has a special character and, by its nature, caters to only a few students), and in the ecclesiastical higher educational institutions. Training of general-school teachers in Hungarian language is provided in a section of the Teacher Training College of Tîrgu Mureş.

After the absorption of Bolyai University, a decrease in the amount of teaching in minority languages, particularly Hungarian, began.[46] The same method that was used to denationalize the universities is still being applied to the rest of the school system: combining Romanian and national-minority schools into a single school with a nationality section. Further efforts are then made to reduce the number of nationality sections as much as possible.

Another method commonly employed was to persuade parents to send their children to Romanian classes. Such parents were concerned that the further education and career prospects of their children might not be as assured if they enrolled them in minority-language schools. Since it was impossible to agitate publicly in favor of education in the mother-tongue, discreet local propaganda in favor of the Romanian section, emphasizing the advantages of learning in Romanian, convinced many parents that it made no sense to education their children in their native language. This conviction was greatly strengthened by the fact that minority-language instruction had been almost completely eliminated from two highly important areas: higher education and vocational education. Often, in an effort to persuade parents, pressure was exerted by the Party, the administration, and individuals' employers. In addition, administrative barriers serving the same aim were employed. All was justified by the argument that insistence on teaching in the mother-tongue is a form of nationalism, indicating lack of loyalty as a citizen and lack of respect for the official language of the state. Changes within the school were ensured by the appointment of nationalist Romanian teachers everywhere, with the deputy teachers being chosen from among the more subservient teachers belonging to the national minorities.

As a result of the educational policy of mergers, all technical education in the minority languages was abolished, even in the apprentice schools, by the end of 1959. Finally, in the wake of the reorganization of the general schools, elementary education in the languages of the national minorities was reduced by a half.

The aim of these measures was to hinder the continuing growth of the minority intellectual leadership and to limit the numbers of skilled minority workers and foremen. This was done partly in order to deprive the national minorities of their leading strata and partly in order to strip the working class of its most militant elements, ensuring that the new generations of workers would get no aid in the development of their class consciousness.

The unification of the schools meant in the vast majority of cases that educational institutions were headed by Romanians, that the language of staff conferences became exclusively Romanian, and that, henceforth, all school ceremonies were conducted in Romanian. Nationality cultural activities in the schools disappeared completely: it was no longer possible for national-minority literary circles, voluntary study groups, or dramatic societies to function. Among the negative effects of the radically altered nationality policy was the fact that the number of national-minority pupils attending Romanian-language general and secondary schools gradually increased.

As the minority languages lost ground, the Romanian language and way of thinking became increasingly predominant. At this point, the ban on importing journals and newspapers from Hungary and Western Europe took on real significance.

The textbooks, which were based on Soviet models, were published by the Ministry of Education or other agencies in charge of education. Their content reflected the proletarian internationalism which was characteristic of the political line of the Eastern European states at that time. Much of their content was devoted to propaganda against American "imperialism" and against the "bourgeois exploiting class," as well as to praise of Soviet "friendship" and the working class.[47]

After 1960, when the unification of the schools had been completed, Romanian statistical yearbooks no longer included data on minority education. Furthermore, the references available in various official sources are not always reliable. According to certain sources, 84.11 percent of the students in 7–8 year schools were Romanian, 11.61 percent were Hungarian, 2.8 percent were German, 0.3 percent were Jewish, and 0.06 percent were Gypsies. In professional schools, 85.6 percent were Romanian, 9.88 percent were Hungarian, 3.29 percent were German, 0.27 percent were Jewish, and 0.03 percent were Gypsies. In middle technical and special schools, 86.75 percent of the student body was Romanian, 9.05 percent was Hungarian, 2.43 percent was German, and 0.66 percent was Jewish. In the lycées, 86.58 percent of the students were Romanian, 8.94 percent were Hungarian, 2.15 percent were German, and 1.25 percent were Jewish, while in the institutions of higher education, the percentages were as follows: 88.72 percent Romanian, 6.10 percent Hungarian, 1.83 percent German, and 2.13 percent Jewish.[48] Thus, the two largest national minorities, the Hungarians and the Germans, were relatively better represented on the primary and intermediate levels, but were under-represented in the lycées and higher educational institutions. The Jewish minority, on the other hand, was much better represented in lycées and institutions of higher learning, relatively speaking, than were the first two groups, and the Romanians were over-represented on all levels of the educational system.

The Educational System of the Romanian Socialist Republic

1968 can be seen as the starting point of a number of tendencies in external and internal politics which have led to profound changes both in Romanian nationality policy and in the Romanian educational system. It was in that year that the new education law, most of which is still in effect, was issued. However, before turning to an analysis of the 1968 education reform, it should be noted that the present-day Romanian educational system is based on the following laws: the educational reform of August 3, 1948, the July 13, 1956 resolution of the Central Committee of the Romanian Communist Party, the Decree of October 7, 1961, the reform-decree concerning the new educational directives issued on May 13, 1968,[49] the decree of May 11, 1973,[50] the June 18-19 resolution of the Central Committee of the RCP,[51] and, finally, the most recent Educational Law, issued on October 11, 1978.[52] These laws have been supplemented by decrees and party resolutions issued in the intervening period. The frequent changes of laws and decrees reflect the contradictory spirit of educational policy and tendencies toward Romanianization.[53]

The Educational Reform Law issued on May 13, 1968, which was later modified by a decree issued on March 8, 1972,[54] brought about both a certain restriction and a certain relaxation in the sphere of education. The law's fundamental provision was the declaration that ten years of general school would henceforth be compulsory, (from age six to sixteen). In practice, however, this measure has still not been fully implemented: pupils who do not go on to higher or continuing education complete only eight years of schooling. This measure was further modified in 1973 by the June 18-19 resolution of the Central Committee of the RCP, which was more restrictive than the 1968 law.

The structure of the present-day Romanian educational system that has emerged, as a result of these modifications, is as follows:

Pre-school (kindergarten) provides education for children between the ages of three and six. During the 1974-75 academic year, 66.5 percent of the children in Romania attended kindergartens. More recently a large-scale program for the further development of the pre-school system was launched. The kindergarten curriculum has placed increasing emphasis on preparing children for school.

The compulsory ten-year general school is divided into the following three stages:

a) classes 1-4: the basic stage (*primas*), or primary school;
b) classes 5-8: the intermediate stage (*gimnasial*);
c) classes 9—10: the lycée stage, grade I (*liceul I*).

Stage b), the elementary school, is the foundation of the entire Romanian school system; Stage c), that is, lycée grade I, opens the way to further secondary education (lycée grade II) or vocational schools.

The general school provides uniform instruction up to the eighth year, after which a greater emphasis is placed on specialization. After the completion of the eighth year, pupils who pass the entrance examinations may enroll in an academic lycée, in a specialized technical lycée, or in a vocational secondary school. Ideally, those students who do not pass such entrance examinations simply complete their education with two more years of general school; after the completion of the ten years they then have the possibility of further vocational education. At the academic lycées, which correspond to the traditional gymnasia, and which are divided into humanities and science lycées, courses last four years. Study in the specialized technical lycées lasts either four or five years; there are six different types of technical lycées, specializing in industry, economics, agriculture and forestry, health, pedagogy, and the arts. Some 55 percent of the pupils of lycée grades I and II attend vocational secondary schools, 27 percent attend the traditional arts or science lycées and 18 percent the specialized technical lycées.[55]

The completion of lycée grade II, either in one of the two types of academic lycées, or in one of the six types of specialized technical lycées, marks the end of secondary education. Success in the final examination, the baccalaureate, entitles pupils to a specialized diploma and an opportunity to go on for higher education. However, admission to college or university also depends on the passing of an entrance examination.

In an era of industrialization, when a large proportion of school children are orienting themselves towards technical training, the significance of the specialized technical lycées is constantly increasing. There had already been experiments in Romania during the 1955-56 academic year, with specialized polytechnical education along the line of Lenin's ideas, but with little result; in the 1958-1959 academic year a press campaign, advocating this model, was launched, and in 1966-67 specialized technical lycées were established.[56]

The number of technical lycées increased at the expense of the academic lycées after 1966. Thus, for example, while during the 1970-71 academic year there were 226 specialized technical lycées and 28 fine-arts lycées with 118,577 and 4,258 pupils, respectively, by the 1978-79 academic year there were 824 technical lycées and 28 fine-arts lycées with 870,128 and 4,622 pupils.[57]

The institutions of further and higher education in Romania can be divided into universities, and other colleges or institutions with courses lasting four to six years for universities, and three years, for teachers' colleges (training teachers for secondary schools) and engineering colleges. Admittance to institutions of further and higher education depends on passing both the baccalaureate examination and the entrance examination. Success in the entrance examination does not depend on talent alone; political reliability, the opinion of local party organs, and participation in ideological life have at least as great a part to play.

Following the resolution of the Ninth Congress of the RCP (1965) and the proclamation of the Romanian Socialist Republic (August 21, 1965), further innovations were introduced in the field of education. Structural changes were introduced primarily on the higher level; these changes were reflected particularly in the "qualitative improvement" of higher education (i.e., more emphasis on technical training and ideological orientation) and in "self-examination based on national traditions." The resolutions of the June 18–19, 1973 plenary session of the RCP Central Committee resulted in a new organization of the higher educational and general educational system. The aim of this reform was the complete integration of education into the economic, social, and political structure. The 1974 annual conference of the teachers and party functionaries of continuing and higher educational institutions introduced further innovations into the Romanian university and college system.

The most profound transformation in Romanian culture and education since the Second World War was produced by the "Little Cultural Revolution" of 1971.[58] Subsequently, in accordance with the November 1971 ideological program of the Party and the resolutions of the XIth RCP Congress (1974) the structure of education—as well as the structure of public administration in general—was reorganized. The purpose of the innovation was to imbue education and cultural and artistic training with a spirit of "loyalty to socialism" and commitment to the "building of communism." The reorganization was most clearly manifested in secondary and higher education, primarily in the rewriting of textbooks and in changes in the curriculum and university lectures. Thus, for example, the history of Romania and of the Romanian Communist Party were made compulsory subjects in every faculty. At the same time, the mass young people's political organizations—the UTM (Union of Working Youth), the Pioneers, and, after 1976, the "Falcons of the Homeland"—increased their activity, aimed at the indoctrination of youth; ideological re-education was accompanied by a special emphasis on Romanian nationalism. The teaching of Latin was given greater emphasis, underlining the Latin origins of the Romanian people, and history was rewritten, with the so-called "Daco-Roman theory" given greater prominence than ever. The negative effects of these Romanian nationalist excesses on the national minorities will be analyzed below.

In order to realize this transformation, the Romanian Communist Party utilized all available organs of the state, subordinating them to itself. Thus, for example, a government decree[59] transformed the Council for Socialist Culture and Education into a state and party organ, subordinating it to the direct control of the Central Committee of the RCP and the Council of Ministers. The principles of complete ideological and educational reorientation were formulated at the "Congress of Political Education and Socialist Culture" in May 1976.[60]

The school system of post-war Romania succeeded in reducing the considerable rate of illiteracy to a minimum by the middle of the 1950s; it also succeeded lessening the great difference in standards between Transylvania and the Regat. Table V-4 illustrates the rate of illiteracy in Romania between 1899 and 1956, comparing the situation in the Old Kingdom (Regat) and in Transylvania. Table V-5 shows the rate of illiteracy according to nationality in Hungary in 1890 and in Romania in 1956.

The Present System of National–Minority Education

In addition to Marxist-Leninist ideological elements, education in Romania is characterized by its stress on the "national," which manifests itself primarily in a disproportionate emphasis on Romanian national history, as well as on Romanian language and literature. The question of national-minority education must be approached with an awareness of these two factors, as well as an awareness of the internal and external political factors shaping nationality policy.

The 1965 Constitution of the Romanian Socialist Republic refers in several places to the equal rights possessed by the nationalities. Among other things, it guarantees the free use of the mother-tongue in education (Article 22). In its words, "education for the nationalities on all levels is in their own languages." The Education Act of May 13, 1968 states that "education for the 'co-inhabiting nationalities' is provided in their own languages at every level of the educational system" (Article

TABLE V-4

Rates of Illiteracy in Romania and in Historical Transylvania 1899-1956

(Figures in percent)

Year	Romania as a Whole	Old Kingdom (Regat)	Historical Transylvania
1899-1900	—	78.0	56.9
1910-1912	—	60.8	50.1
1930	38.2	44.2	33.0
1948	21.1	25.7	18.3
1956	10.1	11.6	7.8

Source: Statistics for 1899-1912 for the Old Kingdom (Regat), from Leonida Colescu, *Recensămîntul general al populaţiei României din dec. 1899.* (The 1899 Census), Bucharest, 1905, pp. 80-331.; *Statistica ştiutorilor de carte din România intocmită pe baza rezultatelor definitive ale recensămîntului general al populaţiei din 1912* (Statistics on literacy in Romania, compiled on the basis of the general census of 1912), Bucharest, 1915; Statistics for Transylvania from Nicolae Albu, *Istoria învăţămîntului românesc din Transilvania pînă la 1800.* (The History of Romanian Education in Transylvania until 1800), Blaj, 1944; Statistics for 1948 from Anton Golopenţia and D.C. Georgescu, "Populaţia Republicii Populare România la 25 ianuarie 1948" (The Population of the Romanian People's Republic on January 25, 1948), *Probleme Economice*, 1948, no. 2, pp. 28-45; on the population over eight years old: *Recensămîntul 1956* (The 1956 Census), Vol. I, p. 426 *et seq.*, for the whole population Vol. I, pp. 576-587.

9, Paragraph 2). The act further stipulates that school textbooks are to be written in the languages of the "coinhabiting nationalities" (Article 45, Paragraph 3) and that, in schools and sections with instruction in minority languages, the teaching and auxiliary staffs will be selected from among those who are familiar with the language in question (Article 9). Furthermore, in minority-language schools or sections, headteachers or deputy heads are to be selected from the nationality in question or at least from among those who speak the language of that nationality (Article 40, Paragraph 2), and in those counties where there are minority-language schools, the staff of the educational

TABLE V-5

Rates of Illiteracy in Hungary and Romania Between 1890 and 1956 According to Nationality
(in percentage)

Nationality	Hungary 1890	Historical Transylvania	Romania (1956)
Jews	—	0.6	3.1
Germans	37.0	0.6	1.1
Hungarians	46.4	3.1	3.1
Romanians	85.9	8.6	10.9
Gypsies	—	31.3	37.7
Other Nationalities	—	5.9	—

Source: *Magyar statisztikai évkönyv 1916-1918* (Hungarian Statistical Yearbook, 1916-1918), p. 10.; *Recensămîntul 1956* (The 1956 Census), Vol. I., pp. 576-582.

administration will be appointed from among the members of these nationalities (Article 46, Paragraph 2).

However, the rights guaranteed by the Constitution have in practice, been implemented quite differently. This is the result, in part, of a lack of clarity in the formulation of the text of the Constitution and, in part, of the clear non-implementation of the rights guaranteed by the text. In outlining the free use of the mother tongue in education, for example, the constitutional text speaks of education "at all levels" but not of "all types." Thus, the text does not exclude the possibility of there being a type of secondary school, such as the specialized technical lycée, where education is carried out exclusively in Romanian. Furthermore, the Constitution does not guarantee minority-language schools, but only "instruction in the mother-tongue." In any case, the educational policy pursued in the years since the proclamation of the constitution has revealed the extent to which these rights have not been observed. This can be seen clearly by examining certain phases of the increasingly disenfranchising and denationalizing educational policy as well as conditions in the most important types of school. An analysis of this problem will be undertaken later.

It cannot be said that the status of national-minority education was in any way stabilized after 1968. After the Czechoslovak events, a policy of temporization was instituted, and a certain degree of relaxation occurred. This was partly the result of internal pressure from the nationalities and partly a result of external pressures (i.e., the Soviet intervention in Czechoslovakia). There were certain concessions made which, though only of secondary significance, with no real effect on the fundamental political line, were nonetheless sufficient to reassure the national minorities and to create a more favorable image of Romania abroad. As a result of internal pressure, minority-language skilled-workers' schools were established; these were later abolished, only to be re-established once more, with great care always taken to ensure the exclusion of non-Romanians from certain key fields. Care was also taken to ensure that these schools functioned in an atmosphere of uncertainty, thus discouraging parents from sending their children to such schools. Pressure was also placed on the head teachers of Romanian schools: it was suggested it was a result of negligence on their part that minority children were not enrolled in Romanian schools.

Once Romania perceived the danger of Soviet invasion to have passed, this system of national oppression and cultural suffocation was reasserted even while measures for the extension of the national-minority school network were formally under discussion. This oppression far surpassed that of the interwar period. Every effort was concentrated on limiting minority education purely to the use of minority language, without permitting any specific nationality content whatsoever.

In 1969 certain concessions were again made in the field of education. A decree of July 3, 1969[61] prescribed that the examination committees for university and other school entrance examinations should include speakers of minority languages. At the March 12, 1971 plenary session of the Council of Working People of Hungarian Nationality, Hungarian delegates were given an opportunity to speak up for the cause of minority education. Furthermore, Nicolae Ceaușescu, General Secretary of the RCP, instructed the Ministry of Education to secure the establishment of Hungarian-language sections or classes in some vocational-training schools and vocational secondary schools beginning in the 1971–1972 academic year, and to expand the amount of teaching in the mother-tongue at Babeș-Bolyai University in Cluj and the Medical and Pharmacological Institute.[62]

And, in fact, a certain measure of improvement did occur in the educational sphere after the 1971 plenary session of the Council of Working People of Hungarian Nationality: educational policy had a positive effect on national-minority culture. In the 1971–72 academic year, the new schools and sections began to function; it must not be forgotten, however, that these measures restored only a tiny proportion of the minority vocational and higher level instructional network that had existed in the 1940s and 1950s. Thus, these new measures did not in any way come near to satisfying the existing needs. Kindergartens and schools teaching in the nationality languages were newly established only in places where their absence was particularly noticeable in view of the size of the national-minority population, or where their establishment had been demanded by local public opinion or by intellectual and political groups. On the other hand, there were still a large number of villages, towns, and new housing developments where, lacking suitable schools, national-minority children could not carry on their studies in their mother-tongue. The recommendation that the "national" subjects—history, geography, and patriotic education—should be taught in the languages of the minorities was not implemented either.

In any case, the 1971 concessions were short-lived. On the basis of higher instructions, issued without any explanation, the vocational schools which had been formed by the new measures were either abolished or reorganized as vocational schools teaching in Romanian. A new decree which ordered the teaching of specialized subjects in Romanian was issued five days before the beginning of the 1971–72 academic year, when school registration had already been completed. A later decree, issued for the following academic year, made the teaching of special subjects in Romanian compulsory in the minority-language specialized technical lycées as well.

Typically, concessions had been motivated largely by considerations of foreign-policy strategy.

During the 1973–74 academic year, new educational laws were adopted,[63] whose purpose was the complete elimination of teaching in the mother-tongue through universal Romanianization. These measures were aimed primarily at the Hungarian and German minorities. In accordance with the new laws, the academic lycées—which correspond more or less to the traditional arts-and-sciences gymnasia of Western Europe—were reorganized: 70 percent became specialized technical lycées or vocational schools, with Romanian as the language of instruction, and 30 percent remained academic lycées, some of them with nationality sections. According to these laws, in order to maintain national-minority sections in general schools between the fifth and tenth grades, at least 25 applications are necessary. Otherwise minority-language instruction can be provided only for the first four grades, and even that only if there are at least seven applicants,[64] except with special approval from the Ministry of Education. As a result of this measure, the minority population scattered in settlements where they are few in number and are unable to receive any education in their own languages. In the lycées and specialized technical lycées (grades 9-10) the minimum number of applicants required to organize a minority-language section is 36. By contrast, no minimum number of students is necessary in order to organize classes taught in Romanian, and the law reinforces this by prescribing that in those secondary and elementary schools where there are classes taught in the languages of the national minorities, Romanian sections must be established, regardless of the number of Romanian pupils. The discriminatory character of the law is not even disguised. In practice, the new education law makes possible the establishment of Romanian sections in all areas inhabited by the national minorities. Thus, the pupil belonging to a national minority who cannot be given a place in his own section because of numbers, finds himself sooner or later in the Romanian section. As a result, in the long run, in those nationality areas which are not entirely homogeneous, education in the vernacular will eventually cease to exist.

It has already been noted that the available data on minority education in Romania during the past decade are far from complete. It should be added that the official statistical data fail to reflect the real situation. Official statistics on the number of minority educational institutions and comparisons drawn with the official percentages of the national minorities do not provide a realistic picture of the geographical distribution of the nationality populations' educational needs. What is more, these statistics cannot indicate the quality or content of minority education nor the direction of new developments. But one cannot ignore such questions as whether, for example, the proportion of minority-language education in the Székler region, 85-95 percent of whose population is Hungarian, merely corresponds to the proportion of Hungarians in the whole of Romania, which is officially 8-9 percent; or, whether in nationality areas where the population belonging to the national minorities is less concentrated, there is any institution teaching in the vernacular at all—as a result of the education act prescribing minimum numbers necessary for the establishment of national-minority classes. This situation is not substantially changed by the fact that, on occasion, in accordance with the needs of foreign policy, the Romanian authorities permit the opening (or rather, reopening) of some national-minority educational institutions.

In my analysis of the issues connected with national-minority education in Romania, I deal mainly with the education of the two largest national minorities, who also happen to have the richest educational traditions—the Hungarians and the Germans; however, on the basis of the data at my disposal I have been able to draw some more general conclusions, as well.

Detailed official data on national-minority education in the Romanian Socialist Republic is provided—as was mentioned—from the 1966 census and various other sources. According to certain sources, during the 1966–67 academic year there were 373 German-language schools or sections attached to Romanian schools in the whole of Romania, consisting of 354 general schools or sections with 1–8 classes, 19 secondary schools or sections with 1–12 classes, and three pedagogical schools (with a total of 314 students), two of which trained teachers and one, nursery nurses.[65] According to that same source, during the 1967–68 academic year there were 1,944 minority-language schools and sections in all of Romania. Of these, 1,480 were Hungarian and 386 German; 78 offered instruction in Serbian, Slovakian, Ukrainian, and Czech.[66]

In the 1969–70 academic year 225,618 pupils attended Hungarian-language educational institutions: of these, 35,177 attended kindergarten, which represents 7.9 percent of all the children in kindergarten in Romania, while in the general schools 168,218 pupils received instruction in Hungarian, which represents only 6 percent of all general-school pupils in Romania; 21,568 pupils were taught in Hungarian academic lycées, 665 in teacher training colleges, 1,425 in specialized technical lycées, and 6,308 in vocational schools.[67] In the same academic year 11,718 children attended German-language kindergartens; in the general schools 44,432 pupils received instruction in German, 3,605 were taught in German secondary schools, and 405 in teacher training colleges.[68]

During the 1970–71 academic year, Hungarian was the language of instruction for 157,000 pupils in 1,337 general schools and for 21,106 pupils in 91 theoretical lycées, representing a total of approximately

179,000 pupils. In the 1971–72 academic year there were 955 Hungarian kindergartens attended by approximately 50,000 children.[69] This represents a significant advance over the situation that existed two years earlier. The reason for it is to be found primarily in the 1967 decree concerning birth control which outlawed abortion and provided incentives for large families. The kindergarten network had to be expanded considerably nationwide in order to meet the increased demand resulting from the higher birth-rate. However, the development of Hungarian-language kindergartens was not proportionate to this growth. In the 1972-73 academic year, the total kindergarten network in Romania was expanded by 1,118 units,[70] while the number of Hungarian-language kindergartens increased by only 42 units.[71] Some of the kindergartens function as Hungarian sections, which means that they share a building with Romanian children. In the 1971–72 academic year, approximately 210,000 Hungarian pupils were enrolled in 1,337 Hungarian-language general schools or general-school sections. This increase in numbers is in part the result of the transition to the ten-year general school.

As a result of the concessions made in 1971, secondary education for the national minorities in Romania became somewhat more extensive in the academic year 1971–72. In the regions with a substantial Hungarian population, Hungarian-language specialized technical lycées, parallel sections, and vocational schools were established in a number of towns, including: Miercurea Ciuc/Csíkszereda, Odorheiu/Székelyudvarhely, Tîrgul Secuiesc/Kézdivásárhely, Sfîntu Gheorghe/Sepsiszentgyörgy, Ciombord/Csombord, Cluj/Kolozsvár, Tîrgu Mureş/Marosvásárhely, Reghin/Szászrégen, and Vlahiţa/Szentegyházasfalu. Beginning in the 1972–73 academic year, Hungarian was the language in a total of 25 specialized schools. At the same time, instruction in Hungarian was offered in several academic lycées, including the Alexandru Moghioroş Lycée in Oradea/Nagyvárad, Lycée No. 1 in Sfîntu Gheorghe, Lycée No. 1 in Miercurea Ciuc, the Bolyai Farkas Lycée in Tîrgu Mureş, Lycée No. 5 in Satu Mare/Szatmár, and the Hungarian-language lycée in Timişoara/Temesvár.

In the 1971–72 academic year the following academic lycées had instruction exclusively in German or had German-language sections: Honterus Lycée in Braşov/Kronstadt, Brukenthal Lycée (now Lycée No. 1) in Sibiu/Hermannstadt, Stephan Ludwig Roth Lycée and Axente Sever Lycée in Mediaş/Mediasch, Nikolaus Lenau Lycée in Timişoara/Temeswar, Josef Haltrich Lycée in Sighişoara/Schässburg and Lycée No. 21 in Bucharest. However, beginning with the 1976–77 academic year, only the lycées in Braşov, Sibiu, Timişoara and Bucharest remained (Lycée No. 6 in Arad is a new institution.)[72]

In this context, it should not be forgotten that minority–language vocational schools simply had not existed after the early 1950s. Likewise, minority-language lycées had existed only in the form of sections, as a result of mergers, and even in that form they operated at a greatly reduced capacity. In addition to this, it is worth mentioning that in the majority of cases such national-minority schools specialize in the fields of construction, textiles, and commerce, not in those industries that require greater skills, such as machine building or the chemical industry. This means that members of the national minorities can generally find positions only in relatively less significant fields. New problems for the minorities have been created in the area of specialized education by the establishment of mammoth schools, providing vocational training in ten to twelve fields within a single specialized technical lycée: there is no possibility of opening classes taught in the minority language for the eight to ten (or even fewer) minority pupils who enter any one of these courses.

The proportion of specialized technical lycées was further increased at the expense of academic lycées by the 1972–73 academic year. On a national scale the relative ratio of specialized technical lycées to academic lycées became 1: 1.5. In the Hungarian minority–school network, for example, only 17 percent of the lycée classes were of the specialized lycée type.

In accordance with need, where the parents and the pupils request it, new minority-language classes can be opened in the areas inhabited by national minorities. In such cases, this request must be included in a student's application for admission and the school is obliged to ensure that there is a teacher on the examination committee who is familiar with the language of the applicant. In many localities, particularly in towns and villages with a mixed population, the school heads are able to ignore this prescription, since Romanian hostility is such that no member of a national minority would dare to apply to take the examination in his or her mother tongue.

It has already been mentioned that entry into the specialized technical lycées and vocational secondary schools requires the passing of examinations in Romanian; this makes secondary and higher education more inaccessible and, in many cases, impossible for minority students. Although, according to a decree issued on July 3, 1969[73] everyone is entitled to take examinations in the mother tongue, this applies only to those subjects studied in the minority language. However, the syllabus for the entrance examination to the specialized technical lycées and vocational secondary schools does not include subjects taught in the minority languages, with the exception of mathematics. There have also been instances where the heads of certain specialized schools have refused to permit entrance examinations in the minority languages. It also happens, on occasion, that the written entrance examination which precedes the oral examination is not taken into consideration at all. Pupils often cannot take advantage of the possibility of taking the entrance examination in a minority language for the simple reason that the examination committees do not always include teachers who can speak those languages.

In a society on the road to industrialization, technical training is also indispensable for national-minority youth. The restriction imposed by the compulsory entrance examination in Romanian particularly hinders national-minority children from participating in the process of urbanization. For that very reason, one of the most serious problems of national-minority education has continued to be the ongoing recruitment of national-minority members of the professional intelligentsia.

In the 1973–1974 academic year, significant changes occurred in secondary education for the national minorities with regard to the number of schools and sections. The number of independent national-minority educational institutions was reduced considerably, while the number of national-minority sections within Romanian schools increased. According to official statistics, the number of Hungarian general-school and lycée pupils in Romania was 190,000 and a total of 2,383 Hungarian-language schools and sections with 220,000 pupils were in operation. Of the kindergartens and general schools, 1,230 were independent and 1,062 were sections within Romanian schools. At the same time, during the 1973–74 academic year, 60,992 German pupils were enrolled in German-language schools or sections: of these, 16,130 were enrolled in kindergarten, 40,071 in general schools, and 4,791 in academic lycées. The total number of German-language schools was 711, including both independent schools and sections.[74] In the same academic year there were 115 Serbian, Slovak, Ukrainian, Czech, Bulgarian, and Greek schools. German-language education was expanded—at least numerically—in the 1974–75 academic year, with the introduction of universal lycée education. In this academic year there were 340 kindergartens and kindergarten sections with 16,087 children, 355 general schools and general-school sections with 41,661 pupils, 28 lycées and lycée sections with 4,696 pupils. The total number of German-language schools was 723.[75]

German was the language of instruction during the 1975–1976 academic year in 324 kindergartens or sections attended by 14,878 children, 338 general schools or sections with 42,043 pupils, and 30 academic or specialized technical lycées or sections with 6,272 pupils. The total number of schools was 692.[76] In the academic year 1976–77 13,748 children were enrolled in 309 kindergartens and kindergarten sections, 41,737 pupils in 335 general schools and general-school sections and 5,689 pupils in 33 lycées and lycée sections. The total number of German-language schools and sections was 677,[77] while in 1977–78, 371 German-language general schools and 37 lycées were in operation.

According to official figures, during the 1976–77 academic year there were only 4,666 Hungarian students in the third year of the lycées entitled to grant graduation (baccalaureate), in contrast to the 8,300 who had completed the second year of lycée during the previous academic year. Hungarian was the language of instruction in a total of 128 lycée classes, including five academic, 48 industrial, eleven agricultural-industrial, one economic, two pedagogical, four sports, and three arts first-year lycée classes. It should be added, however, that of a total of 34,738 secondary school pupils whose mother tongue was Hungarian, 15,591 attended specialized technical lycées where the specialized subjects were taught exclusively in Romanian, because there was no Hungarian-language specialized education available for them. This, moreover, at an age decisive in the development of the individual personality and in laying the foundations for his vocational education. In this area the main problem has been the lack of minority teachers, the result of an absence of programs training minority teachers for the specialized technical lycées. Such a policy ignores the fact that pupils can acquire knowledge best in their native language.

In the academic year 1977–78 there were 1,393 Hungarian-language general schools and general-school sections and 112 lycées, of which 12 were independent and 100 were sections within Romanian schools. If, however, we compare these figures with data for 1947, the decline in numbers is quite clear: in 1947 there were 186 Hungarian secondary schools in Romania; of these, 147 were academic lycées, 17 teacher training colleges, 14 commercial and 8 industrial secondary schools; in Cluj alone there were 14 Hungarian-language lycées in 1947. Of the 147 theoretical lycées 38 had the right to grant the graduation (baccalaureate) degree. To put these figures in perspective, during the 1948–49 academic year there were a total of 217 academic lycées of all types in Romania, whereas in 1968–69 there were 568, to which should be added 53 art lycées and 415 specialized technical lycées as well as 191 vocational schools, making a total of 1,227.[78]

According to official statistics for the academic year 1976–77, 79.7 percent of Hungarian pupils attended Hungarian general schools and 20.3 percent attended Romanian schools;[79] by comparison about a third of German-minority pupils attended Romanian schools in the same academic year, whereby a further decrease has to be noted.

If, however, the proportions of Hungarian pupils in the various counties is taken into consideration, it becomes clear that the official figures falsify the situation: in reality the proportion of Hungarian pupils attending Romanian lycées in the academic year 1976–77 was approximately 30–40 percent; this proportion increased by 1977–78 to 47.83 percent. According to a situation report, in the 1975–1976 academic year, only 60 percent of the Hungarian elementary school pupils, 33 percent of those in secondary schools, and 17 percent of the technical and vocational school students attended Hungarian-language schools.[80]

German was the language of instruction during the 1976–1977 academic year in 309 kindergartens or sections attended by 13,748 children, 335 general schools or sections with 41,737 pupils, and 33 lycées or sections with 5,689 students.[81] In the same academic year there were 2,904 German teachers in the kindergartens and schools.[82] The proportion of German children attending German kindergartens or sections in the 1976–1977 academic year was 1.67 percent, in the general schools and sections 1.34 percent, in the independent lycées or sections 0.56 percent, and in the universities 1.17 percent.[83] At the time of the 1977 census, Germans accounted for 1.66 percent of the population of Romania.[84]

On the basis of an analysis of statistical data on elementary and intermediate education, it can be concluded that the number of minority students in Romania continued to decline in all educational institutions in the decade 1969–1979. While, for example, there were 3,479 minority schools in 1978, by 1980 their number had been reduced to about 3,300.[85] The most drastic reduction was experienced by the Hungarians: a continuous decrease in the amount of instruction in Hungarian, especially in secondary education can be observed. The

Germans are better represented in the lycées, but are under-represented in the lower classes. The losses suffered by the Jews were primarily the result of further emigration.

In contrast to the largest nationalities, smaller ethnic groups have enjoyed more support as a result of educational policy. Elementary schools for Polish and Turkish minorities were established in 1978, and elementary school textbooks have been published in Turkish, Polish, Czech, Bulgarian, and Greek.[86]

The development of higher education for the national minorities in Romania offers a very different, and at the same time, contradictory, picture: the largest nationalities, such as the Hungarians and Germans, have been under-represented on the higher educational level, while smaller ethnic groups—for clear tactical and political reasons—have enjoyed considerable support in this area.

In the academic year 1978–79 there were seven universities, ten technical colleges, four agricultural colleges, four medical schools, seven art academies, five teachers' colleges and four mixed colleges with 134 faculties; there were also four theological institutes of university rank and two theological seminaries.[87]

Teaching in the academic year 1978–79 in the languages of the national minorities was offered only in some sections at the following institutions of higher education: Babeş-Bolyai University in Cluj, the Institute of Medicine and Pharmacology in Tîrgu Mureş, and the István Szentgyörgyi Institute of Dramatic Arts in Tîrgu Mureş; lectures are read in Hungarian or in German at the Sibiu branch of Babeş-Bolyai in Cluj-Napoca and in the German studies program at the universities of Bucharest, Iaşi, and Timişoara. However, there is no separate German-language institution of higher education in Romania. It should be noted, however, that despite a high number of national-minority students, no teaching in their languages is offered at the ten technical colleges, four agricultural colleges, five teachers' colleges, and four mixed colleges. The situation is even worse in the field of technical training. During the 1977–78 academic year, all the arts-oriented academic lycées were reorganized as specialized technical lycées;[88] consequently a large percentage of the national-minority teachers lost their jobs, and the reorganized lycées do not have instruction in the minority languages.

By the end of the 1960's Hungarian-language higher education in Romania had been reduced to a minimum. Reference already been made to the statements of party leader N. Ceauşescu, at the March

12, 1971 plenary session of the Council of Working People of Hungarian Nationality, that Hungarian-language higher education would be expanded.[89] At the same time, the deputy rector of Babeş-Bolyai University in Cluj also admitted that "there were setbacks, mistakes. . ." in providing higher education for the national minorities in their mother tongue.[90]

At the beginning of the 1970s lectures were also given in Hungarian at the Gheorghe Dima Conservatory in Cluj, the Ion Andreescu Institute of Visual Arts and, to some extent, the teachers' college in Tîrgu Mureş. At the Institute of Medicine and Pharmacology of Tîrgu Mureş all teaching was originally in Hungarian; later, Romanian was also introduced, and, by the beginning of the 1960s, teaching in Hungarian ceased. After 1969 some parallel Romanian and Hungarian lectures were introduced. In fact, however, only some of the lectures and seminars of a theoretical nature are given in the two languages, while practical training is in Romanian, a situation which is the source of much difficulty.

The István Szentgyörgyi Institute of Dramatic Arts in Tîrgu Mureş used Hungarian exclusively until 1976; later, however, it was Romanianized, and at present it is under Romanian administration. This is the institute which provides actors and directors for the Hungarian theatre in Romania.

On May 10, 1971, the Ministry of Education issued a document concerning the status of the University of Cluj, which contained a list of subjects that could be taught in Hungarian. According to this document, the social sciences would henceforth have instruction in Hungarian in 17 subjects in 11 faculties (nine in Cluj and two in Sibiu). At the same time, a Hungarian-language lectorate was to be established at the faculty of law for teaching legal terminology. Courses supplementing the main subjects could be offered in either Romanian or Hungarian as needed, and, in the same way, translation from foreign languages could also be made into Hungarian in certain circumstances. The ultimate result of this legislation, however, was that subjects taught in the nationality languages were constantly introduced, abolished, and reintroduced, thereby creating a sense of permanent uncertainty.

Although the 1971 statements appeared to herald a positive move away from the patterns of the previous period, they were never, in fact, implemented. Although teaching in Hungarian did begin for a few groups in some of the subjects listed, these classes were frequently abolished, with the excuse that there were too few applicants. Thus, the teaching of subjects in the languages of the national minorities came to depend entirely on the number of minority students gaining admission to the university. On the other hand, university admission has frequently been based on nationality quotas. Incidentally, practical seminars and the activities of youth organizations within the universities are still conducted exclusively in Romanian.

The Babeş-Bolyai University of Cluj is, on the whole, dominated by a Romanian administration. There is no institutional arrangement to ensure the dual-nationality (Romanian and Hungarian) character of the university, and there are no separate Romanian and Hungarian sections for individual subjects. The only group for whom instruction is entirely in Hungarian are those students studying Hungarian in the Department of Hungarian Language and Literature, which is part of the Faculty of Philology. Teaching in German is offered in the Faculty of German Studies.

There are no precise data on the number of national-minority students attending higher educational institutions; it may be said, however, that their number is very small in comparison with their share of the total population. Thus, while the number of university students in Romania between 1950 and 1979 nearly quadrupled, the number of Hungarian students, for example, rose by only about ten percent.

Out of a total of 108,750 full-time students in higher educational institutions in 1974-75, for example, only 6,188 were Hungarian.[91] It is worth comparing these figures with data relating to the 1950-51 academic year, when 4,082 Hungarian students attended Hungarian-language higher educational institutions; to this must be added 1,000-1,500 Hungarian students enrolled in technical courses at Romanian universities, making a total of 5,500 students out of a national total of 53,007 full-time students in institutions of higher education.[92]

At Babeş-Bolyai University in Cluj there were in 1970-71 6,363 students, distributed among the various nationalities as follows: 4,928 Romanians (72.7 percent), 1,048 Hungarians (16.5 percent), 223 Germans and 164 others. At the beginning of the 1976-77 academic year Babeş-Bolyai University had approximately 6,000 students; of 1,206 first-year students, 269 belonged to the Hungarian minority. However, not all the Hungarian students were able to attend lectures in Hungarian. These were attended by only eight percent of the students; thus, the majority of Hungarians were enrolled in courses taught entirely in

Romanian. Similarly, while 210 of the approximately 900 members of the academic staff were Hungarian, a high proportion of them taught in Romanian.

German students, like Hungarians, are also under-represented in higher educational institutions. Their number in 1976–77 was 1,965, representing 1.17 percent of the students enrolled in higher education in Romania.[93]

An examination of the number of students of other nationalities in higher education reveals a very different development. Jews were represented to a very high degree in Romanian universities and colleges in 1956; however, the 1966 census indicated a considerable reduction on all levels of the educational system. This decline was largely the result of emigration.

The Gypsies are virtually unrepresented in higher educational institutions in Romania, a reflection of the high rate of illiteracy among them. On the other hand, Russians and Serbs are represented to a considerable extent.

Thus, one must conclude that only those intending to become physicians or teachers have a chance of receiving a higher education in a minority language in Romania today. In the faculties of natural science and technology, the proportion of students belonging to the national minorities is much smaller than the proportion of those nationalities in the total population.

In contrast to the period between the two world wars, very few university students belonging to the national minorities can now study abroad. Hungarian–minority students, for example, cannot attend universities in Hungary; a total of twenty students were given permission to study in Hungary in 1971, but now even this number would be out of the question.

The further development of secondary education is determined, in turn, by the system of university education. The difficulties of passing the university entrance examinations, which are in Romanian, means that those who have attended a Romanian secondary school stand a much better chance of getting into a university than those who have attended a nationality–secondary school. Thus, the university situation serves to deter national-minority families from insisting on their children's attending secondary schools with instruction in their native tongue and pressures them to transfer their children to Romanian schools at that stage of the educational process. In any case, only a very few minority-language schools in each town or city have been permitted to set up eleventh and twelfth grades to complement the basic grades, which means that large numbers of minority pupils are forced to complete the last two years of schooling necessary for university admission in a Romanian-language school. In other words, the higher one moves in the educational process, the more Romanian it becomes.

The professional placement of college and university graduates plays an important role in the university policy of the Romanian government. The state places graduates in jobs which they are obliged to accept and does this in such a way that members of the national minorities—and particularly those who have demonstrated their attachment to their nationality by attending classes taught in their own language—inevitably find themselves in a comparatively worse position. For example, a high proportion of Hungarian graduates are given jobs in predominantly Romanian areas, and even if they are employed in areas inhabited by Hungarians, they are generally appointed to teach in primary, not secondary, schools. It has thus happened that the graduates of the Tîrgu Mureş Teacher Training College who received teaching diplomas in mathematics, chemistry, and physics in 1971–72 and the newly qualified pharmacologists from the Medical University were given posts in the Regat, not in Transylvania. As a result of this practice, there are a great number of Hungarian physicians in the villages of Moldavia.

There are two "internal instructions" and several "subsidiary rules" governing the placement of university and college graduates. The first states that the Placement Commission (*Comisia de Repartizare*) is obliged to secure a post for all students upon graduation. The second obliges the student, by means of a written agreement, to accept the post offered by the commission. There are various ways of abusing these measures, and the national minorities are usually placed in a disadvantaged position.

According to the existing regulations, university entrance examinations may be conducted in a minority language at the request of the candidate; however, it is certainly not advisable to try to take advantage of this provision. It is generally accepted that the possibilities of receiving permission to take an entrance examination in a minority language are somewhat more favorable for applicants to universities and colleges outside Transylvania provided, of course, that there are lecturers speaking those languages.

The Educational Status of the Csángó-Hungarians of Moldavia

As was already mentioned, briefly, in Chapter I, the Csángó Hungarians of Moldavia, are a group of ethnic Hungarians numbering approximately 100,000 to 150,000 who live east of the Carpathians. Their educational problems must be included in the education of the Hungarian nationality in Romania, since their national consciousness links them organically with the Hungarians living in Transylvania.

The organization of a school network for the Csángó Hungarians of Moldavia began, by and large, after the end of the Second World War, since in this part of Moldavia, most villages had not previously had any schools at in the vernacular.[94]

The organization of Hungarian schools here met with obstacles from the very beginning, particularly because of the resistance of the Catholic Church of Moldavia, which aimed at the Romanianization of the Csángós. It should be noted that the young priests who had already been used by the Romanian government between the wars to encourage the Romanianization of the Csángó Hungarians were trained at the Romanian Catholic Seminary in Iași.

In the 1947–48 academic year 72 Hungarian schools were established in eight Csángó Hungarian villages; from 1952–53 the Bacău regional people's council organized literacy courses in the Csángó villages. By the 1952–53 academic year, there were Hungarian-language kindergartens in thirteen villages, with 30 to 33 children in each. The schools could have become a means for the development of national consciousness under socialist conditions by the Csángó Hungarians, who had lived under great oppression in the interwar period, but the schools were abolished after three or four years. At first, officials and Church leaders began a campaign against Hungarian education among the population, and then in many cases the Hungarian parents themselves, having been persuaded, appealed to the government, asking that the Hungarian schools be abolished.[95]

At the beginning of the 1950s, Hungarian teachers were trained at the Bacău Teacher Training College. In the 1952–53 academic year, the Hungarian section was attended by 31 students; the teaching staff for this section had two members, and in the following year, four. In the Székler region, eight-month Hungarian-language teacher training courses were organized for Csángó youth. This measure could have helped lay the foundations for a Csángó Hungarian intelligentsia; however, this program was also eliminated in 1958.

For a long time the situation of the Csángó Hungarians in Romania could not even be mentioned in print. The first real reports began to appear only at the beginning of the 1970s, and shortly thereafter, the Romanian authorities banned all further discussion of the Csángó problem.

The Supervision of National-Minority Education.

The direction and supervision of education in Romania at the national level is the responsibility of the Ministry of Education. It is the Ministry which appoints and dismisses teachers, principals, and school inspectors on the recommendation of the county councils. The activities of the school inspectors, however, fall under the control of a central organ, the Inspectors' Directorate. Thus, the system of education in Romania is characterized by a high degree of centralization of administration.

As for the direction of minority education in Romania, after the mergers at the end of the 1950s, the nationality administrative organs, the school inspectorates, ceased to exist, and the administrative reorganization of the counties rapidly excluded members of the national minorities from local educational administration.

The Directorate for Nationality Schools, whose task it is to deal with the special problems of nationality education, was established again within the framework of the Ministry in 1970. This organ, however, is limited to dealing with the problems arising in individual classes within the school system. It does not have general jurisdiction over minority educational problems.

At the county level, the supervision of education is the responsibility of the county school inspectorate, which is under the direct control of the county council on the one hand and of the Ministry of Education on the other. Professional supervision is carried out within the framework of the school inspectorates.

As already mentioned, with the abolition of the national-minority organs for the direction of education, the number of educational specialists belonging to the national minorities in the county school inspectorates was significantly reduced, at least outside the most homogeneous nationality areas. National–minority schools—and even minority sections—are generally directed by Romanian principals or chairmen, with the members of the minorities occupying subordinate posts only.

In 1971, the number of Hungarian principals and assistant principals of general schools was 1,430. In the overwhelming majority of cases, Hungarian principals directed only the independent Hungarian schools, while in jointly directed institutions it was the general practice for the principal to be Romanian and his assistant to be a member of a national minority.

Teachers Training

The system of continuing education for teachers—regulated by the Statute for Teachers[96]—is well developed in Romania; in certain respects, it is linked to professional and financial advancement. Some courses of this kind are organized by the Central Institute for the Continuing Education of Teachers or its branches in the provinces, while others are organized by the county school inspectorates. All teachers are obliged to pass an examination within three years of graduation in order to obtain tenure; with the exception of Hungarian and German language and literature specialists, all teachers must take this examination in Romanian.

The training of kindergarten and primary-school teachers is done in five-year pedagogical lycées. In general, there is one pedagogical lycée in each county. The training of the national-minority teachers in Romanian in most of these institutions is a source of serious problems in national-minority education.

A further supply of Hungarian teachers is provided by the three-year Teacher Training College in Tîrgu Mureş and, in part, also by the University of Cluj-Napoca. Between 1960 and 1965 the number of those who received diplomas in Hungarian language and literature increased from 29 to 39; at the same time, however, the number of those earning degrees in Romanian language and literature increased from 40 to 218.

Since the 1972–73 academic year, there has been a Hungarian-language teacher-training college in Oradea, and similar sections in operation at Aiud/Nagyenyed and the Pedagogical Lycée in Odorhei/Székelyudvarhely. Since 1976, however, no new Hungarian first or third-year classes have been organized at Aiud, and in Odorhei there is now only a class for kindergarten teachers. There are also Hungarian-language schools for training kindergarten teachers in Miercurea Ciuc/Csíkszereda, Odorhei, Oradea, and Aiud. Teachers for the German-language schools are trained in the Pedagogical Lycée in Sibiu/Hermannstadt.

Textbooks

The publication of textbooks for the national minorities in Romania is the responsibility of the Textbook and Educational Publishing House. The vast majority of minority-language textbooks are poor translations of Romanian school textbooks, using vocabulary and modes of expression which are often incomprehensible to the pupils. The situation is much the same with regard to methodological handbooks. Given this, it does not take much imagination to picture for oneself the low quality of instruction in the history of nationality literature, for example. The situation is even worse, however, in the field of history. National-minority pupils are not taught the history of their own people or the true history of Transylvania, but are presented with a distorted and falsified picture that reflects the spirit of Romanian nationalism.[97] In this way, an attempt is made to deprive these children of their natural historical and cultural heritage. After all, the teaching of language and literature is one of the most important aspects of the development of national consciousness. Aside from history, this is the subject which best transmits the cultural traditions of a national minority to students, and the acquisition of the foundations of a national culture is what enables an individual to take part in the life of a national minority. Naturally, the use of the mother-tongue in the teaching of all subjects as well as in extra-curricular activities is also an important part of this process. It is a characteristic reflection on contemporary Romanian historiography that, at textbook conferences attended by historians from the Federal Republic of Germany and Romania, whose purpose is the harmonization and mutual correction of the historiography of those two countries, there are frequently significant differences of opinion about the history of Transylvania. "Every time the three countries (Moldavia, Muntenia, and Transylvania) were discussed," according to the report of one conference, "Transylvania, which belonged to Hungary until 1918, was placed in a light which did not accord with historical reality" by the Romanian historians.[98]

Just as in the case of historiography, the depiction of the literary history of the national minorities leaves out—apart from the private endeavors of a few lecturers—the national historical connections; the pupil thus cannot form a realistic picture of national development over the centuries. The student teachers in the teacher-training colleges can only obtain books which have been arbitrarily prescribed by the educational plan as "compulsory matter" in accordance with the official point of view. Furthermore, there is not a sufficient number of books in the minority languages in the school libraries for the use of minority pupils. The shortage of reading material in the nationality languages also hinders the work of primary and secondary school teachers in the provinces. Because of prescribed quotas, the Kriterion nationality publishing house rarely publishes specialized works or, if it does, publishes them in insufficient numbers.

As for the educational press, the weekly educational journal of the Ministry of Education, is also published in Hungarian (*Tanügyi Újság*); it has, however, little to say about the problems of national-minority education.

Conclusion

In analyzing the educational opportunities provided for the national minorities, not only the number and quality of nationality schools, but also their effective geographical distribution must be considered. From the point of view of Hungarian education, for example,—on a relative scale—qualitatively different conditions exist in the Székler counties, where there is an overwhelming majority of Hungarians. Different conditions also exist in those Transylvanian towns and cities with strong national-minority cultural traditions and a high proportion of national-minority inhabitants (*e.g.*, Cluj-Napoca, Oradea, Brașov, Sibiu, Arad, Timișoara). In those areas where the number of national minorities is fairly small in relation to the total population, conditions are much worse.

The German population still lives in the Transylvanian cities and their environs; its school network is also centered largely in these areas. This means that as the proportion of the German population constantly decreases as a result of German emigration and the Romanianization of the cities, German-language education faces an ever-growing crisis.

More recently, nationality education in Romania reached such a state in the late 1970s that national-minority schools were institutions of nationality education in name only; in reality, the aim of all education in Romania was and is none other than the creation of a "unified socialist nation" whose language is Romanian. Some examples of the educational methods employed in different types of schools in areas inhabited by the national minorities can shed light on the Romanianization and possible elimination of the minority-language school network on all levels.

Let us start with an examination of the history of the chemistry department at the University of Cluj. At the time of the merger of the Hungarian and Romanian universities in 1959, general chemistry was taught in Hungarian at Bolyai University, while at the Romanian-language Babeş University, in addition to general chemistry, physical chemistry was also taught. In the new joint university, up until 1962, general chemistry was taught in parallel classes in both languages. Then, however, in an effort to eliminate instruction in Hungarian, the entire subject was abolished, and replaced by analytical chemistry which was taught, like physical chemistry, in Romanian only. In 1964, general chemistry was reintroduced, and a few courses in Hungarian were introduced in the field of physical chemistry as well. In the 1970s physical chemistry was abolished as a subject in turn, to be replaced by the chemistry of construction materials. Although Hungarian students are enrolled in this course, none of the teaching is in Hungarian. Here, again, the method employed has been to create an atmosphere of insecurity, thereby eliminating resistance and opening the way for the eventual abolition of instruction in Hungarian, by discouraging Hungarian students from requesting classes taught in Hungarian.

Another highly characteristic development can be seen in the training of teachers in the chemistry department of the University of Cluj. Traditionally, after four years of teachers training there has been a fifth year in which students are trained to do scientific research. Only a small proportion of those completing the fourth year are admitted to the fifth year, while the rest are given teaching diplomas. Characteristically, in 1976, while 84 Romanian and 38 Hungarian students were enrolled in fourth-year classes in general chemistry, none of the Hungarians was admitted to the fifth year. This indicates, once more, the tendency of the university system to limit national-minority students to a teaching career, thereby not allowing them to rise above the level of medium-grade intelligentsia.

The universities are under the direction of the so-called University Scientific Council, which issues internal directives regulating university operations. One such directive, for example, prescribed that the students in any one year may be divided into several seminar groups, each consisting of at least 15 students. This measure, too, has been applied in a manner which discriminates against national-minority students, as can be illustrated by the following example: let us assume that the first-year class of a biology department has 60 students and, thus, four study-groups. Of the four groups, three will be Romanian and one will be national-minority and if there have been fewer than 15 national-minority applicants, there will be four Romanian groups and no national-minority groups at all. If, for example, only 11 of the national-minority applicants have been permitted to pass the entrance examination, then four Romanian applicants will be added to the eleven national-minority students and a new Romanian language group will be established for them. In this case there will once again be no national-minority group. The same method has been employed in other faculties as well.

The following illustrations are characteristic of the entire system of secondary education:

At the end of the Second World War there were 11 Hungarian-language gymnasia in Cluj; of these, seven were entitled to issue graduation certificates. There were three more Hungarian-language gymnasia in the county, making a total of 14. By the beginning of the 1973–74 academic year only nine academic lycées in Cluj provided instruction in Hungarian with five more in the surrounding region; altogether this amounts to 14, but, nonetheless, this change in distribution also reflected a qualitative deterioration. At the beginning of the 1976–77 academic year, there were seven Hungarian academic-lycée classes in Cluj-Napoca, and another four in the countryside, making a total of 11. Thus, the deterioration is quite clear. It becomes even more manifest if we take into consideration the fact that the educational system had in the meantime been reorganized, and instead of its traditional, narrower task of training future teachers and intellectuals, it was given the broader task of mass education. In 1973, at the beginning of the academic year, there were 32 Romanian-language academic lycées in the city of Cluj-Napoca and a further 29 in the county, making a total of 61. By 1976, there were 74 Romanian-language classes in the county as a whole.[99] Thus, while education in the languages of the nationalities declined, the development of Romanian-language education was constant and rapid. It should be remembered that at the beginning of the 1970s almost half of the population of Cluj-Napoca was of Hungarian nationality, and it was only the large-scale settlement of Romanians which succeeded in changing the national composition of this traditional Hungarian city.

The school system in Tîrgu Mureş offers a similar picture. At the end of the war, there were three independent Hungarian-language lycées providing instruction up to graduation level, while at present, there are three lycées which also have Hungarian classes. In 1974 there were still three independent Hungarian-language lycées in the city and two in the countryside. The present proportions are as follows: there are twelve Romanian and eight Hungarian sections in the lycées of Tîrgu Mureş. If all the schools are taken into consideration, including the general schools (which count as academic schools), there are eight with instruction in Hungarian, as opposed to 36 teaching in Romanian. Of the three lycées with parallel Romanian and Hungarian classes, one has a Hungarian principal and the other two have Romanians. The direction of development is also indicated by the decline of the number of Hungarian primary and secondary school teachers during the past ten years, while the number of Romanian teachers has increased from 110 to more than a thousand.[100] This process has no relation to nationality needs, since according to the official census of 1956, 73.8 percent of the population of Tîrgu Mureş belonged to the Hungarian nationality.

The situation in the specialized technical lycées in the city and county of Cluj is as follows: at the beginning of the 1973–74 academic year there were 174 first-year classes in the specialized technical lycées of the county. In two of these, the language of instruction was Hungarian. One was a class being trained for work in the textile and ready-made clothing industry and the other was being trained for careers in the construction industry. The Romanian-language schools included classes providing training for careers in such fields as teaching, health, agriculture, engineering, electrical technology, chemical industry, communications, etc. The nature of the differentiation is quite apparent: teaching is offered in Hungarian only in those fields that are low in prestige; in the more "elite" fields, the instruction is entirely in Romanian. In the beginning of the 1976–77 academic year, in Mureş County a specialized education in Romanian was available in 192 specialized technical lycée classes, including 159 concentrating in the field of industry, 13 in the field of agriculture, and 20 in the fields of economics and only nine classes had instruction in Hungarian: one was in the field of agriculture, the other eight in the field of industry. The vocational composition of the latter had been improved by the addition of mechanics, electromechanics, and metallurgy to the earlier list of subjects. It is worth comparing the ratio of specialized technical to academic lycées: in the case of Romanian-language classes, the proportion was 192:72 in favor of the specialized technical lycées, while in the case of Hungarian-language classes, the proportion was 9:11 in favor of the academic ones.[101] On the other hand, it appears that in Mureş County (Hungarian Maros) over 40 percent of Hungarian pupils have to attend Romanian-language schools. It should be noted that, in accordance with official data, as of July 1, 1967 the total population of Mureş County was 567,532, of which 280,495 were Romanian and 252,551, Hungarian.[102] All of these figures reveal the extent to which the official statistics provide a misleading picture of reality.

In Romania the compulsory teaching of the language of the majority nation in the national-minority schools,[103] at the expense of the minority-languages, has become one of the most controversial issues of nationality education. While it is desirable that states inhabited by several nationalities encourage all of their peoples to learn one another's languages, no member of any nationality should be discriminated against for not speaking any language other than his own.

A national-minority child in Romania first encounters the Romanian language in kindergarten, as part of the educational program. Later, beginning with the first grade of general school, Romanian language is a compulsory subject. Some of the teachers who teach Romanian belong to the minorities, but others are Romanian, even though it would be best, in order to ensure effective teaching, if the teachers could speak the same language as their pupils. Incidentally, it is worth mentioning here that, according to regulations, the so-called "pioneer work" (student study groups) must be organized jointly by the Romanian and the nationality students, with Romanian as the common language.[104] Similarly, all other school activities are also organized jointly for the Romanian and the national–minority pupils.

The situation in the general schools varies widely in different areas, depending on whether there is a compact national-minority population, a mixed population, or only a very small amount of national-minority population. In the compact nationality areas, such as the

Székler region (inhabited by Hungarians), young people encounter the Romanian language for the first time in school; in many cases, even in the towns and cities with a mixed population the minority–school child is very rarely exposed to the Romanian language in his daily life, since his family generally only speaks its native language at home. Bilingualism from early childhood is typical primarily in those areas with a very small national-minority population. It is thus a violation of the interests of the inhabitants of compact national-minority areas to expect them to speak perfect Romanian. Furthermore, it is unfortunate that the question of the majority people learning the languages of the co-inhabiting nationalities in those areas with a mixed population or where the minority population predominates has not even been raised. In the Romanian-language schools of the Székler region, for example, optional Hungarian language instruction has yet to be made available.

It is often argued that young people from the national minorities will find themselves in a disadvantaged position unless they become proficient in the official language of the state. As a matter of fact, a young person belonging to one of the national minorities is handicapped if his mother-tongue is in a handicapped position, if it counts as a merely second-class language alongside the "state language." And the words of the General Secretary of the RCP, Nicolae Ceaușescu, make it clear that this is the status of the minority languages in Romania today: "The Romanian language is not a foreign tongue for any young person living in Romania. This is the language of our socialist society and it must be acquired by all Romanian citizens. This is the only way in which the realistic conditions for equality before the law can be fulfilled."[105] On another occasion, speaking about the problems of the Hungarian and German national minorities, the General Secretary declared: "In education we must keep in the forefront of our attention the fact that under present-day conditions we should not concentrate exclusively or primarily on the question of whether education is provided in one language or another, although this also has a certain significance, but—quite apart from the language—we should concentrate on the content of education. . . . Does it transgress against the national sentiments of someone when he is told, for example, that he must learn Arabic to work in an Arab country?"[106]

The complex of issues relating to the minority languages will long continue to be one of the most crucial aspects of national-minority education, judging from past developments. At a time when equal rights in language usage has become an international issue, linguistic intolerance is an incomprehensible anachronism in Central Europe. The national minorities in Romania—as compared with the majority nation—do not have equal opportunities to obtain vocational training or to secure their future through social institutions and organs defending their right to existence and development. It is in the interests of the national minorities to learn the language of the majority nation; however, to make this compulsory and to employ sanctions against those who do not speak the language of the majority nation is irreconcilable with the spirit of the present age.

6

THE CHURCHES OF THE NATIONAL MINORITIES IN ROMANIA

Historical Background and the Period Between the Two World Wars

For centuries Transylvania was outstanding as a land of religious freedom, tolerance and diversity. At a time when religious wars were wreaking havoc elsewhere in Europe, Transylvania became the first land to proclaim freedom of religion. Between 1544 and 1575 no fewer than twenty-two laws guaranteeing freedom of conscience were enacted. In 1557, for example, the first Diet of Torda (Turda) granted Lutherans the right to free religious observance; the same freedom was accorded the Calvinists in 1564. In 1568, four "received" religions were recognized: the Roman Catholic, the Calvinist, the Lutheran, and the Unitarian.

By contrast, before the First World War, the Orthodox Church was the predominant and official religion in Romania. Almost 95 percent of the population of the Old Kingdom belonged to the Orthodox faith;[1] Jews, Catholics (the archbishopric of Bucharest and the bishopric of Iaşi), Protestants, and Unitarians accounted for the rest.

Tensions between the churches and the Romanian state arose as a result of the annexation of new territories after the First World War. The religious homogeneity of the Old Romanian Kingdom was lost with the incorporation of Transylvania and regions of the Banat, Bessarabia, and Bucovina. This development had profound political and social implications. A vital condition for the political consolidation of the new multinational Romania now became the development of close ties between the state and the various churches in the new territories. This was particularly so in light of the fact that the geographical boundaries between the different denominations coincided almost exactly with the boundaries between the various nationalities. Generally, membership in a given faith also meant membership in a given nationality.

Moreover, the churches saw the cultivation of national consciousness as one of their major responsibilities and their historic role in this process made them a force to be reckoned with. The newly-established (1918) Romanian state could therefore not rely exclusively on the traditional guardian of Romanian nationhood, Orthodoxy, in the consolidation of Greater Romania: peaceful coexistence with the national minorities assumed a certain degree of tolerance on the part of the state toward the non-Orthodox churches as well. And, in fact, the churches of the nationalities became, during the period of oppression of the minorities between the two world wars, an even more important factor, not only in the area of religion, but also in the cultural, social and political spheres.

The confessional situation was made even more complex by the presence of one-million-and-one-half Transylvanian Romanians of the Uniate faith.[2] The awakening of Romanian national consciousness had begun among the Transylvanian Uniate clergy, the so-called *Şcoala Ardeleană* (Transylvanian School), in the 18th century.[3]

The Transylvanian Roman Catholic Church presented as great a problem for the post-war Romanian state as did the Uniates. The Roman Catholics, who numbered approximately 1.3 million, mainly of Hungarian nationality, had the oldest traditions. On several occasions this Church had played a decisive role in the internal and external politics of the state; this made the confrontation between the Catholic Church and Romanian Orthodoxy, the official state religion, all the more serious. Like the Uniate Church, the Roman Catholic Church aimed at securing religious equality. With the support of international Catholicism and its own political weight, it proved capable, on the whole, of defending the cultural and political interests of the Hungarian, Banat Swabian and other Catholic national minorities in Romania between the two world wars.

The two main Protestant churches, the Reformed (Calvinist) Church and the Lutheran Church were also a significant factor in Romania between the wars. The adherents of the Calvinist Church numbered over 700,000, almost all of them Hungarian, while the number of Lutherans in the whole of Romania amounted to approximately 400,000, most of them Germans but also including a group of Hungarians. However, from a political point of view, neither the Calvinist nor the Lutheran Church was a factor of great significance; their importance was manifested primarily in the cultural and social spheres. The Lutheran Church did take on political importance from the 1930s onward, as a result of Romania's German orientation.

The historical development, status, and membership of the minority churches and the Romanian Uniate Church during the interwar period will be analyzed more closely in the section that follows. In determining the membership of each, non-Romanian sources as well as Romanian census data will be taken into consideration.

The Roman Catholic Church in Transylvania, as stated, had the oldest traditions. The Bishopric of Gyulafehérvár/Alba Iulia was founded in 1010 and the Bishopric of Nagyvárad/Oradea in 1077. (The oldest data concerning the Catholic population of Transylvania comes from papal taxation lists of 1332–37). Between the two world wars the Roman Catholic Church consisted of one archbishopric in Bucharest and the seven dioceses: Alba Iulia of Transylvania, Oradea, Csanád, Satu Mare/Szatmár, Timișoara/Temesvár, Iași and in Tiraspol; Satu Mare and Oradea were merged into a single bishopric. It had 177 churches, 669 parishes, 21 chapels, 116 monasteries and convents, several welfare and charitable institutions and religious societies, 8 periodical publications, and 6 theological colleges. The number of adherents in the whole of Romania was approximately 1,234,000, of whom 850,000 were Hungarian; the rest was made up of a large number of Germans and some Slovaks, Armenians, Czechs, Poles, and Croats. Hungarian Catholics were concentrated most densely in northwestern Transylvania, along the Hungarian-Romanian border, in the Székler region, and in Bacău and Roman counties of Moldavia (the Csángó Hungarians). The majority of German Catholics lived in the Banat (Swabians of the Banat), around Satu Mare, in the area of the Regat, and in Bessarabia, Bucovina, and various towns.

The traditions of the Transylvanian Lutheran Church dated back to 1542–43, when at the prompting of Johannes Honterus, the Transylvanian reformer (1489–1549), the Catholic Saxons of Kronstadt and Burzenland, adopted the Protestant religion; the rest of the Saxons in Transylvania followed suit in 1547.[4] The oldest body of the Church in Transylvania was the *Evangelische Landeskirche Augsburgischer*

Bekenntnisses in Siebenbürgen (Transylvanian Evangelical National Church of the Augsburg Confession).

The organization encompassing all German adherents of the Lutheran Church in Romania, the *Evangelische Landeskirche A. B. in Rumänien* (The Evangelical National Church A.B. of Romania), was founded in 1926-27. Altogether approximately 350,000 Germans belonged to it, distributed among the different territories as follows: in Transylvania, 240,000; in Bessarabia, 66,000; in Bucovina, 20,000; in the various cities and towns of the Regat and in Dobrugea 16,000; and in the Banat, 8,000. Before the Second World War the Lutheran Church had one bishop in Sibiu/Hermannstadt, 14 deaconries, 332 parishes, and one theological college. The number of adherents in the whole of Romania amounted to approximately 400,000-450,000, almost all of them of the German nationality, but also including a group of Hungarians (12,000), approximately 2,700 Gypsies and about 1,000 Slavs.

The Transylvanian Reformed (Calvinist) Church before the First World War had two episcopal dioceses, whose seats were in Cluj and Oradea, 26 church-districts, 780 churches and parishes. The Church also had one theological college with nine departments, and five periodical publications.[5] Adherents numbered approximately 700,000-750,000, all of them Hungarian.

The Transylvanian Unitarian Church had one bishop, whose seat was in Cluj, eight dioceses, and 113 parishes, with approximately 70,000 adherents, all of them Hungarian. It published two ecclesiastical journals, the *Keresztény Magvető* (Christian Sower) and the *Unitárius Közlöny* (Unitarian Information).

The Jewish faith had no central organization: the 922 synagogues, with 731 rabbis, were dispersed all over the country. The members of the Jewish community numbered approximately 750,000. The Greek Catholic (Uniate) Church consisted almost exclusively of persons of Romanian nationality, with a small number of Hungarians, Greeks, Serbs, and Bulgarians. It comprised one archbishopric and four dioceses with episcopal rank. There were 1,725 churches with 1,594 priests, 34 canons, and 75 prelates. Three theological seminaries were available for the training of the clergy. The number of adherents in the whole of Romania amounted to approximately 1,400,000. In addition, there were a number of smaller religious communities.[6]

After the annexation of Transylvania, the Alba Iulia Resolutions of December 1, 1918 guaranteed in paragraph 2 of Section 3, "equal rights and full ecclesiastical autonomy for all the religions in the state"; the same guarantees were made in Article 2 of the Minorities Treaty of December 9, 1919, according to which "every inhabitant of Romania is entitled to practice freely any faith, religion, or persuasion, publicly or at home, insofar as these practices are not contrary to public order and morality." Article 137 of the Romanian Constitution of 1923 also guaranteed all the rights of the churches, but Article 22 declared the Romanian Orthodox Church to be the dominant, privileged church. The Constitution also gave preference to the predominantly Romanian Greek Catholic (Uniate) Church over the other churches; the Uniate Church, together with the Orthodox Church, formed the "national Church," whereby the privileged position of the two Romanian Churches implied a certain discrimination against the others. A law published on May 6, 1925, relating to the organization of the Orthodox Church, confirmed the status of Orthodoxy as the dominant faith of Romania.

The Law on Cults (No. 1,093), issued on April 22, 1928, regulated relations between the state and the churches, as well as the legal position of the churches in Romania, and relations between the different denominations. With the exception of the small communities— designated by the law as sects— all religious organizations enjoyed equal freedom in the spiritual sphere at this time, but, with the exception of the Roman Catholic Church, the state was to exercise administrative supervision: its permission was required for the establishment of new parishes, and it had control over church educational institutions. Similarly, the state had to approve all ecclesiastical measures and determined the number of senators nominated by the churches.

The 1928 Law on Cults also affirmed the dominant position of Orthodoxy and the privileged position accorded to the Greek Catholic (Uniate) Church; the Roman Catholic, Reformed (Calvinist), Lutheran, Unitarian, Armeno-Gregorian, Jewish, and Mohammedan faiths were referred to as "historic churches." The state exerted stricter control over the non-Romanian churches, particularly over their political activities. Thus, Article 6 of the Law prohibited the creation of political organizations on a confessional basis and prohibited ecclesiastical corporations and institutions from dealing with political issues.

Relations between the Romanian state and the Roman Catholic Church were regulated by the Concordat concluded on May 10, 1927 and ratified after the adoption of the Law on Cults, on July 9, 1929. Although this agreement between the Holy See and the Romanian government guaranteed full freedom for the Roman Catholic Church and seemingly secured its rights vis-à-vis the dominant Orthodox Church, it also limited the almost thousand year-old autonomy of the Church in Transylvania by subordinating the Hungarian bishoprics of the annexed territories to the Romanian archbishopric of Bucharest, which had only a small number of members. Although the state did not extend its direct control over the Catholic educational institutions, it reserved the right to approve the selection of teaching staff and the composition of the syllabus. Charitable and welfare institutions, such as Catholic hospitals, dispensaries, orphanages, homes for the elderly, and nurseries did not come under state supervision. On the other hand, with only a few exceptions, the Roman Catholic Church was not given financial support by the state. It is also worth noting that this Concordat was reached in the face of strong opposition from the Orthodox Church.

At the end of the First World War the national-minority churches in Romania were supported largely by incomes from church property. However, the Romanian agrarian reform of 1921 expropriated a large percentage of these landholdings, thus destroying a large part of the churches' financial base. A total of 277,645 yokes of land were taken from the Roman Catholic bishoprics in Transylvania, leaving them with only 13,104 yokes; 36,686 yokes of land were taken away from the Calvinist bishoprics, leaving them with 44,420.[7] At the same time an additional 58,000 yokes of land were expropriated from the Transylvanian Lutheran Church. According to the Agrarian Reform Act, each parish could keep 32 yokes of land, but of the 240 Saxon parishes, for example, only 42 received their full quota.[8] Among the Roman Catholic parishes, 119 were left without any land.[9]

According to the data of the December 29, 1930 Romanian census—to offer a final bit of statistical data on religious confessions—the population of the whole of Romania and Transylvania was divided among the various denominations as shown in Table VI-1.

The Legal Position After the Second World War

The churches in Romania found themselves in very different circumstances after the Second World War. In general, during the immediate post-war period, the various religious communities were able to retain their prewar administrative status. For the time being, it was in

CHURCHES OF THE NATIONAL MINORITIES

TABLE VI-1

Religion	Romania	Percent	Transylvania	Percent
Orthodox	13,108,000	72.6	1,932,356	34.8
Greek Catholic (Uniate)	1,427,000	7.9	1,385,445	24.9
Roman Catholic	1,234,000	6.8	947,351	17.1
Reformed (Calvinist)	711,000	3.9	696,320	12.6
Lutheran	399,000	2.2	274,415	5.0
Unitarian	69,000	0.4	68,330	1.2
Baptist	61,000	0.3	—	—
Moslem	185,000	1.0	—	—
Jewish	757,000	4.2	192,833	3.5
Other	106,000	0.7	51,313	0.9
Total	18,057,000	100.0	5,548,363	100.0

Source: *Recensământul populatiei României din 29 decemvrie 1930* [The Romanian Census of December 29, 1930] (Bucharest:1939), pp. 70-73. The data relating to Transylvania also include data for the Banat, Crişana and Maramureş.

the interest of the Romanian state to maintain and cultivate the churches of the national minorities; the fundamental aim of its nationality policy at that time was to convince the victorious Powers and world public opinion of its tolerance. This policy was also necessary for the preservation of the territorial integrity of the country.

The Romanian Orthodox Church continued to be the "dominant Church." It was in an advantageous position vis-à-vis the other churches because it had not actively opposed the socialist revolution; in fact, some of the clergy had even participated in the anti-fascist movements. Furthermore, the Romanian Orthodox Church was viewed as a guardian of national culture. Nonetheless, perhaps because, as the state religion, the Orthodox Church had had close ties with the autocratic war-time regime, an ideological campaign was launched against it by the new regime—just as was the case with the other Orthodox churches of Eastern Europe—using the full armory of weapons available to the party and state. The main goal of this campaign was to exclude the influence of Orthodoxy from public life.

The legal status of the minority churches until 1948 was determined by the Nationality Statute of February 6, 1945 and by the Paris Peace Treaty of February 10, 1947. Both guaranteed full religious freedom to every inhabitant of Romania. Likewise, the first communist Constitution of April 13, 1948 guaranteed freedom of religion and the right of churches to organize, as long as this did not "threaten public security and order." Similarly, according to Article 84 of the 1952 Constitution, "the citizens of the Romanian People's Republic can freely determine their religious allegiance and the religious denominations are free to organize and function." The above article also stipulated that no denomination, congregation, or religious community could establish or maintain institutions other than special schools for training clerics. The Constitution of August 21, 1965 of the Romanian Socialist Republic also guaranteed in Article 30 "freedom of conscience for all. Everyone is free to determine his own religious affiliation or whether to have a religious affiliation at all. The free practice of religion is guaranteed. . . church and school are to be separate."

As a result of territorial changes, resettlements, and deportations in post-war Romania, the number of adherents of the various denominations changed significantly. Due to a lack of complete ecclesiastical statistics it is difficult to determine the exact extent of these changes. However, it can be said that the Roman Catholic Church, the Lutheran Church of the Transylvanian Saxons (due to the sharp decline in the German population), and the Jewish community suffered particularly serious losses.

The remainder of this chapter will be an attempt to provide a general picture of the status of the churches of the national minorities in Romania between 1945 and 1980. The year 1945 is important, since it marked the first intervention by the state in the life of the churches, an act which ultimately led to profound transformations.

The land-reform decree issued by the Groza government on March 23, 1945, had grave consequences for the national minorities—especially the Germans and Hungarians—in Romania. The expropriations eliminated the wealth of the minority churches, including, for example, the property of the Transylvanian "Roman Catholic Status."[10]

The first effort by the state to gain political control over the churches was made by the People's Front Government of Groza in October 1945, which sought to win the ecclesiastical leaders over to the cause of socialism, but the experiment failed. The next step taken was aimed at the ideological transformation of the dominant Orthodox Church. The purges carried out in the administration and in every sphere of public life also affected the Orthodox clergy, and a subsequent decree of May 1947 established a mandatory retirement age for Orthodox clergy. Thus, the old guard was more easily dismissed, to be replaced by young clerics who could perhaps be won over more easily to the cause of socialism. The purges, however, were carried out more gradually and carefully in the church than in other institutions, since the state still hoped to use the church as an ideological instrument. A "Union of Democratic Priests" was founded for this purpose; the state's agents were active in this organization from the very beginning. However, various experiments with re-education met everywhere with stubborn resistance from the clergy and, consequently, it proved necessary to seek formal legitimacy for radical change. The first Constitution of the People's Democracy, enacted on April 13, 1948, provided the point of departure for making state control over the churches permanent. The Constitution continued to describe the Romanian Orthodox Church as the "dominant Church" but it did not refer to the Uniate Church as a "national Church." The Constitution abolished the confessional general schools and monastic orders and extended state control over all cultural institutions in the country.

The assertion of state control over the churches was manifested most strikingly in stripping the Roman Catholic Church (which the state viewed as the greatest threat) of its rights. Because of its foreign connections, the great number of its adherents (almost three million Roman Catholics and Uniates), as well as its high degree of organization, the Catholic Church had great strength. Consequently, the government perceived it to be a most dangerous institution, likely to oppose communism and to hinder the creation of a unified national state.

The initial attack on the Catholic Church was still formulated in general terms. The Church was still one of the legally recognized religious bodies of Romania; it was, nonetheless, branded as "reactionary" by the press, the party, and the state. Along with the press campaign, a campaign of intimidation was begun within the hierarchy of the Church, working upwards from the lower ranks. Between May 1947 and March 1948, 92 Catholic priests were arrested.[11] Intimidation, imprisonment, and deportations continued in August and September 1948, in hopes of weakening resistance.[12] At the same time all the Catholic newspapers and publications were abolished. However, further legal action soon proved necessary.

On the basis of the new People's Democratic Constitution, the Grand National Assembly enacted a decree whereby the Romanian

People's Republic revoked, immediately and for all time, the Concordat between the Holy See and Romania of May 10, 1927.[13] As this was an international treaty, it could be revoked only after the abolition of the 1923 Constitution. The annulment of concordats and the breaking off of diplomatic relations with the Vatican occurred all over East Central Europe during this period: in 1945 Poland broke off relations with the Vatican, as did Czechoslovakia in 1950 and Yugoslavia in 1952. Only later did a certain degree of normalization take place.

The annulment of the Concordat brought the almost thousand-year-old independence of the Roman Catholic Church to an end. Furthermore, unlike the other Romanian churches, it thereby lost its legal status as well. At the same time, the Holy See lost its supremacy over the state in ecclesiastical matters, a supremacy hitherto expressed in the fact that the Vatican had been the mediator between the church and the state. At this time the Orthodox was still a privileged Church; and the revocation of the Concordat affirmed its dominant position. Nonetheless, the legal status of the Orthodox Church was soon to be considerably restricted.

The foundations of the new policy towards the churches (a policy still in effect) were laid by the Law on Cults (*Legea cultelor*),[14] of August 4, 1948, which provided a "general regulation of the practice of religion." The new law abolished the decree of 1928, which had defined the legal position of the churches in Romania and had already instituted a certain degree of state control over the churches; in essence, the new law completed the absorption of the churches by the state. This meant that the state subordinated the freedom of action of the churches, which had autonomous rights, to the immediate control of state organs, ordered a revision of the organizational rules of the churches, and took full control of the higher ecclesiastical administrative, financial, and economic institutions, restricting the activity of the churches to liturgical and pastoral matters. Control over the churches was henceforth in the hands of the Ministry of Religious Affairs.

In principle, the law guaranteed freedom of religion (Article 1), as well as the form of organization appropriate to each religious community, so long as "this does not threaten public security and order or morality" (Articles 6 and 7). However, all ecclesiastical organizational activities and functions were to be subject to prior approval by the Presidium of the Grand National Assembly, which meant, in practice, that even the continued existence of legally recognized religious communities was dependent on the good will of the state.

According to Article 13, legal recognition of a religious community could "be revoked at any time in cases where this is justified." According to Article 40, Romanian religious bodies and their representatives were forbidden to have any type of connection with foreign religious communities, institutions, or official personages; foreign contacts—which had still been free at the time of the Concordat—henceforth required the permission of the Ministry of Religious Affairs and the cooperation of the Ministry of Foreign Affairs. This legal measure was aimed primarily at restricting the freedom of the Catholic Church in Romania, abolishing papal jurisdiction over it. According to Article 42, subsidies from abroad were also to be subject to state control. Article 21 stipulated that the heads of the churches could hold office only with the approval of the highest state organs. The members of the clergy were to take an oath of loyalty to the Romanian state, its Constitution and laws.

Decree No. 1,388/1948, which was issued as a supplement to the Law on Cults, and the law relating to educational reform of August 3, 1948, further established the state's right to unrestricted supervision of the activities of the churches.[15] Article 35 of the educational law stipulated that "all ecclesiastical and private schools are to be reorganized as state schools." At the same time, the state expropriated the existing properties of the churches, without compensation. This legal measure destroyed the centuries-old ecclesiastical school system of the national minorities. It is well known that the churches and schools of the Hungarian and German nationalities in Transylvania were traditionally closely linked to one another providing a basis for the continuing cultural survival of those national minorities. The role of the Hungarian churches became even more important after 1918, when most of the leadership of the Hungarian community was drawn from among the clergy.

The educational reform decree instituted complete separation of church and school, a state of affairs which exists in only two other socialist countries—the Soviet Union and Yugoslavia. The Catholic Church protested against this measure at a synod of bishops held in Oradea on August 26–27, 1948.

In further support of the Law on Cults and the educational reform, the government issued a number of administrative measures aimed at the liquidation of the Roman Catholic and Romanian Uniate Churches. In order to break the growing resistance of the Churches, the government issued a decree on September 18, 1948,[16] arbitrarily stipulating (on the basis of Article 22 of the Law on Cults) the number of dioceses of episcopal rank. According to this measure, each diocese had to have at least 750,000 faithful under its jurisdiction; as a result, only five of the hitherto existing ten Catholic dioceses (five Roman Catholic and five Greek Catholic) were retained—three Roman Catholic and two Greek Catholic (Uniate). As a result of the measure, three Uniate and two Roman Catholic bishops were removed from their posts, and even the bishops who retained their sees were exposed to constant attack in the press.

At the end of September 1948 the government called on adherents of the Uniate Church to convert to Orthodoxy; for the time being, however, actions were limited to individuals and small groups. The Cluj Congress of October 1, 1948, sought to mobilize larger masses for the merger.[17] As a result of governmental actions, by November 1948, 600 Uniate clergymen had been arrested; with one exception, all the Uniate bishops perished in prison. In its campaign of conversion by coercion, the government made use of Article 27 of the Law on Cults, which stipulated that after the conversion of adherents of one faith to another, the property of the former was to become that of the latter, in proportion to the percentage of converts. Furthermore, if 75 percent of the adherents of one Church were converted to another, the former Church was to lose all of its wealth, including its buildings, properties and churches.

With these developments, the government of the Romanian People's Republic felt certain of soon achieving its goal of eliminating the Greek Catholic (Uniate) Church. On October 21, 1948, the "return of the Uniate Church into the Orthodox Church as historical act" was celebrated at the Romanian Cathedral in Alba Iulia. Finally, a decree issued on December 1, 1948, officially abolished the Romanian Uniate Church after 250 years of existence, and its property was transferred to the Orthodox Church.[18] Significantly, the 1948 Constitution did not provide specific protection for the Uniates.

The rejection by members of the Greek Catholic Church of the forced unification into the Orthodox Church resulted in a protest demonstration in Cluj. In 1977 the Committee To Save the Romanian Uniate Church sent a letter to state and party chief Ceaușescu, requesting the repeal of the ban on the Uniate Church; the request was rejected by the new Orthodox Patriarch, Justin Moisescu.

As a result of an order of the Minister of Religious Affairs on February 5, 1949,[19] the state finally assumed control over all religious denominations in Romania. Only the Catholic Armenian Church was permitted to maintain its foreign ties (with the Armenian Republic of the USSR).

The Romanian Orthodox Church was the first Romanian church to have its legal status recognized by the government, on October 20, 1948; this was publicly approved by a February 23, 1949 decree of the Grand National Assembly. On June 1 and 6 of the same year the legal status of the following religious communities in Romania was officially recognized: the Reformed (Calvinist) Church, the Saxon Evangelical Church, the Presbyterian Church, the Unitarian Church, the Armeno-Gregorian Church, the Russian Old Believer community, the Jewish and Moslem faiths, and a few, small Neo-Protestant religious communities (Baptists, Adventists, Evangelicals).

After the elimination of the Romanian Uniate Church, new and even more severe attacks were begun against the Roman Catholic Church, which still had no recognized legal status. These attacks, which reached their peak in June and July of 1949, were aimed at the higher clergy. The day after the state's official recognition of the status of the Orthodox Church, on February 24, 1949, Áron Márton, a Hungarian Roman Catholic bishop, submitted a protest to the government over the abolition of the Uniate Church and the extension of arbitrary state power over the Roman Catholic Church.

Finally, between June 20 and 26, 1949, the two Catholic bishops who had remained in their posts were arrested and imprisoned. With the loss of these bishops, Áron Márton and Anton Durcovici, the Catholic Church was left leaderless.[20] According to reports, four of the five Catholic bishops who had remained in the country later died in prison.[21] Soon after the arrest of the Catholic bishops, a decree issued on July 29 by the Council of Ministers dissolved 15 monastic orders and congregations of the Roman Catholic Church, as well as those Catholic charitable and welfare institutions which had provided education, health care, and social services.[22] Two monasteries and three convents were permitted to remain in existence. Most of the deported Catholic priests and nuns were taken to the forced labor camp, and many of them died there.

The state now had a free hand to transform the structure of the Catholic Church, and only the stubborn resistance of the clergy saved the Church from being finally abolished altogether. First the government selected those "progressive" members among the higher clergy who were ready to obey the will of the government, to use them in controlling the rest of the clergy. The government plan was to bring together the more "progressive" ecclesiastics, to separate the Catholic faithful from the hierarchy, and to gain a proclamation of loyalty to the state through the creation of a so-called "Catholic Action Committee." This committee held its first meeting in Tîrgu Mureş on April 27, 1950, under the leadership of the left-wing priest András Ágotha, and it called on the Catholic faithful of Romania to join in the "struggle for peace." In the context of the time "peace" amounted to an acceptance of the measures contained in the Law on Cults of 1948 and general submission to the will of the state. The final aim of the state was the creation, through the destruction of the Catholic Church and with the aid of the "Catholic Action Committee," of a new "national Church," which it could fully control. The committee held a second session on September 6 in Gheorgheni/Gyergyószentmiklós, despite the fact that the Holy See had excommunicated its leaders. In the meantime, the Apostolic Nuncio had been expelled from Romania. Despite the continuous pressure exerted by the state, the Catholic Church expressed its allegiance to the Holy See and world-wide Catholicism. The continued resistance of the Catholic clergy led to further drastic measures by the state. Thus, for example, on September 17, 1951, several Roman Catholic priests were sentenced to life imprisonment or forced labor on the charge of "espionage in the service of the Vatican."

The losses suffered by Catholics living in Romania between 1945 and 1953, according to a survey made by "Documentation Catholique" are listed in Table VI-2.

After the death of Stalin (March 1953) there were signs of liberalization in ecclesiastical policy here as elsewhere in the Soviet bloc. However, at the end of the 1950s, during the "de-Stalinization campaign," the persecution of the churches and the elimination of the monastic orders began again in Romania, as elsewhere in East Europe. In 1963, more than half of the still-existing theological colleges were closed, 1,500 priests, monks, and active laymen were arrested, and approximately 2,000 clergymen were dismissed.[23]

The Romanian Policy of Independence and the Churches

When, in the middle of the 1960s, Romania sought to achieve a certain independence in the political and economic spheres *vis-à-vis* the

TABLE VI-2

Losses Suffered by the Catholic Church in Romania, 1945-1953

	1945	1953	Comments
archbishops and bishops	12		arrested, sentenced, and deported; three died in prison;
priests and monks, nuns	3,331	1,405	55 executed, 250 died or exiled, 200 sentenced to forced labor, 200 imprisoned;
churches and chapels	3,795	700	all the churches of the Uniate Church, numbering 2,734, became the property of the Orthodox Church; a further 300 Roman Catholic churches were expropriated;
parsonages	2,490	683	all the parsonages of the Uniate Church, numbering 1,807, became the property of the Orthodox Church;
Church homes	160	25	85 percent were abolished;
Catholic boys' schools	224		all abolished;
Catholic girls' schools	152		all abolished;
Charitable institutions	160		all abolished;
Catholic journals and press	30		all abolished.

Source: Rev. Don Brunello, "La Chiesa del Silenzio," in *Documentation Catholique*, No. 1156, September 20, 1953; see also P. Gherman, *L'âme roumaine écartelée*, (Paris:1955), p. 197.

Soviet Union, it attempted to establish closer links with the Western countries. As a result, there were certain—even if not very significant—improvements in the status of the churches in Romania. On one hand, there was a need for an internal policy that could mobilize all forces in the cause of national "independence," and, on the other hand, it was important—particularly for economic reasons—to portray Romanian policy as a liberal one for Western audiences. The role of the national-minority churches, which traditionally had ties with the West,—at least superficially—became more important in internal politics; the international connections of the Romanian Orthodox Church were likewise expanded. The representatives of the Romanian Orthodox Church and the Romanian Evangelical Church were able to participate in international ecumenical conferences in the early 1960s. At the beginning of the sixties the Romanian Orthodox Church became a member of the Christian Peace Conference and the Ecumenical Council of Churches and has since participated in the Conference of European Churches.[24] In this regard, it should be noted that the Hungarian Bishop of Alba Iulia, Áron Márton, was permitted to leave his residence for the first time since his release from prison in 1955, on the occasion of a church jubilee celebration. (This did not mean, however, that he was thereafter free from house arrest.)

A subsequent liberalization in the life of the Romanian churches came about as a consequence of the Soviet intervention in Czechoslovakia in August 1968. As long as there was a danger of a Soviet invasion of Romania as well, it was in Ceauşescu's interests to gain the trust of the representatives of the churches and to hold out the prospect of certain concessions. In fact, this liberalization was only apparent and temporary, as was demonstrated by the restrictions introduced shortly thereafter in nationality and religious policy. Thus, in July 1970, an organizational decree, issued on behalf of the Ministry of Religious Affairs, extended the unrestricted authority of state organs over all aspects of the life of every religious community in Romania.[25] The so-called "Little Cultural Revolution," launched on July 6, 1971, brought about even more profound transformations in social, intellectual, and economic life. At the heart of this campaign lay the notion that the primary aim of cultural education should be the service of "socialist patriotism" and the ideology of the party. Obviously, the churches also had to play a role in the realization of these new principles. The first specific step was a 1974 declaration urging religious communities to join the Socialist Unity Front. The "Congress of Political Education and Socialist Culture," held on June 2–4, 1976, announced as its aim the realization of "socialist culture and education" in every sphere of public and private life. There is no doubt whatsoever that the new cultural policy, whose goal was ideological unification, restricted the possibilities of religious education even more than before.

The Minority Churches in Romania Today

The Romanian state has accorded legal recognition to 14 religious communities, in contrast to the approximately 60 recognized religious denominations before 1948. The Roman Catholic Church has two bishoprics: those of Alba Iulia and Iași; the four dioceses which existed in Transylvania between the two world wars have been merged, leaving only that of Alba Iulia. The former Satu Mare-Oradea Diocese has been divided into Hungarian and a Romanian part under a Hungarian and Romanian deputy vicar; the Bishopric of Timișoara is not recognized.

The number of adherents of the Roman Catholic Church in Romania is approximately 1,300,000, of whom approximately 850,000–900,000 are Hungarian, and 240,000–250,000 German, predominantly Swabians of the Banat; the rest include Armenians, Poles, Czechs, Slovaks, Croatians, and a small number of Romanians. The greatest concentrations of Roman Catholics of Hungarian nationality are found: in northwest Transylvania, along the Hungarian border, in the Székler region, in Bucharest, and in the Moldavian counties Bacău and Roman (Csángó Hungarians). The bulk of the Roman Catholics of German nationality live in the Banat and in Satu Mare County (Swabians of the Banat and Sathmar), as well as in Bucharest and, in smaller numbers, in Maramureș and South Bucovina.

There are 875 priests active in the 660 parishes of the Roman Catholic Church; 668 of them receive a state subsidy. There are a total of 967 churches and chapels. By contrast, according to the data from the Romanian Department of Religious Affairs (*Direcțiunea Cultelor*), Hungarian-speaking Roman Catholics have 515 churches and 500 priests.[26] According to data dating from the end of the 1960s, the diocese of the Swabians of the Banat under the leadership of Canon-Vicar Konrad Kernweiss had 164 parishes and 210 priests;[27] their number has now been reduced to 123 (1980). The Diocese of Alba Iulia has approximately 250 parishes and about 320,000 faithful, mostly Hungarian, under the leadership of Bishop Áron Márton, one of the most outstanding leaders of the Hungarians of Transylvania. Áron Márton was imprisoned during the great religious persecutions, on June 21, 1949, and was released only in 1955, and even thereafter was forced to remain under house arrest until 1967. Even for some time after that he was required to obtain official permission in order to leave his residence. His freedom of movement is no longer restricted, but for a decade he was excluded from the ongoing life of the Church. The Roman Catholic Church is one of those religious communities not recognized officially by the state and having no legal statutes or hierarchy. The celebration of the liturgy is only possible under the supervision of the Department of Religious Affairs and the appointment of bishops requires the approval of the state. Roman Catholic priests are appointed by the bishop, subject to the approval of the Department of Religious Affairs.

In accordance with the Law on Cults, priests are state employees and receive salaries of 700 lei per month (approximately 55 US dollars), which the parishioners supplement by payments in kind. Bishops receive salaries of 8,000 lei per month (approximately 620–650 US dollars); they are members *ex officio* of the "National Peace Committee" and of the "National Council of the Socialist Unity Front." Only those priests recognized by the state receive salaries; the rest have to rely on gifts from the faithful. Thus, for example, parishes and settlements with fewer than 400 adherents are not entitled to their own state-subsidized parish priest; these communities become affiliates and their churches, without financial support, eventually fall into disrepair. Between the two world wars, the churches, which still had considerable properties, took care of the payment of the clergy.

The Roman Catholic Theological Institute, an institution of university status with a six-year program for training Roman Catholic priests, continues to function in Alba Iulia, receiving financial support from the state. It has two faculties, one, in Alba Iulia, offering instruction in Hungarian, and the other, in Iași, in Romanian. Admission is on the basis of an entrance examination. The *numerus clausus* introduced in the 1950s is still in effect; this means that the number of students is limited and based on "need", something which the heads of the Theological Institute have little influence in determining. There is even a very small number of scholarships for study abroad (four in 1974–1975). On average, 120–130 Hungarian students of theology attend the Alba Iulia Institute each year;[28] this figure is, however, subject to variation. In general there are fewer departments in the theological faculties than at the universities, a fact which reflects the ecclesiastical policy of the state.

Training for German-speaking Roman Catholic priests has been provided in Alba Iulia, since the abolition of the seminar for priests in Timișoara.

The Iași faculty is formally a branch of the Alba Iulia Theological Institute. It can accept only six to eight students per year, and its function is the training of Romanian-speaking priests. The separation of the two faculties occurred because Hungarian influence was deemed to be too strong in Alba Iulia.

CHURCHES OF THE NATIONAL MINORITIES

The foreign contacts of the Roman Catholic Church in Romania, which were broken off during the great religious persecutions of the 1950s, have been restored to some extent; however, foreign contacts are still possible only with the permission of the Department of Religious Affairs and under the auspices of the Ministry of Foreign Affairs. Thus, for example, the Department of Religious Affairs inspects every ecclesiastical letter sent abroad, and the conditions it sets for the participation of Romanian bishops in synods held abroad are such that the bishops cannot accept them. Although the state no longer regards the Roman Catholic Church as a foreign agent, as it did during the 1950s, the control exerted by the state security organs over the Church is still just as strict.

In sharp contrast to its extensive activity during the interwar period, the Catholic Church press is the poorest among all the Hungarian churches in Romania today.[29] Prayer books are published in very small editions only, and even those are subject to strict censorship.

The small number of Latin-Rite Catholic Armenian parishes in Romania are under the jurisdiction of the Bishop of Alba Iulia. It should be noted, however, that a large number of the Armenians living in Transylvania have been Hungarianized over the course of time.

The Reformed (Calvinist) Church in Transylvania is entirely Hungarian in character and has approximately as many members as there are Hungarian-speaking Roman Catholics, i.e., about 850,000. The other Protestants in Transylvania include 70,000–75,000 Unitarians, about 35,000 Hungarian Lutherans, and 200,000 Neo-Protestants, half of whom are Hungarians. There are, at present, two Calvinist bishoprics in Transylvania: the Diocese of Cluj, headed by Bishop Gyula Nagy and the Diocese of Oradea, led by Bishop László Papp.[30] Above the two bishoprics is the Convent, the highest executive organ of the Hungarian Reformed Church. The two bishoprics consist of thirteen deaneries with 732 parishes, 836 churches, and 773 clergymen.[31] There are 500,000 members in the Diocese of Cluj (formerly the diocese of Transylvania), which has 500 parishes, and 460 clergymen, and is divided into 8 districts.[32] The Diocese of Oradea (formerly the diocese of Királyhágómellék) has 300,000–350,000 faithful in 232 parishes, with 254 clergymen; the diocese is divided into five districts.[33]

The Unified Theological Institute of University Rank in Cluj, founded in 1568, providing the training for Protestant clergy, has two faculties, one in Cluj, where Calvinist, Unitarian, and Hungarian Lutheran theologians are trained, and one in Sibiu, which is attended by Saxon Lutherans. The language of instruction in Cluj is Hungarian, and in Sibiu, German.

At present, the Protestant theological college has 120 Calvinist, 30 Unitarian, and 10 Hungarian Lutheran students; the Sibiu faculty has approximately 50 German-speaking students. Appointments of priests are made by the bishop, but state approval is also required; in recent times, the state has interfered less frequently with appointments. Very few scholarships are awarded for study abroad, and those that are usually go to clergymen with families, since there is a fear that single men might not return to Romania.

The Calvinist and Evangelical Churches jointly publish a journal, the bi-monthly *Református Szemle* (Reformed Church Review) which is produced for internal use only. In any case, it appears in a limited edition of 1,000 copies. There is clear state discrimination in the conditions under which the journal is published; both paper and printing facilities are inadequate.[34]

The Reformed (Calvinist) Church is represented in the World Council of Churches, in the Conference of European Churches, in the World Alliance of the Reformed Church, and in the International Union for Religious Freedom.

The Lutheran Church of the Transylvanian Saxons, the *Evangelische Landeskirche Augsburgischer Bekenntnisses* had, in 1978 approximately 166,000 adherents (162,000 Transylvanian Saxons and approximately 4,000 adherents in Bucovina) with 174 parishes and approximately 162 clergymen under the leadership of Bishop Albert Klein in Hermannstadt and was divided into six church-districts.[35] Historically, the *Evangelische Landeskirche A.B.* has been a major factor in the political and cultural life of the Transylvanian Saxons and amounted in essence, to a national Church.

Since the enactment of the Law on Cults, the Sibiu faculty of the Unified Protestant Theological Institute of Cluj has trained the Lutheran clergy. At the end of the 1960s, the institute had only 29 students, the result of state restrictions on admissions; in 1958, for example, 70–80 students were enrolled in the faculty.[36]

The constant emigration of the Saxon population of Transylvania to the West—in particular, to West Germany—and the conversion of many by some of the newly formed sects has resulted in a serious loss of membership by the Saxon Lutheran Church. The fact that so many of its adherents have joined Neo-Protestant communities reflects the limitations placed on the free practice of religion by the state and the decline in the quality of traditional pastoral care.

State pressure on the Lutheran Church is constantly increasing, as it is against the national-minority churches in general. The Church, the bearer of Transylvanian Saxon national consciousness over centuries, has, however, been able to resist the tendency toward Romanianization. Its journal, the *Kirchliche Blätter,* was banned for some time but was able to resume publication in 1973.

The Unitarian (Anti-Trinitarian) Church, which has an exclusively Hungarian character, is a peculiar feature of Transylvanian Protestantism. Its seat is in Cluj, under the leadership of Bishop Lajos Kovács, once the seat of the only Unitarian bishop in the world. In 1968, the Transylvanian Unitarians celebrated the 400th anniversary of the founding of their Church. The leader of the Church, as President of the International Union for Religious Freedom, has a large number of foreign ties. It is perhaps precisely because of these important foreign connections that the Unitarian Church enjoys certain privileges over and above those accorded to the national minority churches in general.

The Transylvanian Unitarians number approximately 72,000–75,000. Their diocese consists largely of village congregations; 121 parishes are under the jurisdiction of the Bishopric of Cluj. According to the Department of Religious Affairs, the Unitarians have 138 churches and 130 clergymen.[37]

The press organ of the Unitiarian Church is *Keresztény Magvető* (Christian Sower), which appears quarterly in an edition of only 500 copies.[38]

The Hungarian Lutheran Church—a typical diaspora community—is widely scattered; its adherents live mainly in villages around Brașov and are known as the Csángós of Săcele/Hétfalu. The Church has approximately 35,000 adherents under the leadership of their Bishop Pál Szedressy, in Cluj. They recently joined the Lutheran World Federation. The Church has 40 congregations and 30 clergymen, but according to the data of the Department of Religious Affairs, it possesses 46 churches and 44 clergymen.[39]

Due to their small numbers, another community of Hungarian Lutherans who inhabited lands annexed by Romania after the First World War were unable to found a bishopric and instead organized themselves into a superintendency with Arad as its seat. At that time, 25 parishes, with approximately 32,500 adherents belonged to the

Church. A decree issued on March 3, 1940 gave the Church legal recognition and provided it with a state subsidy.

The Protestant religious communities of the national minority churches in Eastern Europe have through the course of history often been victims of oppression, and after the Second World War found themselves isolated. The Neo-Protestant denominations recognized by the Romanian state have been subjected to increased official harassment since 1970. These include the Baptists, Adventists, Pentecostalists, Brethren, and Reformed Adventists. According to scholarly estimates, the Neo-Protestants had a total membership of between 500,000 and 700,000.

The situation of the Romanian Baptists since 1948 is characterized by the same patterns as those typical of the larger churches. State interference has significantly restricted free religious observance, and this is a continuing source of difficulty. Since some of the Romanian Baptists have resisted some measures taken by the state, their Church has been the victim of increasingly arbitrary attacks by the state, which have involved not only arrests but sporadic violence as well. The Romanian Baptist Church has approximately 150,000-200,000 members, 1,300 churches, 150 clergymen and a theological college in Bucharest. The journal of the Church is *Indrumătorul Creștin Baptist* (Baptist Christians' Guide), a Romanian-language monthly which, also publishes some articles in Hungarian.

Among the other officially recognized Neo-Protestant groups, the Seventh-Day Adventists have about 70,000 members, and a theological college in Bucharest. The Pentecostal community numbers approximately 75,000.

In 1976, the Romanian Jewish community numbered approximately 50,000 adherents, with two rabbis serving all the communities.[40] The position of the Jewish faith was regulated not by the 1948 Law on Cults but by a 1949 statute,[41] which stipulated that urban areas whose Jews were members of the Federation of Jewish Communities could have only one Jewish organization.

The other national-minority religious communities in Romania have a combined total of fewer than 100,000 adherents.

A part of the Uniate clergy were kept in prison even after the 1964 amnesty; those who were released were integrated into the Greek Orthodox Church. Even so, the Uniate Church has continued to function to this day as a clandestine community. According to estimates, 600 of the 1,800 clergy who once belonged to that Church not only did not

CHURCHES OF THE NATIONAL MINORITIES 235

convert to Orthodoxy or become Roman Catholics, but have continued to carry out pastoral work and preaching as itinerant clerics, despite the fact that this is against the law.

Relations Between Church and State

Historically, the churches of Romania played an extremely important role in the life of the people. With the establishment of communist power, however, the role of the churches was limited to liturgical affairs. The ultimate goal of the post-war Romanian state has been to exclude the churches entirely from social and political life. On the other hand, the mere existence of the churches has been used by the state to create an external appearance of religious freedom, formally guaranteed by constitutional law. Essentially, the religious allegiance of its citizens is of only secondary concern to the state. At the same time, however, the churches, which have been deprived of their legal identities and, consequently, of their public rights, have become the instrument of the state for the realization of the ideological and political aims of the party and the "building of socialism." Leading members of the clergy in Romania participate in elections and become parliamentary representatives, but in their capacity as private individuals, not as representatives of their churches. The limits of church participation in public life have been clearly determined: the public functions, ceremonies, and other activities of the churches must be of a purely religious character, carried out under state supervision.

State control extends to the most minute phenomena of church life. For example, church conferences are generally attended by party functionaries. The Party also determines the themes for sermons. Pastoral letters and the resolutions of church conferences must be formulated in a "progressive" spirit. Attendance at religious services is not forbidden by law, but mass organizations engaged in ideological propaganda, generally hold their meetings on Sundays and holy days in order to prevent participation in religious services. It is well known that the clergy has been infiltrated by agents of the state, a situation which creates fear and insecurity among the Church leadership. Methods of intimidation include frequent accusations of "national separatism" and "isolationism" against the churches of the national minorities.

During the liberalization at the end of the 1960s, the churches in Romania regained some of their authority, which the state has sought to counteract through an extensive atheist propaganda campaign in the press, mass media, and the schools. On the other hand, although the churches formally have press organs of their own, these are limited to dealing with internal church affairs, their numbers are restricted, and their publication dates uncertain.

In socialist countries, the state has removed all religious instruction from the schools. The strictest measures of this kind are found in the Soviet Union, Romania, and Bulgaria.[42] In Romania, for example, all religious instruction in the schools has been outlawed since 1948. The special schools for training the clergy are an exception to this rule, although the training of the clergy has itself been altered. Socialist doctrine regards religion as a threat to the development of socialism, sees the churches as the one-time allies of capitalism, and assumes that they possess a subversive potential.

Religious instruction for the national minorities between the two world wars was carried out in church schools, as part of the general curriculum. In Romania today, religious instruction is provided voluntarily by members of the clergy, usually on Saturdays or Sundays in a church or other church building. Religious instruction is not compulsory, but, nonetheless, attendance is fairly high. The nature and extent of the catechism are determined by the Department of Religious Affairs, and church leaders are responsible for any irregularity that may occur.

Religious instruction at the theological colleges and seminaries in Romania is permitted in accordance with a syllabus prescribed by a decree of the Ministry of Religious Affairs, issued on November 15, 1948, which stipulated that instruction was to be purely religious in character and was to be aimed at the training of candidates for the clergy and priesthood. The state reserved the right, however, to examine the nature of the lectures and the way in which they were delivered, and to intervene in various ways if—in the opinion of the authorities—"outdated prejudices," contrary to the "progressive spirit," were promoted. There are a relatively large number of theological colleges and seminaries in Romania. At the same time, the communist party has endeavored to develop anti-religious attitudes among the population, primarily among school children and young people. For that reason, on the basis of the resolutions of the "Little Cultural Revolution" of 1971, all organs dealing with educational policy or under the jurisdiction of the Ministry of Education have been placed directly under the control of the propaganda department of the Communist Party Central Committee. This has given a new meaning to the increasing stress placed on Marxism-Leninism throughout the entire educational system. The propagation of atheism is carried out by communist mass organizations, the *Uniunea Tineretului Muncitoresc* (Union of Working Youth) and the Pioneers. More recently, in 1976, a mass organization, "The Falcons of the Homeland," was founded, with the aim of involving children from an early age in communist education. Intensive programs of atheistic "enlightenment" are also carried out at universities and colleges as well as through the so-called "Scientific Brigades."

Following the persecution of the churches in the 1950s, during the "de-Stalinization" campaign of the 1960s, and particularly since the Second Vatican Council, there has been a certain "normalization" in Church affairs in all the socialist countries, including Romania. This has meant an end to the open religious persecution and harassment of earlier periods. The churches have also sought to reach a *modus vivendi* with the state, but problems continue to crop up in church-state relations. The state perceives religious education as a threat to the process of technological and industrial development and even suspects the churches of subversive activities. This provides it with sufficient justification for increasing atheistic propaganda.

Despite the obstacles put in the way of religious activities, there are signs of a religious reawakening within Romania; on the other hand, the restrictions placed on free religious observance have led to a phenomenal growth in the membership of various sects. At any rate, it is clear that under an atheistic state, the survival of the churches depends on their internal vitality and the preservation of their centuries-old traditions. Further, it also depends on how far the clergy goes or can go in reaching compromises with the state. Unquestionably, the process of urbanization and the influx of the rural population into the urban areas is one of the greatest concerns of the churches. Modern ways of life themselves have had a transforming effect on Romanian society; the very existence of the parishes, losing members as a result of migration and legal restrictions, has been threatened.

7

THE NATIONAL-MINORITY PRESS AND PUBLISHING INDUSTRY IN ROMANIA

The Press

The national-minority press and publishing industry in Romania should be examined first of all as an aspect of nationality policy in general, and secondly, in terms of their influence in shaping intellectual, social, and economic life in socialist Romania.

According to the official formulation, press and publishing are among the institutionalized forms of intellectual life guaranteed to the Romanian national minorities. In fact, however, both the press and publishing are state monopolies and as such are under the control of the Romanian Communist Party and serve as instruments of ideological and political propaganda.

Since 1945, the functions of the press and publishing have been constantly changing: the different phases of this process can be closely correlated with the general development of party policy.

It is well-known that the oldest and most venerable publishing traditions in Romania are those of the Transylvanian Germans and Hungarians. The first printing press in Transylvania was established by Transylvanian Saxons in 1528 in Hermannstadt/Nagyszeben/Sibiu. This is where the first Transylvanian printed book, the Latin grammar of Thomas Gemmarius, *Libellus Grammaticus*, was published in 1529, which was, however, not preserved. The first printed book in the Romanian language, Luther's *Catechism,* was published in 1544. That press also issued, in 1546, a Slavonic-Romanian (Old Bulgarian) evangelic book (*Tetraevangheliar*)[1]. The second printing press in Transylvania was founded in 1539 in Kronstadt (Brassó/ Braşov), by one of the outstanding figures of the Transylvanian Reformation, the Saxon Johannes Honterus (1489-1549). Gáspár Heltai (Kaspar Helth 1490 or 1510-1574), a Hungarianized Saxon cleric, printer, and publisher, also established with Georg Hoffgreff a printing press in 1550, in Kolozsvár/ Klausenburg/ Cluj.[2]

A century later, the Hungarian Miklós Kis Tótfalusi (1650-1702) founded a printing press in Kolozsvár, where he published about a hundred books. The first Transylvanian journal, *Theatral Wochenblatt*, began appearing in Hermannstadt in 1778; in 1784 it became the *Siebenbürgische Zeitung* (later *Kriegsbote*, then *Siebenbürger Bote*, and, after 1971, *Hermannstädter Zeitung*). The first scholarly journal in the country, *Siebenbürgische Quartalschrift*, was established in 1790, as was the newspaper *Erdélyi Magyar Hírvivő* (The Transylvanian-Hungarian Messenger), later *Erdélyi Híradó* (Transylvanian Advertiser).[3] In 1814 Gábor Döbrentei published the first Hungarian-language scholarly journal *Erdélyi Múzeum* (Transylvanian Museum). The *Archiv des Vereins für Siebenbürgische Landeskunde*, a more significant scholarly publication, began appearing in 1853.[4]

After the annexation of Transylvania to Romania, the survival of the ethnic press, theater, and educational institutions was possible only through the support of members of the minorities. Cities such as Cluj, Oradea, and Arad, with their overwhelming Hungarian populations and centuries-long Hungarian traditions and, to a lesser extent Braşov, became more important as cultural centers because of their isolation from Hungary. At the same time, Sibiu, Timişoara, and Braşov had the same importance for Germans.

As a result of the suspension of censorship between 1928 and 1933, a new stimulus was provided for the development of a nationality press and literature in Romania. After 1920, 330 newspapers, journals and other periodical publications, as well as 50 literary series in the languages of the national minorities were being published in Transylvania; 243 of them were newly founded. The political press of the nationalities was represented by 18 daily and 53 weekly newspapers.[5] During the interwar period, the journals published in Transylvania in Hungarian-language included: *Erdélyi Helikon* (Transylvanian Helicon), a literary and critical periodical which appeared between 1928 and 1944; the Marxist literary journal *Korunk* (Our Age), published between 1926 and 1940, which reappeared in 1957; *Pásztortűz*

(Shepherd's Fire), another literary and critical journal published between 1921 and 1944; *Erdélyi Irodalmi Szemle* (Transylvanian Literary Review), which appeared between 1924 and 1929 and was later merged with the scholarly journal *Erdélyi Múzeum* (Transylvanian Museum); *Magyar Kisebbség* (Hungarian Minority), a special journal dealing with minority questions; and the cultural-affairs periodical *Hitel* (Credit), published between 1936 and 1944. Among the more important Hungarian-language dailies were *Brassói Lapok* (Brassó Papers), *Ellenzék* (Opposition), and *Keleti Újság* (Eastern Journal), published in Cluj.

The German-language press was also represented during the interwar period in Romania by a large number of newspapers, journals, and other periodicals. Among the most important periodicals were the cultural journal *Ostland* (Hermannstadt, 1919–1921 and 1926–1931) and the literary journal *Klingsor* (Kronstadt, 1924–1939). Among the leading German-language newspapers were the daily *Kronstädter Zeitung,* established in 1849 (Kronstadt, 1849–1944); the leading Transylvanian Saxon conservative daily, *Siebenbürgisch-Deutsche Tageblatt,* established in 1874 (Hermannstadt, 1874–1944); *Banater Deutsche Zeitung* (Temesvar); and another Temesvar daily, *Tageszeitung.*[6] With the rise of the National-Socialist movement, the two great papers *Siebenbürgisch-Deutsche Tageblatt* and *Banater Deutsche Zeitung* were merged to form *Südostdeutsche Tageszeitung* (1941–1944). A cultural-affairs monthly, *Volk im Osten,* similar to *Klingsor,* began appearing in this period as well.

The Hungarian and German-language publications listed above all fell victim to the change of regime at the end of the Second World War, except for the Marxist *Korunk* (Our Age) and the Hungarian-language left-wing daily *Igazság* (The Truth), established in 1940.

The publishing of books in the languages of the national minorities during the interwar period in Romania developed rather freely as a result of the abolition of censorship between 1928 and 1933. Of all the publishing houses in Transylvania, 61.8 percent produced publications in Hungarian and 10.5 percent in German, while only 27.7 percent produced publications in Romanian.[7]

Development Since 1945

In the immediate post-war period the Hungarian and German press and publishing industry in Transylvania continued to be of importance. During this period of political conflict and transition to a communist regime, the national minorities in Romania still retained their autonomous cultural institutions. Out of a total of 2,417 books published by state publishing houses in 1949, 770 were in languages of the national minorities, while in 1950, 953 out of a total of 2,921 books were in minority languages. This ratio was to change dramatically during the ensuing decades. (In 1956 only 519 of 3,168; in 1974, 666 of 4,406; and in 1978, only 554 of 3,774.)

In fact, several new Hungarian and German newspapers and journals were founded during these years. These included the following Hungarian-language publications: *Népi Egység* (Unity of the People), established in Brasov in 1944; *Világosság* (Light), which began publication in Cluj in 1944; *Szabad Szó* (Free Word), founded in Tîrgu Mureș in 1944, and *Erdély* (Transylvania), *Utunk* (Our Path), *Falvak Népe* (People of the Villages), and *Romániai Magyar Szó* (Hungarian Word in Romania), all published in Cluj. Postwar German-language newspaper publishing began in 1949, with the appearance of *Neuer Weg*, which was followed by other periodicals, such as: the literary magazine *Kultureller Wegweiser*, the journal of the German writers' association, *Banater Schrifttum*, published in Timișoara; *Temeswarer Zeitung*, a Banat newspaper, which appeared in Transylvania as well under separate title, and later as *Neue Literatur*, published in Bucharest beginning in 1956. *Die Freiheit* was the organ of the Social Democratic Party. *Neue Welt*, a German-language illustrated magazine published by the Romanian-Soviet Society, also appeared in the postwar period, as did *Volkszeitung*, published in Brașov, and *Die Wahrheit*, published in Timișoara.[8]

During the period of transition to a communist regime the newspapers and journals published in Romania became instruments of communist party propaganda. They owe their continued existence only to this fact. The consolidation of the regime and the general political and social transformations which accompanied it and which had such a decisive effect on nationality relations also exerted a significant influence on the press and book publishing in general.

Soon after the establishment of the People's Front of the Groza Government (March 6, 1945), a decree, issued on May 4, listed those literary and scientific works published between 1917 and 1944 which were considered "subversive" according to the new cultural policy. By 1949 the number of forbidden works had reached 8,000.[9] Censorship was also intensified. In accordance with a new decree,[10] the publication of all literary or scholarly works required preliminary approval from the Ministry of Arts and Information.

With the establishment of the communist regime (December 30, 1947) all cultural institutions came under tight state control and were made instruments of "progressive" culture. At the same time, freedom of the press was abolished. Literature lost its original function and became a mere political tool for furthering the ideas of "class struggle" and "revolution." While Western writers in the years after 1945 were preoccupied with the psychological problem of man shaken by war, writers in East Central Europe were pressured to choose themes that were more propagandistic and agitational in tone. Much of prewar literary tradition fell victim to these new endeavors.

It was easy, under the guise of the ideological struggle, to carry out against the bourgeois regime a policy whose aims included the progressive erosion of the cultural and literary heritage of the national minorities. This began with the dispersion of ethnic cultural centers. In order to solidify central control, not only the majority of publishing houses but also most of the newspaper editorial offices were moved to Bucharest. In 1957, both the Hungarian and the German writers' associations were abolished, and the membership was incorporated into the Romanian Writers' Association, centered in Bucharest. A considerable proportion of the national-minority press and publishing industry was also moved to the capital. At present, ten Hungarian weekly and monthly journals, as well as the largest Hungarian-language daily in Romania, are all edited and published at the Romanian press center in the *Scînteia* Building in Bucharest. These include: *A Hét* (The Week), *Munkásélet* (Workers' Life), *Dolgozó Nő* (Working Woman), *Művelődés* (Education), *Tanügyi Újság* (Education Journal), *Falvak Dolgozó Népe* (Working People of the Villages; formerly *Falvak-Népe—* People of the Villages), *Ifjúmunkás* (Young Worker), *Jóbarát* (Good Friend), *Méhészet Romániában* (Bee-Keeping in Romania), *Matematikai Lapok* (Mathematical Papers), and the daily *Előre* (Forward, formerly *Romániai Magyar Szó*), established in 1953.[11]

The German-language daily, *Neuer Weg*,[12] the chief organ of the Germans in Romania, has been published in Bucharest since 1949. Since that year, a popular-scholarly periodical, *Volk und Kultur,* and *Neue Literatur,* a monthly literary journal publishing the works of German writers and scholars, have also been published in Bucharest; the biannual scholarly periodical *Forschungen zur Volks- und Landeskunde* is published in Sibiu. Other nationality-language periodicals published there include the Armenian weekly *Nor ghiank,* the Ukrainian bi-monthly *Novii Vik* (New Time), the Serbo-Croatian biannual *Knjizevni Zivot* (Literary Life), and a Yiddish newspaper.

In addition to the periodicals listed above, ecclesiastical journals in the languages of the national minorities are also published. These include two Hungarian journals—the bi-monthly publication of the Reformed and Evangelical Churches, *Református Szemle* (Reformed Church Review), and the quarterly of the Unitarian Church, *Keresztény Magvető* (Christian Sower, Cluj, 1861–1944, and 1971–) and the German-language monthly of the Evangelische Landeskirche A.B. in Rumänien, *Kirchliche Blätter.*

In addition to the major minority-language literary and sociopolitical journals and other periodicals published in Bucharest, there are a number of provincial and local newspapers published in Hungarian and German.[13] The Hungarian-language sociopolitical and philosophical journal *Korunk* (Our Age), for example, which was the leading periodical of the interwar left-wing movement is published in Cluj-Napoca. It contains general, abstract studies and specialized professional articles which are dogmatic in their approach and are, with a few exceptions, irrelevant to the real concerns of the Hungarian national minority in Romania. The leading Hungarian-language literary journal, *Igaz Szó* (True Word), is published in Tîrgu Mureş, and the literary weekly *Utunk* (Our Path), founded in 1946, appears in Cluj-Napoca. The German-language cultural weekly *Karpatenrundschau* is published in Braşov, and the sociopolitical weekly *Die Woche,*[14] in Sibiu.

In the 1960s the local papers of the national minorities firmly established themselves in the cultural life of the province and to some extent could fill the place of the missing specialized journals; their institutionalized uniformity, however, led to a decrease in variety. Although restricted to their respective counties, their officially limited editions were not sufficient to fill the needs of their readership. It must be noted here that while the local Romanian papers were published in editions averaging between 20,000 and 30,000 copies, the Hungarian papers, for example, were published in editions of only 5,000 in Covasna and Harghita Counties which had overwhelmingly Hungarian populations.

In the next period of improvement, it was soon obvious that the local press, like all the mass media, owed its existence and was subordinated to the propagation of the ideological tenets of the communist party.

THE NATIONAL-MINORITY PRESS 245

Thirty Hungarian-language publications and eight German-language papers are published in Romania today (1980). By contrast, between the two world wars, a total of 288 such publications appeared in Romania, 181 of them in Hungarian (112 newspapers and 69 journals) and 107 of them in German (77 newspapers and 30 journals).[15] Most of the nationality publications in Romania were established in the second half of the 1940s and 1950s, but the papers serving the area with the largest concentration of Hungarians, the Székler region, and almost all Hungarian-language student papers began to appear only at the end of the 1960s.

The editing and publishing are not always done in the same locality, a situation which makes the coordination of these tasks complicated and difficult. With the exception of the Dacia Publishing House in Cluj-Napoca and a few insignificant provincial publishers, the publishers of the books in the languages of the national minorities are all located in Bucharest.

In the analysis that follows, an attempt will be made to consider the political and cultural aspects of the stages in the history of the national-minority press and publishing industry in post-war Romania. The most significant turning points in Romania's cultural policy since the Second World War are as follows: 1948, with the consolidation of the communist regime; the beginning of the 1950s, with the triumph of "socialist realism" in the arts and letters; the middle of the 1960s; and, finally, 1971 and 1976. Each of these dates can be closely correlated with significant changes in the tone of literature and the press. A periodic loosening and tightening of restrictions and successive periods of liberalism and repression have helped breed confusion and tension in the cultural field.

The Dogmatic Period

As was mentioned, the period of proletarian internationalism in the 1950s inevitably left its mark on the national-minority literature and press as well. By the second half of the 1940s, the minority press had lost a great deal of its specific nationality character and had become a tool of mass propaganda. It became monotonous, colorless, and superficial. There was a real lack of serious writing relating to the fundamental issues of minority life. The literature of the mother countries of the national minorities was also excluded, for all practical purposes, from the Romanian press, as was most world literature. The literary works published during this period were of poor quality, not only in terms of content, but in terms of their external appearance as well. The content of the press and literature were determined almost exclusively by the politics of "class struggle." Writers were obliged to choose topics dealing with workers or peasants, and their works had to be imbued with the spirit of agitation and propaganda. Literature became stereotyped: the written word was made little more than a weapon of dogmatic "proletcult" propaganda. The voices of important Hungarian and German authors were muted in isolation, but not even the best writers were able to avoid having to manifest their political commitment.[16] "Russifying" influences, especially during the Zhdanov period, led ultimately to a rewriting of Romanian history and to official support for a theory proclaiming the Slavonic origin of the Romanian language. Ironically, however, it was this very same anti-nationalist cosmopolitanism which was soon to give rise to a new emphasis on nationalism.

The Desatellitization Process—Liberalizing Trends

Soon after Stalin's death in March 1953, an important transformation of Romanian domestic policy, representing a departure from the strict, dogmatic approach of the early 1950s, could be noted. At the same time, a certain assertion of independence and efforts at emancipation from Russian tutelage were apparent. Characteristic of the new political phase were a kind of controlled liberalization, a certain regeneration of the intellectual life, the return to the literary heritage of the past, and, finally, an opening of the country to Western influences, all, however, carried out within a framework of Marxist-Leninist principles.

Decisive factors in the further development of Romanian cultural policy during the 1960s were the election of Nicolae Ceauşescu as the party's First Secretary (March 22, 1965), the Ninth Congress of the RCP (July 1965), and the Soviet invasion of Czechoslovakia (August 21, 1968). Initially, signs of a more liberal—even if strongly nationalistic-cultural policy could be observed, although the hegemony of the communist party was never put in question. Just as the literature of the 1950s was marked by revolutionary class struggle, so the guidelines of cultural policy in the 1960s were set by patriot-educational and ideological commitment. As is characteristic of the East-bloc mentality, cultural liberalization only meant freedom to criticize the immediate past, which, in this case, meant a condemnation of Stalinist excesses.

The Soviet invasion of Czechoslovakia in 1968 helped usher in a new period of controlled liberalization in Romanian cultural policy, which in turn meant a renewal of the national-minority literatures and press in Romania. The tone of the press became more democratic and liberal; writers belonging to the national minorities were given encouragement to manifest their own national spirit. This period was marked by a vigorous struggle between the leaders of the party and those writers who supported a liberalizing trend of the Czechoslovak type.[17] Journals published foreign literature more regularly, and there was a significant improvement in the material quality of publications. The number of publications in all areas—with the exception of the Yiddish press—also increased as compared with the 1950s.[18]

Between 1968 and 1971 the literature of the national minorities in Romania developed to a greater extent than it had during the preceding twenty-five years. It was during this period of two or three years that the most outstanding works of postwar national-minority literature were published.[19] However, "liberalization" never went so far as to permit a realistic depiction of contemporary problems. Thus, many creative writers sought refuge in historical fiction, using it as a means for discussing problems of the present. This approach has given rise to a whole series of historical plays and novels.

This phase of the renewal bought the Hungarians and Germans in Romania important cultural journals as well as significant county newspapers; some of the daily and critical literary magazines gained manifoldness and a more significant content.

The subsequent hardening of the ideological line, however, showed clearly that the process of liberalization was only a tactical move and was limited. Control over cultural activities also came increasingly into the hands of the Central Committee of the party during this period. Moreover, the primary function of nationality publishing and the nationality press came to be seen as the translation of Romanian works into the languages of the national minorities. Naturally, this has had a markedly negative effect on minority scholarship since publishing houses and press organs can publish only a limited amount of material. The aim of this unvoiced but clear policy has been the reshaping of the patterns of minority intellectual and cultural life, separating the minorities from their own national cultures and implanting the spirit of Romanian culture in their consciousness. This policy has resulted in the creation of a hybrid national consciousness, whose only national characteristic is language. This cultural policy has employed a whole battery of devices—censorship, limitations on the size of editions, material and moral incentives, propaganda, etc.—in its efforts to force national-minority writers to develop a particular form of "nationality" literature. This "nationality" literature should, according to the official view, preserve as little of the traditions of its own classical national literature as possible and, preferably, be completely isolated from the influences of contemporary European literature. Furthermore, it should depict the history of the national-minority and Romanian peoples in accordance with official views, particularly with regard to the development of Transylvania, and last, but not least, it should contain a positive evaluation of present-day nationality policy. Naturally, these principles have never been officially expressed but there can be no doubt about their real significance for the makers of Romanian national-minority policy.

The press and publishing are coming to be weapons of a general nationality policy aimed at the merging of the various national groups in Romania through "homogenization" and uniformization.[20] Thus, for example, the official view, which states—contrary to fact—that there are no compact Hungarian areas in Romania, must be reflected in Hungarian nationality literature, through the compulsory inclusion of Romanian as well as Hungarian characters; writers who do not comply cannot have their work published unless it is rewritten by the censors.[21]

All the major national-minority literary journals have been publishing translations of Romanian works to an increasing extent. In and of itself, this would not be objectionable, so long as it took place on a reciprocal basis, within the framework of a fair and truly effective cultural exchange aimed at the unity of national cultures. However, in fact, Romanian literature, literary history, and literary events are given incomparably more space in the national-minority press than materials on national-minority literature receive in the Romanian press. Moreover, the nationality press cannot even publish articles dealing with its own national history unless they are presented in terms of "mutual fraternity," i.e., from the point of view of official Romanian historiography; even then, minority history must be portrayed as secondary to Romanian history. By contrast, the nationality press must devote a great deal of space to articles on Romanian history. Thus, nationality policy has turned a rightful demand for mutual understanding into a weapon of intellectual enslavement and has played a role in transforming the "national" development of the minorities into a deformed "nationality" development. The national-minority press publications serves in the realization of the same policy. For example, the chief newspaper of the Hungarian minority, *Előre* (Forward), or the German-language *Neuer Weg,* in their leading articles and political commentaries publish, word for word, material from the two leading Romanian dailies, *Scînteia* (Spark) and *România Liberă* (Free Romania). It is therefore not surprising that national-minority papers offer the same articles as Romanian papers, aimed at the distortion of historical consciousness[22] and the promotion of the idea of Romanian national supremacy.[23] Since the Western press has begun to devote more attention to the problems of the national minorities in Romania, the Romanian party leadership has ordered so-called "refutations," articles denying alleged discrimination against the minorities. In general the persons selected for writing these rejoinders are high-ranking party functionaries and other privileged supporters of the regime belonging to the national minorities.[24]

The Cultural Policy of the 1970s

A return to a rigid, dogmatic cultural policy resembling that of the 1950s came with the proclamation of the "Little Cultural Revolution," in July 1971. One aspect of this "revolution" was a re-emphasis on the didactic role of literature and the arts. The new measures began to be implemented after the May 1972 Writers' Conference and the analysis of it issued by the Council for Socialist Culture and Education, and they were given concrete form in the principles and guidelines drawn upon the basis of the resolutions of the Eleventh Congress of the RCP (November 24-27, 1974). Plans for the ideological and political transformation of all of Romanian intellectual and artistic life took on final form in the program of the June 1976 Congress of Political Education and Socialist Culture.

The phases of this campaign for intellectual and ideological transformation can be traced through the various decrees, secret directives, and resolutions of various conferences issued after 1972. Unlike the proletarian internationalism of the 1950s, the guiding principle of the cultural revolution was emphatically nationalist—a total identification with the Party's and the nation's goals.

The "Little Cultural Revolution" heralded the creation of a "new man" and the transformation of all aspects of intellectual and artistic life in order to create a "mass culture," a "socialist culture," and although it was met by opposition from several well-known artists and writers,[25] it soon began to have an impact on the cultural scene. The press, the publishing industry, and mass media became weapons in the proclaimed campaign of ideological and political education: "The press, radio, and television, and all means of mass communication must in the future increase their activities . . . these means of communication must be imbued with . . . more firmness, with a more militant, committed spirit, with a greater intolerance for error."[26]

In 1972 the relationship between the ideological imperatives of the "Little Cultural Revolution" and artistic freedom had not yet been clearly defined.[27] However, there was increasing concern over a growing climate of dogmatism and its potentially crippling effect on artistic creativity. There were explosive debates in the press, a kind of trial of strength between the party and the representatives of the arts.[28] As a result, in November 1972, the Council for Socialist Culture and Education submitted the recalcitrant artists to critical rebuke. Henceforth, free expression was increasingly restricted. The statutes passed by the May 1972 Writers' Conference were openly aimed at the nonconformists among the younger generation of writers.[29]

Before proceeding to a brief analysis of the cultural and artistic development of Romania during the 1970s, it should be noted that the operations of the press, book publishing, radio, television, and filmmaking were, until 1977, regulated by the 1965 Constitution, the 1974 press law, and a decree outlining the activities of the Committee on Press and Printing (*Comitetul pentru presa și tipărituri*).[30]

The first Romanian press law, issued after the Second World War,[31] was drawn up under the direction of party leader Ceaușescu. According to Article 1, Paragraphs 1 and 2, of that law, "the press carries out its activities under the direction of the RCP." In essence, this law represented a radical reorganization of the press, with the aim of increasing the effectiveness of the latter as an educational and propaganda tool. It emphasized, aside from Marxist ideological content, the promotion of a nationalistic point of view. According to Article 4, for example, "workers coming from the ranks of the coinhabiting nationalities have the opportunity to obtain information and express their views through press organs published in their own languages . . ." but only so long as such publications are "in complete harmony with the interests of the Party and the state." Thus, the freedom granted was merely illusory, since it assumed a total obedience to the Party. The law further required journalists to commit themselves fully to the realization of the social, economic and cultural goals prescribed by the Communist Party (Articles 39–57). The strict observance of these regulations was to be ensured by the Committee on Press and Printing. This was a party and state organ whose tasks included coordinating public informational activities and overseeing the implementation of the laws regulating the press and book publishing. Censorship was one of its main tasks. The membership of the committee included leading representatives of newspapers, journals, radio, television, and artists' associations.

The press law of 1974 further restricted the import and sale of foreign publications. These restrictions applied particularly to Hungarian and Western literature. The exclusion of the latter was justified by the party leadership on the grounds of its "subversive influence on Romanian youth."

The resolutions of the Central Committee of the RCP of May 7, 1974[32] contained new measures modifying the structure of the press. Various publications were merged, changes in content were introduced, and censorship was increased. This measure was accompanied by mass dismissals of editorial personnel. Those viewed as "liberal" were replaced by conformists: retaining one's job was based on one's "loyalty," and the degree of governmental control over the press was thereby increased.

The program of the Eleventh RCP Congress, held between November 24 and 27, 1974,[33] reinforced these trends and laid the basis for a cultural and literary policy that was militant and propagandistic in spirit. The Party program reflected Marxist orthodoxy on one hand and nationalistic tendencies on the other.

At the Congress of Political Education and Socialist Culture, held between June 2 and 4, 1976, the approximately 6,000 party functionaries present drew up ideological, educational, and cultural guidelines expressed in the form of resolutions. The Congress called for the total realization of the ideological resolutions of the Eleventh Party Congress—extending to every sphere of public and private life—and the goals of the 1971 cultural revolution; this was aimed at the creation of a "socialist culture"—a decisive factor in cultural development in

Romania in the 1970s. That meant the systematic and dogmatic return to the 1950s.

At the end of 1976, a session of the Council for Socialist Culture and Education formulated the so-called "National Epos," which was intended to further the party's program in literature, the visual arts, music, and dance; in essence, it represented a "mythical, heroic" vision of the Romanian past and socialist present.

Among the consequences of the new press law were changes in personnel and the imposition of restrictions on the use of paper.[34] This restriction, which was made on the grounds of an alleged need to limit the use of paper, applied to both Romanian and national-minority press and book publishing. Most of the national-minority papers were reduced in size by half, some dailies were changed into weekly publications, and some papers were abolished altogether. However, a few of the Romanian papers were later permitted to appear again in their original size, but this opportunity was not made available to any national-minority papers.[35] Discrimination against the minorities can be observed in the remuneration of writers as well; because of the smaller number of books printed, the authors of works written in the languages of the national minorities receive a smaller amount of royalties than do Romanian authors; the amount of remuneration received by writers is also less in the case of national-minority newspapers and periodicals. Romanian publications often provide three times as much in royalties as do national-minority publications.[36] Thus, the low numbers of national-minority books and publications printed doubly handicap writers belonging to those minorities: not only do they have fewer opportunities to publish their work, but they must suffer greater financial hardship as well. Here, as elsewhere, every new measure has meant a new step toward destroying the cultural unity of the national minorities.

Before the new censorship system was introduced in 1977, every text intended for publication was subjected to repeated checks from various points of view and could not be published without permission from the Committee on Press and Printing. All manuscripts had to be submitted to an agency of the committee, the so-called *"Organ de Sinteză,"* which acted as a preliminary censorship body to determine—even before regular censorship—whether or not a given text was "suitable" for publication. Political, ideological, and nationalistic considerations had at least as much weight as other considerations in evaluating the "suitability" of literary works. Manuscripts intended for publication in the languages of the national minorities were submitted to special scrutiny, on the basis of a secret directive. Initially, the principles of censorship were at least clear and definite: the authorities determined which subjects could or could not be written about, which points of view could or could not be adopted, and which words could not be uttered. These guidelines were formulated in secret directives sent to editorial boards and publishing houses in a monthly circular. Not surprisingly, editors and publishers were forbidden to publish these directives or even to mention them, and care had to be taken at the time of typesetting to conceal the omitted parts. The new censorship system, however, brought about important transformations in information and cultural policy. The Committee on Press and Printing was abolished, and the responsibility for censorship was taken over by the Council for Socialist Culture and Education.[37] According to the official statement, this meant that instead of the hitherto existing censorship and control commissions, editors and publishing houses would exercise "self-censorship," thus putting censorship on a "democratic basis." In reality, however, the reorganization of censorship represented further control over the work of editors and publishers. At the same time, all decisions and criteria for pre-censorship and post-censorship, and thus the "ideological responsibility" for the press and publishing as a whole were placed in the hands of the party functionaries of the Council for Socialist Culture and Education.

After the introduction of the new censorship system, contradiction and uncertainty reigned supreme in the cultural sector. In contrast to the situation prevailing under the old censorship system, editors and publishers were forced to change and to mutilate texts already prepared for printing; texts of all kinds were banned without explanation, and even the editors were kept in the dark about the reasons for such actions. The aim was to keep publishers in a state of constant uncertainty so that they would not even consider trying to outwit the censors.

As a result of the above developments, the national-minority press and literatures have declined sharply in terms of quality since 1975: their existence has become increasingly formal, and they have come to differ little from Romanian publications except insofar as they are written in a different language. Their role as transmitters of the cultural heritage of the national minorities has been considerably reduced. Just as the total literary and artistic sector of the country was subordinate to the party's ideological demands, as well as to the promotion of the personality of Ceaușescu and to expressions of loyalty to "socialist patriotism", so did the press publishing industry become an instrument of the nationalities policy which aimed at merging the ethnic minorities. Through the monolithic machinery of unification the content of letters and press publications has been reduced in large part to hackneyed political speeches and translations of works by Romanian authors. In this way, too, the intellectual life of the national minorities has been forced to conform with Romanian socialist intellectual life, with complete disregard for peculiar national characteristics.[38]

The editors of periodicals must devote particular attention to articles, reviews, and commentaries published in *Scînteia,* the organ of the Central Committee of the RCP. These commentaries and reports reflect internal party decisions, and it is possible to deduce the contents of unpublished resolutions from a study of them. Such a study reveals a discrepancy between a proclaimed press policy of "liberalization" and a *de facto* continuation of adherence to traditional party dogma.

There are no signs of change within the foreseeable future in this situation, an outgrowth of the Romanian "cultural revolution" which has left its mark on the entire Romanian intellectual scene. Ultimately, this radical "homogenization" is certain to lead to a complete stifling of the cultural life of the national minorities.

Official statistical data on newspapers, periodicals, and books published in the languages of the nationalities do not reveal the real inadequacies and limitations of the intellectual life of the national minorities in Romania today. On the other hand, publishers' lists provide a basis for the concluding that the nationalities lack independent cultural institutions. In 1975, for example, 27 of the 30 Hungarian-language periodical publications were issued by the RCP or organs directly subordinate to it; two were Hungarian-language papers published by the Romanian Writers' Association; and one was a publication of the Romanian Apiculturists' Association. Eighteen of them were sociopolitical publications; two were illustrated magazines; one was a cultural journal; two were literary journals; four were, in part, specialized scholarly publications; one was a Hungarian-language version of the official gazette; and two were church periodicals.[39]

Book Publishing

At the beginning of 1970 the Ministry of Education reorganized the book publishing industry in Romania:[40] some publishing houses were abolished and new ones were founded. Henceforth, the majority were centered in Bucharest.

Until 1970 national-minority book publishing was concentrated chiefly in the hands of two institutions: the Literary Publishing House and the Youth Publishing House. In 1970 the Literary Publishing House was incorporated into the Kriterion Publishing House, which now has Hungarian, German, Ukrainian, Serbo-Croatian and Yiddish departments. Several other Romanian publishing houses also publish books in minority languages, albeit on a much smaller scale: altogether, eleven publishers print books in Hungarian,[41] and at least five publish German-language books, about a hundred titles per year.[42] However, a high proportion of these books are translations of works by Romanian authors. The directors and editors of the publishing houses which deal in books published in the languages of the national minorities are in part Romanians and in part members of the minorities. In principle, the relative numbers of publications printed in each language are determined by ministerial decrees laid down in the organizational statutes of the publishing houses; these decrees, however, are generally ignored.

The Kriterion Publishing House, the main publisher of books for the national minorities, puts out mostly literary works in the minority languages. It publishes approximately eight or nine books in Hungarian and four or five in German every month. The Dacia Publishing House, located in Cluj-Napoca, has a Hungarian and a German department; it publishes literary and popular scientific works, four or five of them per month, on the average, in languages of the national minorities.

The various phases of nationality policy can be traced precisely in the development of national-minority book publishing. This is best illustrated by the number and content of national-minority publications, as well as by the various genres of books published. For example, after the Hungarian Revolution, from 1957 to 1964, the number of books published in the languages of the national minorities was reduced by half, from 917 titles to 519.[43] It was during the same period that the schools of the minorities were merged with the Romanian schools, and the remaining national-minority institutions were placed in the service of the Romanianization process. Part of this new publishing policy involved more translations of Romanian books into the national-minority languages and an intensified promotion of Romanian literature.[44] At the same time, the minorities were isolated from their own national literatures: the import of books from Hungary was reduced, the free sale of Hungarian newspapers ceased, and there were increasingly fewer references in the Hungarian press in Romania to Hungarian literature or the literature of the Hungarian minorities in Czechoslovakia and Yugoslavia.

During the next period, with the increasing predominance of books with political-ideological themes and literary works translated from Romanian, the number of books published in the national–minority languages increased, although it still remained below the levels of the years between 1949 and 1957.[45] This tendency is best illustrated by data on the output of the Kriterion Publishing House over a period of two years: as opposed to 150 books in 1971, Kriterion published 177 books in Hungarian in 1972, whereas the Literary Publishing House had published only 67 titles in Hungarian in 1962.[46] In 1975, a total of 216 works in Hungarian were published by Kriterion, and in 1976, 223.[47] In 1973, 96 works were published in German. According to a difference source, 158,000 copies of German-language books were published in 1970 and 290,000 in 1974.[48] During the first 10 months of 1975, more than 200 works were published in German.[49]

Through an analysis of the development of publishing houses among the nationalities, it can be determined that a sound picture can be obtained only through an attentive consideration of the official statistics. The relatively high number of publications and the continuing growth of their numbers do not necessarily indicate an improvement in content or in the intellectual opportunities which they provide for the national minorities. On the contrary, while the number of works published in the languages of the national minorities has increased since the reorganization of the publishing industry, the number of copies of books which are interesting from a nationality point of view has not increased proportionally. Such works are sold out within a few days and the small number of copies printed cannot begin to meet the demand of the reading public. Moreover, a very high percentage of the works published in the languages of the national minorities are political or ideological works, collections of official speeches, or translations of books of Romanian authors; another large group of them are works containing general information, and only a very small proportion consists of works dealing with nationality culture, mainly literature and linguistics.[50]

A predominance of literary works and an insignificant number, if not complete absence, of scholarly works has been characteristic of national-minority publishing almost from the very beginning. Works on literary history, sociology, history, art, philosophy, natural science, or economics are hardly ever published in the languages of the minorities. Only in 1972, for example, were any Hungarian books on the history of music published, while works on the visual arts in Hungarian have only recently begun to be published (in very small editions) and many scholarly manuscripts in Hungarian have been awaiting publication for decades. An absence of books on history is most striking. Works dealing with the Hungarian role in the history of Transylvania or with the historic role of the Germans there are only rarely published, and where they do appear, they are much abridged and written from the perspective of Romanian historiography. Between 1949 and 1962, a total of 13 popular books on scholarly topics were published in Hungarian; in other words, one per year. In 1971 none was published. The ratio of such works to works of literature was approximately one to ten. In 1971, only one original Hungarian novel for young people was published.[51] This paucity of works in minority languages is the result of a conscious publishing policy, not the result of any lack of national-minority authors.

The publication of specialized technical works is another highly revealing indicator of the state of Romanian nationality policy. Characteristic of the area are the applied practices of the state: literature for every specialized training in the minority languages is either unavailable or does not supply the demands of a society aiming at modern industrialization, thereby eliminating the nationalities from this process.

Although the national minorities have often raised this issue at official gatherings,[52] the authorities have refused to consider importing such works from Hungary or the Federal Republic of Germany. In light of these facts, it must be concluded that the promises and resolutions of 1971 have had no real results. On the contrary: since 1977, for example, the number of natural science and popular books on scholarly topics published in Hungarian language was reduced by half.[53]

The supply of the nationalities in Romania with imported books and publications, a vital factor for the preservation of their cultural and ethnic existence, is stifled, when not completely stopped, by the current political leadership through extraordinary restrictions. This even applies to imports from socialist states within the East bloc, although there is a cooperation agreement between Hungary and Romania for exchanges of books and between publishing houses. According to the bilateral agreement, the two sides have committed themselves to importing equal numbers of books, newspapers and films. A telling example of the one-sidedness of this agreement is the fact that while on the Hungarian side, the full quota of books to be imported from Romania is made use of, the Romanian state imports books from the neighboring country only in restricted quantities. While Romanian book exports to Hungary average between 11,000 and 12,000 books each year, imports from Hungary are never more than 1,300–1,400 books per year.[54] It should be noted that, while Romania has about 2.3 million Hungarians, the Romanians in Hungary number 12,600. Since the meeting of the Congress of Political Education and Socialist Culture in June 1976, books considered for import from abroad are subject to even more stringent controls, based on ideological considerations.

In 1974, the system of book publishing was reorganized and new restrictions were introduced. The partial decentralization carried out in 1970 was reversed and direction was taken over by a newly founded organ, the Central Publisher (*Centrala Editorială*). Its functions include, among other things, the compilation of publishers' plans and regulation of the size of editions in line with the cultural policy of the RCP and the state.

NOTES

Chapter 1

1. The area of present-day Transylvania is given in Hungarian statistical sources as being between 102,787 and 103,093 square kilometers; the vast majority of Romanian sources give the area as 102,200 square kilometers.
2. Gyula László, "Magánbeszéd a kettős honfoglalásról" ["Monologue on the Dual Conquest of the Homeland"], *Népszava,* Budapest, December 19, 1970; *A honfoglalókról* [On the Conquerors of the Homeland], (Budapest: 1973); *Magyar őstörténeti tanulmányok* [Studies in Hungarian Pre-History] (Budapest: 1977).
3. On the Hungarian conquest of Transylvania, the following works provide detailed information: Bálint Hóman—Gyula Szekfű, *Magyar történet* [Hungarian History], vols. I–VIII, (Budapest: 1935–1936); J. Darkó, *Die Landnahme der Ungarn in Siebenbürgen,* in *Ostmittel-europäische Bibliothek,* no. 24, (Budapest: 1940); E. Moór, *A honfoglaló magyarság megtelepedése és a székelyek eredete* [The Settlement of the Hungarian Conquerors and the Origin of the Székler], (Szeged: 1944).
4. Valuable information on the origin of the Széklers, [Székely], in György Györffy, "Der Ursprung der Székler und ihre Siedlungsgeschichte", in E. Mályusz ed., *Siebenbürgen und seine Völkerschaften,* (Budapest-Leipzig: 1943); K. Schünemann, "Zur Herkunft der Siebenbürger Székler", in *Ungarische Jahrbücher,* vol. IV, 1924; Gy. Sebestyén, *A székelyek neve és eredete* [Name and Origin of the Széklers], (Budapest: 1897); Bálint Hóman, "Der Ursprung der Székler", in *Ungarische Jahrbücher,* vol. II, 1922.

5. While a large proportion of the inhabitants of the districts and seats were free and enjoyed autonomous rights, the inhabitants of the counties, which were based on the feudal system, were nobles and serfs.

6. When the county boundaries were redrawn in 1968, the historical names of three Székler counties were abolished. Udvarhely and Csík Counties were combined under the name of Harghita, and the name of Háromszék County was changed to Covasna.

7. "Csángó" is probably the derivative of an archaic verb that meant "wandering away" or "breaking away."

8. About 13,000 Bucovina-Csángó Magyars were resettled to the Bácska (Hungarian until 1918 and now Yugoslavia) after the annexation of Northern Bucovina by the Soviets in 1941. They were resettled from there to Hungary in 1945.

9. See among others, Mózes Rubinyi, "A moldvai csángók múltja és jelenje" [The Past and the Present of the Csángós of Moldavia], in *Ethnographia,* Budapest, vol. 1901, p. 115; Pál Péter Domokos, *A moldvai magyarság* [The Hungarians of Moldavia], (Csíksomlyó: 1931), p. 15.

10. See László Mikecs, "A Kárpátokon túli magyarság" ["The Hungarians Beyond the Carpathians"], in József Deér and László Gáldi, eds., *Magyarok és románok* [Hungarians and Romanians], (Budapest: 1943), vol. I, p. 446. On the Moldavian and Bucovinan Csángós, the following works provide excellent and detailed information: Ernst Wagner, "Ungarn (Csangonen) in der Moldau und in der Bukowina im Spiegel neuerer rumänischer Quellen-editionen", in *Zeitschrift für Siebenbürgische Landeskunde,* 3. (74) vol., no. 1/80, pp. 27–47; Hugo Weczerka, *Das mittelalterliche und frühneuzeitliche Deutschtum im Fürstentum Moldau,* (München: 1960.)

11. Zoltán Kallós, *Balladák könyve* [Book of Ballads], (Bucharest: 1970.)

12. The name "Saxon" comes quite likely from a word in Latin, the official language of Hungary in the Middle Ages. On the history of the Transylvanian Saxons see, for example, Georg Daniel Teutsch and Friedrich Teutsch, *Geschichte der Siebenbürger Sachsen für das sächsische Volk,* vols. 1–4 (Hermannstadt: 1907–1926); Friedrich Teutsch, *Kleine Geschichte der Siebenbürger Sachsen.* Mit einem Nachwort von A. Möckel (Darmstadt: 1965); Ernst Wagner, *Quellen zur Geschichte der Siebenbürger Sachsen 1191–1975,* (Köln-Wien: 1976); K. K. Klein, *Transsylvanica.* Gesammelte Abhandlungen und Aufsätze zur Sprach—und Siedlungsforschung der Deutschen in Siebenbürgen, (München: 1963).

13. "Königsboden," the name of a large part of the area inhabited by the Saxons, consisted of Saxon seats and districts; but approximately one-third of the Saxon settlers did not live in this area. The Königsboden's inhabitants—Hungarians and Romanians as well as Saxons—were free.

14. See F. Zimmermann and C. Werner, *Urkundenbuch zur Geschichte der Deutschen in Siebenbürgen,* vol. I, document no. 19, p. 11. The Barcaság (in German Burzenland; in Romanian, Ţara Bîrsei) is a flat area in the south-

eastern part of Transylvania, between the Olt River ad the southern Carpathians.

15. Urkundenbuch, doc. 43, p. 32.

16. See F. H. Riedl, *Das Südostdeutschtum in den Jahren 1918-1945*, (München: 1962), p. 46.

17. On the history of the Romanians see, for example, Nicolae Iorga, *Istoria Românilor* [The History of the Romanians], vols. I-X, (Bucharest: 1936-39); C. C. Giurescu and D. C. Giurescu, *Istoria Românilor din cele mai vechi timpuri pînă astăzi* [The History of the Romanians from the Most Ancient Times to the Present], (Bucharest, 2nd ed.: 1975); Robert W. Seton-Watson, *A History of the Roumanians; from Roman Times to the Completion of Unity*, (Cambridge: 1934), 2nd ed. USA: 1963); Georg Stadtmüller, *Geschichte Südosteuropas*, (München: 1950); *Grundfragen der europäischen Geschichte*, (München-Wien: 1965); Alexandru Philippide, *Originea Românilor* [The Origin of the Romanians], vols. I-II (Iaşi: 1923-1927); A. D. Xenopol, *Une énigme historique: les roumains au moyen-âge*, (Paris: 1885); L. Gáldi and L. Makkai, *A románok története* [The History of the Romanians], (Budapest: 1942); André Du Nay, *The Early History of the Rumanian Language*, (Lake Bluff, USA: 1977); Constantin C. Giurescu and Dinu C. Giurescu, *Geschichte der Rumänen, (Bucharest: 1980)*.

18. Historical documents refer to the presence of the Romanians in the territory of Transylvania for the first time: 1222, in: Zimmermann and Werner, *Urkundenbuch,* document 31, p. 18-20; 1223: Silva Blacorum et Bissenorum, am Nordrand der Fogarascher Gebierge, doc. 43, pp. 32-35; the Abbey of Kerz (Kerzer Abtei) as "terra exempta de Blaccis" in: *Urkundenbuch,* doc. 38, pp. 26-28.

19. The word *ispán* came into Hungarian from the Slav *zupan*, meaning, in this case, "lord."

20. For more detail on this see the chapter entitled "The Churches of the National Minorities in Romania".

21. Zoltán I. Tóth, "Román vonatkozású magyar történeti irodalom" ("Hungarian Historical Literature with Romanian Connections"), *Hitel* (Credit), no. 2, Kolozsvár, 1943, p. 125; Elemér, Mályusz, "A magyarság és a nemzetiségek Mohács előtt" ("The Hungarians and the Nationalities before Mohács"), in *Magyar művelődéstörténet* [Hungarian Cultural History], (Budapest: 1942), pp. 105-124.

22. The Hungarians, moving east beyond the Carpathians, inhabited a sizable area of the Romanian voivodship for several centuries. *Secuieni,* for example, was a county inhabited by Széklers and Romanians in Wallachia, the present-day Muntenia; the political division disappeared only in 1845. See C. C. Giurescu, *Judeţele dispărute din Ţara Românească* [Vanished Counties in the Romanian Voivodships], (Bucharest: 1937), pp. 17-18.

23. Elemér Mályusz, "A magyarság és a nemzetiségek Mohács előtt", *op. cit.,* pp. 109-124.

24. See István Bakács, "A török hódoltság korának népessége" ("The Population in the Age of Turkish Domination"), in József Kovacsics, ed., *Magyarország történeti demográfiája* [The Historical Demography of Hungary], (Budapest: 1963), pp. 115-142.

25. See, for example, Zsigmond Jakó, "A románság megtelepülése az újkorban" ("The Settling of the Romanians in the Modern Period") in Elemér Mályusz, ed., *Erdély és népei* [Transylvania and its Peoples], (Budapest: 1941), pp. 118-141; Attila T. Szabó, "A románok újabb kori erdélyi betelepülése" ("The Immigration into Transylvania by the Romanians in the Modern Period"), *Hitel,* June 1942; László Makkai, "Északerdély nemzetiségi viszonyainak a kialakulása" ("The Development of the Nationality Conditions in Northern Transylvania"), *Hitel,* July 1942; G. Müller, "Die ursprüngliche Rechtslage der Rumänen im Siebenbürger Sachsenlande," in *Verfassungs- und Verwaltungsgeschichte der Deutschen in Ungarn,* (Hermannstadt: 1912), vol. I.

26. The Romanian Voivodships or Romanian Principalities (or Danubian Principalities) consisted of the territories of Wallachia and Moldavia, which gained their independence in the fourteenth century. In the fifteenth century they came under Turkish rule; and they merged in 1859. These principalities were formed where the Cumanians and Petchenegues had settled; a part of the principalities, an area that was known as Ungro-Wallachia, was under Hungarian sovereignty during the Middle Ages.

27. The Fanariots were the rulers of the Danubian Principalities from the beginning of the eighteenth to the beginning of the nineteenth centuries. They received the name "Fanariot" from the Fanar district of Constantinople. They were trusted agents of the Turkish court.

28. Zoltán Dávid, "Az 1715-20 évi összeírás" ("The 1715-20 Population Register"), in *A történeti statisztika forrásai* [The Sources of Historical Statistics], (Budapest: 1957), p. 172.

29. The data are based on approximate calculations made from Austrian statistics; see B. Hóman and Gy. Szekfű, *Magyar történet* [Hungarian History], (Budapest: 1936), vol. VI, pp. 443-444; see also R. W. Seton-Watson, *A History of the Roumanians,* (Connecticut: 1963), p. 177.

30. See Nicolae Togan, "Românii din Transilvania la 1733. Conscripția episcopului Ioan In. Klein de Sadu" [The Transylvanian Romanians in 1733. The Population Register of Bishop Ioan In. Klein de Sadu], in *Transilvania,* Sibiu 1898, vol. XXIX.; Augustin Bunea, "Statistica Românilor în anul 1750," in *Transilvania,* no. 32., (1901), pp. 237-292.

31. Based on statistics given by C. A. Macartney, *Hungary and Her Successors,* (London: 1937), p. 264.

32. *Ibid.*

33. On the Swabians of the Banat, the following works provide excellent information: E. Eisenburger, M. Kroner, eds., *Sächsisch-schwäbische Chronik. Beiträge zur Geschichte der Heimat,* (Bucharest: 1976), pp. 81-93,

107-110, 133-139; Johann Wolf, "Wie kamen im 18. Jahrhundert die deutschen Kolonisten ins Banat", in *Forschungen zur Volks- und Landeskunde,* Hermannstadt, vol. 16/2, 1973, pp. 5-20.; Anton Tafferner, *Quellenbuch zur donauschwäbischen Geschichte,* vol. 1, (München: 1974), vol. 2., (Stuttgart: 1977), vol. 3., (Stuttgart: 1978).

34. The Romanian Banat is in the southwestern part of Romania, situated between the Mureş, Tisza and Danube Rivers and comprises Timiş-Torontal and Caraş-Severin Counties.

35. See *Transilvania, Banatul, Crişana şi Maramureşul 1918-1928,* vols. I-III, (Bucharest: 1929), p. 653.

36. See *Die Österreichisch-Ungarische Monarchie in Wort und Bild,* vol. IV, *Hungary,* (Vienna: 1902), pp. 238. *et seq.*

37. Data from E. Wagner's work, *Historisch-statistisches Ortsnamenbuch für Siebenbürgen,* (Cologne-Vienna: 1977), p. 75.

38. In Oradea/Nagyvárad 97.4 percent of the Jews were Hungarian-speaking, in Satu Mare/Szatmár 94.1 percent, in Arad 96.1 percent, in Timişoara/Temesvár 65.3 percent, and in Cluj/Kolozsvár 93.2 percent. See László Fritz, "Az erdélyi magyar anyanyelvű zsidóság" ("The Hungarian-Speaking Jews of Transylvania"), in *Erdélyi Magyar Évkönyv 1918-1929* [Transylvanian Hungarian Yearbook 1918-1929], (Cluj: 1930), pp. 109-117.

39. The data relating to language in the 1910 Hungarian census is published parish by parish in *Magyar Statisztikai Közlemények* [Hungarian Statistical Papers], new series, vol. 42, (Budapest: 1912); also see József Kovacsics, ed., *Magyarország történeti demográfiája. Magyarország népessége a honfoglalástól 1949-ig* [The Historical Demography of Hungary. The Population of Hungary from the Conquest of the Homeland until 1949)], (Budapest: 1963). The Jewish population was not classified according to language in the Hungarian census of 1910. For information on the Romanian census, see R. W. Seton-Watson, *A History of the Roumanians,* new ed., USA 1963, pp. 566-567.

40. Together with Fiume (21,000 square kilometers) as well as Croatia and Slovenia (43,822 square kilometers). Figures relating to the size of the territory of historic Hungary vary according to the source. In the *Magyar Statisztikai Szemle,* nos. 7-8, 1923, p. 289, the 1910 data give the area as 325,411 square kilometers; according to the 1880 data the area was 322,939 square kilometers.

41. See G. Schacher, *Die Nachfolgestaaten—Österreich, Ungarn, Tschechoslowakei—und ihre wirtschaftliche Kräfte,* (Stuttgart: 1932), p. 2; also see *Magyar Statisztikai Szemle,* nos. 7-8, 1923.

42. In Transylvanian usage the term "Regat" does not include Bucovina and Southern Dobrugea.

43. The Bucovina was acquired by the Habsburgs after the first Partition of Poland (1775); it remained an Austrian possession until 1918 when it was attached to Romania. Since 1940, Northern Bucovina has belonged to the Soviet Union.

44. Situated between the Danube, the Balkan Mountains, and the Black Sea, Dobrugea is an area of Romania and Bulgaria. Northern Dobrugea was taken from Bulgaria and granted to Romania by the Treaty of San Stefano (1878), and its modification by the Congress of Berlin (1878). Romania acquired Southern Dobrugea in the 1913 Balkan War; it was, however, returned to Bulgaria by the Craiova Agreement of September 7, 1940.

45. Data by the Hungarian National Refugee Office. This number increased to 260,000 by 1938. Also see H. Bogdan, *Le problème des minorités nationales dans les "États-Successeurs" de l'Autriche-Hongrie*, (Louvain: 1976), p. 13.

46. See E. Mesaroș, "Inceputurile statisticii migrației externe a populației în România" ["The Statistical Beginnings of the External Migrations of the Population of Romania"], *Revista de Statistică* [Statistical Review], 6, Bucharest, 1969, pp. 47–48.

47. See *Nation und Staat*, vol. 14, Vienna, 1940–41, p. 14.

48. See H. Hartl, *Das Schicksal des Deutschtums in Rumänien*, (Würzburg: 1958), p. 35.

49. We find the figure for the German population too low; in our estimation it reached 70,000.

50. See *Recensământul general al României din 6 aprilie 1941: Date sumare provizorii* [The General Romanian Census of April 6, 1941. Preliminary Summary Data], Bucharest, Institutul Central de Statistică, 1944, Table I, p. ix; "Rezultatele Recensământului maghiar 1941" ["The Results of the Hungarian Census of 1941"], *Comunicări Statistice*, no. I, Bucharest, January 15, 1945, Table 18, pp. 14–15; also see Lajos Thirring, "A visszacsatolt keleti terület. Terület és népesség" ["The Re-Annexed Eastern Territory. Territory and Population"], *Magyar Statisztikai Szemle*, nos. 8–9, Budapest, 1940, p. 663.

51. *Magyar Statisztikai Szemle*, nos. 9–12, 1944, pp. 394–410.

52. On the loss of the German population in Romania during World War II the following works provide detailed information: *Dokumentation der Vertreibung der Deutschen aus Ost-Mitteleuropa*. Vol. III: *Das Schicksal der Deutschen in Rumänien*, edited by the Bundesministerium für Vertriebene, Flüchtlinge und Kriegsgeschädigte, (Berlin: 1957); see also *Die deutschen Vertreibungsverluste. Bevölkerungsbilanz für die deutschen Vertreibungsgebiete 1939–1950*, edited by the Statistisches Bundesamt, (Wiesbaden-Stuttgart: 1958), Supplement, W. Krallert; Hans Hartl, *Das Schicksal des Deutschtums in Rumänien*, (Würzburg: 1958).

53. See Krallert's findings in *Die deutschen Vertreibungsverluste*, p. 473.

54. *Dokumentation der Vertreibung der Deutschen aus Ost-Mitteleuropa*, p. 80 E.

55. *Ibid.*, p. 112 E.

56. *Ibid.*

57. Data by the Bundesausgleichsamt.

NOTES   265

58. The population data of some of the territories (Bessarabia, Northern Bucovina, Southern Dobrugea) lost in 1940 by Romania are not included in this figure.

59. Sabin Manuilă and W. Filderman, "Regional Development of the Jewish Population in Romania," *Genus*, vol. XIII, nos. 1-4, Rome, 1957, p. 162.

60. See E. Wagner, *Historisch-statistisches Ortsnamenbuch für Siebenbürgen*, p. 75.

61. S. Fischer-Galati, ed., *Romania*, p. 38.

62. For more detail on this, see Matatias Carp, *Cartea neagră—fapte și documente—suferințele evreilor din România 1940-1944* [Black Book—Facts and Documents—The Sufferings of the Romanian Jews, 1940-1944], (Bucharest: 1946); Oscar I. Janowsky, *People at Bay: The Jewish Problem in East Central Europe*, (London: 1938); Peter Meyer, *The Jews in the Soviet Satellites*, (Syracuse, N.Y.: 1953).

63. Data is cited from S. Fischer-Galati, ed., *Romania*, p. 38.

64. See *The Statistical Bulletin of Israel*, vol. 3, October-April, 1952-1953.

65. S. Fischer-Galati, ed., *Romania*, p. 39.

66. See *Los Angeles Times*, November 11, 1976.

67. See RFE (Radio Free Europe) Special, Washington, January 18, 1977.

68. See the preliminary results of the official Romanian census of January 5, 1977, in *Scînteia* (The Spark), the official daily of the Romanian Communist Party, Bucharest, June 14, 1977, and in *Revista de Statistică*, June, 1977.

69. According to some sources approximately 250,000 Jews in the Regat had already become fully assimilated before the First World War. (See C. A. Macartney and A. W. Palmer, *Independent Eastern Europe*, (London-New York: 1962), p. 168.

Chapter 2

1. See Coriolan Suciu, *Dicționar istoric al localităților din Transilvania* [Historical Dictionary of Transylvanian Localities], (Bucharest: 1967); Ernst Wagner, *Historisch-statistisches Ortsnamenbuch für Siebenbürgen*, Studia Transylvanica 4, (Cologne: 1977), p. 30.

2. Wagner, *Historisch-statistisches Ortsnamenbuch*, p. 30.

3. The county was the largest unit of public administration in Hungary; in Romanian it is known as *"județ"* and in Hungarian *"megye"*, or *"vármegye"*.

4. *Monitorul Oficial*, no. 220, October 7, 1925.

5. Coșna/Kosna and Cârlibaba Nouă/Radnalajosfalva were transferred to Suceava County in Moldavia. Similar regroupings of parishes, some of them of a temporary nature, occurred later as well. Larger-scale transfers of territory to the Regat were barred by the high Carpathian Mountain chain.

6. See "Legea administrativă" ("Public Administration Law"), *Monitorul*

Oficial, no. 187, August 14, 1938. It is characteristic of the spirit of the law that according to Article 58, only those with pure Romanian origins going back at least three generations could become royal governors.

7. See S. Fischer-Galati, ed., *Romania,* p. 32.

8. Maramureş, Crişana, Banat, and Transylvania.

9. The parishes from Székler region, Ghimeş Făget/Gyimesbükk, Bicazul Ardelean/Gyergyóbékás, Bicaz-Chei/Békás, and Poiana Sărată/Sósmező, as well as the town and neighborhood of Orşova/Orsova, with approximately 515 square kilometers were attached to administrative centers of the Old Kingdom, to Neamţ, respectively Mehedinţi Counties.

10. Law No. 5, 1950, *Buletinul Oficial,* no. 77, September 8, 1950. This law established 28 regions, 177 districts (raions), 4,056 parishes, and 148 towns and cities in the area of post-World War II Romania.

11. Arad, Bacău, Bârlad, Bucureşti, Constanţa, Craiova, Galaţi, Hunedoara, Iaşi, Cluj, Baia Mare, Oradea, Piteşti, Ploieşti, Suceava, Stalin (Brassó/Kronstadt), Timişoara, and the Hungarian Autonomous Region.

12. The regions of Arad and Bârlad were abolished; at the same time the Hungarian Autonomous Region was changed to the Mureş-Magyar Autonomous Region.

13. *Buletinul Oficial,* February 17, 1968; see also *Judeţele României Socialiste* [The Counties of Socialist Romania], 2nd ed., (Bucharest: 1972).

14. For example, the town and surrounding area of Baia Mare/Nagybánya, which had a preponderantly Hungarian population, were attached to and thereby almost doubled the area of Maramureş County, which had a Romanian majority; Satu Mare/Szatmár and Sălaj/Szilágy Counties where the Hungarians comprised almost half the population, were considerably decreased. The town of Schässburg/Sighişoara and its environs, which had a Saxon population, were attached to Mureş County with its Romanian majority. One of the three Székler counties, Odorhei/Udvarhely was abolished and most of its territory attached to the former Ciuc/Csík County, from which it is separated by the Hargita Mountain chain; the new county thus formed has the name of Harghita; and finally the historical name of the Háromszék/Trei Scaune County was changed to Covasna/Kovászna.

15. Făgăraş/Fogaras, Târnava Mică/Kisküküllő, Târnava Mare/Nagyküküllő, Someş/Szolnok Doboka, Turda/Torda-Aranyos, and Odorhei/Udvarhely Counties.

16. With about 550,000 people more than the last two censuses had given. The differences between the official census data and the author's figures is clear from the texts given by the author.

17. *Recensământul populaţiei şi locuinţelor din 15. martie 1966* [The Census of the Population and Dwellings of March 15, 1966], vol. I, Part I, Bucharest, 1969, pp. 153, 154, 158, 159.

18. Monica Barcan and Adalbert Millitz, *Die deutsche Nationalität in Rumänien,* (Bucharest: 1977), pp. 45–48.

19. The sources for the results of the 1920 compilation of demographic statistics: G. Martinovici and N. Istrati, *Dicționarul Transilvaniei, Banatului și celorlalte ținuturi alipite* [The Dictionary of Transylvania, the Banat, and the Other Annexed Regions], (Cluj: 1921). This data has been corrected on several occasions by tables published in the periodicals, *Anuarul Statistic al României* (Statistical Yearbook of Romania) and *Buletinul Statistic al României* (Statistical Bulletin of Romania). Right up to 1925 all the official Romanian statistical publications and lectures gave the demographic and mobility data of the one-time Hungarian territories under the heading "Transilvania."

20. See *Recensământul general al populației României din 29 decemvrie 1930* [The General Census of the Romanian Population of December 29, 1930], Sabin Manuilă, ed., Bucharest, 1938, vol. II, pp. 1-180: *neam, limba maternă, religie* (nationality, mother tongue, religion).

21. See V. Moldovan, "Le nouveau régime des cultes en Roumanie," *Revue de Transylvanie*, 1934, no. 8.

22. Between 1921 and 1930 some 42,000 Germans emigrated overseas from the Banat. See *Nation und Staat*, 13 (1939-1940).

23. See *The 1941 Census*, Budapest, 1947; conducted January 31, 1941.

24. See *Recensământul general al României din 6 aprilie 1941. Date sumare provizorii* [The General Romanian Population Census of April 6, 1941. Preliminary Summary Data], Bucharest, 1944, vol. XIV, p. 300.

25. On the 1948 census see A. Golopenția and D. C. Georgescu, "Populația Republicii Populare Române la 25 ianuarie 1948. Rezultatele provizorii ale recensământului" ["The Population of the Romanian People's Republic on January 25, 1948. The Preliminary Results of the Census"] in *Probleme Economice* (Economic Problems), R. Manescu, ed., Bucharest, 1948, paper 2, pp. 28 ff.

26. *Recensământul populației din 21 februarie 1956. Volumul III. Structura populației după naționalitate și limba maternă* [The Population Census of February 21, 1956. The Structure of the Population in Accordance with Nationality and Mother Tongue], Bucharest, 1961, XVIII-XXI. The term "nationality" or *"naționalitate"* has been in use in Romania only since the 1956 census.

In none of the censuses, however, has an attempt been made to show the ethnic communities—the Hungarian, German, Russian, and other nationalities according to dialect, historical origin, religious denomination or other criteria—as independent ethnic groups.

27. *Republica Socialistă România, Recensământul populației și locuințelor din 15, martie 1966* [The Census of the Population and Dwellings of the Romanian Socialist Republic of March 15, 1966], vol. I, Part I, Bucharest, 1969, pp. 153, 154, 158. Direcția Centrală de Statistică (Central Statistical Board).

28. See G. D. Satmarescu, "The Changing Demographic Structure of the Population of Transylvania," *Eastern European Quarterly*, vol. VIII, no. 4, Jan-

uary 1975, p. 432. It must be noted that in the 1920s, for example, 50,000 Hungarian workers immigrated to Bucharest and other towns and cities in the Regat. (See Sándor Turnowsky, "A társadalom" ["Society"], in *Metamorphosis Transilvaniae*, ed. István Györi Illés, (Cluj: 1937).

29. G. D. Satmarescu, "The Changing Demographic Structure," p. 426.
30. *Ibid.*, p. 436.
31. See S. Fischer-Galati, ed., *Romania*, pp. 43–44.
32. See G. D. Satmarescu, "The Changing Demographic Structure," p. 426.
33. *Demographic Yearbook*. Direcţiunea Centrală de Statistică, Bucharest, 1967, Table 13; and *Statistical Yearbook*, Bucharest, 1970.
34. G. D. Satmarescu, "The Changing Demographic Structure," p. 435.
35. See S. Fischer-Galati, ed., *Romania*, p. 49.
36. References to this process are also to be found in some Romanian demographic studies. See I. Measnicov, "Migraţia internă în perioada 1948–1956" ["Internal Migration in the 1948–1956 Period"], *Revista de Statistică*, 2 *(1969), p. 22;* Measnicov-Bîrsan, "Unele aspecte ale migraţiunii interne a populaţiei în corelaţia cu desvoltarea economică a ţării noastre" ["Certain Aspects of the Internal Migration of the Population in Connection with the Economic Development of Our Country"], *Revista de Statistică*, 2 (1963), p. 30; V. Nini, "Populaţia Regiunii Banat la recensămîntul din 15 martie 1966" ["The March 15, 1966 Census of the Population of the Banat Region"], *Revista de Statistică*, 6, (1967), p. 62.
37. The counties that significantly exceed the average are Braşov with 86.4 percent, Cluj with 65.8 percent, Mureş with 45.1 percent, Sibiu with 52.4 percent, and Maramureş with 42.2 percent.
38. See M. Stănescu and I. V. Stoichiţa, "Evoluţia natalităţii în România în anii 1958–1964" ["The Development of the Birthrate in Romania in the Years 1958–1964"], *Revista de Statistică*, 8 (1966), p. 56.
39. E. Wagner, *Historisch-statistisches Ortsnamenbuch*, p. 63.
40. The preliminary results were published by the Central Census Committee in the June 14, 1977 issue of *Scînteia*.
41. See Decree No. 770/1966 forbidding abortion and Decree No. 771/1966 which amended several clauses of the criminal code. The National Demographic Commission was established in March 1971 to promote a higher birthrate.
42. See also Trond Gilberg, *Modernization in Rumania since World War II*, (New York: 1975), pp. 213, 214, 217.; George Cioranescu and P.M.: *Official Romanian Documentary Material on Minority Affairs*, in *Radio Free Europe Research*, RAD Background Report/75 (Romania), April 19, 1978; Mihnea Berindei, "Les minorités nationales en Roumanie" in *L'Alternative*, Paris, vol. 1980, no. 3, pp. 39-40.
43. See J. F. Neigebauer, *Beschreibung der Moldau und Walachei*, (Leipzig: 1848), pp. 288–298.
44. See Virgil N. Mădgearu, *Zur industriellen Entwicklung Rumäniens*, (Weida i. Th.: 1911), pp. 10, 14; *Populaţie şi societate. Studii de demografie*

NOTES

istorică [Population and Society. Studies in Historical Demography], vol. I, Ş. Pascu, ed., (Cluj: 1972), p. 250.

45. *Recensămîntul general 1930*, vols. V-VI.

46. See G. Retegan, "Evoluţia populaţiei urbane a României" ["The Development of the Urban Population of Romania"], *Revista de Statistică*, 7 (1965), p. 66, V. Trebici, *Populaţia României şi creşterea economică* [The Population of Romania and Economic Growth], (Bucharest: 1971), pp. 264–265.

47. See G. D. Satmarescu, "The Changing Demographic Structure," p. 425.; T. Gilberg, *op cit.*, p. 209.

48. See *Dokumentation der Vertreibung der Deutschen aus Ost-Mitteleuropa*, p. 6E.

49. Sándor Vita, "Tallózás az 1930. évi román népszámlálás köteteiben", ["Gleaning in the Volumes of the Romanian Census of 1930"] in *Hitel*, Kolozsvár, vol. 2, 1936, pp. 34–35.

50. See N. Istrate, "Ardealul şi Banatul în lumina cifrelor," ["Transylvania and the Banat in the Light of Numbers"] in *Transilvania, Banatul, Crişana şi Maramureşul 1918-1928*, I-III, (Bucharest: 1929), p. 677.

51. G. D. Satmarescu, "The Changing Demographic Structure," p. 433.

52. An average of 17,000 people, for example, immigrated into Arad, Braşov, Cluj-Napoca, Oradea, and Timişoara during this period. See G. R. Şerbu, "Căile de creştere numerică a populaţiei oraşelor mari ale R.P.R." ["The Paths of the Numerical Growth of the Population in the Larger Cities of the R.P.R."], *Revista dē Statistică*, no. 5, 1961, pp. 26–34.

53. On the new Romanian settlers in the Transylvanian cities with predominate Hungarian or German population see Franz Ronneberger, "Sozialstruktur", in *Rumänien. Südosteuropa Handbuch*, Klaus-Detlev Grothusen, ed., (Göttingen: 1977), p. 415.

54. See "The Hungarian Minority Problem in Rumania," *Bulletin of the International Commission of Jurists*, no. 17, December 1963, Geneva, p. 74.

55. Through a State Council Decree of October 16, 1974 Cluj/Kolozsvár received an additional mark of Daco-Romanian continuity—its name was changed to "Cluj-Napoca".

56. Sources: *The 1910 Census*, in *Magyar Statisztikai Közlemények*, Budapest, 1912; the population register of 1920, in *Dicţionarul Transilvaniei*, Cluj, 1921; *Recensămîntul general 1930; Recensămîntul general 1941;* the results of the 1948 census in *Probleme Economice*, 1948, no. 2; *Recensămîntul populaţiei 1956*.

57. The population of Cluj-Napoca, for example, numbered 273,199 in 1979, and that of Timişoara 277,779; of Braşov 268,226; of Oradea 179,780; of Arad 174,411, and of Tîrgu Mureş 136,679. See *Anuarul Statistic al RSR 1979*. (Statistical Yearbook of the Romanian Socialist Republic 1979), Bucharest, pp. 50–53.

58. *Enciclopedia României* [The Encyclopaedia of Romania]. (Bucharest: 1937), vol. III, p. 42; *Institutul Central de Statistică* (Central Institute of

Statistics), Populația Republicii Populare Române la 25 ianuarie 1948 [Population of the Romanian People's Republic, January 25, 1948], Bucharest, 1948, p. 12; Virgil Ioanid, "Factori al sistematizării localităților urbane și rurale" ["The Factors for the Systematization of the Urban and Rural Settlements"], *Lupta de Clasă*, (Class Struggle), Bucharest, no. I, 1968, pp. 44–45.

59. *Anuarul Statistic al Republicii Socialistă România* (The Annual Statistics of the Romanian Socialist Republic), 1975, pp. 5, 9.

60. See Mihai Dulea, "România—țara socialistă în curs de desvoltare" ["Romania—a Socialist Country in the Process of Development"], *Era Socialistă* (Socialist Age) (previously *Lupta de Clasă*), Bucharest, no. 3, 1973, pp. 21–24.

61. Petru Deica, "Structura populației pe clase și ramuri de activitate" [The Structure of the Population According to Classes and Occupation], in *Monografia Geografică al RPR*, Bucharest vol. II, pp. 43–53.

62. *Recensământul populației din 21 februarie 1956* [The Census of February 21, 1956], vol. III. The Structure of the Population, pp. 296, et. seq.; *Recensământul populației și locuințelor din 15 martie 1966*, vol. I, p. 157.

63. A graphic representation of this demographic aging can be found in *Breviarul Statistic al Republicii Socialiste România* [The Statistical Summary of the Romanian Socialist Republic], (Bucharest: 1970).

Chapter 3

1. Hugh Seton-Watson, *Osteuropa zwischen den Kriegen 1918–1941*, (Paderborn: 1948), p. 91.

2. Excellent and detailed data are provided in Theodor Veiter, *Nationalitätenkonflikt und Volksgruppenrecht im 20. Jahrhundert*, vol. I: Entwicklungen, Rechtsprobleme, Schlussfolgerungen, (Vienna: 1977).

3. See below for a fuller discussion of the Resolutions of Alba Iulia and the Paris Minorities Treaty.

4. Ciucea is a village in western Transylvania.

5. László Fritz, "Az erdélyi magyar anyanyelvű zsidóság" [The Hungarian-speaking Transylvanian Jewry], in Sulyok-Fritz eds., *Erdélyi Magyar Évkönyv 1918–1929* [Transylvanian-Hungarian Yearbook], vol. I, (Cluj: 1930), pp. 109–117.

6. See, among others, C. A. Macartney and A. W. Palmer, *Independent Eastern Europe*, (London: 1932); Arnold Werner, "Rumäniens Volksgruppenpolitik von den Karlsburger Beschlüssen 1918 bis zur Gegenwart," in *Monatshefte für Auswärtige Politik*, vol. 5, 1938, p. 1070; *Dokumentation der Vertreibung der Deutschen aus Ost-Mitteleuropa*, vol. III, *Das Schicksal der Deutschen in Rumänien*, ed. by the Bundesministerium für Vertriebene, Flüchtlinge und Kriegsgeschädigte, (Berlin: 1957), specially pp. 20 E-27 E.

7. The national minorities in Romania had contacts with the Interparliamentary Union, the Nationality League, the International Union of the Association for the League of Nations, the International Association of Minority Newspapermen, and various church and religious movements. They could direct their appeals to and through these organizations to publicize their complaints.

8. Imre Mikó, *Huszonkét év* [Twenty-Two Years], (Budapest: 1941), p. 303. In neutralizing the complaints of its national minorities to the League of Nations Romania counted from the very beginning on the support of France. Thus, for example, the French Department of the League of Nations remarked in a note written for the Political Department of the Quai d'Orsay on April 6, 1923, that "although the Hungarian complaint is justified, the Romanians are our friends." (Archives du Ministère des Affaires Étrangères Paris, série Z, Roumanie, t.43, p. 81. Quoted in H. Bogdan, *Le problème des minorités nationales dans les "États-Successeurs" de l'Autriche Hongrie*, (Louvain: 1976), p. 11. See also Pablo de Azcarate y Florez, *League of Nations and National Minorities*, (Washington, D.C.: 1945); Arthur Balogh, "Die Autonomie in Religions- und Schulfragen der széklerischen und sächsischen Gemeinschaften in Siebenbürgen", in *Nation und Staat*, 5/1931–1932, pp. 531–542.

The League of Nations' system for the protection of minorities ceased to function for all practical purposes with the outbreak of the Second World War and formally came to an end with the signing of the 1947 peace treaties. Further literature on the nationality subject: C. A. Macartney, *National States and National Minorities*, (London: 1934); Arthur Balogh, *Der internationale Schutz der Minderheiten*, (Munich: 1928); Felix Ermacora, "Innerstaatliche, regionale und universelle Struktur eines Volksgruppenrechtes," in Th. Veiter, ed., *System eines internationalen Volksgruppenrechts*, II part, (Vienna-Stuttgart: 1972); Hugo Wintgens, *Der völkerrechtliche Schutz der nationalen, sprachlichen und religiösen Minderheiten*, (Stuttgart: 1930).

9. The essay of Otto Folberth in the Hungarian-language literary journal, *Erdélyi Helikon* (Cluj: 1928), p. 66. The German-language literary journal, *Klingsor* (Brașov/Kronstadt) advocated a spiritual reconciliation between the three Transylvanian nations—the Romanians, Saxons, and Hungarians. See, for example, Heinrich Zillich, "Siebenbürgen und der Curentul," *Klingsor*, August 1928, vol, 5, pp. 314–316; Egon Hajek, "Von siebenbürgischen Menschen," *Klingsor*, vol. 3, 1926, pp. 137–139.

10. An attempt to represent Transylvanism, was the foundation of the Romanian journal *Cultura*, in Cluj, January 1924, published in four languages—Romanian, Hungarian, German and French.

11. Quoted in *Dokumentation der Vertreibung der Deutschen aus Ost-Mitteleuropa, op. cit.*, p. 32E.

12. *Ellenzék* [Opposition] Cluj, January 10, 1932.

13. The Iron Guard was an extreme Romanian nationalist and fascist terrorist organization. It was founded in 1927 as the "Legion of the Archangel Michael," and the name "Iron Guard" was adopted in 1930. It was abolished in 1935 but reconstituted later as the "All for the Fatherland" organization. This strongly anti-minority and particularly anti-Semitic organization came to power in 1940. After their open rebellion in January 1941, General Antonescu liquidated them ; their leaders were executed. See also M. Fătu and I. Spălățelu, *Garda de fier, organizație teroristă de tip fascist* [The Iron Guard, a Fascist Terror Organization], (Bucharest: 1971); Corneliu Zelea Codreanu, *Eiserne Garde,* (Berlin: 1939); *Pentru legionari* [For Legionaries], (Bucharest: 1940). A valuable source of information on Romanian fascism is Eugen Weber, "Romania," in Hans Rogger and Eugen Weber, eds., *The European Right. A Historical Profile.* (Berkeley, Calif.: 1965), pp. 501–574.

14. "Vásárhely" is the short version of Marosvásárhely/Tîrgu Mureș.

15. Ernst Wagner, *Quellen zur Geschichte der Siebenbürger Sachsen 1191–1975,* (Cologne-Vienna: 1976), p. 259.

16. The decree of September 15, 1940. The term was abolished after the fall of the Iron Guard on February 15, 1941.

17. *Monatshefte für Auswärtige Politik,* vol. 7, no. 9 (September 1940), p. 706. Important data on German-Romanian relations are found in Andreas Hillgruber, *Hitler, König Carol und Marschall Antonescu. Die deutsch-rumänischen Beziehungen 1938–1944,* 2nd ed., (Wiesbaden: 1965).

18. Decree-Law No. 830/1940, "über die Konstituierung der Deutschen Volksgruppe in Rumänien," in *Monitorul Oficial* [Official Gazette], part I, no. 275/1940, November 21, 1940, p. 6530.

19. Turnu Severin is a Romanian town on the Danube.

20. See Petru Groza, *L'École du pouvoir,* (Paris: 1947), p. 202 and *In the Darkness of Prison,* p. 291; see also C. A. Macartney, *October Fifteenth,* (Edinburgh: 1957), vol. II, p. 351; Amelia C. Leiss—R. Dennet, *European Peace Treaties after World War II,* (New York: 1954), p. 102.

21. The Craiova (Oltenia) Agreement, September 7, 1940.

22. A documented analysis on the Second Vienna Award by E. Wagner, *op. cit.,* p. 295, note 14; see also C. A. Macartney, *op. cit.,* vol. I, pp. 419–424.

23. *General Census of Romania,* April 6, 1941, Central Statistical Office, Bucharest, 1944, Table 1, p. ix.; "Rezultatele Recensământului Maghiar 1941" ["The Results of the Hungarian Census"], in *Comunicări Statistice* [Statistical Publications], no. 1, January 15, 1945, Table 18, pp. 14–15.

24. See S. Fischer-Galati, ed., *Romania,* (New York: 1956), p. 121.

25. Important information of these points may be found in A. D. Finkelstein, *Fénysugár a rémület éjszakájában* [A Ray of Light in the Night of Horrors], (Tel-Aviv: 1958).

26. Finkelstein, *op cit.,* p. 15.

27. Eduard Beneš, President of Czechoslovakia, represented the exiled Czechoslovak government in London from 1941 onward; the émigré politicians

from Central Europe gathered around his English-language journal, *Central European Observer.*

28. From the report to the Hungarian Ministry of Foreign Affairs and documentation relating to Transylvania in the Archives of Department II (Minorities) of the Prime Minister's Office, 15008/1944 and the Archives of the Party History Institute Attached to the Central Committee of the Hungarian Socialist Workers' Party, R 25046/1944, 17060/1944.

29. A. C. Leiss-R. Dennet, *European Peace Treaties after World War II,* pp. 101-102., 299; A. Cretzianu, "Rumanian Armistice Negotiations," in *Journal of Central European Affairs,* (Boulder, Colorado), October 1951, pp. 243-258.

30. A. Cretzianu, *Captive Rumania,* (New York: 1956), pp. 18-20.

31. The Transylvanian Party was founded in May 1941 by a group of Transylvanian deputies. It supported the Hungarian government of the time.

32. Alba Iulia is a town in central Transylvania. Its Hungarian name is Gyulafehérvár; and its old German name Weissenburg, from 1715 Karlsburg.

33. Great Britain, France, Russia, Belgium, and Serbia; later also Italy, the USA, and Japan. Treaties for the protection of the minorities were concluded with Poland, Romania, Yugoslavia, Czechoslovakia, and Greece. See Theodor Grentrup, *Das Deutschtum an der mittleren Donau in Rumänien und Jugoslawien,* (Münster: 1930), pp. 3-13.; Erwin Viefhaus, *Die Minderheitenfrage und die Entstehung der Minderheitenschutzverträge auf der Pariser Friedenskonferenz 1919. Eine Studie zur Geschichte des Nationalitätenproblems im 19. und 20. Jahrhundert,* (Marburg: 1960).

34. See F. Ermacora, "Über den Minderheitenschutz in den Friedensverträgen der Donaustaaten nach dem Zweiten Weltkrieg", in *Der Donauraum,* vol. 11, nos. 1-2, 1966, p. 67.

35. Valuable data are provided in David Hunter-Miller, *My Diary at the Peace Conference of Paris,* (New York: 1924-1926), vol. XIII, New States, (Minorities).

36. *Gazeta Oficială* (Official Gazette), no. 3, December 31, 1918. The original text of the Alba Iulia Resolutions is contained in Ioan Clopoțel, *Revoluția din 1918 și unirea Ardealului cu România* [The 1918 Revolution and Transylvania's Union with Romania], (Cluj: 1936), pp. 121-123; the German text in E. Wagner, *Quellen zur Geschichte der Siebenbürger Sachsen, op. cit.* p. 264.

37. The Romanian national minorities are referred to as the "coinhabiting peoples" (*popoarele conlocuitoare*) in the Alba Iulia Resolutions; the present official terminology also refers to "coinhabiting nationalities" (*naționalitățile conlocuitoare*).

38. The proclamation of protest issued by the Hungarian-Székler National Council on December 18, 1918, and the self-determining national assembly of the Transylvanian Hungarians on December 22. See Imre Mikó, *op cit.,* p. 11.

39. A documented analysis by Walter König "Haben die Siebenbürger Sachsen und die Banater Schwaben 1918/1919 bedingungslos dem Anschluss

an Rumänien zugestimmt?", in *Zeitschrift für Siebenbürgische Landeskunde,* vol. 2/73, no. 1/79, pp. 101–110. See also C. A. Macartney and A. W. Palmer, *Independent Eastern Europe, op. cit.,* note 2.

40. See, among others, the criticism of the report by M. Constantinescu, L. Bányai, V. Curticăpeanu, and C. Göllner, Romanian historians, by Soviet Academician V. M. Turok, among the contributions in "Zur nationalen Frage in Österreich-Ungarn 1900–1918," in *Die nationale Frage in der Österreichisch-Ungarischen Monarchie 1900–1918,* (Budapest: 1966), pp. 307–309. The Romanian daily *Universul,* published in Bucharest, contained a revealing article on October 8, 1930, according to which Alexandru Vaida-Voevod, a well-known Romanian politician in those days, had published a secret pamphlet in Vienna in 1922 under the title "Ardealul Ardelenilor" [Transylvania Belongs to the Transylvanians], which stated, among other things, "The circumstances under which the Alba Iulia Resolutions came about clearly prove that the union of Transylvania with Romania was proclaimed only as the result of a certain amount of pressure." The content of the pamphlet is published in German in Herbert van Leisen, *Das siebenbürgische Problem,* (Geneva: 1943), pp. 101–102.

41. H. van Leisen, *Das siebenbürgische Problem* [The Transylvanian Question], pp. 104–105.

42. Valuable data are provided in H. Seton-Watson, *op. cit.* p. 229, note 1. The fulfillment of a secret agreement, which promised Romania a large part of the Hungarian Plain, almost as far as Szeged and Debrecen, was hindered by the treaty concluded in the meantime between Bucharest and the Central Powers.

43. See among others Theodor Grentrup, *Das Deutschtum an der mittleren Donau in Rumänien und Jugoslawien, op. cit.,* p. 16; Henry Bogdan, *Le problème des minorités nationales, op. cit.,* spec. pp. 12–14; *Dokumentation der Vertreibung der Deutschen, op. cit.,* p. 27 E.

44. Romul Boila, *Organizația de stat* [The Organization of the State], (Cluj: 1929), p. 135; Radu Budișteanu, *Un capitol nou în dreptul internațional public și privat: Minoritățile etnice* [A New Chapter in International Public and Civil Law: the Ethnic Minorities], (Bucharest: 1928), p. 49; Gheorghe Sofronie, "Actul dela Alba Iulia și valoarea sa internațională" [The Act of Alba Iulia and its International Value], *Transilvania,* LXXIV, 1943, pp. 866–875.

45. See Silviu Dragomir, *La Transylvanie roumaine et ses minorités ethniques,* (Bucharest: 1934), p. 260.

46. Concerning the original text of the Paris Minorities Treaty, see in *Protection des minorités de langue, de race et de religion par Société des Nations. Recueil des stipulations,* (Geneva: 1927).

47. W. König, *op. cit.,* p. 107, note 39. See further Zsombor Szász, *The Minorities in Roumanian Transylvania,* (London: 1927), p. 22 *et seq.,* 319 *et seq.;* Th. Grentrup, *Das Deutschtum, op. cit.,* p. 15.

48. *Nouă Constituție a României, 1923. Prelegeri organizate de Institutul Social Român* [Romania's New Constitution, 1923. Lectures Organized by the Romanian Social Institute], (Bucharest: n.d.), pp. 27-28.

49. The Hungarian representative of the Entente remarked: "I have no doubt whatsoever that the Romanian authorities, with or without the knowledge of the Bucharest government, use all available means to oppress the Hungarians living in the country." (Archives du Ministère des Affaires Étrangères Paris, série Z, Roumanie, t. 41, Tg du 6 novembre 1919, Sir George Clerk au Conseil Suprême Paris). Quoted in H. Bogdan, *op. cit.*, p. 12, note 6.

50. The agrarian reform had already been planned in 1919, but it was carried out only from 1921 onward. The Decree-Law 3911 of September 10, 1919, was replaced by the law of July 30, 1921 (*Monitorul Oficial*, no. 82, July 30, 1921).

51. On the Romanian agrarian reform and its political aspects, see C. A. Macartney, *Hungary and Her Successors. The Treaty of Trianon and its Consequences 1919-1937.* (London, New York, Toronto: 1937), pp. 316-320; I. L. Evans, *The Agrarian Revolution in Rumania*, (Oxford: 1930); D. Mitrany, *The Land and the Peasant in Roumania*, (Cambridge: 1924); E. Wagner, *Historisch-statistisches Ortsnamenbuch für Siebenbürgen*, (Cologne: 1977), p. 99.

52. Miklós Endes, *Erdély három nemzete és négy vallása autonómiájának története* [The History of the Autonomy of the Three Nations and Four Religions of Transylvania], (Budapest: 1935), p. 487.

53. See Archives du Ministère des Affaires Étrangères Hongrie, 13/pol. du 31 décembre 1921 à Haut Commissaire de France Budapest. Quoted in H. Bogdan, *op. cit.*, p. 14, note 6.

54. *Ibid.*, serie Z., Roumanie t. 43, Rapport Consul de France à Cluj d'Affaires Étrangères, Paris, 3 février 1923.

55. P. de Azcarate, *La Société des Nations et la protection des minorités*, (Geneva: 1969), pp. 35-44. Quoted in *Ibid*.

56. See Lajos Jordáky, *Az erdélyi társadalom szerkezete* [The Structure of the Transylvanian Society], (Kolozsvár: 1946), pp. 5-6.

57. *Monitorul Oficial*, no. 282, March 29, 1923.

58. Archives du Ministère des Affaires Étrangères Paris, série Z, Roumanie, t. 41. Mémoire du 13 janvier 1920 de l'Église presbytérienne d'Angleterre adressé au Conseil Suprême; *Ibid.* t. 41, Lt. no. 102, Ministre de France Bucarest á Archives du Ministère des Affaires Étrangères, Paris, 12 septembre 1920. Quoted by H. Bogdan, *op. cit.*, p. 12, note 6.

59. See a document of the Union Internationale des Associations pour la Société des Nations with the signature of Secretary General Th. Ruyssen, *Archives de la Société des Nations* 1481/58 075/R, 1630. Quoted by H. Bogdan, *op. cit.*, p. 13, note 6.

60. *Monitorul Oficial*, no. 60, June 19, 1923.

61. For the text of the decree concerning the dismissal of railway employees, see Imre Mikó, *Huszonkét év*, p. 128.

62. See *Pandectele Române*, XV, 1936, III, p. 50. According to the January 1936 report of the leader of the Transylvanian Saxons, Hans Otto Roth, more than 580 German civil servants were dismissed. The losses suffered by the Hungarians were considerably greater. (Quoted in C. A. Macartney, *Hungary and Her Successors*, p. 296.)

63. Imre Mikó, *Huszonkét év*, p. 148.

64. Legea pentru unificarea administrativă [The Law Concerning the Unification of Public Administration], *Monitorul Oficial*, no. 128, July 14, 1925.

65. One last attempt was made to restore local self-government on the basis of the new public administration law enacted in 1929. In February–March 1930, the first—and the last—village and county elections to self-governing bodies were held in Romania. In these, the national minorities gained representation in proportion to their numbers. However, the newly elected organs could not begin to function, since a change of government led to the final abolition even of the principle of local self-government.

66. See, E. Ammende, *Die Nationalitäten in den Staaten Europas*. Sammlung von Lageberichten. (Vienna, Leipzig: 1931; supplement Vienna; 1932), 415 *et. seq.*

67. H. Hartl, *Das Schicksal des Deutschtums in Rumänien*, (Würzburg: 1958), p. 57. According to the data provided by Hartl, at the end of the 1930's the Transylvanian Saxons had 135 credit cooperatives, 36 consumers' cooperatives, 2 wine-growers cooperatives, and other types of cooperatives as well. Following the foundation of the joint cooperative union of the Transylvanian Saxons and the Swabians of the Banat, the National Union of German Cooperatives in Romania (*Landesverband der deutschen Genossenschaft in Rumänien*), comprised 262 credit cooperatives, 167 purchasing and marketing cooperatives, 47 consumers' cooperatives, and 28 other types of cooperative.

68. The Transylvanian Hungarian Economic Federation (*Erdélyi Magyar Gazdasági Egyesület*), the Transylvanian Hungarian Banking Syndicate (*Erdélyi Magyar Bankszindikátus*), the Federation of Credit Cooperatives (*Hitelszövetkezetek Szövetsége*) and the Hangya Cooperative Center (*Hangya Szövetkezetek Központja*) were all sizeable economic organizations.

69. The law was to have been issued on June 7, 1937, but it was withdrawn on the protest of the national minorities. Quoted by E. Wagner, *Quellen zur Geschichte der Siebenbürger Sachsen*, p. 291.

70. See "Legea pentru pregătirea profesională și exercitarea meșeriilor" [The Law Concerning Vocational Training and the Practice of a Vocation], *Monitorul Oficial*, no. 99, April 30, 1936.

71. "Statistica impozitelor directe pe 1924" [The Statistics of Direct Taxes for the Year 1924]. Ministerul Finanțelor, Direcțiunea Statisticei general al Finanțelor [Ministry of Finance, The General Statistical Directorate of Finances], (Bucharest: 1926, 1927). "Lei" is the Romanian monetary unit.

72. Cernăuți County in Bucovina, for example, where Jews and Germans lived in large numbers. *Anuarul Statistic al României 1937–38* [Romanian Statistical Yearbook, 1937–1938], published by Institutul Central de Statistică [Central Office of Statistics], (Bucharest: 1939), pp. 260–261; "Statistica impozitelor directe pe anii 1925 și 1926" [Statistics on Direct Taxes, 1925–1926], by L. Fritz, in *Magyar Kisebbség* [Hungarian Minority], (Lugoj), June 26, 1928; *Anuarul Statistic al României 1937–1938* [Romanian Statistical Yearbook 1937–1938].

73. The Austrian "Joch" (yoke) is 0.575 hectares, or about 1.42 acres.

74. C. A. Macartney, *Hungary and Her Successors*, p. 319.

75. The Minority Statute contained three Decree-Laws: part I, in *Monitorul Oficial* no. 101, May 4, 1938; part II, in *Monitorul Oficial* no. 178, August 4, 1938; and part III. *ibid.*

76. Article 18. *Monitorul Oficial*, no. 178, Aug. 4, 1938.

77. *Monitorul Oficial*, no. 49, March 1, 1938.

78. See A. Cretzianu, *Captive Rumania*, p. 21.

79. See Fischer-Galati, ed., *Romania*, p. 64.

80. See *Szakszervezet* [Trade Union; Hungarian-language press organ published in Cluj], no. 128, March 1945; see also *Monatshefte für Auswärtige Politik*, (Berlin), vol. 11, 1944, p. 550.

81. For the text of the Romanian Armistice Agreement, see E. C. Ciurea, *Le traité de paix avec la Roumanie du 10. février 1947*, (Paris: 1954).

82. See *Munkások és földművesek naptára* [Calendar for Workers and Farmers], (Cluj: 1945), p. 136.

83. A. Cretzianu, *Captive Rumania*, p. 32.

84. *Scânteia*, (Bucharest), March 11, and 12, 1945; see also Keesing's *Archiv der Gegenwart*, vol. 15 (1945), pp. 135 D, 137 A, 138 B. *Scînteia* [The Spark], the chief journal of the RCP, named in honor of Lenin's *Iskra*, was founded in 1931 and resumed publication in 1944. The original spelling, "Scânteia," was changed to "Scînteia" as part of the program of "de-Russification."

85. See *Roumania at the Peace Conference: Paris 1946* (Romanian Government Publication), Switzerland, 1946, pp. 35–41 and Annex I, pp. 49–78.

86. See Ferenc Nagy, *The Struggle behind the Iron Curtain*, (New York: 1948), pp. 204, 209–210, 218–219.

87. S. D. Kertesz, *Diplomacy in a Whirlpool. Hungary between Nazi Germany and Soviet Russia*, (Notre Dame, Ind.: 1953), p. 181.

88. Source of information in *A Szovjetunió története 1926–1945*. Válogatott dokumentumok. [The History of the Soviet Union 1926–1945, Selected Documents], (Budapest: 1967).

89. S. D. Kertesz, *Diplomacy in a Whirlpool*, (Indiana: 1953), p. 182.

90. Ghița Ionescu, *Communism in Rumania, 1944–1962*, (London: 1964), p. 129; F. Nagy, *The Struggle behind the Iron Curtain*, p. 214.

91. The Paris Peace Conference was proceeded by a conference of the foreign ministers of the four great powers in May 1946, which discussed the conditions for the peace conference with the satellite states (Bulgaria, Finland, Hungary, Italy, and Romania) and made recommendations as well as preempting certain decisions for the peace conference.

92. C. L. Sulzberger, "Rumania Gets Rule in Transylvania," *The New York Times,* May 8, 1946, p. 1.

93. Report of the British Commissioner in Rumania, Le Rougetel, to Foreign Secretary Anthony Eden, on his visit to Cluj on July 19, 1945: FO 371, R 451/451/21, 6.1.1945. London, Foreign Office.

94. Its official name is not peace conference but the Paris Conference (Conférence de Paris 1946).

95. *Paris Peace Conference 1946: Selected Documents,* Department of State, Publication 2868, Conference Series 103. (Washington, D.C.: 1947).

96. Gyula Juhász, "Az üszkös pillanat. Magyar-angol titkos tárgyalások 1943-ban. II. rész." [The Smouldering Moment. Secret Anglo-Hungarian Negotiations in 1943. Part II], in *Új Írás* [New Writing], (Budapest), June 1977, pp. 54–80.

97. For the text of the Paris Peace Treaty, see World Peace Foundation, *European Peace Treaties After World War II,* 1954, pp. 298–321. For the German text of the Paris Peace Treaty see E. Menzel, *Die Friedensverträge nach 1947 mit Italien, Ungarn, Bulgarien, Rumänien und Finnland,* (Oberursel: 1948). The Peace Treaty with Romania see E. C. Ciurea, *Le traité de paix avec la Roumanie du 10 février 1947,* (Paris: 1954). By signing the peace treaty Romania *de facto* became one of the satellite states of the Soviet Union.

98. Ghiţa Ionescu, *Communism in Rumania 1944–1962,* p. 131.

99. Decree-Law No. 363/1947 on the Proclamation of the Romanian People's Republic, *Monitorul Oficial,* Part I, no. 300, 1947.

100. Law No. 393.

101. See *Siebenbürgisch-Deutsches Tageblatt* [Transylvanian German Daily], (Hermannstadt), vol. 71, no. 201, September 1, 1944, quoted in *Dokumentation der Vertreibung der Deutschen aus Ost-Mitteleuropa. p. 83 E.*

102. Decree-Law No.485/1944, October 8, concerning the abolition of Law No. 830/1940 on the institutionalization of the German ethnic group in Romania. *Monitorul Oficial,* part I, no. 233/1944.

103. Further literature on the deportation of the German population: Alfred Bohmann, *Menschen und Grenzen,* vol. 2: *Bevölkerung und Nationalitäten in Südosteuropa. Rumänien,* pp. 101–218, (Cologne: 1969), p. 189; *Dokumentation der Vertreibung der Deutschen aus Ost- Mitteleuropa,* vol. III, pp. 79 E, 80 E, and 85 E; Nicolas Spulber, *The Economics of Communist Eastern Europe,* (Cambridge, Mass.: 1957), p. 237; S. Fischer-Galati, ed., *Romania,* p. 38; *Die deutschen Vertreibungsverluste. Bevölkerungsbilanz für die deutschen Vertreibungsgebiete 1939–1950.* Edited by Statistisches Bundesamt. (Wiesbaden: 1958), Contribution W. Krallert, p. 482.

104. Hans Hartl, *Das Schicksal des Deutschtums in Rumänien*, p. 121.
105. Decree No. 826/1946, *Monitorul Oficial*, part I, no. 243/1946.
106. Dániel Csatári, *Forgószélben. Magyar-román viszony 1940-1945*, [In the Whirlwind. Hungarian-Romanian Relationship 1940-1945], (Budapest: 1968), p. 432.
107. Valuable information is provided in Titus Popovici, *Străinul* [The Alien], (Bucharest: 1972), pp. 438-444; P. Séqueil, *Le dossier de la Transylvanie*, (Paris: 1967), p. 120; Dániel Csatári, *Forgószélben*, p. 441. The so-called Maniu-Guard (named after Maniu's Peasant Party), consisted of approximately 10,000 men, armed by the Romanian Military High Command. They followed the Soviet and Romanian regular troops into the Hungarian-inhabited Transylvanian villages where, under the pretext of "restoring law and order," they massacred the defenseless population.
108. Left-wing movement consisting largely of workers and intellectuals, between the two world wars. It was abolished in 1944.
109. *The New York Times*, March 11, 1945.
110. From the text of the proclamation of the Tîrgu Mureş/Marosvásárhely meeting of the Hungarian People's Alliance, held on November 15-18, 1945, published in the December 2, 1945 issue of the Hungarian newspaper, *Falvak Népe* [The People of the Villages], (Cluj). The three-day conference summarized the grievances of the Hungarians in Romania in eleven points.
111. See *A nemzetiségi politika három éve a demokratikus Romániában*, [Three Years of Nationality Policy in Democratic Romania], (Bucharest: 1948), p. 26.
112. See Articles 17 and 22 of Part I of the Nationality Statute issued on February 6, 1945.
113. See the April 12, 1945 issue of the Hungarian-language periodical *Népi Egység* [The Unity of the People], published in Braşov.
114. Decree No. 847/1945. See the April 3, 1945 issue of *Erdély* [Transylvania], the journal of the Transylvanian Social Democratic Party, published in Kolozsvár.
115. See *Magyar Nemzet* [Hungarian Nation], (Budapest), July 29, 1945.
116. See Sándor Kelemen, *Az erdélyi helyzet* [The Transylvanian Situation], (Budapest: 1946).
117. Ghiţa Ionescu, *Communism in Rumania*, p. 184. T. Gilberg estimated the number of Jews who emigrated from Romania between 1947 and 1975 at 300,000 (Cf., T. Gilberg, *Modernization in Rumania Since World War II*, (New York: 1975), p. 267.
118. László Rajk, one-time member of the Hungarian Communist Party, Minister of Internal (1946-1948) and later of Foreign Affairs (1948-1949). He was a victim of the purges carried out by means of Moscow-instigated show-trials; in 1949 he was sentenced to death and executed on the basis of fabricated charges.

119. See T. Gilberg, *Modernization in Rumania Since World War II*, (New York: 1975), p. 211; a discussion of anti-Semitism in Romania can be found in Peter Meyer, *et al., The Jews in the Soviet Satellites*, (Syracuse: N.Y.: 1953), and H. Seton-Watson, *Eastern Europe between the Wars 1918-1941*. (Cambridge, England: 1945) pp. 288-296.

120. Detailed data are provided in E. Viefhaus, *Die Minderheitenfrage und die Entstehung der Minderheitenschutzverträge auf der Pariser Friedenskonferenz 1919, op. cit.;* see A. C. Leiss—R. Dennet, *European Peace Treaties After World War II*, (New York: 1954); Peter Pernthaler, *Der Schutz der ethnischen Gemeinschaften durch individuelle Rechte*, (Vienna-Stuttgart: 1964).

121. See F. Ermacora, "Über den Minderheitenschutz in den Friedensverträgen der Donaustaaten nach dem Zweiten Weltkrieg", in *Der Donauraum,* vol. 11, nos. 1-2, p. 70.

122. Romania recognized the Universal Declaration of Human Rights at the time of its admission to the UN on December 14, 1955. See V. Duculescu, *Romania la Organizația Națiunilor Unite* [Romania in the UN Organization], (Bucharest: 1973).

123. Information on the activity of the Subcommission of the UN, in Josef Niset, "La Sous-Commission de la lutte contre les mesures discriminatoires et la protection des minorités des Nations Unies à sa vingtième session Genève, 3 au 21 septembre 1973", in *Revue des droits de l'homme—Human Rights Journal,* Paris vol. VI, no. 3-4/1973. See also Felix Ermacora, *Der Minderheitenschutz in der Arbeit der Vereinten Nationen,* (Vienna—Stuttgart: 1974).

124. See Decree-Law No. 575/1944 of November 13, in *Monitorul Oficial,* part I, no. 264/1944, November 14.

125. See Decree-Law No. 85/1945, *Monitorul Oficial,* part I, no. 30/1945, February 7, 1945, p. 819 *et seq.*

126. Decree-Law No. 630/1945 of August 3, 1945. *Monitorul Oficial,* I, no. 176/1945.

127. See Decree-Law No. 629/1945 of August 3, in *Monitorul Oficial,* part I, no. 176/1945, August 6, p. 6794. The concept of "coinhabiting nationalities" (*"naționalități conlocuitoare"*) is also part of the people's democratic Constitution of 1948.

128. Decree-Law No. 187/1945, *Monitorul Oficial,* I, no. 68 II/1945, March 23, 1945. Edict No. 4/1945 of April 11, 1945, relates to the execution of the law, *Monitorul Oficial,* no. 85/1945, April 12, 1945.

129. Sándor Kelemen, *Az erdélyi helyzet,* p. 20. Contains only Hungarian data; for the German data, see *Dokumentation der Vertreibung der Deutschen, op. cit.,* pp. 85 E-91 E.

130. See *Comunicări Statistice* [Statistical Publications], Bucharest, 1947, no. 17, table 6.

131. For more detail, see Hans Bergel, *Die Sachsen in Siebenbürgen nach dreissig Jahren Kommunismus,* (Innsbruck: 1976), p. 7. Further literature on the 1945 agrarian reform: Costin Murgescu, *Reforma agrară din 1945* [The

Agrarian Reform of 1945], (Bucharest: 1956), p. 270; *Dokumentation der Vertreibung der Deutschen*, pp. 85 E-91 E; E. Wagner, *Quellen zur Geschichte, op. cit.*, pp. 343-351.

132. See Decree-Law No. 91/1945, April 2, 1945.

133. Law No. 261. *Monitorul Oficial*, I, no. 78, April 4, 1945.

134. Decree No. 12 of August 13, 1945 in *Monitorul Oficial*, I, no. 182, August 13, 1945.

135. The term "Romanian Communist Party" has come into use again since the Ninth Party Congress (1965). The Romanian Communist Party was established in 1921 with the name "Communist Party in Romania" and was outlawed three years later.

136. *Monitorul Oficial*, I, no. 87/1948, April 13, 1948. The English text of the Constitution can be found in *Constitutions of Nations*, ed. A. J. Peaslee, vol. III, (Concord: 1950), p. 37 *et seq.*

137. Decree No. 119/1948 in *Monitorul Oficial*, I, no. 133 II/1948, June 11, 1948, p. 5047 *et seq.*

138. S. Fischer-Galati, ed., *Romania*, p. 107.

139. For more detail, see the chapter "National-Minority Education in Romania".

140. The predecessor of the Union of Working Youth was the Union of Communist Youth (UTC, *Uniunea Tineretului Comunist*), which was founded in 1922. At present, it has approximately 2.3 million members. 70 percent of the 9-14 age group, approximately 1.3 million young people, belong to the Pioneers.

141. The term is derived from the name of Michael Roller, author of the *History of the Romanian People's Republic* (Bucharest: 1948 and 1952), *Probleme de istorie* [Problems of History], (Bucharest: 1951) and *Scrieri istorice și social-politice* [Historical and Sociopolitical Writings], (Bucharest: 1957). On the "Roller period," see Michael Rura, *Reinterpretation of History as a Method of Furthering Communism in Rumania*, (Washington, Georgetown: 1961).

142. Law No. 5/1950. *Buletinul Oficial* [Official Bulletin], no. 77, September 8, 1950. *Buletinul Oficial* is the successor to the *Monitorul Oficial;* the name was introduced after 1949.

143. The first law relating to the establishment and organization of people's councils (*Sfaturi populare*) was issued on January 15, 1949, while the final decree, 259/1950, was issued on December 28, 1950. *Buletinul Oficial*, no. 14/1950.

144. The old police and gendarme units were abolished on January 23, 1949, and the Miliția was established. However, the organization of the police had already begun in 1945; in 1955 the *Securitate* (Security Police) was formed.

145. *Buletinul Oficial*, no. 1/1952. On the text of the Constitution, see A. J. Peaslee, ed., "Constitution of the Romanian People's Republic" in *Constitutions of Nations*, (The Hague: 1965), second edition, vol. III, p. 251.

146. Article 18. Arad, Bacău, Bârlad, București, Constanța, Craiova, Galați, Hunedoara, Iași, Cluj, Baia Mare, Oradea, Pitești, Ploiești, Suceava, Stalin, Timișoara, and the Hungarian Autonomous Region.

147. On the power struggles of the period, the following works provide excellent and detailed information: Ghița Ionescu, *Communism in Rumania 1944-1962,* (London: 1964); Stephen Fischer-Galati, ed., *Romania,* (New York: 1956); Alexandre Cretzianu, *Captive Rumania,* (New York: 1956).

148. The Soviet Union placed primarily non-Romanian elements at the head of the government: Ana Pauker was a Romanian-speaking Soviet citizen of Jewish origin, László Luca was Hungarian, Pintilie Bodnarenko and Emil Bodnăraș (Botnarcsjuk) were Soviet citizens of Ukrainian origin; Sándor Mogyorós, who was of Hungarian origin, became an assimilated Romanian and assumed the name Moghioroș. Ana Pauker and Teohari Georgescu were sentenced to lengthy prison terms in 1952. László Luca was executed. It is characteristic that until 1952 his name appeared as Luca (the Romanian spelling) in the Romanian press but thereafter as Luka, emphasizing his Hungarian origins.

149. The construction of the Danube-Black Sea Canal began in 1949, using almost exclusively political prisoners. (Cf., Cretzianu, *Captive Rumania,* pp. 37, 40, 78.) According to estimates, the canal project employed 40,000 prisoners and an additional 40,000 so-called "volunteers." (Cf., Ionescu, *Communism in Rumania,* pp. 199-200). A large proportion of the prisoners came from the middle class, particularly from among the intellectuals. In many cases, they were sent there without being sentenced and were often not released even after completing their term. (Cf. N. G. Shuster, *Religion hinter dem Eisernen Vorhang,* (Würzburg: 1954), p. 251.) The construction of the canal was abandoned in 1954.

150. The 1952 Constitution changed the term "coinhabiting nationalities" to "national minorities"; later "coinhabiting nationalities" was reintroduced.

151. *Scânteia,* June 22, 1948.

152. Quoted in Gh. Ionescu, *Communism in Rumania,* p. 182.

153. The quote is from *Dokumentation der Vertreibung der Deutschen aus Ost-Mitteleuropa,* p. 101 E, note 6.

154. See *Dokumentation . . . ,* p. 101 E.

155. Relating the Romanianization between 1944 and 1958, see R. W. Burks, *Die Dynamik des Kommunismus in Osteuropa,* German edition, (Hannover: 1969), p. 240.

156. *Evidence of Violation of Peace Treaty, Guarantees of Human Rights,* (Washington, D.C.: 1951). See also A. Cretzianu, *Captive Rumania,* p. 36.

157. At that time, four counties belonged to the Székler region: Trei Scaune/ Háromszék, Ciuc/Csík, Odorhei/Udvarhely and Mureș-Turda/Maros-Torda.

158. *Scânteia,* September 26, 1952.

159. According to the 1956 census, the Hungarian Autonomous Region had 731,387 inhabitants, of which 77.3 percent (565,510) were Hungarian, 20.1

NOTES

percent (146,830) were Romanian, 0.4 percent were German, 0.4 percent were Jewish, 1.5 percent were Gypsy, and 0.3 were other nationality. The population other than Hungarian or Romanian numbered altogether 19,047. *Recensământul Populaţiei din 21 februarie 1956. Rezultate generale,* Bucureşti, Direcţia Centrală de Statistică, 1959 [The Census of February 21, 1956, General Results. Bucharest. Central Statistical Directorate, 1959], pp. 558–559, and *Anuarul Statistic al R.P.R.* 1961, p. 74.

The districts of Sepsi and Kézdi in Trei Scaune/Háromszék County, with Hungarian populations of 85.3 percent and 90.2 percent respectively, were removed from the region and added to Braşov Region (Regiunea Braşov), which had a Romanian majority. At the same time Tîrnăveni (Dicsőszentmárton), which had belonged to Braşov Region, and Luduş (Marosludas) and Şarmaş (Sármás), which had belonged to the Cluj Region, with Hungarian populations of only 25.6, 22.1, and 13.7 percent respectively, were added to the Magyar Autonomous Region.

160. Decree No. 2/1968.

161. Marshal Tito, whose real name was Josip Broz, party and state chief of Yugoslavia, was expelled from Cominform in June 1948 because of his refusal to recognize Soviet hegemony over Yugoslavia.

162. The barren area between the Danube and Ialomiţa Rivers, southeast of Bucharest.

163. For more detailed information see: *Dokumentation der Vertreibung der Deutschen aus Ost-Mitteleuropa,* p. 112 E.

164. Decree of February 9, 1952, published in *Buletinul Oficial,* no. 9/1952, February 16, 1952.

165. See *Dokumentation ...* , p. 113 E.

166. As a result of a decree issued in the summer of 1956, some of the Romanian citizens of Hungarian or German origin were given back their confiscated real estate. (Cf., *Dokumentation ...* , p. 117 E.)

167. Gh. Gheorghiu-Dej, "A népi demokratikus rendszer további erősödése a Románia Népköztársaságban" [The Further Strengthening of the System of People's Democracy in the Romanian People's Republic], in *Igazság* [Justice; Hungarian-language publication, Cluj], 1953, I, p. 29.

Chapter 4

1. *The New York Times,* October 30 and November 3, 1956; *Daily Mail* (London), November 2, 1956.

2. T. Gilberg, *Modernization in Rumania since World War II,* (New York: 1975), p. 213; see also A. Bohmann, *Menschen und Grenzen,* vol. 2, p. 180.

3. "Ethnic and Political Persecution in Rumania," *The Congressional Record,* (Washington, D.C.), August 8, 1964.

4. E. Crankshaw, "Hungarian Minority Fears Rumanian Age," in *The New York Herald Tribune*, April 15, 1963.

5. For an extensive discussion of Romanian nationalism, see Stephen Fischer-Galati, "Romanian Nationalism", in Peter F. Sugar and Ivo J. Lederer eds., *Nationalism in Eastern Europe*, (Seattle, London: 1969), pp. 373–395; Karl W. Deutsch, *Nationalism and Social Communication*, (Cambridge, Mass.: 1966), Chapters 5 and 6, pp. 107–153; John C. Campbell, *French Influence and the Rise of Romanian Nationalism*, (Harvard University: 1940).

6. *Statement on the Stand of the Romanian Workers' Party Concerning the Problems of the International Communist and Working-Class Movement*, (Bucharest: 1964). The text was also published in *Lupta de Clasă* [Class Struggle], the theoretical and political journal of the CC of the RCP, (Bucharest), 1964, no. 4, pp. 3–35.

7. R. Alison Remington, *The Warsaw Pact. Case Studies in Communist Resolution*, (Cambridge: 1971).

8. E. B. Valev, "Problemy économiceskogo razvitija pridunajskich rajonov Rumynii, Bolgarii i SSSR" [Problems of the Economic Development of the Romanian, Bulgarian and Soviet Danube Region], in *Vestnik Moskovskogo Universiteta*, Serija V–Geografija, no. 2/1964, pp. 56–64, with 2 maps.

9. The Romanian answer appeared in no. 24, June 12, 1964, of the economics weekly, *Viaţa Economică* [Economic Life], (Bucharest), pp. 5–12.

10. A detailed and comprehensive analysis by V. Socor, "The Limits of National Independence in the Soviet Bloc: Rumania's Foreign Policy Reconsidered," in *Orbis*, (Philadelphia periodical of the Foreign Policy Research Institute), vol. 20 (1976), no. 3, pp. 701–723.

11. *Anuarul Statistic al R.S.R. 1979*. [The Statistical Yearbook of the Romanian Socialist Republic 1979], p. 489.

12. *Scînteia* [The Spark], December 14, 1974.

13. *Scînteia*, April 3, 1975. The U.S. Congress accorded Romania "most favored nation" trading status on August 3, 1975.

14. *Radio Free Europe Report*, December 2, 1976; Romania owes approximately 3 billion dollars to the West, and it has a chronic balance of payments deficit. (The data comes from the December 13, 1976 issue of the *Christian Science Monitor*, published in London. See also *The Washington Post*, October 11, 1976.)

15. E. R. Rafael, *"Entwicklungsland" Rumänien*, (Munich: 1977), p. 28.

16. V. Socor, "The Limits of National Independence in the Soviet Bloc," p. 731.

17. In August 1977, the workers in the coal mines of the Jiul Valley rebelled because of bad conditions and poor wages and went on strike; when this was put down, thousands of workers and their families were deported to other parts of the country. A very high proportion of the miners were Hungarian. On the damage caused by the strike, see *Scînteia*, December 23, 1977.

18. Decree No. 12/65, Article 2.

19. *Radio Free Europe, Romanian Situation Report,* no. 3, February 9, 1978, p. 11; *Scînteia,* April 4, 1973; *România Liberă,* April 5, 1973.

20. See N. Ceaușescu, *Raport cu privire la proiectul de Constituție a Republicii Socialiste România* [Report Concerning the Constitution's Project of the Socialist Republic of Romania], (Bucharest: 1965); S. Fischer-Galati, *The New Romania: From People's Democracy to Socialist Republic,* (Cambridge, Mass.: 1967); Dionisie Ghermani, "Nationalistischer 'Internationalismus' am Beispiel Rumäniens", in *Canadian Review of Studies in Nationalism,* 2/1975, pp. 279–296.

21. Reports of the Ninth Congress in *Scînteia,* no. 20, 24, July 1965.

22. Ceaușescu's principal speech at the Congress may be found in *Scînteia,* July 20, 1965. See also *The Ninth Congress of the Romanian Communist Party,* (Bucharest: 1966).

23. *Buletinul Oficial* [Official Bulletin], no. 1, part I, August 21, 1965. For the text of the Constitution, see *Constitution of the Socialist Republic of Romania,* (Bucharest: 1965), p. 34. The Constitution was reprinted in *Buletinul Oficial,* I, no. 31, 1969. The Constitution of 1965 reintroduced the spelling "România" in place of "Romînia," which had been introduced by the orthographical Law of 1952 as part of the Slavonicization (Russification) campaign.

24. *Scînteia,* August 22, 1968.

25. *Theses of the Central Committee of the Romanian Communist Party Concerning the Tenth Congress of the Party,* (Bucharest: 1969).

26. *Előre* [Forward—a Hungarian-language daily published in Bucharest], March 14, 1971.

27. See the text of the article "The Shaping of History," published in the Hungarian-language press: "There has hardly been a party document published in recent years which did not call attention to the fact of the legal equality of the citizens of our country and that the leading force in our society, the party, is consistent in the nationality question. . . Those few people who have been unable as yet to alter their psychological conditioning, their national prejudices, must also take this to heart. . ." (*Korunk* [Our Age—Hungarian-language monthly],) (Cluj), August, 1970, p. 1,141.

28. See "The Source of Lessons to be Learned," published in the Hungarian-language press: ". . . the development of culture in the vernacular, the cultivation of socialist Hungarian nationality consciousness, taking cognizance of its values, particular features, and possibilities, at the same time assumes a more thorough acquaintance with the Romanian language, Romanian literature, and Romanian national traditions, their popularization and study. . ."; quoted in *Igaz Szó* [True Word], (Tîrgu Mureș), September 1969, p. 446.

29. In Romania a law, the highest legal authority, is generally enacted by the Grand National Assembly. A Decree-Law, a decree of legal force issued by the State Council, the highest organ of state power, is a secondary legal source, as

is a resolution issued by the Council of Ministers (*Hotărirea Consiliului de Miniștri*). Resolutions issued jointly by the RCP Central Committee and the Council of Ministers count as a special source of law. Laws are generally published in Romanian, but *Buletinul Oficial,* which publishes the laws, also appeared in the languages of the various national minorities. (Decree-Law No. 716/1965).

30. Until 1975 place-names were bilingual in the almost entirely Hungarian-inhabited Székler region, but this practice has ceased.

31. For example: Dej (Romanian)-Dés (Hungarian), Satu Mare (Romanian)-Szatmár (Hungarian), etc. For the use of place names in Romania, see *Radio Free Europe, Situation Report* no. 41, November 3, 1971, p. 16.

32. Act No. 1/1968, *Scînteia,* February 1968.

33. See F. Mayer, G. H. Tontsch, I. Iovănaș (Cluj-Napoca), "Staat—Verfassung—Recht—Verwaltung", in *Rumänien. Südosteuropa-Handbuch,* vol. II, ed. by K. D. Grothusen, (Göttingen: 1977), p. 56.

34. More detail on this in Chapter II.

35. *Scînteia,* July 20, 1972. See also *Die sozialistische Nation.* Dokumente der Rumänischen Kommunistischen Partei, (Bucharest: 1973); "Raport prezentat la Conferința Națională a Partidului Comunist Român—19 iulie 1972" [Report on the National Conference of the Romanian Communist Party—July 19, 1972], in Nicolae Ceaușescu, *Reden und Artikel,* vol. 7, (Bucharest: 1973), p. 464 *et seq.*

36. S. Fischer-Galati, "The Socialist Republic of Rumania," in Peter A. Toma, ed., *The Changing Face of Communism in Eastern Europe,* (The University of Arizona: 1970), pp. 28–32.

37. "L'écrivain roumain Paul Goma est à Paris pour amplifier les cris de révolte et de désespoir de ses concitoyens," *Le Monde,* (Paris), November 26, 1977; see also Virgil Tanase, *Le Dossier Paul Goma: L'écrivain face au socialisme du silence,* (Paris: 1977).

38. Andrei Sida, "Die Nation und die sozialistische Demokratie," in *Era Socialistă,* (Bucharest), no. 20/1973; see also Dumitru Mazilu, "Die sozialistische Nation, ein Faktor des Fortschritts innerhalb der zeitgenössischen Welt," in *Revista de Filozofie,* (Bucharest), no. 9, 1973.

39. A regulation concerning "nationality composition" (*componența națională*) was issued on April 12, 1974, stipulating that members of the national minorities were not to occupy positions of leadership in public or economic life. The regulation was not made public.

40. Valuable data are provided in Robert R. King, *Minorities under Communism. Nationalities as a Source of Tension among Balkan Communist States,* (Cambridge, Mass.: 1973), p. 13.

41. Statement by Pál Bodor, Editor-in-Chief of the Hungarian-language service of Romanian Television. For the text see *Korunk* no. 3, 1978, p. 195.

42. T. Gilberg, *Modernization in Rumania, op. cit.,* p. 214.

43. Excerpts from Ceaușescu's speech at a joint session of the Councils of Working People of Hungarian and German Nationality. Cf., *Neuer Weg* [New

Path—German language daily], (Bucharest), March 17, 1978. See also *Radio Free Europe, Romanian Situation Report* No. 7, March 19, 1978.

44. *BBC Research,* EE/5766/B/3, March 17, 1978.

45. E. Bondor-Deliman, "Naționalitățile conlocuitoare în istoria și viața social-politică a României socialiste" [The Coinhabiting Nationalities in the History and Sociopolitical Life of Socialist Romania], in *Lupta de Clasă,* [Class Struggle], no. 7, 1971. The name *Lupta de Clasă* was later changed to *Era Socialistă.*

46. "Raport prezentat la Conferința Națională a Partidului Comunist Român—19 iulie 1972" [Report to the July 19, 1972 National Conference of the Romanian Communist Party], in Nicolae Ceaușescu, *Speeches and Articles,* vol. 7, (Bucharest: 1973), p. 464 *et seq.*

47. *The RCP Program for the Creation of a Multilaterally Developed Socialist Society and Romania's Advance Toward Communism,* (Bucharest: 1974), pp. 158–162.

48. Quoted by H. Bergel, *Die Sachsen in Siebenbürgen nach dreissig Jahren Kommunismus,* p. 16.

49. Decree No. 278, May 11, 1973. These decrees will be discussed in more detail in the chapter dealing with national-minority education in Romania.

50. "Legea ocrotirii patrimoniului cultural național al Republicii Socialiste România," in *Buletinul Oficial,* Part I, no. 137. November 2, 1974. The text of the law was published in the November 3, 1974 issue of *Előre.* Part of the German text in E. Wagner, *Quellen zur Geschichte der Siebenbürger Sachsen, op. cit.,* pp. 386–396.

51. *Buletinul Oficial,* Part I, no. 131, October 31, 1974.

52. *Buletinul Oficial,* Part I, no. 155, December 10, 1974 (a new version).

53. "Bürokratische Schikanen gegen die Kirche Rumäniens," *Neue Zürcher Zeitung,* February 6, 1975; H. Bergel, "Die Entwicklung der Siebenbürger Sachsen seit 1945 als Problem der Volksgruppen im Donauraum," in *Donauraum* (Vienna), 1976, p. 156.

54. *Tribuna României* [The Romanian Tribune], (Bucharest) February 15, 1975.

55. R. Staar, *Die kommunistischen Regierungssysteme in Osteuropa,* (Stuttgart-Degerloch: 1977), p. 207.

56. *Buletinul Oficial,* no. 156, December 16, 1974.

57. *Buletinul Oficial,* Part I, no. 152, December 6, 1974.

58. Decre-Law No. 255/1974.

59. Decree No. 372/1976.

60. More detail on this in Chapter II. Decrees Nos. 24 and 25 of November 5, 1976 enable the authorities to allocate manpower forcibly for "useful" construction projects in Romania. These two decrees replaced two other administrative laws and regulations enacted between 1953 and 1972 regarding administrative banishment and confinement to places of forced labor. (See *Romania* [an Amnesty International USA Publication], p. 4).

61. *Neue Zürcher Zeitung,* August 3, 1978. N. Ceauşescu promised to remedy the grievances of the national minorities regarding dispersal at the joint national session of the Councils of Working People of Hungarian and German Nationality. The text of Ceauşescu's speech was published on March 17, 1978 in the German-language *Neuer Weg* (Bucharest) and the Hungarian-language *Előre* (Bucharest).

62. T. Gilberg, *Modernization in Rumania since World War II,* (New York: 1975), p. 224.

63. "Gemeinsame Sitzung der Räte der Werktätigen ungarischer und deutscher Nationalität. Rede des N. Ceauşescu," in *Neuer Weg,* March 17, 1978, pp. 1 and 3.; on the Romanian cultural revolution see T. Gilberg, "Ceauşescu's kleine Kulturrevolution", in *Osteuropa,* no. 22, 1972.

64. *Ibid.* (Gemeinsame Sitzung...)

65. Gordon Brook-Shepherd's interview with N. Ceauşescu in *Sunday Telegraph* (London), May 9, 1978; see also Mihnea Berindei, "Les minorités nationales en Roumanie," (II), *L'Alternative,* (Paris), no. 4-5, 1980, p. 36.

66. Ervin Mikó, "The Force of Our Brotherhood," in *România Liberă* [Free Romania], (Bucharest), May 10, 1978.; *Agerpress* (Romanian News Agency), May 10, 1978. (English 0948 gmt., London)

67. *România Liberă* [Free Romania], February 21, 1978.

68. *Contemporanul* [Contemporary], (Bucharest), no. 7, February 17, 1978.

69. *Romanian News,* (Bucharest), May 11, 1978.

70. Radio Bucharest, February 22, 1978.

71. Dacia Publishing House, (Cluj-Napoca: 1974).

72. Dacia Publishing House, (Cluj-Napoca: 1975).

73. Miklós Horthy was Regent of Hungary from 1920 to 1945; the 1940-1944 "Horthy-period" refers to the period of Hungarian rule in Northern Transylvania. On the anti-Hungarian campaign by Romanian historians, see Manuel Lucbert, "La minorité hongroise de Transylvanie est méconté de son sort," in *Le Monde,* (Paris), May 5, 1978.

74. See the novel *Delirul* [Delirium] by the Romanian author, Marin Preda, which in essence rehabilitates the head of the Romanian fascist government between 1940 and 1944, Ion Antonescu. On the rehabilitation and its political implications, see "Bukarest rehabilitiert die 'Gestrigen'," *Wissenschaftlicher Dienst Südosteuropa,* (Munich), vol. 1965, no. 6/7, pp. 89-92; "Nationale Geschichte—neu gesehen. Bukarest rehabilitiert die rumänische Vergangenheit," *Ibid.,* vol. 1965, no. 8/9, pp. 123-126. Dionisie Ghermani, "Neue 'grossrumänische' Bekenntnisse", *Ibid,* vol. 1978, no. 819, p. 218.

75. *Scînteia,* November 16, 1977: Party Resolution on 2,050th Anniversary of Dacian State (EE/5653/Cl/l); see also "Istoria şi terminologia istorică" [History and Historical Terminology], *Scînteia,* May 18, 1976.

76. In this connection I quote the RCP resolution: "Bei der Behandlung der nationalen Frage ging die Rumänische Kommunistische Partei von der Tatsache aus, dass sich im Laufe der Geschichte auf dem Gebiet des Vater-

landes auch andere Nationalitäten—Ungarn, Deutsche, Serben und andere—niedergelassen haben" (In dealing with the nationality question, the Romanian Communist Party begins from the fact that in the course of history other nationalities—Hungarians, Germans, Serbs, and others—also settled in the territory of our country.) "Resolution der Landeskonferenz der RKP von Juli 1972," (Excerpts), quoted by E. Eisenburger, in *Heimatbilder*, (Cluj-Napoca: 1976), p. 314.

77. *Europa Ethnica*, vol. 35, 2/1978, pp. 75–80.; Paul Lendvai, "Achilles Heel of Romanian Nationalism," *Financial Times* (London), January 31, 1978.; "Tales from Transylvania," *The Economist* (London), February 4, 1978.; Dessa Trevisan, "Minority Leader Taken to Task," *The Times* (London), February 8, 1978; Pol Mathil, "La Transylvanie: une marmite rouge," *Le Soir* (Brussels), February 1978; Dusko Doder, "Minority Issue Splits Bloc States," *The Washington Post*, February 23, 1978.

78. *The Washington Post*, February 23, 1978.

79. Michael Dobbs, "Romania Suppresses Hungarian Minority's Protest," *The Guardian* (London), March 2, 1978; Dessa Trevisan, "Letter Telling Plight of Hungarian Minority Answered by Repression," *The Times*, (London) March 2, 1978.

80. *A Hét* [The Week—Hungarian-language weekly published in Bucharest], no. 25 June 2, 1978; Radio Bucharest and *Agerpress* (Romanian News Agency), June 24, 1978.

81. See Pál Bodor's article in *România Liberă*, March 3, 1978, and the poem by the Hungarian poet, László Miklós, in *Scînteia*, March 12, 1978.

82. The March 14, 16, and 17, 1978 issues of *Neuer Weg* and *Előre*.

83. "Charter 77" is a movement for the protection of human and civic rights which began in Czechoslovakia; several European writers have joined it.

84. *Deutsche Presse Agentur*, December 14, 1977; Rudolf Krämer-Badoni, "Der Schriftsteller Goma klagt Ceauşescu an," *Die Welt*, (Hamburg), December 15, 1977; "Druck auf die Minderheiten," *Frankfurter Rundschau*, December 15, 1977; "Schwere Vorwürfe gegen rumänische Regierung," *Frankfurter Allgemeine Zeitung*, December 16, 1977.

85. Report on the "Seminar on the Multi-National Society", Ljubljana, Yugoslavia, 8 to 21 June 1965, Doc. ST/TAO/HR 23.

86. United Nation Seminar on the Promotion and Protection of Human Rights of National, Ethnic and Other Minorities, Ohrid, Yugoslavia, 25 June-8 July 1974.

87. Francesco Capotorti, *Study on the Rights of Persons Belonging to Ethnic, Religious and Linguistic Minorities*, UNO-Doc ECOSOC E/CN. 4/Sub. 2/L. 564, June 27, 1972 and E/CN 4/Sub. 2/384, June 20, 1977. See also Th. Veiter, *Nationalitätenkonflikt und Volksgruppenrecht im 20. Jahrhundert*, vol. I, p. 138.

88. *KSZE-Dokumentation* (Helsinki Conference on Security and Cooperation in Europe), edited by Presse und Informationsamt der Bundesregierung, Bonn 1975, pp. 38, 101, 133.
89. *Népszabadság,* (Budapest), January 28, 1958.
90. *Radio Bucharest,* February 27, 1958.
91. *Népszabadság,* October 6, 1968.
92. *Népszabadság,* June 25, 1971.
93. *Scînteia,* July 9, 1971.
94. *Népszabadság,* August 1, 1975.
95. See the reply of János Szász, a Hungarian writer in Romania, to the articles in the May 15 and June 15, 1968 issues of *Élet és Irodalom* [Life and Literature], (Budapest), in the July 25, 1968 issue of *Gazeta Literară* [Literary Gazette], (Bucharest).
96. *Magyar Nemzet* [Hungarian Nation], (Budapest), December 25, 1977, and January 1, 1978.
97. *Luceafărul* [Hesperus], monthly review published in Bucharest, May 6, 1978.
98. *Élet és Irodalom,* July 8, 1978.
99. According to Romanian and certain other historiographers, the Romanian people grow out of the intermingling of Dacians with Romans.
100. C. Giurescu, "Probleme der zeitgenössischen Historiographie—Die Geschichte der Rumänen vor dem Hintergrund einiger neuer ausländischer Arbeiten," in *Revista de Istorie* [Historical Review] (Bucharest), no. 6, 1975.
101. László Makkai, "Egy kis szakmai ördögűzés" [A Little Professional Exorcism], in *Történelmi Szemle* [Historical Review], (Budapest), no. 4, 1975, p. 725.
102. *Magyar Tudomány* [Hungarian Scholarship—publication of the Hungarian Academy of Sciences], (Budapest), vol. XXII, no. 2, February 1977, p. 151.
103. *Magyar Hírlap* [Hungarian News—Budapest daily], no. 303, December 25, 1977 and April 3, 1978.
104. D. Berciu and C. Preda, "In the Spirit of Historical Truth," in *Contemporanul,* February 10, 1978.
105. *Radio Free Europe Research, Romania,* November 2, 1979, pp. 4–7.
106. Those asking to emigrate lose their jobs. (Cf., Bergel, *Die Entwicklung. . . , op. cit.,* p. 159.) See also *Europa Ethnica,* vol. 33, 1976, p. 181.

Chapter 5

1. Hans Hartl, *Das Schicksal des Deutschtums in Rumänien,* (Würzburg: 1958), p. 36. For more detail on the education of the Transylvanian Saxons see Otto Folberth, "Das Schulwesen der Siebenbürger Sachsen. Rückblick auf

eine abendländische Kulturleistung", in *Südostdeutsche Vierteljahresblätter,* 9/1960, pp. 194-202; Friedrich Teutsch, *Die Siebenbürgisch-sächsischen Schulordnungen,* vols. 2, Berlin: 1888-1892.

2. For more detail on this, see Ernst Wagner, *Historisch-statistisches Ortsnamenbuch für Siebenbürgen. Studia Transylvanica,* (Cologne-Vienna: 1976), pp. 84-88; see further T. Gilberg, *Modernization in Rumania since World War II,* (New York: 1975), p. 210. In the so-called Obere Vorstadt of Brașov (Bolgárszeg/Scheii Brașovului) there was a Romanian Orthodox school in the 15th century.

3. Elemér Jancsó, *Az erdélyi magyarság életsorsa nevelésügyének tükrében 1914-1934* [The Fate of the Hungarians in Transylvania as Reflected by their Educational Situation 1914-1943], (Cluj: 1935).

4. István Dolmányos, "Kritik der Lex Apponyi" (Die Schulgesetze vom Jahre 1907), in *Die nationale Frage in der Österreichisch-Ungarischen Monarchie 1900-1918,* (Budapest: 1966), pp. 233-304.

5. Among others T. Gilberg, *Modernization in Rumania,* p. 209; F. Ronneberger, "Sozialstruktur," in K. D. Grothusen ed., *Rumänien. Südosteuropa Handbuch,* vol. II, (Göttingen: 1977), p. 414.

6. *Monitorul Oficial,* [Official Gazette], Part I, no. 161, July 26, 1924.

7. *Monitorul Oficial,* Part I, no. 283, December 22, 1925.

8. Decrees 100,088 and 100,090/1923, issued by C. Angelescu, Minister of Education in the Liberal government.

9. Decree No 771/1924, and paragraph 40 of Law No. 159. Ten Transylvanian counties, about a half of them with a majority of Hungarian inhabitants, belonged to the so-called "cultural zone": Bihor/Bihar, Sălaj/Szilágy, Satu Mare/Szatmár, Maramureș/Máramaros, Turda/Torda Aranyos, Hunedoara/Hunyad, Odorhei/Udvarhely, Ciuc/Csík, Trei Scaune/Háromszék, and Mureș/Maros-Torda.

10. Lajos Nagy, *A kisebbségek alkotmányjogi helyzete Nagyromániában* [The Constitutional Position of the Minorities in Greater Romania], (Kolozsvár: 1944), p. 123.

11. For more detail, see: Endre Barabás, *A romániai magyar nyelvű oktatás első tíz éve* [The First Ten Years of Hungarian-language Education in Romania], (Lugos: 1929); see also: István Sulyok and László Fritz eds. *Erdélyi Magyar Évkönyv 1918-1929,* vol. I, (Cluj: 1930), pp. 73-84.

12. *Monitorul Oficial,* March 8, 1925. The term "baccalaureate" refers to the final examinations at the end of secondary education of the gymnasium (grammar school) type. Passing this examination was a precondition for university entrance.

13. For more detail, G. A. Dima, *Școala secundară în lumina bacalaureatului* [Secondary Education in the Light of the Baccalaureate], (Bucharest: 1928); see also Theodor Grentrup, *Das Deutschtum an der mittleren Donau in Rumänien und Jugoslawien,* (Münster: 1930), p. 204 *et seq.*

14. *Nation und Staat,* (Vienna), March 1935, p. 404.

15. Alfred Bohmann, *Menschen und Grenzen. Bevölkerung und Nationalitäten in Südosteuropa. Rumänien*, pp. 101–218 (Cologne: 1969), p. 120.

16. *La Transylvanie demande a être écoutée. Aide-Mémoire presenté à la Conférence de la Paix par le Comité Hongrois de Transylvanie*, (Paris: 1946), p. 11.; see also *Information sur la situation de la minorité hongroise en Roumanie*, (Geneva: 1934), p. 11.

17. E. Ammende, *Die Nationalitäten in den Staaten Europas*, 1931, p. 386, *et seq*.

18. *Monitorul Oficial* no. 101, May 4, 1938; *Ibid.*, Part II, no. 178, August 4, 1938, and Part III.

19. *Gesetz No. 977 "über die Einrichtung des deutschen Schulwesens in Rumänien"* [The Law Relating to the Institution of German Education in Romania], November 8, 1941, *Monitorul Oficial* no. 266, November 8, 1941, p. 7,000 *et seq*.

20. Endre Barabás, "A magyar iskolaügy helyzete Romániában 1918–1941" [The State of Hungarian Education in Romania, 1918–1941], *Kisebbségi Körlevél* [Minority Circular], no. 5, 1943, p. 273.

21. *Sächsisch-schwäbische Chronik*, eds., E. Eisenburger and M. Kroner, (Bucharest; 1976), p. 169.

22. *Ibid*.

23. Franz H. Riedl, *Das Südostdeutschtum in den Jahren 1918–1945* (Munich: 1962), p. 52; see also E. Wagner, *Historisch-statistisches Ortsnamenbuch, op. cit*., p. 91, Table 19.

24. For more detail see Trond Gilberg, "Ethnic Minorities in Romania Under Socialism," *East European Quarterly*, vol. VII, no. 4, January 1974, p. 439.

25. For more detail, *Dokumentation der Vertreibung der Deutschen aus Ost-Mitteleuropa*, vol. III: *Das Schicksal der Deutschen in Rumänien*, edited by the Bundesministerium für Vertriebene, Flüchtlinge und Kriegsgeschädigte, (Berlin: 1957), p. 92 E. *et seq*.

26. *Ibid*.

27. Wilhelm Reiter, "Die nationalitätenpolitik der Rumänischen Volksrepublik im Spiegel ihrer Statistik," *Osteuropa*, vol. 11, 1961, no. 3, p. 194.

28. *Monitorul Oficial*, Part I, no. 177, August 3, 1948, p. 6,322 *et seq*.

29. Decree No. 176/1948, relating to the nationalization of the school-properties, and Decree No. 175/1948, relating to the nationalization of the schools, in *Monitorul Oficial*, August 3, 1948, Part I, no. 177, p. 6,322 *et seq*.

30. On the "Daco-Roman continuity-theory" see the explanation in Chapter IV, note 99.

31. *Istoria României. Manual unic pentru școlile generale* [The History of Romania. Uniform Textbook for the General Schools], (Bucharest: 1949); see also the textbook by Dumitru Almaș and Eleonora Fotescu, *Geschichte des Vaterlandes* (Bucharest, 1977); Walter König, "Die gegenwärtigen Schulverhältnisse der Deutschen in Rumänien," in *Korrespondenzblatt des Arbeitskreises*

für siebenbürgische Landeskunde, III, vol. 7, nos. 3-4, pp. 122-123, Cologne-Vienna, 1977.

32. Decree-Law No. 159, July 21, 1948, concerning the Foreign Schools in the Romanian People's Republic, in *Monitorul Oficial,* Part I, no. 167, July 22, 1948.

33. For more detail see: Stephen Fischer-Galati, ed., *Romania,* (New York: 1956), p. 162.

34. Alfred Bohmann, *op. cit.,* p. 200.

35. Sándor Kelemen, *Az erdélyi helyzet* [The Transylvanian Situation], (Budapest: 1946), p. 27.

36. *Ibid.*

37. Report prepared on the instructions of the Executive Committee of Bolyai University in Cluj, December 1954 and March 1955. (Manuscript).

38. The first pioneer units were established at the end of April 1949 on the basis of the resolution of the Romanian Workers' Party at its plenary session on December 22-24, 1948. *Scînteia* [The Spark], the central organ of the RCP, (Bucharest), May 4, 1949.

39. Robert Schultz, *Deutsche in Rumänien. Das Nationalitätenproblem in der Rumänischen Volksrepublik,* (Leipzig-Jena: 1955), pp. 85, 88. Quoted from *Dokumentation,* p. 104 E.

40. Resolution No. 1003 of the Council of Ministers on July 26, 1957. See also Constantin Sporea, "Probleme des Hochschulwesens in Rumänien", special number of *Wissenschaftlicher Dienst Südosteuropa,* (Munich), vol. 8, 1959, no. 3, p. 7.

41. Resolution of the Council of Ministers, No. 3,886 of November 17, 1953, in *Colecţia de legi şi decrete* [Collection of Laws and Decrees], (Bucharest).

42. Hans Bergel, *Die Sachsen in Siebenbürgen nach dreissig Jahren Kommunismus* [The Transylvanian Saxons after Thirty Years of Communism], (Innsbruck: 1976), p. 12.

43. For more detail, see Randolf L. Braham, *Education in the Rumanian People's Republic,* U.S. Department of Health, Education and Welfare. DE-14,087. Washington, D.C., U.S. Government Printing Office, 1963, p. 75.

44. For a detailed discussion, see Hans Bergel, "Die Entwicklung der Siebenbürger Sachsen seit 1945 als Problem der Volksgruppen in Donauraum", in *Der Donauraum* (Vienna: 1976), pp. 151-160.

45. The history of the present-day Babeş-Bolyai University began in the 16th century, with the foundation of a Hungarian Jesuit Academy in Kolozsvár (Cluj) by the Transylvanian Prince Stephen Báthori (1581). This institution became a university with Ferenc József University in 1872; in 1919, this university was expropriated by the Romanian state and renamed Ferdinand I University. Between 1940 and 1958, it was again a Hungarian university. See among others Ştefan Pascu, *A Kolozsvári "Babeş-Bolyai" Egyetem,* [The University "Babeş-Bolyai" of Kolozsvár], (Kolozsvár/Cluj: 1972).

46. A. Bohmann, *op. cit.*, p. 180.

47. Mihail Roller, *The History of the Romanian People's Republic*. Textbook for the secondary classes, (Bucharest: 1952).

48. I took this information from T. Gilberg, *Modernization in Rumania since World War II, op. cit.*, p. 227, Table 8 and 10.

49. Legea nr. 11/1968 privind învățămîntul în Republica Socialista România [Law No. 11/1968 relating to education in the Romanian Socialist Republic], in *Buletinul Oficial*, Part I, no. 62, May 13, 1968.

50. Decretul nr. 278 din 11 mai 1973 privind stabilirea normelor unitare de structura pentru instituțiile de învățămînt [Decree No. 278 of May 11, 1973, relating to the regularization of structural norms for educational institutions], in *Buletinul Oficial*, no. 67, May 13, 1973, p. 818.

51. Resolution on the Development and Completion of Education in the Romanian Socialist Republic, *Buletinul Oficial*, Part I, no. 100, July 9, 1973.

52. *Scînteia*, October 14, 1978. For more detail, see D. Ghermani, "Das neue rumänische Schulgesetz," in *Wissenschaftlicher Dienst Südosteuropa*, (Munich) November 1978, vol. 27, no. 11, pp. 274–279.

53. *Ibid.*, p. 277.

54. Decree No. 80/1972, *Buletinul Oficial*, no. 28, March 8, 1972.

55. D. Ghermani, "Das rumänische Schul-und Hochschulwesen," in *Wissenschaftlicher Dienst Südosteuropa*, 1975, no. 10, p. 206.

56. Law No. 2/1966 "Concerning the establishment, organization, and function of technical lycées."

57. *Anuarul Statistic al Republicii Socialiste România 1979*, pp. 547–548.

58. For more details, see Chapter VII.

59. Decree No. 301/1971, *Buletinul Oficial* [Official Bulletin], no. 108, September 21, 1971.

60. For more details, see Chapter VII.

61. Decree No. 371/1969.

62. These statements were made at the session of Council of Working People of Hungarian Nationality by István Péterfi, in his presidential address. See *Előre* [Forward—Hungarian—language journal published in Bucharest], March 14, 1971.

63. Decretul nr. 278 din 11 mai 1973 [Decree No. 278 of May 11, 1973], in *Buletinul Oficial*, no. 67, May 13, 1973, p. 818.

64. Decree No. 278/1973, Article 3, Paragraphs 2 and 3.

65. A. Bohmann, *op. cit.*, p. 202.

66. Nicolae Ceaușescu, *Romania on the Way to the Construction of the Multilateral Developed Socialist Society*, (Bucharest: 1976), vol. III, p. 700.

67. János Demeter, in *Korunk* [Our Age], 1970/11, p. 1627.

68. *Ibid.*

69. *Tanügyi Újság* [Education Journal], (Bucharest), no. 31, 1971; *A Hét* [The Week], (Bucharest), no. 37, 1971.

70. Traian Pop in *Tanügyi Újság*, no. 38, 1972.

71. *Előre* [Forward], no. 7,588, 1972.
72. It should be noted that after 1945 the historical names of the majority of the national-minority lycées were abolished and were replaced by numbers or Romanian names.
73. Decree No. 371/1969.
74. Eduard Eisenburger, *Wegzeichen der Heimat*, (Cluj: 1974), p. 163. See also the information issued by the Ministry of Education in March 1977.
75. Walter König, *Die gegenwärtigen Schulverhältnisse der Deutschen in Rumänien*, (Köln-Wien: 1977), pp. 124–125.
76. *Sächsisch-schwäbische Chronik*, E. Eisenburger and M. Kroner, (Bucharest: 1976), p. 194; see also data issued by the Romanian Ministry of Education, volumes 1947–1946.
77. W. König, *Die gegenwärtigen Schulverhältnisse, op. cit.* pp. 124–125.
78. From data issued by the Ministry of Education.
79. From data issued by the Ministry of Education: Árpád Debreczi, *Előre*, March 31, 1972.
80. *Europa Ethnica*, vol. 32, 2/1975, p. 106.
81. W. König, *op. cit.*, p. 90.
82. Monica Barcan and Adalbert Millitz, *Die deutsche Nationalität in Rumänien*, (Bucharest: 1977), p. 85.
83. W. König, *op. cit.*, p. 103.
84. The 1977 Census, *Scînteia*, June 14, 1977.
85. I took this information from Mihnea Berindei, "Les minorités nationales en Roumanie" (II), in *L'Alternative*, (Paris), May-August 1980, p. 41.
86. *Ibid.*
87. *Wissenschaftlicher Dienst Südosteuropa*, no. 10, 1975, pp. 207–208; see also *Anuarul Statistic al Republicii Socialiste România 1979*. [Statistical Yearbook of the RSR 1979], p. 557 *et seq.*
88. Decree No. 207/1977 of the State Council "Concerning the organization and function of the lycées", in *Buletinul Oficial*, no. 67, July 12, 1977, and Decree No. 208/1977 " Concerning the organization and function of the vocational schools."
89. From the speech of N. Ceauşescu at the March 12, 1971 session of the Council of Working People of Hungarian Nationality in *Előre* [Forward], Bucharest, March 14, 1971.
90. János Demeter in *A Hét* [The Week], no. 28, 1971.
91. *The Hungarian Nationality in Romania*, Institute of Political Science and the Study of Nationality Questions, Bucharest, 1976, p. 17.
92. Quoted from a Memorandum of Lajos Takács, former Rector of the Babeş-Bolyai University, Cluj. (Manuscript).
93. W. König, *Die gegenwärtigen Schulverhältnisse*, p. 111.
94. György Kovács writes about the difficulties of organization and the resistance of the Church in his report, *Az igazság útján* [Along the Path of Truth], (Bucharest: 1949).

95. György Beke, *Magunk keresése* [Quest of Ourselves], (Bucharest: 1972), p. 28.

96. Law No. 6, March 14, 1969 in *Buletinul Oficial,* Part I, no. 33, March 15, 1969.

97. *Istoria României. Manual pentru clasa a XII-a, partea a II-a.* [The History of Romania. Textbook for the XIIth Class, Part. II], ed. Florea Dragne, (Bucharest: 1968); see also W. König, *op. cit.* pp. 122–123.

98. Gotthold Rhode, "Deutsche Einheit und rumänischer Nationalstaat" [German Unity and the Romanian National State], in *Südosteuropa Mitteilungen,* Munich, 1975, no. 2, p. 48.

99. Data published by the Ministry of Education, March 1977.

100. George Lázár, "Jelentés Erdélyből" [Report from Transylvania], in *Irodalmi Újság* [Hungarian Literary Gazette—a Hungarian-language monthly], (Paris), March-April issue, 1977.

101. *Ibid.*

102. *Județele României Socialiste* [The Counties of Socialist Romania], (Bucharest: 1969), p. 368.

103. Decree No. 278 of May 11, 1973, in *Buletinul Oficial,* Part I, no. 67, May 13, 1973, p. 818.

104. Paragraph *a* in Section II of Decree No. 278 of May 11, 1973.

105. "Az oktatás fejlesztéséről és tökéletesítéséről" [On the Development and Improvement of Education], in *Előre* [Forward], (Bucharest), June 21, 1973.

106. From the text of a speech given at the joint session of the Council of Working People of Hungarian and German Nationality published in *Neuer Weg* [New Path], (Bucharest), April 7, 1974, pp. 1 and 3.

Chapter 6

1. Stephen Fischer-Galati, ed., "Religion," in *Romania,* (New York: 1956), p. 132.

2. The Uniates, or Greek Catholics, had officially broken away from the Orthodox Church by a Union with the Roman Catholic Church, formalized by a Charter issued on February 16, 1699, by the Austrian emperor Leopold I. Valuable information on the Uniate Church can be found in J. Crisian, *Beitrag zur Geschichte der kirchlichen Union der Romänen in Siebenbürgen unter Leopold I,* (Hermannstadt: 1882), and in *Biserica Română Unită. Două sute cincizeci de ani de istorie,* [The Romanian Uniate Church. Two Hundred and Fifty Years of History], (Madrid: 1952). See further S. Fischer-Galati, *L'église unie de Roumanie. Dix ans de persécution 1948–1958,* (Paris: 1959); Silviu Dragomir, *"Romînii din Transilvania și unirea cu biserica Romei"* [The Transylvanian Romanians and the Union with the Roman Church], in *Studii și materiale de istorie medie,* no. 3, 1959, pp. 323–337.

3. Keith Hitchins, "Samuel Clain and the Rumanian Enlightenment in Transylvania", in *Slavic Review,* XXIII, no. 4, December 1964, pp. 660–675.

4. For a detailed discussion, see Friedrich Teutsch, *Geschichte der evangelischen Kirche in Siebenbürgen,* vol. 1: 1150–1699, vol. 2: 1700–1917 (Hermannstadt: 1921 and 1922).

5. For a detailed discussion, see *Erdélyi Magyar Évkönyv 1918-1929,* [Transylvanian Hungarian Yearbook, 1918–1929], volume I, eds., István Sulyok and László Fritz, (Cluj: 1930), pp. 38–39, 62.

6. The Moslem community had four muftis and 307 ecclesiastics, all in the area of Dobrugea. The number of adherents was approximately 180,000. The Baptist Church also lacked a central organization. It had approximately 105 congregations with 3,113 chapels. The number of adherents was approximately 50,000 throughout Romania. The small community of Seventh-Day Adventists had seven congregations with 520 meeting-houses and about 15,000 members. The congregations of the Lipovan Church (Old Believers) were concentrated in Bucovina, Bessarabia, and Dobrugea and had approximately 50,000 members. The superintendency of the Presbyterian Church possessed three church-districts, 25 parishes, and 32,648 adherents. The Armeno-Gregorian Church had one bishopric (Bucharest) and 50,000 adherents. A valuable source of information on the distribution of denominations in Romania can be found in *Recensământul populației din 29 decemvrie 1930* [The Census of Romania on December 29, 1930], pp. 70–73; the data relating to Transylvania includes the Banat, Crișana and Maramureș. See further Stephen Fischer-Galati, ed., "Religion," in *Romania,* (New York: 1956), pp. 132, 135–137; also R. L. Wolff, *The Balkans in our Time,* (Cambridge, Mass.: 1956), pp. 559–561.

7. *Erdélyi Magyar Évkönyv 1918–1929, op. cit., p. 72.*

8. *Die Nationalitäten in den Staaten Europas,* ed., E. Ammende, (Vienna: 1931), [Nachtrag, 1932], p. 416.

9. *Roumania Ten Years After,* issued by the American Committee on the Rights of Religious Minorities, (Boston: 1928), p. 100.

10. The representative of the Transylvanian Roman Catholic Church at the local level and, later, the manager of its wealth was the "Status Catholicus Transylvaniae," founded in 1698; a large part of its property was expropriated by the Romanian state between the two world wars; in 1948 it was nationalized and its name was changed to "Status Romano-Catholicus Romaniae."

11. For more detail, see Alexandre Cretzianu, *Captive Rumania,* (New York: 1956), p. 176.

12. Protest note of the Apostolic Nuncio to the Ministry of Foreign Affairs of the RPR, October 2, 1948.

13. Decree No. 358.

14. Law No. 177/1948. *Monitorul Oficial* [Official Gazette], Part I, August 4, 1948.

15. Cf., Ernst Chr. Suttner, "Kirchen und Staat," in *Rumänien,* ed. Klaus-Detlev, Grothusen, *Südosteuropa Handbuch,* vol. II, (Göttingen: 1977), p. 462.

16. *Monitorul Oficial,* September 18, 1948.

17. The Verbal Protest of Mgr. Gerard Patrick O'Hara, Apostolic Nuncio in Bucharest to the Ministry of Foreign Affairs, No. 2130/1948 (October 2, 1948).

18. Decree No. 358.

19. Decree-Law No. 37, *Monitorul Oficial,* February 5, 1949.

20. Cf., R. Janin, "L'Église Catholique en Roumanie," in *La Documentation Catholique,* no. 1092, April, 1951.

21. On the names and fates of the various bishops, see *Radio Free Europe Situation Report, Romania,* December 10, 1965.

22. Decree No. 810/1949, issued by the Council of Ministers on August 1, 1949.

23. For more detail, see *Kirchen im Sozialismus. Kirche und Staat in den osteuropäischen sozialistischen Republiken,* edited and revised by Giovanni Barberiñ, Martin Stöhr, and Erich Weingartner, (Frankfurt am Main: 1977).

24. For more detail, see E. C. Suttner, "50 Jahre rumänisches Patriarchat. Seine Geschichte und die Entwicklung seines Kirchenrechts," *Ostkirchliche Studien,* no. 24, 1975; no. 25, 1976.

25. Decree No. 334/1970. Cf. E. C. Suttner, "Kirchen und Staat," in *Rumänien, Südosteuropa-Handbuch,* vol. II, p. 471.

26. Cf., *The Hungarian Nationality in Romania,* The Institute of Political Science and the Study of the Nationality Question, (Bucharest: 1976), p. 23.

27. Quoted by Alfred Bohmann, *Menschen und Grenzen,* vol. 2, *Bevölkerung und Nationalitäten in Südosteuropa, Rumänien,* pp. 101–218, (Cologne: 1969), p. 198.

28. Cf., *The Hungarian Nationality in Romania,* p.23.

29. Between the two world wars, two Catholic weeklies, a monthly and five other journals were published.

30. The Reformed Church communities along the Hungarian-Romanian border, which did not belong to the Transylvanian bishopric, organized themselves into a separate bishopric, with its seat in Arad, after the First World War (December 14, 1920). The newly formed bishopric was only recognized by the Romanian state in a law issued on November 22, 1939.

31. For data relating to the Churches and clergy, see *The Hungarian Nationality in Romania,* p. 23.

32. Brașov/Brassó, Alba Iulia/Gyulafehérvár, Cluj/Kolozsvár, Dej/Dés, Tîrgu Mureș/Marosvásárhely, Tírnăveni/Dicsőszentmárton, Odorhei/Székelyudvarhely, and Sfîntu Gheorghe/Sepsiszentgyörgy.

33. Carei/Nagykároly, Baia Mare/Nagybánya, Zălău/Zilah, Oradea/Nagyvárad and Timișoara/Temesvár.

NOTES   299

34. Between the two world wars, the Reformed Church had three well edited monthly publications and the regularly published *Református Naptár* (Reformed Church Calendar).

35. Bistritz, Hermannstadt, Kronstadt, Mediasch, Mühlbach, and Schässburg. A source of information on the Lutheran Church is E. Wagner, *Quellen zur Geschichte der Siebenbürger Sachsen 1191-1975*, (Cologne-Vienna: 1976), pp. 425-426.

36. A. Bohmann, *Menschen und Grenzen*, p. 198.

37. *The Hungarian Nationality in Romania*, p. 23.

38. Between the two world wars *Unitárius Közlöny* [Unitarian Gazette] was an important journal, published in an edition of 8,000-10,000 copies, while *Keresztény Magvető* appeared in an edition of 5,000-6,000 copies.

39. *The Hungarian Nationality in Romania*, p. 23.

40. Richard F. Staar, *Die Kommunistischen Regierungssysteme in Osteuropa*, (Stuttgart: 1977), pp. 218-219.

41. *Monitorul Oficial*, July 12, 1949.

42. Cf., *Kirchen im Sozialismus, op. cit.*, p. 33.

Chapter 7

1. Zsigmond Jakó, "Die Hermannstädter Druckerei im 16. Jahrhundert und ihre Bedeutung für die rumänische Kulturgeschichte," in *Forschungen zur Volks- und Landeskunde*, vol. 9, no. 1, 1966, pp. 31-58.

2. Pál Binder, "Kulturbeziehungen auf dem Gebiet des Buchdruckes", in *Archiv des Vereins für Siebenbürgische Landeskunde*, no. 12, 1976.

3. For more detail, see Hans Meschendörfer, *Das Verlagswesen der Siebenbürger Sachsen. Ein Überblick*, (Munich: 1979), p. 21.

4. Published under the title *Korrespondenzblatt des Vereins für siebenbürgische Landeskunde* from 1878 to 1930, as *Siebenbürgische Vierteljahresschrift* from 1931 to 1941, from 1971 to 1978 as *Korrespondenzblatt des Arbeitskreises für siebenbürgische Landeskunde* in the Federal Republic of Germany, and after 1978 as *Zeitschrift für Siebenbürgische Landeskunde*.

5. Lajos György, *Az erdélyi magyarság szellemi élete. Az erdélyi magyar irodalom bibliográfiája 1919-1924* [The Intellectual Life of the Hungarians in Transylvania. Bibliography of Hungarian Literature in Transylvania 1919-1924] (Cluj: 1925), pp. 8-9; see further Alfred Bohmann, *Menschen und Grenzen*, vol. 2: *Bevölkerung und Nationalitäten in Südosteuropa*, (Cologne: 1969), p. 203; see also H. Meschendörfer, *op. cit.* p. 70.

6. Meschendörfer, *op. cit.*, pp. 58-70.

7. Lajos György, *op. cit.*, 5-12.

8. For more detail, see Alfred Bohmann, *op. cit.*, p. 203; *Dokumentation der Vertreibung der Deutschen aus Ost-Mitteleuropa*, vol. III, *Das Schicksal der Deutschen in Rumänien*, (Berlin: 1957), p. 105E.

9. See Stephen Fischer-Galati, ed., *Romania*, (New York: 1956), p. 172; Alexandre Cretzianu, *Captive Rumania*, (New York: 1956), p. 128; see also Anneli Ute Gabanyi, "Literatur," in *Rumänien, Südosteuropa Handbuch*, vol. II, ed., Klaus-Detlev Grothusen (Göttingen: 1977), p. 527.

10. *Monitorul Oficial* [Official Gazette], no. 11, January 14, 1949.

11. Data from Council for Socialist Culture and Education, in *A magyar nemzetiség Romániában* [The Hungarian Nationality in Romania], (Bucharest: 1976), Appendix no. 3.

12. *Neuer Weg* was the daily of the so-called German Anti-Fascist Committee in Romania in 1948. It appeared at a time when the first wave of discrimination against the Germans in Romania had abated and the support of the nationalities was important for the communist regime, then in the process of consolidating its authority. At the time of its founding, *Neuer Weg* bore the subtitle *Organ des Antifaschistischen Komitees der deutschen Werktätigen in Rumänien;* from 1953 onwards, it was designated *Organ der Volksräte der Rumänischen Volksrepublik;* at present, it is known as *Organ des Landesrates der Front der Sozialistischen Einheit;* and, as a political daily, like the Hungarian-language *Előre* [Forward], it is the leading German-language newspaper of the RCP and the Romanian Socialist Republic.

13. The following is a list of other Hungarian-language publications in Romania:

Daily papers: *Előre* [Forward], Bucharest; *Fáklya* [Torch], Oradea; *Igazság* [Truth], Cluj-Napoca; *Vörös Zászló* [Red Banner], Tîrgu Mureș; *Szabad Szó* [Free Word], Timișoara.

Weeklies: *Vörös Lobogó* [Red Flag], Arad; *Brassói Lapok* [Brassó Papers], Brașov; *Megyei Tükör* [County Mirror], Sfîntu Gheorghe; *Hargita*, Miercurea Ciuc; *Bányavidéki Fáklya* [Bányavidék Torch], Maramureș; *Szatmári Hírlap* [Szatmár Journal], Satu Mare.

Monthlies: *Napsugár* [Sunlight], Cluj-Napoca.

Irregularly published periodicals: *Új Élet* [New Life], Tîrgu Mureș and *Nyelv- és Irodalomtudományi Közlemények* [Publications in Linguistics and Literary Science], Cluj-Napoca. The *Buletinul Oficial* [Official Bulletin] is also published in the languages of the national minorities. The daily paper of the Swabians of the Banat, *Neue Banater Zeitung*, is published in Timișoara.

14. Until October 29, 1971, *Die Woche* appeared under the title *Hermannstädter Zeitung;* the name fell the victim to the measure officially banning the use of certain significant national-minority place names, the text of which has never been published. In accordance with a further secret directive, Hungarian or German place names may be used only if they resemble Romanian place names or if the national-minority population amounts to at least 30 percent of the inhabitants of the localities in question. Concerning the use of the place

names in the language of the nationalities in Romania, see *Radio Free Europe: Situation Report, Romania,* no. 41, November 3, 1971, p. 16.

15. Joseph S. Rouček, *Contemporary Roumania and her Problems,* (Stanford: 1932), pp. 208-209.

16. Some German and Hungarian writers and poets in Romania stopped writing during the years of rigid literary formalism, but in addition to those writers who committed themselves to "proletcult" propaganda, a few well-known minority writers were also published. One frequently encounters the names of the Germans Erwin Wittstock and Oskar Walter Cissek, or the Hungarians Ferenc Szemlér, László Szabédi, Jenő Kiss, Imre Horváth and—from the younger generation—András Sütő on the pages of the literary journals of the 1950s. For more detail, see Lajos Kántor and Gusztáv Láng, *Romániai magyar irodalom 1944-1970* [Hungarian Literature in Romania 1944-1970], (Bucharest: 1973).

17. It was at this time that novels were published by: Paul Goma, *Ostinato;* Marin Preda, *Intrusul* [The Intruder]; and Fănuș Neagu, *Ingerul a strigat* [The Angel has Called].

18. *Romanian Statistical Pocket Book 1964,* published by the Romanian People's Republic, Central Statistical Board, 1964, pp. 266-268.

19. From among Hungarian prose writers: András Sütő, *Anyám könnyű álmot ígér* [My Mother Promises a Light Sleep], 1970; Tibor Bálint, *Zokogó majom* [Sobbing Monkey], 1969. From among the poets: Sándor Kányádi, *Fától fáig* [From Tree to Tree], 1970; Árpád Farkas, *Jegenyekör* [Poplar Circle], 1971; Domokos Szilágyi, *Búcsú a trópusoktól* [Farewell to the Tropics], 1969. From among the German writers: the posthumous work of Erwin Wittstock, *Das Jüngste Gericht in Altbirk,* 1971; and Arnold Hauser, *Der fragwürdige Bericht Jakob Bühlmanns,* 1968, the first work to depict the fate of Germans of Transylvania since the war.

20. Cf., the statement of Hungarian writers in Romania, made according with the official instructions: "We do not intend to slice up Romanian education and, within it, our own Hungarian nationality literature and culture into regional units because—in the words of Ceaușescu—the unity of Romanians, Hungarians, Germans and other nationalities around the party and government is indivisible." *Igaz Szó* [True Word] Tîrgu Mureș monthly, no. 12, 1970, p. 795. For a discussion of national assimilation, see Karl W. Deutsch, *Nationalism and Social Communication,* (Cambridge, Mass.: 1966); Chapters 5 and 6, pp. 107-153.

21. One of the pre-war novels of the Hungarian writer György Kovács and a work by the Romanian author Lucia Demetrius, on a Transylvanian theme, could only be published after being revised by the office of censorship.

22. The Hungarian-language daily published in Bucharest, *Előre* [Forward], published a long article in its February 15, 1975 issue on the "liberation" of Budapest by Romanian and Soviet troops; the August 1975 issue of *Vörös*

Zászló [Red Banner], Tîrgu Mureș, published photographs taken 35 years earlier of mass demonstrations against the Second Vienna Award.

23. *Scînteia* [The Spark], the central organ of the RCP, published an article in its May 18, 1976 issue on the "2,050-year-old independent, centralized state of the Dacians," thereby emphasizing the historic primacy of the Romanian people in Transylvania. The article had to be published by the nationality papers as well.

24. Cf., László Hegedüs, "Szocialista kultúránk—a testvériség szolgálatában" [Our Socialist Culture—in the Service of Fraternity], in *A Hét* [The Week], March 17, 1978, p. 2; also Franz Storch, "A szocialista építés szerves része," *Ibid.,* p. 3.

25. "Grundfragen der rumänischen Kulturpolitik," in *Wissenschaftlicher Dienst Südosteuropa,* Munich, 1974, no. 4, p. 74.

26. "From the Report submitted by Comrade Nicolae Ceaușescu on behalf of the Central Committee of the Romanian Communist Party at the 11th Congress," in *Korunk* [Our Age], a Cluj-Napoca Hungarian-language monthly, vol. 12, 1974, p. 1208.

27. For more detail, see A. U. Gabanyi, " Die rumänische Literaturpolitik seit 1972," in: *Wissenschaftlicher Dienst Südosteuropa,* no. 9, 1975, pp. 180–184. See also T. Gilberg, "Ceaușescu's kleine Kulturrevolution in Rumänien", in *Osteuropa,* no. 22, 1972.

28. On the resistance and the realization of the policy of the party see *Osteuropa,* Stuttgart, 10/1972, pp. 717–728.

29. The statutes passed at the May conference of the Writers' Association contain a supplementary clause regarding young writers: "while, in accordance with the 1968 regulations, admission to the Writers' Association was possible after the publication of a single book, from 1972 onwards this shall require the publication of two books." (Cf. A. U. Gabanyi, "Die rumänische Literaturpolitik seit 1972," *op. cit.,* pp. 180–184.)

30. Decree No. 53/1975, *Buletinul Oficial,* no. 51, May 30, 1975.

31. Law No. 3, published in *Buletinul Oficial,* no. 48, I, April 1, 1975.

32. Resolution of the Secretary of the CC of the RCP, published in *Neuer Weg,* May 8, 1974.

33. Congresul al XI-lea al Partidului Comunist Român [The 11th Congress of the RCP], (Bucharest: 1974).

34. Resolution of the Secretary of the CC of the RCP, published in *Neuer Weg,* May 8, 1974.

35. Malcolm W. Brown, "Repression Rise Seen in Rumania," in *The New York Times,* May 30, 1976.

36. Report commissioned by the party office of Bolyai University of Cluj, December 1954–March 1955, p. 64 (Manuscript).

37. Decree No. 422 in *Buletinul Oficial,* no. 127, November 28, 1977.

38. Characteristic of the Romanian government's view of the merging of cultures is the statement of RCP Chief N. Ceaușescu: "It does not matter in

which language the nationalities sing, recite, or play-act, or in which language they write: the important thing is what they say and what they write." "From Nicolae Ceaușescu's 1976 New Year's Speech", in *Igaz Szó*, Tîrgu Mureș, no. 1, 1976. A valuable source of information on cultural assimilation—specially among the Hungarians—is Trond Gilberg, "Ethnic Minorities in Romania under Socialism," in *East European Quarterly*, vol. VII, no. 4, January 1974, p. 439; see also Karl W. Deutsch, *Nationalism and Social Communication*, (Cambridge, Mass.: 1966), Chapters 5 and 6, pp. 107-153; see further Stephen Fischer-Galati, "The Socialist Republic of Rumania", in Peter A. Toma, ed., *The Changing Face of Communism in Eastern Europe*, (University of Arizona: 1970), pp. 28-32.

39. Cf., *A magyar nemzetiség Romániában* [The Hungarian Nationality in Romania], Appendix 3.

40. Resolution of the Council of Ministers No. 2,215, *Buletinul Oficial*, December 9, 1969.

41. Among others the Dacia Publishing House in Cluj-Napoca, the Ion Creangă, Ceres, Eminescu, and Albatros Publishing Houses in Bucharest, and the Faclă Publishing House in Timișoara. See also note 39, p. 17.

42. Cf., *Sächsisch-schwäbische Chronik*, eds., E. Eisenburger and M. Kroner (Bucharest: 1976), p. 198.

43. Cf., *Anuarul Statistic al RPR 1965* [Statistical Yearbook of the Romanian People's Republic, 1965], Bucharest, Central Statistical Directorate, 1965, Table 256, p. 532; *Anuarul Statistic al RPR 1957* [Statistical Yearbook of the Romanian People's Republic, 1957], Central Directorate, Bucharest, 1957, Table 138, p. 222.

44. S. Fischer-Galati, ed., *Romania*, pp. 164-165; L. Deáky and N. Rădulescu, "Fighters of the Socialist Struggle", in *Scînteia, March 6, 1964*.

45. *Anuarul Statistic al RPR 1965*, Table 256; and *op. cit., 1957*, Table 138, p. 222.

46. See *Igaz Szó*, Tîrgu Mureș, no. 5, 1972, p. 640.

47. Cf., László Hegedüs, "Szocialista kultúránk—a testvériség szolgálatában" [Our Socialist Culture—in the Service of Fraternity] in *A Hét*, Bucharest, March 17, 1978; see also *A magyar nemzetiség Romániában* [The Hungarian Nationality in Romania], p. 18.

48. See, *Neuer Weg Kalender 1977*, (Bucharest: 1976), p. 22.

49. The joint session of the Councils of Working People of Hungarian and German Nationality, December 3, 1975, *Scînteia*, December 4, 1975.

50. See, *Project de plan editorial* [Editorial Project], 1971-1977.

51. *Ibid.*, 1971.

52. The text of the contributions is published in the March 14, 1971 issue of the Hungarian-language daily *Előre*.

53. *Korunk* [Our Age], Cluj-Napoca, no. 9., 1981, pp. 710-711.

54. Sándor Pezderka, "Magyar könyvek—a számok tükrében" [Hungarian Books—a Quantitative Study], in *A Hét*, Bucharest, February, 17, 1978.

SELECTED BIBLIOGRAPHY

1. BIBLIOGRAPHICAL WORKS

Bakó, Elemér and William Solyom-Fekete: *Hungarians in Rumania and Transylvania:* A Bibliographical List of Publications in Hungarian and West European Languages Compiled from the Holdings of the Library Congress. [Mimeographed], (Washington, D.C.: Library of Congress, 1966).
Bibliographie courante d'articles de périodiques postérieurs à 1944 sur les problèmes politiques, économiques et sociaux, (Boston: 1968).
Bibliographie européenne des travaux sur l'URSS et l'Europe de l'Est. Vol. I, 1975, ed., Thomas Hnik, (Birmingham: 1977).
Bibliografia istorică a României [Historic Bibliography of Romania], vol. I, 1944–1969.
Bibliografia literară română ilustrată 1944–1970 [Illustrate Romanian Literary Bibliography 1944–1970], (Bucharest: 1971).
Braham, Randolph L.: *Jews in the Communist World: A Bibliography 1945–1960*, (New York: 1961).
Byrnes, Robert F.: *Bibliography of American Publications on East Central Europe, 1945–1957,* (Bloomington, Indiana: 1958).
Deutsch, Robert: *Istoricii şi ştiinţa istorică din România 1944–1969* [Historians and the Science of History in Romania 1944–1969], (Bucharest: 1970).
Fischer-Galati, S.: *Rumania. A Bibliographic Guide,* (Washington, D.C.: 1963, New York: 1968).
Horecky, P. L. ed.: *Southeastern Europe. A Guide to Basic Publications,* (Chicago, London: 1969).
Magyar Történeti Bibliográfia 1925–1967 [Hungarian Historical Bibliography 1925–1967], (Budapest: 1950–1959).

Newspapers, periodicals and magazines from Rumania, (Bucharest: 1955).
Roberts, Henry L. et al. eds.: *Foreign Affairs Bibliography.* A Selected and Annotated List of Books on International Relations 1952-1962. Council on Foreign Relations, (New York: 1964).
Südosteuropa-Bibliographie, ed. by Südost-Institut, compiled by Gertrud Krallert-Sattler, Munich. Vol. I 1956: Rumania 1945-1950; vol. II 1962: Rumania 1951-1955; vol. III 1964: Rumania 1956-1960; vol. IV 1969: Rumania 1961-1965.
U.S. Bureau of the Census. Bibliography of Social Science Periodicals and Monograph Series: Rumania, 1947-1960, Washington, D.C.: 1961. [Foreign Social Science Bibliographies, Series P-92, no. 1].
U.S. Library of Congress. Division of Bibliography. The Balkans: IV Rumania, (Washington, D.C.: 1943).
U.S. Library of Congress. Division of Bibliography. The Balkans; a Selected List of References. Compiled by Helen Conover, (Washington, D.C.: 1943).
U.S. Library of Congress. Slavic and Central European Division. Newspapers of East Central and Southeastern Europe in the Library of Congress. Edited by Robert G. Carlton, (Washington, D.C.: 1965).
U.S. Library of Congress. Slavic and Central European Division. The USSR and Eastern Europe: Periodicals in Western Languages. Compiled by Paul L. Horecky and Robert G. Carlton, 3d ed., (Washington, D.C.: 1967).

2. HISTORICAL SOURCES

Documenta Historiam Valachorum in Hungaria illustrantia, edited by Antal Fekete Nagy and László Makkai, (Budapest: 1941).
Documente privind istoria României [Documents Concerning the History of Romania], B. Wallachia, vol. I 1247-1500, (Bucharest: 1953); C. Transylvania, XI, XII and XIII centuries, vol. I, (Bucharest: 1951); XIII century, vol. I, (Bucharest: 1952).
Documenta Romaniae Historica. C. Transylvania, vol. X, 1351-1355 edited by Ştefan Pascu, (Bucharest: 1977).
Hurmuzaki, Eudoxiu de: *Documente privitoare la Istoria Românilor,* [Documents Concerning the History of the Romanians], vol. I 1199-1345, compiled by Nicolae Densuşianu, (Bucharest: 1887).
Lukinich, Imre and László Gáldi: *Documenta Historiam Valachorum in Hungaria illustrantia usque ad annum 1400 p. Chr.,* edited by Antal Fekete-Nagy et László Makkai, (Budapest: 1941).
Monumenta Vaticana historiam regni Hungariae illustrantia. Series I, vols. I-IV, (Budapest: 1885-1889).
Popa-Lisseanu, G.: *Izvoarele istoriei românilor* [Sources of the History of the Romanians], vols. I, V-VI, and VII, (Bucharest: 1934-1935).

Urkundenbuch zur Geschichte der Deutschen in Siebenbürgen, vol. I 1191–1342, compiled by Franz Zimmermann and Carl Werner, (Hermannstadt: 1892); vol. II 1391–1415, (Hermannstadt: 1902).
Urkundenbuch zur Geschichte Siebenbürgens, Part I until 1301, compiled by G. D. Teutsch and Fr. Firnhaber, (Vienna: 1857). Fontes Rerum Austriacarum, 2 Sect., 15 vol.

3. GENERAL DEPICTIONS—REFERENCE WORKS

Austrian History Yearbook. Volumes IV-V, 1968–1969, IX-X, 1973–1974, (Houston, Texas, Rice University: 1970, 1975).
Bergel, Hans: *Rumänien. Porträt einer Nation,* (Munich, Esslingen: 1969).
Bohmann, Alfred: *Menschen und Grenzen,* II. vol.: Bevölkerung und Nationalitäten in Südosteuropa, (Cologne: 1969).
Brown, James F.: *The New Eastern Europe: The Khrushchev Era and After,* (New York: 1966).
Brzezinski, Z. K.,: *The Soviet Bloc,* rev. ed., (New York: 1967).
Burks, Richard V.: *The Dynamics of Communism in Eastern Europe,* (Princeton, N.J.: 1961).
Byrnes, Robert F. ed.: *East Central Europe Under the Communists,* (New York: 1956–1957).
Campbell, John C.: "The European Territorial Settlement", in: *Foreign Affairs,* Oct. 1947, pp. 196–218.
Campbell, John C.: *The United States in World Affairs 1945–1947,* (New York: 1947).
Chambers Twentieth Century Dictionary. New edition, ed. A.M. Macdonald, (Edinburgh: 1974).
Churchil, Sir Winston: *The Second World War.* Vols. I-VI, (Boston: 1948–1953).
Cretzianu, Alexandre, ed.: *Captive Rumania. A decade of Soviet Rule,* (New York: 1956).
Csatári, Dániel: *Forgószélben. Magyar-román viszony 1940–1945* [In the Whirlwind. Hungarian-Romanian Relationship 1940–1945], (Budapest: 1968).
Dicționar enciclopedic romîn [Encyclopaedical Romanian Dictionary], vols. I-IV, (Bucharest: 1962–1966).
Dicționarul Transilvaniei, Banatului și celorlalte ținuturi alipite [The Dictionary of Transylvania, the Banat and the Other Annexed Regions], eds. G. Martinovici and N. Istrati, (Cluj: 1921).
Djilas, Milovan: *The New Class: An Analysis of the Communist System,* (New York: 1957).
Dokumentation der Vertreibung der Deutschen aus Ost-Mitteleuropa. Vol. III: Das Schicksal der Deutschen in Rumänien, ed. by the Bundesminis-

terium für Vertriebene, Flüchtlinge und Kriegsgeschädigte. Compiled by Theodor Schieder, (Berlin: 1953-1962).

East Central and Southeast Europe. A handbook of library and archival resources in North America. Ed. by Paul L. Horecky and David H. Kraus, (Santa Barbara, Calif., Oxford Egl. Clio Press: 1977). [The Joint Committee on Eastern Europe Publications series 3.].

Eisenburger, Eduard: *Wegzeichen der Heimat.* Bilder, Berichte, Zeitdokumente über die Rumäniendeutschen, (Cluj: 1974).

Eisenburger, Eduard: *Heimatbilder.* Bekanntes und weniger Bekanntes über die Rumäniendeutschen, (Cluj-Napoca: 1976).

Enciclopedia României, vols. I-IV, (Bucharest: 1938-1943).

Fischer-Galati, Stephen: *The New Rumania: From People's Democracy to Socialist Republic,* (Cambridge, Mass.: 1967).

Fischer-Galati, Stephen, ed.: *Romania,* (New York: 1957).

Fischer-Galati, Stephen, ed.: *Eastern Europe in the Sixties,* (New York—London: 1963).

Fischer-Galati, Stephen: "The Origins of Modern Rumanian Nationalism", in: *Jahrbücher für Geschichte Osteuropas* 12., 1964, pp. 48-54.

Fischer-Galati, Stephen: *The Socialist Republic of Rumania,* (Baltimore: 1969).

Fischer-Galati, Stephen: *Twentieth-Century Rumania,* (New York—London: 1970).

Floyd, David: *Rumania, Russia's Dissident Ally,* (New York: 1965).

Forster, Kent: *Recent Europe. A Twentieth-Century History,* (New York: 1965).

Gibson, Hugh, ed.: *The Ciano Diaries 1939-1943,* (New York: 1946).

Gilberg, Trond: *Modernization in Romania Since World War II,* (New York: 1975).

Great Britain. Foreign Office. Historical Section. Rumania, (London H.M. Stationery Office: 1920). [Handbooks. . ., no. 23].

Grentrup, Th.: "Das Deutschtum an der mittleren Donau in Rumänien und Jugoslawien", in: *Deutschtum im Ausland,* (Münster: 1930).

Griffith, William E. ed.: *Communism in Europe,* (Cambridge, Mass.: 1964).

Grothusen, Klaus-Detlev, ed.: *Rumänien.* Südosteuropa Handbuch, vol. II, (Göttingen: 1977).

Hartl, Hans: *Das Schicksal des Deutschtums in Rumänien,* (Würzburg: 1958).

Hoffmann, George W.: *The Balkans in Transition,* (Princeton N.J., Toronto, London, New York: 1963).

Illyés, Elemér: *Erdély változása. Mítosz és valóság* [Change in Transylvania. Myth and Reality], (Munich: 1975, 2nd edition 1976).

Illyés, Elemér: *Nationale Minderheiten in Rumänien. Siebenbürgen im Wandel,* (Vienna-Stuttgart: 1981).

Indicatorul alfabetic al localităților din R.P.R. [Alphabetical Register of the Localities of the Romanian People's Republic], (Bucharest: 1965).

Indicatorul localităţilor din România [Register of the Localities of Romania], (Bucharest: 1974).
Ionescu, Ghiţa: *Communism in Rumania 1944-1962*, (London, New York, Toronto: 1964).
Ionescu, Ghiţa: *The Breakup of the Soviet Empire in Eastern Europe*, (Baltimore: 1965).
Iordan, I.; Gâştescu, P.; Oancea, D. I.: *Indicatorul localităţilor din România* [Place-Register of Romania], (Bucharest: 1974).
Jászi, Oszkár: "Visszaemlékezés a Román Nemzeti Komitéval folytatott aradi tárgyalásaimra" [Reminiscence on my Debate with the Romanian National Committee in Arad], in: *Napkelet*, (Budapest: 1921), II, pp. 1345-1356.
Jowitt, Kenneth: *Revolutionary Breakthroughs and National Development: The Case of Romania, 1944-1965*, (Berkeley and Los Angeles: 1971).
Judeţele României Socialiste [The Counties of the Socialist Romania], (Bucharest: 1967, 2nd. ed. 1972).
Kane, Robert S.: *Eastern Europe. A to Z: Bulgaria, Czechoslovakia, East Germany, Hungary, Poland, Romania, Yugoslavia, and the Soviet Union*, (Garden City, N.Y.: 1968).
Kann, Robert A.: *The Multinational Empire*. Nationalism and National Reform in the Habsburg Monarchy 1848-1919, vols. I-II, (New York: 1964).
Kertesz, D., Stephen: *Diplomacy in a Whirlpool. Hungary Between Nazy Germany and Soviet Russia*, (Notre Dame, Indiana: 1953).
Kertesz, D. Stephen ed.: *East Central Europe and the World. Developments in the Post-Stalin Era*, (Notre Dame: 1962).
Klein, Karl Kurt: *Transsylvanica*. Gesammelte Abhandlungen und Aufsätze zur Sprach- und Siedlungsforschung der Deutschen in Siebenbürgen, (Munich: 1963).
Kormos, C.: *Rumania: Basic Handbook*. British Survey Handbooks, vols. I-III, (Cambridge: 1944).
Korunk Évkönyv 1973-1980 [The Korunk-Yearbook 1973-1980]. (Cluj-Napoca).
Kósa, László and Filep, Antal: *A magyar nép táji-történeti tagolódása* [Regional-historical Division of the Hungarian People], (Budapest: 1975).
Lenk von Treuenfeld, Ignaz: *Siebenbürgens geographisch-, topographisch-, statistisch-, hydrographisch und orographisches Lexikon...*, vols. I-IV, (Vienna: 1839).
London, Kurt: *Eastern Europe in Transition*, (Baltimore: 1966).
Macartney, C. A.: *The Danubian Basin*. Oxford Pamphlets of World Affairs, no. 10, 1939.
Magyar Néprajzi Lexikon [Hungarian Ethnographical Lexicon], Vol. I A-E (Budapest: 1977); vol. II F-Ka, (Budapest: 1979); vol. III K-Né, (Budapest: 1980); vol. IV N-Szé, (Budapest: 1981).
Mately, I. M.: *Romania: A Profile*, (London: 1970).

Mellor, R.E.H.: *Eastern Europe.* A Geography of the Comecon Countries, (New York: 1975).
Nagybaczoni Nagy, Vilmos: *Végzetes esztendők 1938–1945,* [Fatal Years 1938–1945], (Kispest: 1947).
Orbán, Balázs: *A Székelyföld leírása történelmi, régészeti, természetrajzi s népismei szempontból* [The Description of the Székler Region According to Historical, Archaeological, Scientific, and Ethnological Aspects], vols.I-VI, (Pest: 1868–1873). Re-edited by Elemér Illyés (Munich-Firenze: 1981).
Osborne, R. H.: *East Central Europe,* (New York: 1967).
Pounds, Norman J. G.: *Eastern Europe,* (Chicago-London: 1969).
Riedl, Franz H.: *Das Südostdeutschtum in den Jahren 1918–1945,* (Munich: 1962).
Roberts, Henry L.: *Rumania: Political Problems of an Agrarian State,* (New Haven: 1951).
Romania in the 1980s, edited by Daniel N. Nelson. Westview Special Studies on the Soviet Union and Eastern Europe, (Boulder, Colorado: 1981).
Rouček, Joseph S.: *Contemporary Roumania and Her Problems; a Study in Modern Nationalism,* (Stanford: 1932).
Rouček, Joseph S.: *Central Europe. Crucible of World Wars,* (New York: 1946).
Savadjian, Léon, ed.: *Encyclopédie balkanique permanente,* (Paris: 1936), I. vol. Société générale d'imprimerie et d'édition.
Seton-Watson, Hugh: *Eastern-Europe Between the Wars 1918–1941,* (Cambridge: 1945), 2nd. edit., (Hamden, Connect.: 1962).
Seton-Watson, R. W.: *Transylvania: A Key Problem,* (Oxford: 1943).
Seton-Watson, Hugh: *The East European Revolution,* 2nd. edit., (New York: 1968).
Seton-Watson, Hugh: *Nationalism and Communism,* (London: 1964).
Siegert, H.: *Rumänien heute,* (Vienna-Düsseldorf: 1966).
Staar, F. Richard: *The Communist Regimes in Eastern Europe: An Introduction,* (Stanford, Calif., The Hoover Institution: 1967).
Suciu, Coriolan: *Dicţionar istoric al localităţilor din Transilvania* [Historical Dictionary of Transylvanian Localities], vols. I-II, (Bucharest: 1967–68).
Sugar, Peter F. and Ivo J. Lederer: *Nationalism in Eastern Europe,* (Seattle: 1970).
Sulyok, István and Fritz, László: *Erdélyi Magyar Évkönyv 1918–1929* [Transylvanian Hungarian Yearbook 1918–1929], vol. I, (Cluj: 1930).
Szabó, T. Attila: *Erdélyi magyar szótörténeti tár* [Transylvanian Hungarian Historical Thesaurus of Words], vol. I A-C, (Bucharest: 1976), vol. II Cs-Elsz, (Bucharest: 1978).
Toma, A. Peter ed.: *The Changing Face of Communism in Eastern Europe,* (The University of Arizona: 1970).
Wagner, Ernst: *Historisch-statistisches Ortsnamenbuch für Siebenbürgen.* Studia Transylvanica 4, (Cologne-Vienna: 1977).

Wittstock, Oskar: *Die Siebenbürger Sachsen und der gesamtdeutsche Gedanke*, (Brünn, Munich, Vienna: 1943).
Wolff, Robert Lee: *The Balkans in Our Time*, (Cambridge, Mass.: 1956).
Yearbook of the United Nations 1963-1968. Office of Public Information, UN, (New York: 1965-1971).

4. GENERAL HISTORICAL BIBLIOGRAPHY

Arató, Endre: *Kelet-Európa története a 19. század első felében* [The History of Eastern Europe in the First Half of the 19th Century], (Budapest: 1971).
Asztalos, Miklós: *A Történeti Erdély* [Historic Transylvania], (Budapest: 1936).
Bányai, László: *Közös sors—testvéri hagyományok. Történelmi vázlat* [Common Fate—Fraternal Traditions. A Historical Sketch], (Bucharest: 1973).
Berend, Iván and Ránki, György: *East Central Europe in the 19th and 20th Centuries*, (Budapest: 1977).
Bernath, Mathias: *Habsburg und die Anfänge der rumänischen Nationsbildung.* Studien zur Geschichte Osteuropas. Studies in East European History, (Leiden: 1972).
Bogdan, Henry: *Histoire de la Hongrie*, (Paris: 1966).
Bogdan, Henry: *De Varsovie a Sofia. Histoire des Pays de l'Est*. Collection "Documents", (Paris: 1982).
Brătianu, Gheorghe I.: *Ein Rätsel und ein Wunder der Geschichte: das rumänische Volk*, (Bucharest: 1942).
Chronological History of Romania, 2nd edit., (Bucharest: 1974).
Constantinescu, Miron et. al.: *Études d'histoire contemporaine de la Roumanie*, (Bucarest: 1970).
Constantinescu, M.; Daicoviciu, C.; Pascu, Ş eds.: *Istoria României*, [The History of Romania], 2nd ed., (Bucharest: 1971).
Constantinescu, M. and Pascu, Ş. eds.: *Unification of the Romanian National State. The Union of Transylvania with Old Romania*, (Bucharest: 1971).
Dálnoki Veress, Lajos: *Magyarország honvédelme a II világháború előtt és alatt 1920-1945*, [Hungary's Defensive Military Operation Before and During World War II], I-III vols., (Munich: 1973).
Darkó, J.: *Die Landnahme der Ungarn und Siebenbürgen.* In: *Ostmitteleuropäische Bibliothek*, no. 24, (Budapest: 1940).
Deér, József and Gáldi, László: *Magyarok és románok* [Hungarians and Romanians], vols. I-II, (Budapest: 1943-1944).
Dinić, M.: "The Balkans, 1018-1499. Principalities of Wallachia and Moldavia", in: *The Cambridge Medieval History*, vol. IV. The Byzantine Empire, Part I. Byzantinum and its Neighbours, edited by M. Hussey (Cambridge: 1966).

Din istoria Transilvaniei, eds. Constantin Daicoviciu, Ștefan Pascu, Victor Cherestețiu, Ștefan Imreh, Alexandru Neamțu, Tiberiu Morariu, I-II vols., (Bucharest: 1963).

Droz, J.: *L'Europe Centrale*, Evolution historique de l'idée de" Mitteleuropa," (Paris: 1960).

Gáldi, L. and Makkai, L.: *A románok története* [The History of the Romanians], (Budapest: 1942).

Gamillscheg, E.: *Über die Herkunft der Rumänen*, (Berlin: 1940).

George, Pierre and Tricart, Jean: *L'Europe Centrale*, I, (Paris: 1954).

Ghermani, Dionisie: *Die kommunistische Umdeutung der rumänischen Geschichte unter besonderer Berücksichtigung des Mittelalters*, (Munich: 1967).

Ghermani, Dionisie: "Wandlungen der rumänischen Historiographie im Spiegel der ersten vier Bände der 'Istoria României', in: *Südostforschungen* 26, 1967, pp. 354-367.

Ghermani, Dionisie: *Die nationale Souveränitätspolitik der SR Rumänien*. Part 1. Im Rahmen des sowjetischen Bündnissystems, (Munich: 1981).

Giurescu, Constantin, ed.: *Istoria României in date* [History of Romania in Dates], (Bucharest: 1972).

Giurescu, C. Constantin: *Transsilvanien in der Geschichte des rumänischen Volkes*, (Bucharest: 1968).

Giurescu, C. C. and Giurescu, D. C.: *Istoria Românilor din cele mai vechi timpuri pînă astăzi* [The History of the Romanians From the Earliest Times to our Day], 2nd ed., (Bucharest: 1975).

Göckenjan, Hansgerd: *Hilfsvölker und Grenzwächter im mittelalterlichen Ungarn*, (Wiesbaden: 1972).

Gündisch, Gustav: "Siebenbürgen in der Türkenabwehr 1395-1526", in: *Revue Roumaine d'Histoire*, 13, 1974, pp. 415-443.

Gündisch, Gustav: "Die Türkeneinfälle in Siebenbürgen bis zur Mitte des 15. Jahrhunderts", in: *Jahrbücher für die Geschichte Osteuropas*, 2, 1937, pp. 393-412.

Györffy, György: "Adatok a románok XIII. századi történetéhez és a román állam kezdeteihez" [Data on the History of the Romanians in the 13th Century and on the Beginning of the Romanian State], in: *Történelmi Szemle* 7, 1964, pp. 1-25, 537-568.

Györffy, György: "Der Ursprung der Székler", in: *Ungarische Jahrbücher* XXII, 1942.

Halecki, Oscar: *Borderlands of Western Civilization. A History of East Central Europe*, (New York: 1952).

Hillgruber, Andreas: *Hitler, König Carol und Marschall Antonescu. Die deutsch-rumänische Beziehungen 1938-1940*, (Wiesbaden: 1954).

Hitchins, Keith: *Orthodoxy and Nationality. Andrei Șaguna and the Rumanians of Transylvania 1846-1873*, (Cambridge, Mass., London: 1977).

Hóman, Bálint and Szekfű, Gyula: *Magyar történet* [Hungarian History], vols. I-VIII, (Budapest: 1935-1936).
Hóman, Bálint: "Der Ursprung der Siebenbürger Székler", in: *Ungarische Jahrbücher* II, 1922.
Hóman, Bálint: *Geschichte des ungarischen Mittelalters,* vols. I-II, (Berlin: 1941-43).
Horedt, Kurt: *Untersuchungen zur Frühgeschichte Siebenbürgens,* (Bukarest: 1958).
Hurdubeţiu, I.: *Die Deutschen über die Herkunft der Rumänen* [von Johann Thunmann bis Ernst Gamillscheg], (Breslau: 1943).
Hurmuzaki, E. de: *Fragmente zur Geschichte der Rumänen,* vols. I-V, (Bucharest: 1878-1886).
Iordan, I.: *Originea românilor* [The Origin of the Romanians], (Bucharest: 1950).
Iorga, Nicolae: *Istoria Românilor* [The History of the Romanians], vols. I-X, (Bucharest: 1936-1939).
Iorga, Nicolae: *Histoire des Roumains et de leur civilisation,* (Paris: 1920).
Jakó, Zsigmond: "Bihar megye a török pusztítás előtt" [Bihar County Before the Turkish Devastation], in: *Település-és népiségtörténeti Értekezések* 5, (Budapest 1940).
Jászi, Oszkár: *The Dissolution of the Habsburg Monarchy,* (Chicago: 1929).
Karp, Hans-Jürgen: *Grenzen in Ostmitteleuropa während des Mittelalters. Ein Beitrag zur Entstehungsgeschichte der Grenzlinie aus dem Grenzsaum,* XXIV, (Cologne-Vienna: 1972).
Kőváry, László: *Erdély története* [History of Transylvania], vols. I-VI, (Kolozsvár: 1859-1866).
László, Gyula: *Vértesszöllőstől Pusztaszerig. Élet a Kárpát-medencében a magyar államalapításig* [From Vértesszöllős to Pusztaszer. Life in the Carpathian Basin Until the Magyar State-Establishment], (Budapest: 1974).
László, Gyula: *A honfoglalókról* [On the Magyar Conquerors], (Budapest: 1973).
Lot, Ferdinand: *Les invasions barbares et le peuplement de l'Europe,* (Paris: 1937).
Lükő, Gábor: *A moldvai csángók* [The Moldavian Csángos], (Budapest: 1936).
Lupaş, Ion: *Zur Geschichte der Rumänen,* (Hermannstadt: 1943).
Macartney, C. A.: *Hungary: A Short History,* (Chicago, 1949).
Macartney, C. A.: *Hungary and Her Successors. The Treaty of Trianon and Its Consequences, 1919-1937,* (London, New York, Toronto: 1937).
Macartney, C. A.: *October Fifteenth: A History of Modern Hungary 1929-1945,* vols. I-II, (Edinburgh: 1956, 1961).
Macartney, C. A.: *The Magyars in the Ninth Century,* (Cambridge: 1930).
Macartney, C. A. and Palmer, A. W.: *Independent Eastern Europe. A History,* (London: 1962).

Makkai, László: *Magyar-román közös múlt* [Hungarian-Romanian Common Past], (Budapest: 1948).
Makkai, László: *Histoire de Transylvanie*, (Paris: 1946).
Makkai, László: *Szolnok-Doboka megye magyarságának pusztulása a XVII század elején* [The Extinction of the Magyars of Szolnok-Doboka County at the Beginning of the 17th Century], (Kolozsvár: 1942).
Marczali, Henrik: *Erdély története* [The History of Transylvania], (Budapest: 1935).
Melich, János: "A honfoglaláskori Magyarország" [Hungary at the Time of the Magyar Conquest], in: *A magyar nyelvtudomány kézikönyve* I, 6., (Budapest: 1925–1929).
Mikecs, László: *Csángók* [The Csángos], (Budapest: 1941).
Mittelstrass, Otto: *Beiträge zur Siedlungsgeschichte Siebenbürgens im Mittelalter*, (Munich: 1961).
Mittelstrass, Otto: "Die Besitzergreifung Siebenbürgens durch die Arpadenkönige", in: *Neue Beiträge zur siebenbürgischen Geschichte und Landeskunde*, [Siebenbürgisches Archiv. Archiv des Vereins für Siebenbürgische Landeskunde. Dritte Folge, edited by Arbeitskreis für Siebenbürgische Landeskunde, vol. I], (Cologne-Graz: 1962).
Moór, E.: "Studien zur Früh- und Urgeschichte des ungarischen Volkes", in: *Acta Ethnographica Academiae Scientiarum Hungaricae* II, 1951.
Müller, G. E.: "Die ursprüngliche Rechtslage der Rumänen im Siebenbürger Sachsenlande", in: *Archiv des Vereins für Siebenbürgische Landeskunde*, N.F. 38 (1912), 85–314.
Musset, Lucien: *Les invasions. Le second assaut contre l'Europe.* [VIIe-XIe siècles], (Paris: 1971).
Mutafčiev, P.: *Bulgares et Roumains dans l'histoire des pays Danubiens*, (Sofia: 1932).
Nägler, Thomas: *Die Ansiedlung der Siebenbürger Sachsen*, (Bukarest: 1979).
Niederhauser, Emil: *A nemzeti megújulási mozgalmak Kelet-Európában* [National Renewalmovements in East Europe], (Budapest: 1977).
Pascu, Ştefan: *Voievodatul Transilvaniei* [The Voivodship of Transylvania], vol. I (Cluj: 1971), vol. II (Cluj: 1979).
Pascu, Ştefan: "Die mittelalterlichen Dorfsiedlungen in Siebenbürgen" (bis 1400), in: *Nouvelles études d'Histoire*, Bucharest 1960, pp. 135–148.
Philippide, Alexandru: *Originea Românilor* [The Origin of the Romanians], vol. I (Iaşi: 1925), vol. II (Iaşi: 1928).
Pippidi, D. M.: *Contribuţii la istoria veche a României* [Contributions to the Old History of Romania], (Bucharest: 1967).
Prodan, David: *Supplex Libellus Valachorum*, or The Political Struggle of the Romanians in Transylvania During the 18th Century [Translated by Mary Lazarescu], (Bucharest: 1971).
Roesler, R.: *Romänische Studien*, (Leipzig: 1871).

Roller, Mihail: *Istoria Republicii Populară Române* [The History of the Romanian People's Republic], (Bucharest: 1952).
Rura, Michael J.: *Reinterpretation of History as a Method of Furthering Communism in Rumania. A Study in Comparative Historiography,* (Washington, D.C., Georgetown: 1961).
Schünemann, K.: "Zur Herkunft der Siebenbürger Székler", in: *Ungarische Jahrbücher* IV, 1924, VI, 1926.
Seton-Watson, Robert W.: *A History of the Roumanians from Roman Times to the Completion of Unity,* (Cambridge: 1934), new edit. (Connecticut: 1963).
Sinor, Dénes: *History of Hungary,* (London: 1959).
Stadtmüller, Georg: *Grundfragen der europäischen Geschichte,* (Munich-Vienna: 1965).
Stadtmüller, Georg: *Geschichte Südosteuropas,* (Munich: 1950).
Stadtmüller, Georg: *Forschungen zur albanischen Frühgeschichte,* 2nd edition, (Wiesbaden: 1966).
Szilágyi, Sándor: *Erdélyország története* [The History of Transylvania], vols. I-II, (Budapest: 1866).
Tamás, Lajos: *Romains, Romans et Roumains dans l'histoire de Dacie Trajane.* Études sur l'Europe Centre-Orientale 1, (Budapest: 1936).
Taylor, A.J.P.: *The Hapsburg Monarchy,* (London: 1957).
Teleki, Pál: *The Evolution of Hungary and Its Place in European History,* (New York: 1923).
Teutsch, Georg Daniel and Teutsch, Friedrich: *Geschichte der Siebenbürger Sachsen für das sächsische Volk,* vols. I-IV, (Hermannstadt: 1907-1926).
Teutsch, Friedrich: *Kleine Geschichte der Siebenbürger Sachsen.* Mit einem Nachwort von Andreas Möckel, (Darmstadt: 1965).
Tóth, Zoltán, I.: *Magyarok és románok. Történelmi tanulmányok.* [Hungarians and Romanians. Historical Studies], (Budapest: 1966).
Tóth, Zoltán I.: *Az erdélyi román nacionalizmus első százada 1697-1792* [The First Century of the Transylvanian Romanian Nationalism 1697-1792], (Budapest: 1946).
Wagner, Ernst: "Ungarn [Csangonen] in der Moldau und in der Bukowina im Spiegel neuerer rumänischer Quelleneditionen", in: *Zeitschrift für Siebenbürgische Landeskunde,* 3. (74) vol., no. 1/80, pp. 27-47.
Weczerka, Hugo: *Das mittelalterliche und frühneuzeitliche Deutschtum im Fürstentum Moldau,* (Munich: 1960).
Xenopol, Alexandru D.: *Une énigme historique: les roumains au moyen-âge,* (Paris: 1885).
Zillich, Heinrich: *Siebenbürgen. Ein abendländisches Schicksal,* (Königstein i. Ts.: 1976).

5. STATE AND POLITICS

Antonescu, Ion: *Către români. Chemări — Cuvîntări — Documente* [To the Romanians. Proclamations — Speeches — Documents], (Bucharest: 1941).

Aspects des relations sovieto-roumaines 1967–1971. Sécurité européenne, (Paris: 1971).
Bányai, László: *Hosszú mezsgye. Esszék, jegyzetek 1928–1968* [Long Border. Studies, Notes 1928–1968], (Bucharest: 1970).
Berindei, D.: *Din începuturile diplomației românești moderne* [From the Beginning of the Modern Romanian Diplomacy], (Bucharest: 1965).
Bobocea, G.: "Organizarea administrativ-teritorială a Republicii Socialiste România și sistematizarea localităților rurale" [Administrative-Territorial Organization of the Romanian Socialist Republic and the Systematization of the Rural Localities], in: *Stat, democrație, legalitate,* (Bucharest: 1968).
Braham, R. L.: "Romania: On the Separate Path", in: *Problems of Communism,* 13., 1964.
Brătianu, Gheorghe: *Acțiunea politică și militară a României în 1919* [The Military Action of Romania in 1919] 2nd ed., (Bucharest: 1940).
Ceaușescu, Nicolae: *Die führende Rolle der Partei in der Etappe der Vollendung des Aufbaues des Sozialismus,* (Bucharest: 1967).
Ceaușescu, Nicolae: *Rumänien auf dem Weg des Sozialismus.* Reden, Aufsätze, Interviews, (Freiburg/Br.: 1971). [Sozialwissenschaft in Theorie und Praxis, vol. 15th].
Ceaușescu, Nicolae: *La Roumanie sur la voie de l'édification de la société socialiste multilatéralement développée.* Rapports, discours, articles. Mars-novembre 1974, (Bucharest: 1976).
Ceaușescu, Nicolae: *Rumänien auf dem Weg der Vollendung des sozialistischen Aufbaues.* Berichte, Reden, Artikel, vols. I-II, (Bucharest: 1968–1976).
Ceterchi, I.: *Națiunea și contemporanitatea* [Nation and Contemporaneity], (Bucharest: 1971).
Cioranescu, C. et al.: *Aspects des relations russo-roumaines,* (Paris: 1967).
Ciurea, E. C.: *Le traité de paix avec la Roumanie du 10 février 1947,* (Paris: 1954).
Collection of Documents of the Paris Conference, vols. I-IV, 1957 et seq.
Congresul al III-lea al Partidului Muncitoresc Romîn 20–25 iunie 1960 [The Third Congress of the Romanian Workers' Party, June 20–25, 1960], (Bucharest: 1961).
Congresul al IX-lea al Partidului Comunist Român, 19–24 iulie 1965, (Bucharest: 1966).
Congresul al X-lea al Partidului Comunist Român 6–12 august 1969 [The Tenth Congress of the Romanian Communist Party], (Bucharest: 1969).
Congresul al XI-lea al Partidului Comunist Român [The Eleventh Congress of the Romanian Communist Party], (Bucharest: 1975).
Constitution of the Romanian People's Republic, (Bucharest: 1958).
Constitution of the Romanian Socialist Republic, (Bucharest: 1965).
Daicoviciu, C. et al.: *Republica Populară Romînă* [The Romanian People's Republic], (Bucharest: 1960).

Drost, P.: *Contracts and Peace Treaties,* (Leyden: 1948).
Duculescu, V.: *România la Organizaţia Naţiunilor Unite* [Romania in the United Nations Organization], (Bucharest: 1973).
Fischer-Galati, Stephen: "Rumänien", in: *Sowjetsystem und demokratische Gesellschaft.* Die kommunistischen Parteien der Welt, (Freiburg, Basel, Vienna: 1969).
Fischer-Galati, Stephen: *Man, State and Society in East Europe History,* (New York: 1970).
Foreign Relations. The Paris Peace Conference, vols. I-XIII, 1919; Documents ed. by US-State-Department.
Frenzke, D.: *Rumänien, der Sowjetblock und die europäische Sicherheit.* Die völkerrechtlichen Grundlagen der rumänischen Aussenpolitik, (Berlin: 1975).
Gafencu, G.: *Les préliminaires de la guerre a l'Est,* (Fribourg: 1946).
Gheorghe, Ion: *Rumäniens Weg zum Satellitenstaat,* (Heidelberg: 1952).
Gheorghiu-Dej, G. "A népi demokratikus rendszer további erősödése a RNK-ban" [The Further Strengthening of the People's Democratical System in the Romanian People's Republic], in: *Igazság* (Truth), Kolozsvár, 1953, I, p. 29.
Gheorghiu-Dej, G.: *Articole şi cuvântări* [Articles and Speeches], (Bucharest: 1956-1962).
Ghermani, Dionisie: "Rumäniens Nahostpolitik. Bestandsaufnahme einer diplomatischen Vermittlertätigkeit", in: *Südost-Europa,* no. 1, 1982, pp. 28-45.
Gilberg, Trond: "Ceauşescu's 'kleine Kulturrevolution' in Rumänien", in: *Osteuropa,* 22, 1972.
Great Britain, Foreign Office and U.S. Department of State: *Documents on German Foreign Policy 1918-1945, from the Archives of the German Foreign Ministry,* Series D, 1937-1945, London HMSO, 1949.
Gsovski, Vladimir ed.: *Church and State Behind the Iron Curtain,* (New York: 1955).
Hale, Julian: *Ceauşescu's Roumania. A Political Documentary,* (London, Toronto, Wellington: 1971).
Hartl, Hans: *Nationalismus in Rot.* Die patriotischen Wandlungen des Kommunismus in Südosteuropa, (Stuttgart-Degerloch: 1968).
Hungary and the Conference of Paris. Ministry of Foreign Affairs. (Budapest: 1947).
Ionescu, Ghiţa: *The Politics of the European Communist States, (New York: 1967).*
Juhász, Gyula: *Magyarország külpolitikája 1919-1945* [The Foreign Policy of Hungary 1919-1945], 2nd ed., (Budapest: 1975).
Kertesz, D. Stephen: *Diplomacy in a Whirlpool. Hungary Between Nazy Germany and Soviet Russia,* (Notre Dame, Indiana: 1953).
Legea şi statutele cultelor religioase din Republica Populară Română [Law and Statutes of the Religious Cults in the Romanian People's Republic], (Bucharest: 1949).

Leiss, Amelia C. and Dennet, Raymond eds.: *European Peace Treaties After World War II,* (Worcester, Mass.: 1954).
Making the Peace Treaties 1941-1947. Department of State, Publication 2774, European Series 24, US Department of State, (Washington, D.C.: 1947).
Meier, Viktor E.: *Neuer Nationalismus in Südosteuropa,* (Opladen: 1968).
Meissner, Boris ed.: *Oststaaten und europäische Sicherheit 1972-1975.* Analysen und Dokumente, (Cologne: 1975/76).
Menzel, E.: Die *Friedensverträge nach 1947 mit Italien, Ungarn, Bulgarien, Rumänien und Finnland,* (Oberursel: 1948).
Miller, D. H.: *My Diary at the Peace Conference of Paris,* (New York: 1924-1926).
Muşat, Mircea and Ardeleanu, Ion: *Viaţa politică în România 1918-1921* [Political Life in Romania 1918-1921], (Bucharest: 1976).
Nagy, Ferenc: *The Struggle Behind the Iron Curtain,* (New York: 1948).
Naţiunea socialistă [The Socialist Nation], (Bucharest: 1972).
Paris Peace Conference 1946: Selected Documents. Department of State, (Washington, D.C.: 1947).
Partidul Muncitoresc Român [The Romanian Workers' Party], Comitetul Central. Institutul de Istorie al Partidului, (Bucharest: 1957).
Peaslee, A. J. ed.: *Constitutions of Nations,* (Concord: 1950).
Pop, Nicolae: *Kirche unter Hammer und Sichel. Die Kirchenverfolgung in Rumänien 1945-1951,* (Berlin: 1953).
Prost, H.: *Destin de la Roumanie* [1918-1945], (Paris: 1945).
Pundeff, Marin: *Recent Publications on Communism,* (Los Angeles: 1962).
Remington, Alison R.: *The Warsaw Pact.* Case Studies in Communist Resolution, (Cambridge: 1971).
Report From a Meeting of the Councils of Working People of Hungarian and German Nationality in the Socialist Republic of Romania, March 13-14, 1978, (Bucharest: 1978).
Romanian People's Republic: Ministry of Public Education. Îndrumătorul Învăţătorului, (Bucharest: 1948).
Romanian Workers' Party, Central Committee, Historical Institute of the Party. *Documente din Istoria Partidului Comunist din România 1917-1922,* (Bucharest: 1953).
Rotschild, Joseph: *East Central Europe Between Two World Wars,* (Seattle: 1974).
Schroeder, F. C. and Meissner, B.: *Verfassungs- und Verwaltungsreformen in den sozialistischen Staaten,* (Berlin: 1978).
Schultz, L.: "Die verfassungsrechtliche Entwicklung der Sozialistischen Republik Rumänien seit dem Zweiten Weltkrieg", in: *Jahrbuch des öffentlichen Rechts der Gegenwart,* N. F. 15., 1966.
Seton-Watson, Hugh: *Nations and States: An Inquiry Into the Origins of Nations and the Politics of Nationalism,* (London: 1977).

Socor, V.: "The Limits of National Independence in the Soviet Bloc: Rumania's Foreign Policy Reconsidered", in: *Orbis* (Philadelphia periodical of the Foreign Policy Research Institute), vol. 20., no. 3., pp. 701–723.

Spector, Sherman D.: *Rumania at the Paris Peace Conference: A Study of the Diplomacy of Ion C. Brătianu,* (New York: 1962).

Sporea, C.: "Entstalinisierung in Rumänien", in: *Osteuropa,* December 1962.

Stadtmüller, Georg: *Kommunismus und Nationalismus im Donauraum.* Tschechoslowakei, Ungarn, Jugoslawien, Rumänien, Bulgarien 1956–1962. In: *Moderne Welt,* 4., 1963.

Sugar, Peter F.: *Native Fascism in the Successor States, 1918–1945,* (Santa Barbara: 1971).

Tanase, V. ed.: *Dossier Paul Goma. L'écrivain face au socialisme du silence,* (Paris: 1977).

Temperley, Harold W. H.: *A History of the Peace Conference at Paris,* (London, New York, Toronto: 1969).

The RCP Program for the Creation of a Multilaterally Developed Socialist Society and Romania's Advance Toward Communism, (Bucharest: 1974).

Tilea, Viorel: *Acţiunea diplomatică a României 1919–1920* [Diplomatic Action of Romania 1919–1920], (Sibiu: 1925).

Titulescu, Nicolae: *Documente diplomatice,* ed. by George Macovescu et al., (Bucharest: 1967).

Traian, I.: *Die neue Verfassung der Sozialistischen Republik Rumänien vom 21. August 1965,* in: *Der Staat,* vol. 5th., (Bucharest: 1966).

Triska, Jan F., ed.: *Constitutions of the Communist Party-States,* (Stanford, Hoover Institution: 1968).

Ulam, Adam B.: *Expansion and Co-existence: A History of the Soviet Foreign Policy 1917–1967,* (New York: 1968).

United States: *Treaties of Peace with Italy, Bulgaria, Hungary, Roumania, and Finland,* (Washington, D.C.: 1947). Publ. 2743.

Yearbook on International Communist Affairs 1968–1973, (Stanford: 1968–1973).

6. CULTURE AND SCIENCE

Albu, Nicolae: *Istoria învăţământului românesc din Transilvania pînă la 1800* [The History of the Romanian Education in Transylvania until 1800], (Blaj: 1944).

Asztalos, Miklós ed.: *Jancsó Benedek Emlékkönyv* [Benedek Jancsó Memorial Album], (Budapest: 1931).

Balan, Ştefan: *Desvoltarea învăţămîntului în Republica Socialistă Romînă* [The Development of Education in the Romanian Socialist Republic], (Bucharest: 1968).

Barabás, Endre: *A romániai magyar nyelvű oktatás első tíz éve* [The First Ten Years of Hungarian-Language Education in Romania], (Lugos: 1929).
Barabás, Endre: "A magyar iskolaügy helyzete Romániában 1918-1941" [The Situation of Hungarian Education in Romania 1918-1941], in: *Kisebbségi Körlevél,* nos. 5-6, 1943, p. 2733 *et seq.*
Barberini, Giovanni; Stöhr, Martin; Weingartner, Erich eds: *Kirchen im Sozialismus.* Kirche und Staat in den osteuropäischen sozialistischen Republiken. Eine Dokumentation zum Verhältnis von Kirche und Staat in den osteuropäischen Staaten, (Frankfurt a.M.: 1977).
Barcan, Monica and Millitz, Adalbert: "Verlagstätigkeit." In: *Die deutsche Nationalität in Rumänien,* (Bukarest: 1977).
Beiträge zur siebenbürgischen Kulturgeschichte. Compiled by Gebhard Blücher et. al., edited by Paul Philippi, (Cologne-Vienna: 1974), VIII.
Benkő, Samu: *Sorsformáló értelem.* Művelődéstörténeti dolgozatok [Fate Formed by Intellect. Studies on Cultural History], (Bucharest: 1971).
Binder, Paul: "Interferenzen auf dem Gebiet des Buchdrucks in Siebenbürgen im 16. Jahrhundert", in: *Studien zur Geschichte der deutschen Nationalität und ihrer Verbrüderung mit der rumänischen Nation,* (Bukarest: 1976), vol. I, pp. 274-297.
Binder, Ludwig: *Grundlagen und Formen der Toleranz in Siebenbürgen bis zur Mitte des 17. Jahrhunderts.* Siebenbürgisches Archiv, vol. II, (Cologne-Vienna: 1976).
Biserica Română Unită. Două sute cincizeci de ani de istorie [The Romanian Uniate Church. Two Hundred and Fifty Years of History], (Madrid: 1952).
Bisztray, Gyula; Szabó, T. Attila; Tamás, Lajos eds.: *Erdély magyar egyeteme.* Az erdélyi egyetemi gondolat és a M.Kir. Ferenc József Tudományegyetem története [Transylvania's Hungarian University. The History of the Idea of a Transylvanian University and of the Hung. Roy. Francis Joseph University], (Kolozsvár: 1941).
Braham, L. Randolph: *Education in the Rumanian People's Republic.* Office of Education. U.S. Department of Health, Education and Welfare. OE-14087, Bulletin 1964, 1, (Washington, D.C.: 1963).
Braham, L. Randolph: *Education in Romania. A Decade of Change,* (Washington, D.C.: 1972).
Braham, L. Randolph: "The Rumanian Schools of General Education", in: *Journal of Central European Affairs,* XXI, no. 3, October 1961, pp. 319-349.
Ceauşescu, Nicolae: Rede auf dem Plenum des ZK der RKP vom 18. bis. 19. Juni 1973 über die Entwicklung und Vervollkommnung des Unterrichts, (Bukarest: 1973).
Crisian, J.: *Beitrag zur Geschichte der kirchlichen Union der Rumänen in Siebenbürgen unter Leopold I,* (Hermannstadt: 1882).
"*Cultele în România*" [Cult-Communities in Romania], in: *Enciclopedia României,* vol. I, (Bucharest: 1976), pp. 417-422.

Cultele religioase în Republica Populară Română [Religious Communities in the Romanian People's Republic], (Bucharest: 1949).

Curticăpeanu, Vasile: *Die rumänische Kulturbewegung in der Österreichisch-Ungarischen Monarchie,* (Bukarest: 1966).

Dávid, N. Ildikó: "A kolozsvári egyetem építészeti oktatása" [Education for Architecture on the University of Kolozsvár], in Zádor-Szabolcsi, *Művészet és felvilágosodás,* [Kunsthistorische Studien], (Budapest: 1978), pp. 301–351.

Der Unterricht in der Sozialistischen Republik Rumänien, edited by the Institut für Pädagogische Wissenschaften, (Bukarest: 1973).

Die Evangelische Landeskirche A.B. in Siebenbürgen mit den angeschlossenen evang. Kirchenverbänden Altrumänien, Banat, Bessarabien, Bukowina, Ungarisches Dekanat. Festschrift, (Jena: 1923).

Directivele CC al PCR privind dezvoltarea învăţămîntului în RSR aprobate de Plenara al PCR din 22-25 aprilie 1968 [Directions of the CC of the RCP Concerning the Development of the Education in the RSR, approved by the Plenary Session on April 22–25, 1968, (Bucharest: 1968).

Dragomir, Silviu: *Romînii din Transilvania şi unirea cu biserica Romei. Documente apocrife privitoare la începuturile unirii cu catolicismul roman (1607–1701)* [The Transylvanian Romanians and the Union with the Roman Church. Apocryphal Documents About the Beginnings of the Union with Roman Catholicism], (Bucharest: 1963).

Duţu, Alexandru: *Romanian Humanists and European Culture.* A Contribution to Comparative Cultural History, (Bucharest: 1977).

Fischer-Galati, Stephen: *L'église unie de Roumanie. Dix ans de persécution 1948–1958,* (Paris: 1959).

Gabanyi, Anneli Ute: *Partei und Literatur in Rumänien seit 1945.* Untersuchungen zur Gegenwartskunde Südosteuropas 9., (Munich: 1975).

Gabanyi, Anneli, Ute: "Die rumänische Literaturpolitik seit 1972", in: *Wissenschaftlicher Dienst Südosteuropa,* Munich 1975, no. 9, pp. 180–184.

Gáldi, László: "Az erdélyi magyar tudományosság és a kolozsvári egyetem hatása a román tudományra" [Transylvanian Hungarian Scholarship and the Influence of the University of Kolozsvár Upon Romanian Scholarship], in: *Erdély magyar egyeteme,* pp. 285–304.

"Grundfragen der rumänischen Kulturpolitik", in: *Wissenschaftlicher Dienst Südosteuropa,* Munich 1974, no. 4, p. 74.

Gündisch, Gustav; Klein, Albert; Krasser, Harald eds.: *Studien zur siebenbürgischen Kunstgeschichte,* (Bukarest: 1976).

Hitchins, Keith: *Cultură şi naţionalitate în Transilvania* [Culture and Nationality in Transylvania], (Cluj: 1972).

Hitchins, Keith: "Samuel Clain and the Rumanian Enlightenment in Transylvania", in: *Slavic Review,* XXIII, no. 4, December 1964, pp. 660–675.

Iorga, Nicolae: *Études roumaines,* I. Influences étrangères sur la nation roumaine, (Paris: 1923).

Istoria învăţămîntului din România [The History of the Romanian Education], edited by The Ministry of Education, (Bucharest: 1971).

Jakó, Zsigmond: *Írás, könyv, értelmiség. Tanulmányok Erdély történelméhez* [Script, Book, and Intelligentsia. Studies on the History of Transylvania], (Bucharest: 1977).

Jakó, Zsigmond: "Die Hermannstädter Druckerei im 16. Jahrhundert und ihre Bedeutung für die rumänische Kulturgeschichte," in: *Forschungen zur Volks- und Landeskunde,* 9, 1966, 1, pp. 31–58.

Jakó, Zsigmond: "Újabb adatok a kolozsvári Heltai-nyomda kezdeteihez" [New Data to the Beginning of the Heltai-Press in Kolozsvár], in: *Magyar Könyvszemle,* Budapest 1961, vol. 77, pp. 60–65.

Jancsó, Elemér: *Az erdélyi magyarság életsorsa nevelésügyének tükrében 1914--1934* [The Fate of the Hungarians in Transylvania as Reflected in its Educational Situation 1914–1934], (Cluj: 1935).

Kántor, Lajos and Láng, Gusztáv: *A romániai magyar irodalom 1944–1970* [Hungarian Literature in Romania 1944–1970], (Bucharest: 1971, 2nd edition 1973).

Kelemen, Lajos: *Művészettörténeti tanulmányok* [Cultural Historical Studies], (Bucharest: 1977).

König, Walter: *Die gegenwärtigen Schulverhältnisse der Deutschen in Rumänien.* Sonderdruck aus Korrespondenzblatt des Arbeitskreises für Siebenbürgische Landeskunde, III. Folge, 7, vol., no. 3–4, (Cologne-Vienna: 1977).

König, Walter: "Die Geschichte der Siebenbürger Sachsen in den rumänischen Schulbüchern", in: *Zeitschrift für Siebenbürgische Landeskunde,* 3. (74), vol., no. 2/80.

Kroner, Michael ed.: *Interferenzen.* Rumänisch-ungarisch-deutsche Kulturbeziehungen in Siebenbürgen, (Cluj: 1973).

Legea privind învăţămîntul in R.S.R. [Educational Law of the Romanian Socialist Republic], in: *Buletinul Oficial,* no. 28, March 8, 1972.

Lendl, Egon: *Die mitteleuropäische Kulturlandschaft im Umbruch der Gegenwart,* (Marburg: 1951).

Leonhardt, P.: "Das rumänische Presserecht nach dem Gesetz vom 28.3.1974", in: *Jahrbuch für Ostrecht,* 15., 1974.

Ligeti, Ernő: *Súly alatt a pálma.* Egy nemzedék szellemi élete. 22 esztendő kisebbségi sorsban [Palm under Pressure. The Intellectual Life of a Generation. Twenty-Two-Years in Minority Destiny], (Kolozsvár: 1942).

Mályusz, Elemér: "A magyarság és a nemzetiségek Mohács előtt" [The Hungarians and the Nationalities Before Mohács], in: *Magyar Művelődéstörténet,* vols. I-V, (Budapest: 1939–1942).

Meschendörfer, Hans: *Das Verlagswesen der Siebenbürger Sachsen. Ein Überblick,* (Munich: 1979).

Miclescu, Maria: *Sekundarabschlüsse mit Hochschulreife im rumänischen Bildungswesen* [Secondary School Leaving with Qualifications for Entering

Higher Education in the Romanian Educational System], (Frankfurt am Main: 1976).

Mitter, W.: "Pädagogische Studienreise nach Rumänien", in: *Die Deutsche Schule,* no. 68., 1976.

Mitter, W.: "Strukturfragen der osteuropäischen Bildungssysteme", in: *Osteuropa,* no. 26., 1976.

Molnár, József: "A Mester és a Tanítvány. Tótfalusi Dirk Voskens betűmetsző—és betűöntő műhelyében" [The Master and the Pupil. Miklós Tótfalusi Kis in the Stamp-Engraving and Type Foundry of Dirk Voskens], in: *Új Látóhatár,* Munich, April 30, 1975. Further Studies in *Új Látóhatár,* November 30, 1971, December 15, 1976.

Niedermaier, Paul: *Siebenbürgische Städte.* Forschungen zur städtebaulichen und architektonischen Entwicklung von Handwerksorten zwischen dem 12. und 16. Jahrhundert, (Cologne-Vienna: 1979).

Oschliess, W.: *Gegenwartsprobleme der Jugend und Bildungspolitik Rumäniens,* in: Berichte des Bundesinstituts für ostwissenschaftliche und internationale Studien, no. 3, 1973.

Oschliess, W.: "Schulfunk und Schulfernsehen in Rumänien", in: *Südosteuropa Mitteilungen,* no. 3, 1975.

Pascu, Ştefan: *Die "Babeş-Bolyai" Universität aus Klausenburg,* (Cluj-Kolozsvár: 1972).

Radu, I.: *Sisteme de învăţămînt general-obligatoriu* [Compulsory General Educational Systems], (Bucharest: 1974).

Reformed Church in the Socialist Republic of Romania, (Bucharest: 1976).

Schunemann, K.: *Die Entstehung des Stadtwesens in Südosteuropa,* (Berlin: 1929).

Shuster, N. G.: *Religion hinter dem Eisernen Vorhang,* (Würzburg: 1954).

Sporea, Constantin: "Probleme des Hochschulwesens in Rumänien", in: *Wissenschaftlicher Dienst Südosteuropa,* no. 3, 1959.

Sporea, Constantin: "Kommunistische Erziehung in Rumänien", in: *Der Europäische Osten,* no. 83, September 1961, pp. 517–523.

Studien zur siebenbürgischen Kunstgeschichte. Von Gustav Gündisch, Albert Klein, Harald Krasser, Theobald Streitfeld, (Bucharest: 1976).

Suttner, E. Ch.: "50 Jahre rumänisches Patriarchat. Seine Geschichte und die Entwicklung seines Kirchenrechts", in: *Ostkirchliche Studien,* no. 24, 1975, no. 25, 1976.

Suttner, E. Ch.: "Kirchen und Staat", in: *Rumänien.* Südosteuropa-Handbuch, vol. II, ed. K. D. Grothusen, (Göttingen: 1977), pp. 458–483.

Szalay, Jeromos: *Márton Áron erdélyi püspök* [Áron Márton Transylvanian Bishop], (Paris: 1953).

Teutsch, Friedrich: *Geschichte der evangelischen Kirche in Siebenbürgen,* vol. I, (Hermannstadt: 1921), vol. II, (Hermannstadt: 1922).

"Zur Situation der christlichen Kirchen in Rumänien." Länderbericht. In: *Herder Korrespondenz,* no. 25, 1971.

7. ECONOMICS

Beck, Sam: *Transylvania: The Political Economy of a Frontier,* (Ph.D. dissertation, University of Mass., Amherst: 1979).
Berend, T. Iván and Ránki, György: *Kelet-Közép-Európa gazdasági fejlődése a 19.-20. században* [Economic Development in East-Central Europe in the 19-20th Centuries], (Budapest: 1969; an English ed. New York: 1974).
Bogdan, T. et al.: *Procesul de urbanizare în România. Zona Braşov,* [The Process of Urbanization in Romania. The Area of Braşov], (Bucharest: 1970).
Dezvoltarea economiei R.P.R. pe drumul socialismului 1948-1957, [The Development of Economics of the Romanian People's Republic on the Path of Socialism 1948-1957], (Bucharest: 1964).
Faber, B. ed.: *The Social Structure of Eastern Europe.* Transition and Process in Czechoslovakia, Hungary, Poland, Romania, and Yugoslavia, (New York: 1967).
Ghermani, Dionisie: "Rumäniens Wirtschaftskrise", in: *Südost-Europa,* no. 3/4, 1982, pp. 207-219.
Ionescu, Constantin ed.: *Omogenizarea socială în Republica Socialistă România. Proces şi Factori,* (Bucharest: 1977).
Jordáky, Lajos: *Az erdélyi társadalom szerkezete* [The Structure of the Transylvanian Society], (Cluj: 1946).
Leonties, Demetrius: *Die Industrialisierung Rumäniens bis zum Zweiten Weltkrieg,* (Munich: 1971).
Mitrany, David: *The Land and the Peasant in Rumania: The War and Agrarian Reform 1917-1921,* (New Haven: 1930).
Montias, John Michael: *Background and Origins of the Rumanian Dispute with Comecon,* in: Soviet Studies, 16, 1964.
Moore, W. E.: *Economic Demography of Eastern and Southeastern Europe.* League of Nations, (Geneva: 1945).
Oschliess, W.: *Soziale Mobilisierung in Rumänien.* Berichte des Bundesinstituts für ostwissenschaftliche und internationale Studien, (Cologne: 1973/74).
Pascu, Ştefan: *Meşteşugurile din Transilvania pînă în secolul al XVI-lea* [Handicrafts in Transylvania up to the XVIth Century], (Bucharest: 1954).
Rafael, R. Edgar: *"Entwicklungsland" Rumänien—Zur Geschichte der "Umdefinierung" eines sozialistischen Staates.* (Munich: 1977).
Sampson, Steven: *National Integration Through Socialist Planing: An Anthropological Study of a Romanian New Town,* (Ph.D. dissertation, Univ. of Mass., Amherst: 1980).
Schacher, G.: *Die Nachfolgestaaten—Österreich, Ungarn, Tschechoslowakei—und ihre wirtschaftlichen Kräfte,* (Stuttgart: 1932).
Spulber, Nicholas: *The Economics of Communist Eastern Europe,* (New York-London: 1958).

Spulber, Nicholas: *The State and Economic Development in Eastern Europe,* (New York: 1966).
United Nations. Economic Commission for Europe. Economic Development in Rumania. Bulletin for Europe. Geneva, vol. 13, no. 2, January 1961, pp. 55-107.

8. LAND AND POPULATION

Acsády, Ignác: *Magyarország népessége a Pragmatica Sanctio korában 1720-1721* [The Population of Hungary in the Time of the Pragmatic Sanction 1720-1721], (Budapest: 1896).
Anuarul demografic al R.S. România 1974 [The Demographic Yearbook of the Romanian Socialist Republic 1974], Direcţia Centrală de Statistică, (Bucharest: 1975).
Anuarul statistic al R.P.R. 1961-1965 [Statistical Yearbook of the Romanian People's Republic, vols. I-V., (Bucharest: 1961-1965).
Anuarul statistic al Republicii Socialiste România 1965 [Statistical Yearbook of the R.S.R. from 1965], Direcţia Centrală de Statistică, Bucharest.
Breviarul statistic al R.P.R. [Pocket Book of the R.P.R.], Republica Populară Română, 1-1960, Bucharest.
Breviarul statistic al R.P.R. 1961-1965, Republica Populară Română, vols. I-V, (Bucharest: 1961-1965).
Breviarul statistic al Republicii Socialiste România 1970-1974, Direcţia Centrală de Statistică, Bucharest.
Buletinul demografic al României [The Demographic Bulletin of Romania], Institutul Central de Statistică, Bucharest 1932-
Buletin statistic trimestrial, Republica Populară Română, Bucharest 1959-
Ciobanu, V.: *Statistica Românilor din Ardeal făcută de administraţia austriacă la anul 1760-1762* [The Statistics of the Romanians of Transylvania compiled by the Austrian Administration 1760-1762], in: Anuarul Institutului de Istorie Naţională, Cluj 3, 1924/25, pp. 616-700.
Colescu, Leonida: *Analiza rezultatelor recensământului general al populaţiei României 1899* [An Analysis of the Results of the General Census of the Population of Romania in 1899], Institutul Central de Statistică, (Bucharest: 1944).
Cucu, Vasile: *Oraşele României* [Towns and Cities of Romania], (Bucharest: 1970).
Dávid, Zoltán: *Az 1715-20 évi összeírás. A történelmi statisztika forrásai,* [The Conscription of 1715-20. The Sources of the Historical Statistics], (Budapest: 1957).
Die deutschen Vertreibungsverluste. A Contribution of Wilfried Krallert, (Wiesbaden-Stuttgart: 1958).

Fényes, Elek: *Magyarország statisztikája* [The Statistics of Hungary], (Budapest: 1842, 1843).
Frumkin, G.: *Population Changes in Europe Since 1939,* (London: 1952).
Golopenţia, Anton—Georgescu, D.C.: "Populaţia Republicii Populare România la 25 ianuarie 1948" [The Population of the Romanian People's Republic on January 25, 1948], (Bucharest: 1948), in: *Probleme Economice,* pp. 28–45.
Györffy, György: *Einwohnerzahl und Bevölkerungsdichte in Ungarn bis zum Anfang des XIV. Jahrhunderts.* Studia Historica Academiae Hungaricae 42, (Budapest: 1960).
Györffy, György: *Magyarország népessége a honfoglalástól a XIV. század közepéig* [The Population of Hungary from the Magyar Conquest to the Middle of the 14th Century], in: Magyarország történeti demográfiája, (Budapest: 1963).
Hartl, H. — Kiefer, D. — Gassner, J: *Bevölkerungsentwicklungen in Südosteuropa. Jugoslawien, Ungarn, Rumänien.* Südost-Institut, (Munich: 1964).
Heller, W.: *Bevölkerungsgeographische Betrachtung Rumäniens* [*seit dem 2. Weltkrieg*], in: Hans-Grant-Festschrift, ed. by Eichler, H. and Musall, H., (Heidelberg: 1974).
Jakabffy, Elemér: *Erdély statisztikája* [The Statistics of Transylvania], (Lugos, 1923).
Jinga, Victor: "Migraţiunile demografice şi problema colonizărilor în România" [Demographic Migration and the Problem of Settlements in Romania], in: *Extras din Analele Academiei de Inalte Studii Comerciale şi Industriale din Cluj* [Excerpts from the Yearbooks of the Cluj Academy of Industry and Commerce], vol. I, 1939–1940. (Braşov, 1941).
Judeţele României Socialiste [The Counties of the Socialist Romania], (Bucharest: 1967, 2nd edition 1972).
Kniezsa, István: *Magyarország népei a XI. században* [The Peoples of Hungary in the 11th Century], (Budapest: 1938).
Kovacsics, József ed.: *Magyarország történeti demográfiája. Magyarország népessége a honfoglalástól 1949-ig* [Historical Demography of Hungary. The Population of Hungary from the Conquest of the Homeland till 1949], (Budapest: 1963).
Länderbericht Rumänien 1974. Allgemeine Statistik des Auslandes. Statistisches Bundesamt, (Wiesbaden, Stuttgart, Mainz: 1975).
Magyar Statisztikai Hivatal: 1949-es népszámlálás [Hungarian Statistical Board: The 1949 Census], (Budapest: 1949).
Magyar Statisztikai Közlemények. Uj sorozat [Hungarian Statistical Communications. New Serie], (Budapest: 1910).
Magyar Statisztikai Zsebkönyv [Hungarian Statistical Pocket Book], (Budapest: 1948).
Mályusz, Elemér ed.: *Erdély és népei* [Transylvania and its Peoples], (Budapest: 1941).

Manuila, Sabin: *Studiu etnografic asupra populației României* [Ethnographical Study on the Population of Romania], (Bucharest: 1940).
Manuila, Sabin and Georgescu, D. C.: *Populația României* [The Population of Romania], (Bucharest: 1938).
Manuila, Sabin: *Aspects démographiques de la Transylvanie*, (Bucharest: 1938).
Mesaroș, E.: "Începuturile statisticii migrației externe a populației în România" [The Statistical Beginnings of the External Migrations of the Population of Romania], in: *Revista de Statistică*, Bucharest, no. 6, 1969.
Ortvay, Tivadar: *Magyarország egyházi földleírása a XIV század elején a pápai tizedjegyzékek alapján feltüntetve* [The Survey of Church-Owned Land in Hungary at the Beginning of the 14th Century Based on the Papal "Zehntliste"], (Budapest: 1891–1892).
Pascu, Ștefan: *Populație și societate*. Studii de demografie istorică [Population and Society. Studies on Historical Demography], vol. I, (Cluj: 1972).
Recensământul general al populației României din 29 decemvrie 1930 [The General Census of the Population of Romania of December 29, 1930], edited by Sabin Manuila, vols. I-II: *neam, limba maternă, religie* [Nationality, Vernacular, Religion], (Bucharest: 1938–1941).
Recensământul populației al României dela 6 aprilie 1941 [The Census of April 6, 1941], vol. XXIV, (Bucharest: 1944).
Recensământul populației și locuințelor din 21 februarie 1956 [The Census of the Population and Dwellings of February 21, 1956], vol. I, (Bucharest: 1959–1961).
Recensământul populației și locuințelor din 15 martie 1966 [The Census of the Population and Dwellings of March 15, 1966], vol. I, (Bucharest: 1969).
Retegan, G.: "Evoluția populației urbane a României" [The Development of the Urban Population of Romania], in: *Revista de Statistică*, Bucharest, 7, 1965.
Satmarescu, G.: "The Changing Demographic Structure of the Population of Transylvania", in: *East European Quarterly* [Boulder, Colorado University], 8., 1975.
Schlechtmann, Joseph B.: *Postwar Population Transfers in Europe 1945–1955*, (Philadelphia: 1962).
Semlyén, István: "Országos és nemzetiségi népességgyarapodás" [Population Growth in Romania Generally and According to National Origin], in: *Korunk Évkönyv* [Korunk-Yearbook], 1980, pp. 41–55.
Șerbu, G. R.: "Căile de creștere numerică a populației orașelor mari ale R.P.R." [The Paths of the Numerical Growth of the Population in the Larger Cities of the R.P.R.], in: *Revista de Statistică*, Bucharest, no. 5, 1961, pp. 26–34.
Stănescu, Maria and Stoichița, I. V.: "Evoluția natalității în România în anii 1958–1964" [The Development of the Natality in Romania Between 1958–1964], in: *Revista de Statistică*, 1966/8., p. 56.

Statistical Yearbook. Statistical Office of the United Nations, New York.
Statistical Yearbook. United Nations Educational, Social, and Cultural Organization [UNESCO], Paris.
Statistisches Taschenbuch der Sozialistischen Republik Rumänien [Statistical Pocket-Book of the R.S.R.], (Bucharest: 1969).
Thirring, Gusztáv: *A magyar városok statisztikai évkönyve* [The Statistical Yearbook of the Hungarian Cities], (Budapest: 1912).
A történeti statisztika forrásai [The Sources of the Historical Statistics], ed. by József Kovacsics, (Budapest: 1957).
Wagner, Ernst: "Die päpstlichen Steuerlisten 1332–1337", in: *Forschungen zur Volks- und Landeskunde,* 11/1968, 1., pp. 37–52.

9. NATIONAL MINORITY QUESTIONS

Ammende, Ewald ed.: *Die Nationalitäten in den Staaten Europas,* (Vienna: 1931, supplement 1932).
Amnesty International. Romania. USA Publication, 1978.
Arató, Endre: "A nemzetfogalom vitája a Szovjetunióban" [Discussion of the Conception of the Nation in the Soviet Union], in: *Párttörténeti Közlemények* [Publications of Party History], (Budapest: 1969/1).
Ardeleanu, Josif: *A nemzetiségi kérdés alapelvei Romániában* [The Principles of the Nationality Question in Romania], (Bucharest: 1957).
Azcarate y Florez, Pablo de: *League of Nations and National Minorities; An Experiment,* (Washington D.C.: 1945).
Balogh, Artur: *A kisebbségek nemzetközi védelme* [The International Protection of the Minorities], (Berlin: 1928).
Bányai, László: *Harminc év. Jegyzetek a romániai magyarság útjáról* [Thirty Years. Notes on the History of the Hungarians in Romania], (Bucharest: 1949).
Barcan, Monica and Adalbert Millitz: *Die deutsche Nationalität in Rumänien,* (Bucharest: 1977).
Bergel, Hans: "Die Entwicklung der Siebenbürger Sachsen seit 1945 als Problem der Volksgruppen im Donauraum", in: *Der Donauraum,* vol. 1976, pp. 151–160.
Bergel, Hans: *Die Sachsen in Siebenbürgen nach dreissig Jahren Kommunismus,* (Innsbruck: 1976).
Bogdan, Henry: *Le problème des minorités nationales dans les "États-Successeurs" de l'Autriche-Hongrie,* (Louvain: 1976).
Bulletin de la Commission Internationale des Juristes, (Geneva, December: 1963).
Buza, László: *A kisebbségek jogi helyzete* [The Legal Position of the Minorities], (Budapest: 1930).
Cabot, J. M.: *The Racial Conflict in Transylvania,* (Boston: 1926).

Ceauşescu, Nicolae: "Beszéd a Magyar Nemzetiségű Dolgozók Országos Tanácsának plenáris ülésén 1971. március 12" [Speech on the Plenary Session of the Council of Working People of Hungarian Nationality March 12, 1971], in: *Előre* [Forward], Bucharest, March 13, 1971.
Dami, Aldo: *Destin des minorités*, (Paris: 1936).
Demeter, János, Eisenburger, Eduard, Lipatti, Valentin: *Sur la question nationale en Roumanie. Faits et chiffres*, (Bucharest: 1972).
Dragomir, Silviu: *The Ethnical Minorities in Transylvania*, (Geneva: 1927).
Enloe, Cynthia: *Ethnic Conflict and Political Development*, (Boston, Mass.: 1972).
Ermacora, Felix: *Innerstaatliche, regionale und universelle Struktur eines Volksgruppenrechtes*, in: Theodor Veiter ed.: System eines internationalen Volksgruppenrechts, II. part, (Vienna-Stuttgart: 1972).
Ermacora, Felix: *Menschenrechte in der sich wandelnden Welt*, vol. I: Historische Entwicklung der Menschenrechte und Grundfreiheiten, (Vienna: 1974).
Ermacora, Felix: *Über den Minderheitenschutz im europäischen Südosten*. Sonderdruck aus dem Jahrbuch für Internationales Recht, (Göttingen: 1967).
Ermacora, Felix: "Über den Minderheitenschutz in den Friedensverträgen der Donaustaaten nach dem Zweiten Weltkrieg," in: *Der Donauraum*, vol. 11, no. 1-2, 1966, pp. 64–74.
Ethnicity and Nationalism in Southeastern Europe, Sam Beck and John W. Cole eds., (Amsterdam, University of Amsterdam, forthcoming).
Gáll, Ernő: *Nemzetiség, erkölcs, értelmiség* [Nationality, Morals, Intelligentsia], (Budapest: 1978).
Ghibu, Onisifor: *Politica religioasă şi minoritară a României. Fapte şi documente carii impun o nouă orientare.* [The Religious and the Minority Policy of Romania. Facts and Documents for a new Orientation], (Cluj: 1940).
Gilberg, Trond: "Ethnic Minorities in Romania under Socialism," in *East European Quarterly*, vol. VII, no. 4, January 1974, pp. 435–458.
Gower, Sir Robert: *The Hungarian Minorities in the Succession States*, (London: 1936).
Gütermann, Christoph: *Das Minderheitenschutzverfahren des Völkerbundes*, (Berlin: 1979).
Hartl, Hans: *Die Nationalitätenfrage im heutigen Südosteuropa*, Südost-Institut, (Munich: 1973).
The Hungarian Nationality in Romania. Institute of Political Science and for the Study of the Nationality Question, (Bucharest: 1976).
Illyés, Elemér: *Nationale Minderheiten in Rumänien. Siebenbürgen im Wandel*. Ethnos, (Vienna: 1981).
Jászi, Oszkár: *A nemzeti államok kialakulása és a nemzetiségi kérdés* [The Development of the National States and the Nationality Problem], (Budapest: 1912).

Kann, Robert: *Das Nationalitätenproblem der Habsburgermonarchie,* vols. I-II, (Graz-Cologne: 1964).
Kelemen, Sándor: *Az erdélyi helyzet* [The Transylvanian Situation], (Budapest: 1946).
Kemény, G. Gábor: *A magyar nemzetiségi kérdés története* [The History of the Hungarian Nationality Question], Compendium, (Budapest: 1946).
Kemény, G. Gábor: *Iratok a nemzetiségi kérdés történetéhez Magyarországon a dualizmus korában 1867–1918* [Documents Concerning the History of the Nationality Question in Hungary in the Dualist Period 1867–1918], vols. I-V, (Budapest: 1952–1971).
King, Robert R.: *Minorities under Communism, Nationalities as a Source of Tension among Balkan Communist States,* (Cambridge: 1973).
Kolarz, Walter: *Die Nationalitätenpolitik der Sowjetunion,* (Frankfurt a.M.: 1956).
Kővágó, László: *Kisebbség, nemzetiség* [Minority, Nationality], (Budapest: 1977).
Lahav, Yehuda: *Soviet Policy and the Transylvanian Question 1940–1946,* Research paper no. 27, (Jerusalem: 1977).
Ludányi, Andrew: *Hungarians in Rumania and Yugoslavia.* A Comparative Study of Communist Nationality Policies. A dissertation, published by University Microfilms, (Michigan: 1971).
Macartney, C. A.: *National States and National Minorities,* (London: 1934).
Magyar Külügyminisztérium. A magyar kérdés Románia viszonylatában [Hungarian Foreign Office. The Hungarian Question in Relation to Romania], (Budapest: 1946).
Mandelstam, A.: *La protection internationale des minorités,* (Paris: 1931).
Meissner, Boris: *Das Selbstbestimmungsrecht der Völker in Osteuropa und China,* (Cologne: 1968).
Mester, Miklós: *Az autonóm Erdély és a román nemzetiségi követelések az 1863-64. évi nagyszebeni országgyűlésen* [Autonomous Transylvania and the Romanian Demands at the 1863–64 Diet of Nagyszeben], (Budapest: 1936).
Mikó, Imre: *Huszonkét év. Az erdélyi magyarság politikai története 1918 december 1-től 1940 augusztus 30-ig* [Twenty-Two Years. The Political History of the Transylvanian Hungarians from December 1, 1918 until August 30, 1940], (Budapest: 1941).
Mikó, Imre: *Nemzetiségi jog és nemzetiségi politika* [Nationality Law and Nationality Policy], (Kolozsvár: 1944).
Mikó, Imre: *Változatok egy témára.* Tanulmányok. [Variances on a Theme. Studies], (Bucharest: 1981).
Les minorités ethniques en Europe Centrale et Balkanique. Études et Documents, Série B-2, (Paris: 1946).
Nagy, Lajos: *A kisebbségek alkotmányjogi helyzete Nagyromániában* [The Constitutional Position of the Minorities in Greater Romania], (Kolozsvár: 1944).

A nemzetiségi politika három éve a demokratikus Romániában [Three Years Nationality Policy in the Democratical Romania], (Bucharest: 1948).
Pernthaler, Peter: *Der Schutz ethnischer Gemeinschaften durch individuelle Rechte,* (Vienna: 1964).
Pircher, Erich, H.: *Der vertragliche Schutz ethnischer, sprachlicher und religiöser Minderheiten im Völkerrecht,* (Bern: 1979).
Protection of Minorities. Special Protective Measures of an International Character for Ethnic, Religious or Linguistic Groups. United Nations, Sales no.: 67, XIV, 3, (New York: 1967).
Reiter, Wilhelm: "Die Nationalitätenpolitik der Rumänischen Volksrepublik im Spiegel ihrer Statistik", in: *Osteuropa,* vol. 11, no. 3, 1961.
A romániai magyar nemzetiség [The Hungarian Nationality in Romania], ed. Sándor Koppándi, (Bucharest: 1981).
Roumania Ten Years After. The American Committee on the Rights of Religious Minorities, ed. by Louis Cornish, (Boston: 1928).
Scheiner, H. "Zur Lage des Deutschtums in Rumänien", in: *Der Europäische Osten,* Munich, no. 2, 1954.
Schultz, Robert: *Die Lösung der nationalen Frage in Rumänien.* Untersuchungen über Probleme und Erfolge marxistischer Nationalitätenpolitik, (Leipzig: 1953).
Schultz, Robert: *Deutsche in Rumänien.* Das Nationalitätenproblem in der Rumänischen Volksrepublik, (Leipzig-Jena: 1955).
Séqueil, Pierre: *Le dossier de la Transylvanie,* (Paris: 1967).
Simonds, George W. ed.: *Nationalism in the USSR and Eastern Europe in the Era of Brezhnev and Kosygin,* (Detroit: 1977).
Straka, Manfred [compiled],: *Handbuch der europäischen Volksgruppen,* (Vienna-Stuttgart: 1970).
Straka, Manfred: *Karte der europäischen Volksgruppen,* (Graz: 1979).
Studien zur Geschichte der mitwohnenden Nationalitäten in Rumänien und ihrer Verbrüderung mit der rumänischen Nation. *Die deutsche Nationalität.* Vol. I, compiled by Carl Göllner, (Bucharest: 1976).
Szász, Zsombor: *The Minorities in Roumanian Transylvania,* (London: 1927).
Szekfű, Gyula: *Állam és nemzet.* Tanulmányok a nemzetiségi kérdésről [State and Nation. Studies on the Nationality Question], (Budapest: 1942).
Szenczei, László: *Az erdélyi magyarság harca 1940–1941* [The Struggle of the Hungarians in Transylvania 1940-1941], (Budapest: 1946).
Szenczei, László: *Magyar-román kérdés* [Hungarian-Romanian Problem], (Budapest: 1946).
Tanulmányok a romániai együttlakó nemzetiségek történetéből és testvéri együttműködéséről a román nemzettel. *A magyar nemzetiség története* és testvéri együttműködése a román nemzettel [Studies on the History and Fraternal Cooperation of the Coexisting Nationalities in Romania with the Romanian Nation. The History of the Hungarian Nationality and its Fra-

ternal Cooperation with the Romanian Nation], vol. I, edited by László Bányai, (Bucharest: 1976).
La Transylvanie demande a être écoutée. Aide-Mémoire presenté à la Conférence de la Paix par le Comité Hongrois de Transylvanie, (Paris: 1946).
United Nation Working Paper: Rehák, László: The Right of National and Ethnic Minorities to Protect and Develop their Culture and Ethnic Tradition. United Nation SO 216/3 (26), WP 18.
United States, Dept. of State: Evidence of Violations of Human Rights Provisions of the Treaties of Peace by Romania, Bulgaria and Hungary, submitted. . . to the Secretary General of the United Nations pursuant to the Resolutions of the General Assembly of November 3, 1950, (Washington D.C.: 1951), Publ. 4736.
Veiter, Theodor: *Nationalitätenkonflikt und Volksgruppenrecht im 20. Jahrhundert,* Teil 1: Entwicklungen, Rechtsprobleme, Schlussfolgerungen, (Vienna: 1977).
Veiter, Theodor ed.: *System eines internationalen Volksgruppenrechts.* Völkerrechtliche Abhandlungen, vol. 3, part I and II, (Vienna-Stuttgart: 1970, resp. 1972).
Viefhaus, Erwin: "Die Nationalitätenfrage in den ostmitteleuropäischen Nationalstaaten nach 1919". Eine Übersicht, in: *Archiv des Vereins für Siebenbürgische Landeskunde,* 6, 1967, pp. 116–144.
Viefhaus, Erwin: *Die Minderheitenfrage und die Entstehung der Minderheitenschutzverträge auf der Pariser Friedenskonferenz 1919.* Eine Studie zur Geschichte des Nationalitätenproblems im 19. und 20. Jahrhundert, (Marburg: 1960), Marburger Ostforschungen 11.
Wintgens, Hugo: *Der völkerrechtliche Schutz der nationalen, sprachlichen und religiösen Minderheiten,* (Stuttgart: 1930).

10. PERIODICALS

Acta Musei Napocensis, Muzeul de istorie, Cluj-Napoca.
American Slavic and East European Review, (New York: 1961–).
Anale de Istorie. The theoretical journal of the Historical and Sociopolitical Institute, (Bucharest).
Analele Institutului de Istorie a Partidului de pe lângă CC al RCP.A Periodical of the Institute for Party-History, (Bucharest).
A.W.R.-Bulletin. Quarterly for Refugees, edited by the Research-Society on the Problem of World-Refugees, (Vienna).
Berlin. Freie Universität, Osteuropa-Institut. Bibliographische Mitteilungen, (Berlin: 1952–).
B.I.R.E. Bulletin d'information pour les Roumaines en Exil, (Paris).
Buletinul Oficial al Republicii Socialiste România, Part I, II, III, (Bucharest: 1965–).

Cahiers de l'est, literary and cultural three monthly review, (Paris).
Canadian-American Slavic Studies, (Pittsburgh).
Canadian Review of Studies in Nationalism—Revue Canadienne des Études sur le Nationalisme. [University of Prince Edward Island], (Charlottetown: 1972–).
Canadian Slavic Studies, quarterly, (Montreal: 1967–).
Colecţie de legi, decrete, hotăririi şi decizii [Collection of Laws, Decrees, Resolutions, Decisions], (Bucharest: 1949–).
Comunicări Statistice [Statistical Communications], (Bucharest: 1945–).
Contemporanul [The Contemporary], weekly cultural-political journal, (Bucharest).
Deutsche politische Hefte aus Grossrumänien, monthly journal, (Sibiu/Hermannstadt: 1921–1927).
Documentation sur l'Europe Centrale, scientific quarterly, (Leuven/Louvain: 1962–).
Der Donauraum, monthly journal of the Research Institute for Questions of the Danube Region, (Vienna: 1956–).
East European Quarterly, Boulder, Colorado, (University of Colorado: 1967–).
Eastern European Studies in History, (New York: 1967–).
The Economist, (London).
Élet és Irodalom [Life and Literature], literary weekly, (Budapest: 1957–).
Era Socialistă [Socialist Era], theoretical and political journal of the CC of the RCP [former "Lupta de Clasă", (Bucharest: 1965–).]
Erdélyi Helikon [Transylvanian Helicon], literary and critical monthly, (Cluj/-Kolozsvár: 1928–1944).
Erdélyi Múzeum [Transylvanian Museum], scientific journal of the Association of the Transylvanian Museum, (Pest: 1814–1818, Kolozsvár: 1874–1917, 1930–1947).
Erdélyi Tudományos Füzetek [Transylvanian Scientific Papers], (Cluj/Kolozsvár: 1932–1944).
Études balkaniques. (Sofia: 1965–).
Forschungen zur Volks- und Landeskunde, scientific German-language semiannual journal, (Hermannstadt: 1949–).
A Hét [The Week], Hungarian-language social, political, cultural weekly, (Bucharest: 1970–).
Hitel [Credit], political and scientific monthly journal, (Cluj/Kolozsvár: 1936–1944).
Igaz Szó [True Word], literary monthly review, (Tîrgu Mureş/Marosvásárhely: 1953–).
Irodalmi Szemle [Literary Review], monthly journal, (Bratislava-Slovakia: 1958–).
Irodalmi Újság [Literary Gazette], literary and critical monthly, (Budapest: 1950–1956, London: 1957– , later Paris).

Jahrbücher für Geschichte Osteuropas, quarterly, Osteuropa-Institut, neue Folge, (Munich: 1-1953-).
Journal of Central European Affairs, (Boulder, Colorado: 1941-1964).
Justiția Nouă [New Justice], bimonthly publication of the Society of Juridical Science, (Bucharest).
Karpatenrundschau, social, political and cultural weekly in German-language, (Brașov/Kronstadt: 1949-).
Katolikus Szemle, [Catholic Review], a quarterly for catholic theology and Hungarian culture, (Budapest: 1887-1944, Rome: 1947-).
Klingsor, German-language literary monthly journal, (Brașov/Kronstadt: 1924-1939).
Korrespondenzblatt des Arbeitskreises für Siebenbürgische Landeskunde, series III, Cologne-Vienna: 1971-1977). [See also "Zeitschrift für Siebenbürgische Landeskunde].
Kortárs [The Contemporary], monthly literary journal, (Budapest: 1957-).
Korunk [Our Age], monthly social and cultural journal, (Cluj/Kolozsvár: 1926-1940 and 1957-).
Kritika [Critique], monthly literary, critical and scientific review, (Budapest: 1963-).
Licht der Heimat, published as supplement to the "Siebenbürgische Zeitung", (Munich 1951-), monthly publication, Munich: 1956-).
Luceafărul [Hesperus], weekly literary review, (Bucharest: 1958-).
Lumea [The World], weekly publication, (Bucharest: 1964-).
Lupta de Clasă [Class Struggle], political and theoretical publication of the CC of RCP, (Bucharest: 1921-1965, see also "Era Socialistă").
Magazin Istoric [Historical Review], (Bucharest).
Magyar Kisebbség [Hungarian Minority], monthly political and cultural review, (Lugos/Banat: 1922-1942).
Magyar Statisztikai Közlemények [Hungarian Statistical Communications], (Budapest).
Magyar Statisztikai Szemle [Hungarian Statistical Review], monthly publication for statistics, (Budapest: 1923-).
Magyar Tudomány [Hungarian Scholarship], (Budapest: 1956-).
Mitteilungen des österreichischen Staatsarchivs, (Vienna: 1948-).
Mitteilungen der Südosteuropa-Gesellschaft, [only as headline: "Südosteuropa-Mitteilungen], quarterly, (Munich: 1961-).
Monitorul Oficial [Official Monitor]. (The name was changed in March 1949 to "Buletinul Oficial"). Part I.: laws and decrees; part II.: communications about laws; part III.: parliamentary debates, (Bucharest).
Nation und Staat, political monthly, (Vienna-Leipzig: 1927-1928, -1944).
Neue Literatur, German-language literary monthly, (Bucharest: 1949-).
Österreichische Ost-Hefte, bimonthly publication, (Vienna: 1959-).
Osteuropa, monthly periodical for East-European contemporary topics, (Stuttgart: 1951-).

Ostkirchliche Studien, quarterly on ecclesiastical topics, (Würzburg: 1952–).
Ost-Probleme, (Bonn: 1949–), weekly until 1956.
Pandectele Române, jurisprudential, scientific periodical and a monthly repertory for laws, vols. I-XVIII, (Bucharest: 1922–1939).
Probleme Economice [Economic Problems], (Bucharest: 1949–).
Radio Free Europe. Situation Report: Romania.
Revista Economică [Economic Review], monthly, (Bucharest).
Revista de Istoire, [Historical Review], (Bucharest: 1947–).
Revista de Statistică [Statistical Review], monthly, (Bucharest: 1956–).
Revue des études roumaines, (Paris: 1953–).
Revue des études slaves, annual publication, (Paris: 1921–).
Revue des études sud-est européennes, quarterly, (Bucharest: 1963–).
Revue Roumaine d'Histoire, (Bucharest).
România Literară, weekly, (Bucharest).
Slavic Review, quarterly, (Seattle, Washington: 1940–).
Slavonic and East European Review, h.-yearly, (London: 1922–).
Studies for a New Central Europe, quarterly, (New York: 1963–).
Südostdeutsche Vierteljahresblätter, [vols. 1-6 under the title: "Südostdeutsche Heimatblätter"], quarterly, (Munich: 1952–).
Südosteuropa-Jahrbuch, annual publication, (Munich: 1957–).
Südosteuropa Mitteilungen, quarterly, (Munich: 1961–).
Südost-Forschungen, annual publication, (Munich: 1936–).
Survey, a journal of Soviet and East European studies, quarterly, (London: 1956–).
Századok [Centuries], journal of the Hungarian Historical Association, (Pest-Budapest: 1867–).
Társadalmi Szemle [Social Review], the ideological and scientific monthly of the Hungarian Communist Party, (Budapest: 1946–).
Tiszatáj [Tisza Region], literary and cultural monthly, (Szeged-Hungary: 1947–).
Történelmi Szemle [Historical Review], (Budapest: 1958–).
Történeti Szemle [Historical Review], (Budapest: 1912–1930).
Új Látóhatár [New Horizon], literary and political bi-monthly journal, (Munich: 1958–; from 1949 until 1958 under the name "Látóhatár").
Utunk [Our Path], literary weekly, (Cluj-Napoca: 1945–).
Valóság [Reality], public scientific monthly journal, (Budapest: 1945–1948, 1958–).
Viața Economică [Economic Life], weekly, (Bucharest: 1963–).
Viața Românească [Romanian Life], monthly review of the Writers' Association, (Bucharest: 1906–1916, 1920–1940, 1944–).
Volk und Kultur, German-language popular scientific journal, (Bucharest: 1949–).
Wissenschaftlicher Dienst Südosteuropa. Sources and Reports on State, Administration, Law, Population, Economics, Science and Publications in South-East Europe. (Munich: 1952–).

Die Woche, German-language social, cultural, political weekly, (Sibiu/Hermannstadt: 1949–). [Until 1971 appeared under the title "Hermannstädter Zeitung"].
Zeitschrift für Ostforschung, quarterly, (Marburg/Lahn: 1952–).
Zeitschrift für Siebenbürgische Landeskunde, series I.: 1878–1930 under: "Korrespondenzblatt des Vereins für siebenbürgische Landeskunde"; series II.: 1931–1941 under: "Siebenbürgische Vierteljahresschrift"; series III.: 1971–1977 under: "Korrespondenzblatt des Arbeitskreises für Siebenbürgische Landeskunde"; from 1978 Cologne-Vienna.

11. NEWSPAPERS

The Christian Science Monitor, (London).
Előre [Forward], Hungarian-language daily newspaper, (Bucharest: 1953–).
The Financial Times, (London).
Frankfurter Allgemeine Zeitung, daily newspaper.
The Guardian, (London).
Magyar Nemzet [Hungarian Nation], daily newspaper, (Budapest: 1899–1913; re-edited 1938–).
Le Monde, daily newspaper, (Paris).
Népszabadság [Freedom of People], daily newspaper of the Hungarian Socialist Workers' Party, (Budapest: 1956–).
Neuer Weg, German-language political daily newspaper, (Bucharest: 1948–).
Neue Zürcher Zeitung, daily newspaper.
The New York Herald Tribune.
The New York Times.
Die Presse, daily paper, (Vienna).
România Liberă [Free Romania], daily newspaper of the People's Councils in the Romanian Socialist Republic, (Bucharest: 1943–).
Scînteia [The Spark], daily paper of the Central Committee of the RCP, (Bucharest: 1932; legal from 1944–).
Tribuna României, political daily newspaper, (Bucharest).
Vörös Zászló [Red Banner], Hungarian-language daily newspaper, (Tîrgu Mureş/Marosvásárhely: 1952–).
Die Welt, daily newspaper, (Hamburg).
Die Weltwoche, (Zürich).

NAME INDEX

Acsády, Ignác, 325
Ágotha, András, 226
Albu, Nicolae, 319
Almaş, Dumitru, 292
Ammende, Ewald, 276, 292, 297, 328
Angelescu, Constantin, 74, 162, 291
Anna, the author's wife, 7
Antonescu, Ion, 27, 78, 79, 81, 82, 83, 109, 272, 288, 315
Arató, Endre, 311, 328
Ardeleanu, Josif, 328
Árpád Dynasty, 11
Asztalos, Miklós, 311, 319
Azcarate y Florez de, Pablo, 271, 275, 328

Bakács, István, 262
Bakó, Elemér, 305
Balan, Ştefan, 319
Bălcescu, Nicolae, 5
Bálint, Tibor, 301
Balogh, Arthur, 271, 328
Bánffy, Dániel, 85
Bányai, László, 274, 311, 316, 328, 332
Barabás, Endre, 291, 292, 320
Barberini, Giovanni, 298, 320
Barcan, Monica, 266, 295, 320, 328
Bartha, Antal, 153
Basta, George, Habsburg General, 17
Báthori (Báthory), István (Stephen), 158
Beck, Sam, 324, 329

Beke, György, 296
Beneš, Eduard, 83
Benkő, Samu, 320
Berciu, Dumitru, 153, 290
Berend, T. Iván, 311, 324
Bergel, Hans, 280, 287, 290, 293, 307, 328
Berindei, Dan, 316
Berindei, Mihnea, 268, 288, 295
Bernath, Mathias, 311
Bethlen, Gábor (Gabriel), Prince of Transylvania, 3
Binder, Ludwig, 320
Binder, Pál, 299, 320
Bisztray, Gyula, 320
Bitay, Árpád, 77
Bobocea, G., 316
Bodnăraş, Emil, 102, 282
Bodnarenko, Pintilie, 282
Bodor, Pál, 286, 289
Bogdan, Henry, 264, 271, 274, 275, 311, 328
Bogdan, Tiberiu, 324
Bohmann, Alfred, 278, 283, 292, 293, 294, 298, 299, 300, 307
Boila, Romul, 274
Bondor-Deliman, Ecaterina, 287
Braham, L. Randolph, 293, 305, 316, 320
Brandsch, Rudolf, 73, 77
Brătianu, Gheorghe, 311, 316
Brătianu, Ion, 87, 89

NAME INDEX

Brătianu, Vintilă, 89
Bratoloveanu, Liviu, 147
Brezhnev, Leonid, 128
Brook-Shepherd, Gordon, 288
Brown, F. James, 307
Brown, W. Malcolm, 302
Brunello, Don, 227
Brzezinski, Z. K., 307
Budișteanu, Radu, 274
Bunea, Augustin, 262
Burks, Richard, 282, 307
Buza, László, 328
Byrnes, F. Robert, 98, 305, 307

Cabot, J. M., 328
Campbell, C. John, 284, 307
Capotorti, Francesco, 108, 289
Carlton, G. Robert, 306
Carol II de Hohenzollern-Sigmaringen, King of Romania, 30, 77, 78, 79, 93
Carp, Matatias, 265
Ceaușescu, Elena, 142
Ceaușescu, Nicolae, 127–130, 132, 141, 142, 146, 149, 152, 154, 177, 187, 210, 224, 228, 246, 250, 254, 285, 286, 288, 294, 295, 301–303, 316, 320, 329
Ceterchi, I., 316
Charlemagne, 10
Cherestești, Victor, 312
Chișinevski, Josif, 114
Churchill, Sir Winston, 307
Ciobanu, V., 325
Cioranescu, C., 316
Cioranescu, George, 268
Cissek, Oskar Walter, 301
Ciurea, E. C., 277, 278, 316
Clerc, Sir George, 275
Clopotel, Ioan, 273
Codreanu, Corneliu Zelea, 272
Cole, W. John, 329
Colescu, Leonida, 325
Conover, Helen, 306
Constantinescu, Miron, 114, 274, 311
Cornish, Louis, 331
Crankshaw, E., 284
Cretzianu, Alexandre, 273, 277, 282, 297, 300, 307
Crisian, J., 296, 320

Csatári, Dániel, 279, 307
Cucu, Vasile, 325
Curticăpeanu, Vasile, 274, 321
Cuza, C. Alexandru, 77, 78

Daicoviciu, Constantin, 311, 312, 316
Dálnoki Veress, Lajos, 311
Dami, Aldo, 329
Darkó, J., 259, 311
Dávid, N. Ildikó, 321
Dávid, Zoltán, 262, 325
Deáky, L., 303
Debreczi, Árpád, 295
Deér, József, 260, 311
Deica, Petru, 270
Demeter, János, 294, 295, 329
Demetrius, Lucia, 301
Dennet, Raymond, 272, 273, 280, 318
Densușianu, Nicolae, 306
Deutsch, W. Karl, 284, 301, 303
Deutsch, Robert, 305
Dima, G. A., 291
Dinić, M., 311
Djilas, Milovan, 307
Dobbs, Michael, 289
Döbrentei, Gábor, 240
Doder, Dusko, 289
Dolmányos, István, 291
Domokos, Pál Péter, 260
Dragne, Florea, 296
Dragomir, Silviu, 274, 296, 321, 329
Drost, P., 317
Droz, J., 312
Duculescu, V., 280, 317
Dulea, Mihai, 270
Du Nay, André, 261
Durcovici, Anton, 225
Duțu, Alexandru, 321

Eden, Anthony, 278
Eisenburger, Eduard, 262, 289, 292, 295, 303, 308, 329
Endes, Miklós, 275
Endre II, Hungarian King, 13
Enloe, Cynthia, 329
Ermacora, Felix, 271, 273, 280, 329
Evans, I. L., 275

NAME INDEX

Faber, B., 324
Fabritius, Fritz, 76
Farkas, Árpád, 301
Fătu, M., 272
Fazekas, János, 148
Fekete-Nagy, Antal, 306
Fényes, Elek, 326
Ferdinand I de Hohenzollern-Sigmaringen, King of Romania, 87
Filderman, W., 265
Filep, Antal, 309
Finkelstein, A. D., 272
Firnhaber, Fr., 307
Fischer-Galati, Stephen, 7, 265, 266, 268, 272, 277, 278, 281, 282, 284, 285, 286, 293, 296, 297, 300, 303, 305, 308, 317, 321
Floyd, David, 308
Folbert, Otto, 75, 271, 290
Forster, Kent, 308
Fotescu, Eleonora, 292
Frenzke, D., 317
Fritz, László, 263, 270, 277, 291, 297, 310
Frumkin, G., 326

Gabanyi, Anneli Ute, 300, 302, 321
Gafencu, Grigore, 317
Gáldi, László, 260, 261, 306, 311, 312, 321
Gáll, Ernő, 329
Gamillscheg, E., 312
Gassner, J., 326
Gâștescu, P., 309
Gemmarius, Thomas, 239
George, Pierre, 312
Georgescu, D. C., 267
Georgescu, Teohari, 97, 114, 282
Géza II, King of Hungary, 12, 13
Gheorghe, Ion, 317
Gheorghiu-Dej, Gheorghe, 96, 97, 102, 111, 113, 114, 119, 124, 128, 129, 151, 283, 317
Gheorghiu, Mihnea, 153
Gherman, P., 227
Ghermani, Dionisie, 285, 288, 294, 312, 317, 324
Ghibu, Onisifor, 329
Gibson, Hugh, 308
Gigurtu, Ion, 78, 80

Gilberg, Trond, 268, 279, 280, 283, 286, 288, 291, 292, 294, 302, 303, 308, 317, 329
Giurescu, C. Constantin, 153, 261, 290, 312
Giurescu, C. Dinu, 261, 312
Göckenjan, Hansgerd, 312
Goga, Octavian, 77, 78
Göllner, Carl, 274, 331
Golopenția, Anton, 267, 326
Goma, Paul, 148, 149, 286, 301
Gower, Sir Robert, 329
Grentrup, Theodor, 273, 274, 291, 308
Griffith, E. William, 308
Grothusen, Klaus-Detlev, 269, 286, 291, 300, 308
Groza, Petru, 96, 97, 99, 104, 105, 108, 110, 114, 116, 166, 220, 242, 272
Gsovski, Vladimir, 317
Gündisch, Gustav, 312, 321, 323
Gütermann, Christoph, 329
Györffy, György, 259, 312, 326
György, Lajos, 299
Györi Illés, István, 268

Habsburg Dynasty, 3, 4, 5, 15, 18, 19
Hajek, Egon, 271
Hale, Julian, 317
Halecki, Oscar, 312
Hartl, Hans, 264, 276, 279, 290, 308, 317, 326, 329
Hauser, Arnold, 301
Hegedüs, László, 302, 303
Heller, W., 326
Heltai (Helth), Gáspár, 240
Hillgruber, Andreas, 272, 312
Hitchins, Keith, 297, 312, 321
Hitler, Adolf, 79, 80, 81, 83, 101, 109
Hnik, Thomas, 305
Hoffgreff, Georg, 240
Hoffmann, W. George, 308
Hóman, Bálint, 17, 259, 262, 313
Honterus, Johannes, 158, 240
Horecky, L. Paul, 305, 306, 308
Horedt, Kurt, 313
Horthy, Miklós (Nicholas), 81, 84, 85, 147, 288
Horváth, Imre, 301

Hunter-Miller, David, 273
Hurdubeţiu, Ion, 313
Hurmuzaki, Eudoxiu de, 306, 313

Iancu, Avram, 5
Illyés, Elemér, 308, 310, 329
Illyés, Gyula, 153
Imreh, István, 312
Ioanid, Virgil, 270
Ionescu, Constantin, 324
Ionescu, Ghiţa, 277, 278, 279, 282, 309, 317
Iordan, I., 309, 313
Iorga, Nicolae, 76, 261, 313, 321
Iovănaş, I., 286
Istrate, N., 269
Istrati, N., 267, 307

Jakabffy, Elemér, 326
Jakó, Zsigmond, 262, 299, 313, 322
Jancsó, Elemér, 291, 322
Janin, R., 298
Janowsky, I. Oscar, 265
Jászi, Oszkár, 309, 313, 329
Jinga, Victor, 326
Jordáky, Lajos, 275, 324
Joseph II, Habsburg Emperor, 4, 13
Jowitt, Kenneth, 309
Juhász, Gyula, 278, 317

Kádár, János, 151, 152
Kállai, Gyula, 152
Kallós, Zoltán, 260
Kane, S. Robert, 309
Kann, A. Robert, 309, 330
Kántor, Lajos, 301, 322
Kányádi, Sándor, 301
Karp, Hans-Jürgen, 313
Kelemen, Lajos, 322
Kelemen, Sándor, 279, 280, 293, 330
Kemény, G. Gábor, 330
Kernweiss, Konrad, 229
Kertesz, D. Stephen, 277, 309, 317
Kiefer, D., 326
King, R. Robert, 286, 330
Király, Károly, 148, 149
Kiss, Jenő, 301
Klein, Albert, 232, 323

Klein, Karl Kurt, 260, 309
Kniezsa, István, 326
Kolarz, Walter, 330
Komócsin, Zoltán, 152
König, Walter, 273, 274, 292, 295, 296, 322
Koppándi, Sándor, 331
Kormos, C., 309
Kós, Károly, 72
Kósa, László, 309
Kossuth, Lajos, 5
Kovács, György, 295, 301
Kovács, Lajos, 233
Kovacsics, József, 262, 263, 326, 328
Kővágó, László, 330
Kőváry, László, 313
Krallert-Sattler, Gertrud, 306
Krallert, Wilfried, 264, 278, 325
Krämer-Badoni, Rudolf, 289
Krasser, Harald, 323
Kraus, H. David, 308
Krenner, Miklós, 75, 77
Kroner, Michael, 262, 292, 295, 303, 322

Lahav, Yehuda, 330
Lakatos, Géza, 84, 85
Láng, Gusztáv, 301
László, Gyula, 259, 313
Lázár, György (George), 296
Lederer, J. Ivo, 284, 310
Leisen van, Herbert, 274
Leiss, C. Amelia, 272, 273, 280, 318
Lendl, Egon, 322
Lendvai, Paul, 289
Lenin, Vladimir Ilyich Ulyanov, 277
Lenk Treuenfeld von, Ignaz, 309
Leonhardt, P., 322
Leonties, Demetrius, 324
Leopold I, Habsburg Emperor, 296
Leopold II, Habsburg Emperor, 13
Ligeti, Ernő, 322
Lipatti, Valentin, 329
London, Kurt, 309
Lot, Ferdinand, 313
Lucbert, Manuel, 288
Ludanyi, Andrew, 330
Luka (Luca), László, 102, 114, 282
Lukinich, Imre, 306
Lükő, Gábor, 313

NAME INDEX

Lupaș, Ion, 313
Luther, Martin, 239

Macartney, Carlile Aymler, 262, 265, 270, 271, 272, 274, 275, 276, 277, 309, 313, 330
Macdonald, A. M., 307
Mădgearu, N. Virgil, 268
Makkai, László, 153, 261, 262, 290, 306, 312, 314
Mályusz, Elemér, 259, 261, 262, 322, 326
Mandelstam, A., 330
Manescu, R., 267
Maniu, Iuliu, 82, 83, 97, 99, 101, 279
Manuilă, Sabin, 265, 267, 327
Marczali, Henrik, 314
Martinovici, G., 267, 307
Márton, Áron, 225, 228, 229
Mately, I. M., 309
Mathil, Pol, 289
Matthias (Mátyás) Corvinus, Hungarian King, 13
Maurer, Ion Gheorghe, 148
Mayer, F., 286
Mazilu, Dumitru, 286
Meașnicov, I., 268
Meier, Viktor, 318
Meissner, Boris, 318, 330
Melich, János, 314
Mellor, R.E.H., 310
Menzel, E., 278, 318
Mesaroș, E., 264, 327
Meschendörfer, Hans, 299, 322
Mester, Miklós, 330
Meyer, Peter, 280
Michael I, King of Romania, 79, 84, 95, 96, 99
Michael the Brave, Prince of Wallachia, 17
Miclescu, Maria, 322
Mihalache, Ion, 99
Mikecs, László, 260, 314
Miklós László, 289
Mikó, Ervin, 288
Mikó, Imre, 271, 273, 275, 330
Miller, David Hunter, 318
Millitz, Adalbert, 266, 295, 320, 328
Mitrany, David, 275, 324

Mittelstrass, Otto, 314
Mitter, W., 323
Möckel, Andreas, 260, 315
Moisescu, Justin, 224
Mogyorós (Moghioroș), Sándor, 282
Moldovan, V., 267
Molnár, József, 323
Molotov, Vyacheslav Mikhailovich, 98
Montias, John Michael, 324
Moór, Elemér, 259, 314
Moore, W. E., 324
Morariu, Tiberiu, 312
Müller, G. E., 262, 314
Murgescu, Costin, 280
Mușat, Mircea, 318
Musset, Lucien, 314
Mutafčiev, P., 314
Muth, Kaspar, 73

Nägler, Thomas, 314
Nagybaczoni Nagy, Vilmos, 310
Nagy, Ferenc, 97, 277, 318
Nagy, Gyula, 231
Nagy, Lajos, 291, 330
Neagu, Fănuș, 301
Neamțu, Alexandru, 312
Neigebauer, J. F., 268
Nelson, N. Daniel, 310
Niculescu-Mizil, Paul, 152
Niederhauser, Emil, 314
Niedermaier, Paul, 323
Nini, V., 268
Niset, Josef, 280

Oancea, D. I., 309
O'Hara, Gerard Patrick, 298
Orbán, Balázs, 310
Ortvay, Tivadar, 327
Osborne, R. H., 310
Oschliess, W., 323, 324

Pach, Zsigmond Pál, 153
Păcurariu, Francisc, 147
Palmer, A. W., 265, 270, 274
Papp, László, 231
Pârvulescu, Constantin, 102
Pascu, Ștefan, 293, 306, 311, 312, 314, 323, 324, 327

Pătrășcanu, Lucrețiu, 95, 96, 97, 102, 104, 113
Pauker, Ana, 102, 114, 282
Peaslee, A. J., 281, 318
Pernthaler, Peter, 280, 331
Péterfi, István, 294
Petőfi, Sándor (Alexander), 5
Pezderka, Sándor, 303
Philippide, Alexandru, 261, 314
Pippidi, D. M., 314
Pircher, H. Erich, 331
Pop, Nicolae, 318
Pop, Traian, 294
Popa-Lisseanu, G., 306
Popovici, Titus, 279
Pounds, J. G. Norman, 310
Preda, Constantin, 153, 290
Preda, Marin, 288, 301
Prodan, David, 314
Prost, H., 318
Pundeff, Marin, 318

Rădeceanu, Lotar, 104
Rădescu, Nicolae, 96
Radu, I., 323
Rădulescu, N., 303
Rafael, R. Edgar, 284, 324
Rajk, László, 106, 113, 116, 119, 279
Rákóczi, Ferenc II, 4
Ranghet, Josif, 102
Ránki, György, 311, 324
Rehák, László, 332
Reiter, Wilhelm, 292, 331
Remington, R. Alison, 284, 318
Retegan, G., 269, 327
Rhode, Gotthold, 296
Ribbentrop von, Joachim, 80
Riedl, H. Franz, 261, 292, 310
Roberts, Henry, 306, 310
Roesler, Robert, 314
Roller, Mihail, 112, 281, 294, 315
Ronneberger, Franz, 269
Roth, Hans Otto, 73, 74, 100, 276
Roth, Stephan Ludwig, 5
Rotschild, Joseph, 318
Rouček, S. Joseph, 301, 310
Rubinyi, Mózes, 260

Rura, J. Michael, 281, 315
Ruyssen, T., 275

Sampson, Steven, 324
Sănătescu, Constantin, 84, 95, 96, 108
Satmarescu, G. D., 267, 268, 269, 327
Savadjian, Léon, 310
Schacher, G., 263, 324
Scheiner, H., 331
Schieder, Theodor, 308
Schlechtmann, B. Joseph, 327
Schmidt, Andreas, 76
Schmidt, Helmut, 154
Schroeder, F. C., 318
Schultz, L., 318
Schultz, Robert, 293, 331
Schunemann, K., 323
Schünemann, K., 259, 315
Sebestyén, Gyula, 259
Semlyén, István, 327
Séqueil, Pierre, 279, 331
Șerbu, G. R., 269, 327
Seton-Watson, Hugh, 270, 274, 280, 310, 318
Seton-Watson, W. Robert, 261, 262, 263, 310, 315
Shuster, N. G., 282, 323
Sida, Andrei, 286
Siegert, H., 310
Sima, Horia, 79
Simonds, W. George, 331
Sinor, Dénes, 315
Socor, V., 284, 319
Sofronie, Gheorghe, 274
Solyom-Fekete, William, 305
Spălățelu, Ion, 147, 272
Spector, D. Sherman, 319
Sporea, Constantin, 293, 319, 323
Spulber, Nicholas, 278, 324, 325
Staar, F. Richard, 287, 299, 310
Stadtmüller, Georg, 261, 315, 319
Stalin, Josif Vissarionovich Dzhugashvili, 97, 98, 103, 106, 113, 114, 115, 119, 226 246
Stănescu, Maria, 268
Stephen (St. Stephen, Szent István) King of Hungary, 30

NAME INDEX

Stöhr, Martin, 298
Stoica, Chivu, 151
Stoichiţa, I. V., 268, 327
Storch, Franz, 302
Straka, Manfred, 331
Streitfeld, Theobald, 323
Suciu, Coriolan, 265, 310
Sugar, F. Peter, 284, 310, 319
Sulyok, István, 270, 291, 297, 310
Sulzberger, C. L., 278
Sütő, András, 148, 301
Suttner, Chr. Ernst, 298, 323
Szabédi, László, 177, 301
Szabó, T. Attila, 262, 310, 320
Szalay, Jeromos, 323
Szász, János, 290
Szász, Zsombor, 274, 331
Szedressy, Pál, 233
Szekfű, Gyula, 17, 259, 262, 313, 331
Szemlér, Ferenc, 301
Szenczei, László, 331
Szilágyi, Domokos, 301
Szilágyi, Sándor, 315
Sztójay, Döme, 84

Tafferner, Anton, 263
Takács, Lajos, 148, 295
Tamás, Lajos, 315
Tamás, Lajos, 320
Tanase, Virgil, 286, 319
Taylor, A.J.P., 315
Teleki, Béla, 85, 86
Teleki, Pál, 315
Temperley, W. V. Harold, 319
Teutsch, Friedrich, 260, 291, 297, 315, 323
Teutsch, Georg Daniel, 260, 307, 315
Thirring, Gusztáv, 328
Thirring, Lajos, 264
Tilea, Viorel, 319
Tito (Josip Broz), 119, 283
Titulescu, Nicolae, 319
Togan, Nicolae, 262
Toma, A. Peter, 286, 303, 310

Tontsch, G. H., 286
Tótfalusi Kis, Miklós, 240
I. Tóth, Zoltán, 315
Traian, I., 319
Trajan, 10
Trebici, V., 269
Trevisan, Dessa, 289
Tricart, Jean, 312
Triska, F. Jan, 319
Turnowsky, Sándor, 268
Turok, V. M., 274

Ulam, Adam, 319

Vaida, Voevod, Alexandru, 274
Valev, E. B., 126, 130, 284
Veiter, Theodor, 270, 271, 289, 332
Verdeţ, Ilie, 149
Viefhaus, Erwin, 273, 280, 332
Vishinsky, Andrei Januarevich, 96, 104
Vita, Sándor, 269

Wagner, Ernst, 7, 260, 263, 265, 268, 272, 273, 275, 276, 287, 291, 292, 299, 310, 315, 328
Weber, Eugen, 272
Weczerka, Hugo, 260, 315
Weingartner, Erich, 298
Werner, Arnold, 270
Werner, Carl, 260, 261, 307
Wintgens, Hugo, 271, 332
Wittstock, Erwin, 301
Wittstock, Oskar, 311
Wolf, Johann, 263
Wolff, Robert Lee, 297, 311

Xenopol, D. Alexandru, 261, 315

Zhdanov, Andrei Alexandrovich, 246
Zichy, Ladomér, 85
Zillich, Heinrich, 271, 315
Zimmermann, Franz, 260, 261, 307

PLACE NAME INDEX

Aachen, 12
Aiud-Nagyenyed-Strassburg, 203, 204
Alba-Alsófehér-Weissenburg (County), 39
Alba Iulia-Gyulafehérvár-Karlsburg, 6, 224, 228, 229, 230, 231, 298
Albania, 63, 126
Altland, 13
Ankara, 83
Arad (Town), 62, 64, 97, 154, 192, 205, 233, 240, 266, 269, 282, 298
Arad (County), 18, 26, 32, 39
Aranyosszék, 11
Ardeal-Erdély-Transilvania, 2
Arieş-Aranyos River, 33
Austria, 4, 18, 22, 24, 25, 50
Austria-Hungary, 89
Austro-Hungarian Dual Monarchy, 93
Austro-Hungarian Empire, 22
Austro-Hungarian Monarchy, 5, 6, 71, 138
Avar Empire, 10

Bacău-Bákó (County), 201, 215, 229, 266, 282
Bácska (Region), 260
Baia Mare-Nagybánya, 266, 282, 298
Balkan Peninsula, 17, 84
Banat-Bánság, 6, 18, 19, 20, 21, 25, 30, 32, 33, 38, 45, 50, 56, 60, 72, 76, 82, 84, 110, 115, 119, 159, 163, 164, 165, 213, 215, 216, 219, 229, 242, 263, 266, 297
Bánát Hegyvidék-Banater Bergland, 18
Bărăgan Steppes, 25, 119
Barcaság-Ţara Bîrsei-Burzenland, 16, 260
Bârlad (Region), 266, 282
Bavaria, 12, 18
Belgium, 135
Berlin, 25, 76, 78, 82
Bessarabia, 22, 23, 24, 25, 27, 40, 78, 80, 81, 83, 95, 125, 126, 170, 213, 265, 297
Bicaz Chei-Békás, 266
Bicazul Ardelean-Gyergyóbékás, 266
Bihar-Bihor (County), 9, 291
Bihor-Bihar (County), 19, 20, 32, 39
Bistriţa-Beszterce-Bistritz (Town), 64
Bistriţa Năsăud-Beszterce-Naszód (County), 30, 39
Bistritz-Bistriţa-Beszterce (Town), 13, 299
Black Sea, 264
Bohemia, 18
Braşov-Brassó-Kronstadt (Town), 11, 33, 64, 166, 191, 192, 205, 233, 240, 242, 244, 298
Braşov-Brassó-Kronstadt (County), 39, 48, 94, 268, 269, 283
Bucegi Province, 94
Bucharest (Bucureşti), 25, 28, 32, 59, 62, 76, 87, 94, 126, 129, 147, 170, 192, 215,

345

Bucharest (continued)
229, 234, 242, 243, 245, 266, 268, 274, 275, 282, 283
Bucovina, 11, 22, 24, 25, 32, 83, 213, 215, 216, 232, 263, 277, 297
Budapest, 151, 152
Bulgaria, 22, 80, 107, 126, 236, 264, 278
Burzenland-Barcaság-Ţara Bîrsei, 13, 215
Byzantinum, 55

Canada, 50
Caraş-Krassó (County), 39
Caraş-Severin-Krassó—Szörény (County), 30, 263
Carei-Nagykároly-Gross Karol, 19, 298
Cârlibaba Nouă-Radnalajosfalva, 265
Carpathian Basin, 10, 11, 16
Carpathian Mountain, 2, 11, 13, 14, 16, 32, 86, 201, 265
Central Europe, 3, 15, 25, 94
Cernăuţi (County), 277
China, 152
Cibinburg, 2
Ciombord-Csombord, 191
Ciuc-Csík (County), 39, 282, 291
Ciucea-Csucsa, 270
Cluj-Kolozs (County), 32, 33, 39, 104, 207, 208, 268, 269, 282
Cluj-Napoca-Kolozsvár-Klausenburg (Town), 62, 64, 76, 104, 105, 116, 162, 164, 166, 170-173, 177, 178, 187, 191, 196-198, 203, 205-208, 216, 224, 231-233, 240, 241, 242, 244, 245, 255, 263, 266, 269, 271, 298
Cologne, 12
Constanţa, 266, 282
Coşna-Kosna, 265
Covasna-Kovászna (County), 32, 48, 135, 136, 244, 260, 266
Craiova, 266, 272, 282
Crişana-Körösvidék-Kreischgebiet, 30, 56, 60, 72, 219, 266, 297
Croatia, 263
Csanád (County), 215
Csík-Ciuc (County), 11, 260, 266
Czechoslovakia, 71, 129, 130, 131, 152, 187, 222, 228, 246, 247, 289

Dacia, 10, 288
Danube-Black Sea Canal, 225, 282
Danube Delta, 124
Danube River, 80, 124, 126, 143, 153, 263, 264, 272, 283
Danubian Principalities, 17, 55, 262
Debrecen, 274
Dej-Dés, 286, 298
Dobrugea, 21, 22, 25, 216, 264, 297
Dual Monarchy of Austria-Hungary, 15
Dumbrăveni-Erzsébetváros-Elisabethstadt, 19

East Berlin, 125
East Central Europe, 17, 21, 26, 71, 78, 83, 154, 222, 243
East Europe, 25, 66, 112, 113, 123, 180, 226, 234
East Germany, 50
Erdély, 2
Erdőelve, 2
Europe, 9, 17, 63, 71, 108, 213

Făgăraş-Fogaras, 33, 39, 266
Federal Republic of Germany, 26, 154, 204, 257
Finland, 107, 278
Fiume, 23
Focşani, 83
France, 271
Franconia, 12, 18

Galaţi-Galac, 266, 282
Geneva, 74
German Empire, 19
German Federal Republic, 25, 26, 50
German Reich, 78
Germany, 24, 79, 80, 81, 82, 83, 86, 95, 109, 110, 154
Gheorgheni-Gyergyószentmiklós, 19, 226
Gherla-Szamosújvár-Neuschloss, 19
Ghimeş-Făget-Gyimesbükk, 266
Grand Principality, 4
Great Britain, 95
Great Hungarian Plain, 9, 17
Greater Romania (România Mare), 6, 22, 30, 75, 89, 214
Grossschenk-Nagysenk-Cincul Mare, 13

PLACE NAMES INDEX

Gyimes-Ghimeş, 11
Gyulafehérvár-Alba Iulia-Karlsburg, 215

Habsburg Empire, 3
Habsburg Monarchy, 17
Harghita-Hargita (County), 32, 48, 135, 136, 244, 266
Hargita Mountain, 266
Háromszék-Trei Scaune (County), 11, 136, 260, 266
Helsinki, 150, 290
Hermannstadt-Nagyszeben-Sibiu, 2, 4, 12, 13, 158, 232, 239, 240, 241, 299
Herţa District, 27, 80
Hesse, 12
Hétfalu-Siebendorf, 11
Historic Transylvania, 6, 9, 16, 18, 30, 31, 56, 60, 185, 186
Hunedoara-Hunyad-Eisenmarkt (County), 39, 48, 266, 282, 291
Hungarian Autonomous Region, 136, 282
Hungarian Kingdom, 3, 10, 16
Hungarian Plain, 274
Hungary, 2-4, 6, 9, 22, 24, 27, 50, 71-72, 77, 80-81, 84, 86, 95, 98, 99, 104-107, 109-110, 113, 116, 145, 148, 151-154, 162, 184, 186, 258, 263, 278, 288

Ialomiţa River, 283
Iaşi-Jászvásár-Jassy, 27, 196, 201, 215, 229, 230, 266, 282
Israel, 27, 28, 106
Italy, 79, 107, 135, 278

Japan, 79
Jiul-Zsil River, 33

Kalotaszeg-Calata, 33
Kolozsvár-Cluj-Klausenburg, 158, 240, 293
Körösvidék-Crişana-Kreischgebiet, 6, 21, 30
Kővár (Region), 10
Közép-Szolnok, 10
Kraszna, 10
Kronstadt-Braşov-Brassó, 13, 158, 215, 240, 241, 299
Kroschowa-Karasova District, 20

Leschkirch, 12
Ljubljana, 150
London, 83
Lorraine, 18
Luduş-Marosludas, 283
Lüttich, 12
Luxembourg, 12

Magyar Autonomous Region, 117, 118, 283
Magyar Kingdom, 30
Máramaros-Maramureş, 6, 10, 21, 30
Maramureş-Máramaros (County), 20, 30, 32, 39, 56, 60, 72, 219, 229, 266, 268, 291, 297
Maros-Magyar Autonomous Region, 118
Maros-Torda-Mureş (County), 11
Marosvásárhely-Tîrgu Mureş-Neumarkt, 158
Mediasch-Medgyes-Mediaş, 6, 158, 191, 299
Mehedinţi (County), 266
Mezőség-Câmpia Transilvaniei-Siebenbürgische Heide, 33
Miercurea Ciuc-Csíkszereda, 191, 204
Moldavia, 11, 12, 21, 27, 80, 105, 201, 204, 215, 229, 262, 265
Moscow, 25, 95, 97, 111, 114, 152, 279
Moselle River, 12
Mühlbach, 299
Muntenia, 21, 204
Mureş-Magyar Autonomous Region, 266
Mureş-Turda-Maros-Torda (County), 39, 208, 209, 266, 268, 282, 291
Mureş-Maros River, 33, 263

Nagyenyed-Aiud-Strassburg, 158
Nagyvárad-Oradea-Grosswardein, 215
Neamţ (County), 266
Northern Bucovina, 23, 24, 27, 40, 78, 80, 83, 95, 260, 265
Northern Dobrugea, 24, 32, 53, 264
Northern Transylvania, 22, 24, 27, 31, 40, 78, 80, 81, 84, 85, 95, 97, 99, 101, 102, 109, 110, 147, 162, 164, 166, 288
Nösnerland, 13

348 PLACE NAMES INDEX

Odorhei–Udvarhely (County), 39, 266, 282, 291
Odorhei–Székelyudvarhely, 191, 203, 204, 298
Ohrid, 150
Old Kingdom (Regat), 21, 29, 32, 33, 43, 45, 48, 58, 67, 89, 92, 146, 159, 165, 184, 185, 266
Old Romania, 2
Oltenia, 21
Oradea–Nagyvárad–Grosswardein, 62, 64, 97, 154, 164, 191, 203, 204, 205, 216, 223, 229, 231, 240, 263, 266, 269, 282, 298
Orsova, 266

Palestine, 106
Partium, 9, 33
People's Republic of Hungary, 152
Pitești, 266, 282
Ploiești, 266, 282
Poiana Sărată–Sósmező, 266
Poland, 222, 263
Poznań, 125
Prussia, 5
Pruth River, 83

Regat (Old Kingdom), 21, 23–25, 27, 30, 32–33, 42, 46, 48–50, 55, 58, 59, 62, 67, 89, 90, 93, 124, 146, 161, 178, 184, 200, 215–216, 263, 265, 268
Reghin–Szászrégen, 191
Rhineland-Palatinate, 18
Rhine River, 12, 18
Rodna–Radna, 13
Roman (County), 215, 229
Romania, 2, 6, 9, 11, 13, 22–28, 30–36, 40–47, 49–55, 58–59, 62–63, 66–68, 71–72, 76–84, 86–93, 95–96, 98–101, 103–104, 106–110, 112–113, 116–118, 125–128, 133, 137–138, 145, 148, 151, 153–154, 186, 216, 218, 228, 236–237, 245, 258, 278
Romanian Kingdom, 141, 213
Romanian People's Republic, 31, 111–115, 133, 167, 169, 175, 176, 220, 221–222, 224
Romanian Principalities, 17, 262

Romanian Socialist Republic, 133, 134, 142, 144, 180, 183, 184, 190, 220, 295
Russia, 22

Săcele–Szecseleváros, 11, 233
Sächsisch Regen–Reghin–Szászrégen, 13
Sălaj–Szilágy (County), 32, 39, 266, 291
Șarmaș–Sármás, 283
Satu Mare–Szatmár (Town), 97, 154, 191, 215, 229, 263, 286
Satu Mare–Szatmár–Sathmar (County), 19, 20, 32, 39, 164, 215, 229, 266, 291
Schässburg–Segesvár–Sighișoara, 299
Secuieni (County), 261
Severin–Szörény (County), 39
Sfîntu Gheorghe–Sepsiszentgyörgy, 167, 191, 298
Sibiu–Szeben (County), 39, 268
Sibiu–Nagyszeben–Hermannstadt, 33, 65, 89, 160, 191, 192, 196, 197, 204, 205, 216, 231
Siebenbürgen, 2
Sighișoara–Segesvár–Schässburg, 65, 191
Siret–Szeret River, 11, 83
Slovakia, 18
Slovenia, 263
Someș–Szamos River, 33
Someș–Szamos (County), 39, 266
Southeastern Europe, 84, 94
Southern Bucovina, 24, 27, 229
Southern Dobrugea, 40, 78, 80, 263, 264, 265
Southern Tirol, 135
Southern Transylvania, 22, 24, 27, 40, 80–82, 84–85, 109, 162
Soviet-Carpatho-Ukraine, 32
Soviet Union, 25, 27, 31, 47, 79, 80, 82, 83–84, 95–96, 98, 100, 101, 103, 111, 113, 123–128, 130, 151, 152, 154, 223, 227, 236, 263, 282
Stalin (Brașov–Brassó), 266, 282
Suceava (County), 30, 265, 266, 282
Switzerland, 135
Szatmár–Satu Mare–Sathmar, 6, 10, 21
Szeged, 274
Székelyudvarhely–Odorhei, 158
Székler region (Hung. Székelyföld), 11, 32, 33, 38, 48, 62, 115–117, 119, 135,

PLACE NAMES INDEX

136, 138, 161, 170, 174, 189, 201, 205, 210, 215, 229, 245, 266, 282, 286

Târnava Mare–Nagyküküllő–Gross Kokeln, 39, 266
Târnava Mică–Kisküküllő–Klein Kokeln, 39, 266
Teheran, 83
Temesvár–Timişoara–Temeschburg, 241
Thracian-Geto-Dacian State, 10
Thuringia, 12
Timişoara–Temesvár–Temeschburg, 65, 73, 159, 164, 166, 167, 191–192, 205, 214, 229, 230, 240, 242, 263, 266, 269, 282, 298
Timiş–Temes (County), 39
Timiş-Torontal–Temes-Torontál (County), 18, 263
Tiraspol, 215
Tîrgul Secuiesc–Kézdivásárhely, 191
Tîrgu Mureş–Marosvásárhely–Neumarkt, 33, 65, 124, 167, 170, 172, 178, 191, 196, 197, 200, 203, 208, 226, 242, 244, 269, 272, 279, 298
Tîrnăveni–Dicsőszentmárton, 283, 298
Tisza River, 263
Torda–Turda–Thorenburg, 213
Transilvania, 2
Transylvania, 1–4, 6, 9–25, 29–33, 35–39, 41–45, 48–50, 55, 58, 59, 62, 63, 72–75, 80, 81, 83–85, 87, 88–93, 95, 97–99, 102–104, 109, 110, 115–117, 123–124, 130, 138, 146–148, 157–159, 162–163, 169, 184, 200, 201, 204, 213, 215–216, 218–219, 229, 231, 239–240, 259, 266, 274

Transylvanian Principality, 3, 9
Trei Scaune–Háromszék (County), 39, 94, 282, 283, 291
Trier, 12, 18
Trotuş–Tatros River, 11
Turda–Torda-Aranyos (County), 39, 85, 266, 291
Turkish Empire, 3
Turnu Severin, 79, 272

Udvarhely–Odorhei (County), 11, 136, 260
Ugocsa, 10
Ungro-Wallachia, 262
USA, 50, 95, 127
USSR, 225

Vatican, 222, 226
Vechiul Regat, 21
Vienna, 4, 274
Vlahiţa–Szentegyházasfalu, 191

Wallachia, 17, 21, 262
Western Europe, 180
Westfalia, 12
West Germany, 232
Württemberg, 18, 19

Yugoslavia, 63, 71, 222, 223, 283

Zălău–Zilah, 298
Zaránd, 10

SUBJECT INDEX

Adventists, 225, 234
Agrarian reform, 109, 218, 220, 275
Alba Iulia Resolutions (see Resolutions of Alba Iulia)
Allied and Associated Great Powers, 6
Allied Control Commission, 95, 101–102
Allied Powers, 83, 86, 95, 107
Andreanum, 13
Anti-Fascist Committee of German Workers in Romania, 115
ARLUS, Soviet-Romanian cultural association, 126
Armenians, 19, 20, 229, 231
Armenian Catholic Church, 225, 231
Armeno-Gregorian Church, 217, 225
Armistice Agreement, 95, 98, 101, 110, 277
Ausgleich (The Compromise), 5
Axis Powers, 79, 80, 81, 82, 100

Banat Swabians, 6, 25, 26, 45, 73, 100, 119, 159, 214, 229
Baptists, 225, 234
Bloc of Democratic Parties, 97
Bulgarians, 32, 46, 50

Capotorti Reports, 108, 150
Comes Saxonum, 13
Cominform (Communist International Information Bureau), 283

Committee on Press and Printing, 250, 251, 252, 253
Conclave of Vásárhely, 77
Concordat, 76, 160, 217, 218, 222, 223
Congress of Political Education and Socialist Culture, 184, 228, 249, 251
Council for Mutual Economic Assistance (COMECON), 126
Council for Socialist Culture and Education, 184, 249, 250, 252, 253, 300
Council of Working People, 131, 132, 136, 139, 146, 149, 187, 188, 197
Count of the Saxons, 13
Croat-Karashovans, 32
Csángó-Hungarians, 11, 12, 53, 105, 201–202, 229, 233, 260
Cultural zone, 161
Cumanians, 2, 13, 15, 16
Czechs, 32, 50

Dacians, 14, 290
Dacia Publishing House, 245, 255
Daco-Roman continuity theory, 14, 125, 153, 168, 184, 290, 292
Declaration of Alba Iulia (see Resolutions of Alba Iulia), 6
Declaration of Union of Mediasch, 6
Democratic Committee of Jews, 106
De-Russification, 125, 133
De-Stalinization, 123, 226, 237

351

SUBJECT INDEX

Dictatorship of King Carol II, 77, 93
Diet of Hermannstadt-Nagyszeben, 5
Diet of Torda, 213

Eastern Orthodox Church, 37
Economic and Social Council (ECOSOC), 107
Entente, 87
European Convention for Protection of Human Rights and Basic Freedoms, 107
Evangelical Church in Transylvania, 76, 144, 163, 165, 225, 228, 232, 244
Evangelische Landeskirche A.B. in Rumänien, 216
Evangelische Landeskirche Augsburgischer Bekenntnisses in Siebenbürgen, 215-216, 232

Falcons of the Homeland, 183, 237
Fanariots, 17, 262
Federation of Germans in Romania, 73
Federation of Romanian Jews, 106
First World War, 6, 22, 33, 94, 162, 213, 218, 233

German Party (*Deutsche Partei*), 73
German-Romanian economic treaty, 80
Germans, 1-2, 14, 16, 17-18, 23-26, 31-32, 36, 38, 40-42, 44-45, 50-51, 53-55, 58-59, 63, 67, 73-74, 78-79, 84, 87, 90, 92, 100-101, 109-111, 136, 154, 163, 165-166, 191-192, 193-196, 199, 205-206, 216, 239, 240, 241-242
German-Soviet agreement, 24
Golden Charter, 13
Goldener Brief, 13
Governing Council (*Consiliul Dirigent*), 89, 160
Great Powers, 2, 99, 100, 108
Great Romanian National Council (*Marele Sfat Naţional Român*), 89
Greek Catholic (Uniate) Church, 4, 15, 36, 37, 214, 216, 217, 221, 223-224, 225, 234-235, 296
Gubernium, 4
Gyimes Csángós, 11
Gypsies, 20, 24, 36, 54, 199

Helsinki Conference on Security and Cooperation in Europe, 150-151, 152
Holy See, 76, 217, 222
Hungarian Federation (*Magyar Szövetség*), 72
Hungarian Lutheran Church, 233-234
Hungarian National Party, 72
Hungarian National Workers' Federation (*MADOSZ*), 75, 102, 103
Hungarian People's Alliance in Romania (*Romániai Magyar Népi Szövetség*), 103, 104, 111, 116, 117, 166, 279
Hungarian People's Community (*Magyar Népközösség*), 78
Hungarian People's Party, 72, 75
Hungarian Revolution, 123-124, 173, 255
Hungarians, 1, 10, 14-18, 24, 28, 31-32, 41, 46-49, 51, 53-55, 58, 59, 63, 67, 72, 74-75, 79, 84-85, 87, 90, 92, 97, 101, 102-105, 109-111, 116-118, 136, 158, 166, 169-171, 177-178, 190-191, 193, 194-200, 205, 229-233, 239-240, 242-245
Hungarian Smallholders' Party, 75

Iron Guard, 77, 79, 105, 272

Jews, 1, 20, 25-28, 36-37, 41, 45, 50, 54, 55, 58-59, 63, 67, 74, 79, 82-82, 92, 105-106, 199, 216, 217, 225, 234
Jewish Party, 106
Judeţ (County), 31

Kiáltó Szó (Warning Cry), 72
Knezen, 15
Königsboden, 12, 158, 260
Kriterion Publishing House, 205, 255
Kulaks, 119
Kuruces, 4
League of Nations, 74, 75, 86, 107, 271
Leopoldine Diploma, 4
Lipovans, 32, 50, 53
Literary Publishing House, 255
Little Cultural Revolution, 183, 228, 236, 249, 250
Lutheran Church, 213, 215-216, 217, 218, 220, 232-233

SUBJECT INDEX

353

Magyar Conquest, 10, 11
Maniu Guards, 101
Marxism-Leninism, 108, 112, 115, 117, 128, 140, 141, 168, 184, 237, 246, 250, 251
Ministry of Nationality Affairs, 108
Minorities Treaty, 72, 73, 86, 88–89, 91, 94, 160, 162, 217, 273, 274
Minority Statute, 93
Mohammedans, 217, 225
Moldavian Csángós, 11
Moldavian Hungarians, 11
Moldavian Magyars, 12

National Christian Defense, 77
National Democratic Bloc, 96
National Democratic Front, 96
Nationale Selbsthilfebewegung der Deutschen in Rumänien (NSDR), 76
National Hungarian Party (*Országos Magyar Párt*), 73
National Hungarian Party Opposition, 75
Nationality Statute, 108, 109, 114, 166, 219
National Legionary State, 79
National Liberal Party, 74, 96, 97, 160
National Peasant Party, 74, 96, 97, 99, 160
National Regeneration Front, 78
Nationalsozialistische Deutsche Arbeiterpartei (NSDAP), 76
Nationalsozialistische Erneuerungsbewegung der Deutschen in Rumänien (NEDR), 76
Nationsuniversität, 73, 78, 158
Neo-Protestants, 225, 234

Orthodox Church (Romanian), 15, 36, 78, 213, 214, 217, 218, 219, 220, 221, 222, 224, 225, 227, 228, 235
Ottoman Turks, 17

Pact of Ciucea–Csucsa, 73
Paris Peace Conference, 96, 98, 100, 278
Paris Peace Treaties, 23, 278
Paris Peace Treaty, 99, 107, 219
Peace Treaty of Karlowitz, 4
Peace Treaty of Trianon, 6, 9, 21, 72, 86, 98

People's Community of the Germans in Romania, 78
People's Councils, 31, 111, 113, 133, 201, 281
People's Democratic Front, 111
Petchenegues, 2, 15
Pioneer organization, 112, 171, 183, 293
Placement Commission (*Comisia de repartizare*), 200
Ploughmen's Front, 96, 111
Presbyterian Church, 225

Reformation, 13, 16, 240
Reformed (Calvinist), Church, 37, 144, 213, 215, 216–218, 225, 231–232, 244, 298
Resolutions of Alba Iulia, 6, 73, 79, 86–88, 94, 160, 216
Revolution of 1848–1849, 4, 5
Roller period, 112
Roman Catholic Church, 37, 76, 116, 144, 159, 160, 163, 165, 166, 201, 213, 214, 215, 217, 218, 220, 221, 222, 223–224, 225, 226, 229, 230, 231, 235
Roman Catholic Status, 220
Romanian Anti-Revisionist League, 77
Romanian Communist Party (RCP), 111, 120, 127, 128–129, 130, 131, 140, 141, 142, 148, 181, 183, 184, 246, 249, 250–251, 254, 281
Romanian coup d'état, 24, 84, 95, 100, 101, 105, 106
Romanianization, 12, 17, 48, 58–63, 120, 133, 188–189, 206–211, 247–249, 255
Romanian nationalism, 116
Romanian Orthodox Church, 90
Romanian Principalities, 17
Romanians, 2, 5, 14–16, 17–18, 24, 46, 47, 49, 75, 97, 261
Romans, 14
Romanian Workers' Party, 111, 113, 115, 125, 128, 167
Romanian Writers' Association, 131, 254
Russian Old Believer, 225
Russians, 45, 46, 50, 53
Ruthenians, 24, 45, 46, 51

Sachsengraf, 13
Sachsentag, 13, 73, 76
Sächsische Nationsuniversität, 13
Saxon Assembly, 13
Saxon Lutheran Church, 78
Saxon National University (*Nationsuniversität*), 13, 93
Saxons (Transylvanian), 12–14
Şcoala Ardeleană, 4
Seat (*szék, Stuhl*), 11
Second Vienna Award, 22, 24, 80, 83, 95, 101, 162, 272
Second World War, 14, 22, 23, 25, 26, 31, 32, 41, 42, 48, 59, 94, 95, 99, 106, 107, 164, 165, 183, 207, 216, 218, 234, 241, 245, 250
Selbsthilfe organization, 76
Serbians, 32, 50
Serbo-Croatians, 50
Seven Judges (*Sieben-Richter-Waldungen*), 93
Siebenbürger Sachsen (Saxons), 12–14
Sieben-Richter-Waldungen, 78
Slavs, 15, 20, 50, 54, 58
Slovaks, 24, 45, 50
Socialist Cultural and Educational Council, 184
Socialist Unity Front (F.U.S.), 130, 136, 141, 228, 230
Soviet (Stalin) Constitution, 111, 113
Soviet Military High Command, 95
SOVROMS, Soviet-Romanian economic associations, 126
Subcommission on Prevention of Discrimination and Protection of Minorities, 108
Supplex Libellus Valachorum, 4
Swabians of the Banat, 18–19, 53, 119, 215, 229, 262
Szatmár–Sathmar Swabians, 19, 164, 229
Széklers (Hung. Székely), 11, 53, 90, 116–118, 161, 259

Tatar invasion, 16
Tatars, 45
Teutonic Order, 13
Tito-crisis, 119

Transylvanian Hungarian Council (*Erdélyi Magyar Tanács*), 85–86
Transylvanian Jewish National Federation, 74
Transylvanian Party (Erdélyi Párt), 84–86, 273
Transylvanian School, 4
Transylvanian Saxon Evangelical Church, 14
Transylvanian Saxons, 2, 4, 5, 6, 12, 13, 14, 17, 25, 26, 73, 75, 78, 90, 100, 158, 163, 169, 232, 239–240, 260
Transylvanism, 75
Treaty of Neuilly, 22
Trianon Peace Treaty, 86, 152
Turkish-Tatars, 32, 47
Turks, 14, 45

Ukrainians, 45
Ukrainians-Ruthenians, 32, 37, 51
UN-Charter, 107, 108
UN-Commission on Human Rights, 107
UN-Convention Against Discrimination in Education, 107
UN-Convention for Prevention and Punishment of Genocide, 107
Undersecretary for Minorities, 77
Union of Working Youth (*UTM*), 112, 171, 183, 237, 281
Unitarian Church, 37, 144, 213, 216, 217, 225, 231, 233
United Nations, 107
Universal Declaration of Human Rights, 107
Universitas Saxonum, 13
University of the Saxon Nation (*Nationsuniversität*), 13, 14, 158
UN-World Pact on Civil and Political Rights, 107
Uzes, 2

Valev plan, 126
vármegye (County), 30
Vienna Award, 30
voivod, 15

Warsaw Pact Organization, 126, 129, 152
World War I, 21, 30, 71, 106

SUBJECT INDEX

World War II, 28, 35, 107
World Wars, 1, 21, 25, 73

Yalta Conference, 96
Yaziges, 2
Youth Publishing House, 255

WITHDRAWN